HOW TO
WRITE IT

HOW TO
WRITE IT

A COMPLETE GUIDE TO
EVERYTHING YOU'LL EVER WRITE

Second Edition

Sandra E. Lamb

TEN SPEED PRESS
Berkeley | Toronto

Copyright © 1998, 2006 by Sandra E. Lamb

Ten Speed Press
PO Box 7123
Berkeley, California 94707
www.tenspeed.com

Distributed in Australia by Simon and Schuster Australia, in Canada by Ten Speed Press Canada, in New Zealand by Southern Publishers Group, in South Africa by Real Books, and in the United Kingdom and Europe by Publishers Group UK.

Cover design by Katy Brown, based on an original design by Gary Bernal
Text design by Bonnie Monohan

The Library of Congress has cataloged the first edition as follows:
Lamb, Sandra E.
	How to write it: A complete guide to everything you'll ever write
	over 250 models / Sandra E. Lamb
		p. cm.
	ISBN 1-58008-024-3 (alk. paper)
	1. Commercial correspondence. 2. Business report writing. 3. Technical writing
	4. Letter writing I. Title.
 HF5720.L36		1998		98-8420
 651.7'4–dc21				CIP

ISBN-13 (2nd ed.): 978-1-58008-572-4
ISBN-10 (2nd ed.): 1-58008-572-5

Printed in the United States of America

First printing, 2006
1 2 3 4 5 6 7 8 9 10 — 10 09 08 07 06

CONTENTS

PREFACE

Two weeks after starting my first job as a technical writer, my boss called me into his office. "Sit down," he commanded. Mr. A. owned a reputation as a hard-bitten, ex-military training manual writer.

He immediately started expounding on the necessity of clear communications in our medical instrumentation manuals. Some forty minutes into this monologue he said, "The military has the right approach. There is a precise test for evaluating the ultimate effectiveness of communications. In the Army we call it 'the fog count.'" He picked up a copy of the first manual draft I had written from his desk and began riffling the pages, a look of deep concern spreading over his face. "Let's apply the fog-count method to this, for example," he elevated one eyebrow before continuing, "starting with the first paragraph."

I started to sputter something about how I felt this introduction with equipment names like gaschromatography, instrumentation, and analyses might skew the results just a bit.

He held up a hand like a traffic cop and began to silently lip numbers.

After five minutes and a number of written calculations on his yellow pad (which he shielded from my view), Mr. A. held up his pad and pointed at his scrawls. Solicitously he explained that he had taken the total number of syllables in the first paragraph and divided by the total number of words. "Your fog count," he announced with a grief-stricken look, "is three." He rolled his lips tight, making a small tuft of hair on his chin point accusingly at me. "Much too high," he said, shaking his head. His expression darkened and became so pained, in fact, I thought he might cry from the sheer magnitude of my transgression.

After several nervous and silent minutes, I suggested we try the test on the final draft of the introduction to a manual *he* had just finished. Quickly I pulled two copies from the file on my lap.

". . . Well . . . ," Mr. A. cleared his throat, pointed the tuft of chin hair at me, and with a blush began to move his lips in time with his finger. I, of course, did my own count on the second copy. "Fog count," Mr. A. cleared his throat while his face flushed a bright red, "five!"

I learned two important lessons about writing that day:

1. Make your writing simple, clear, and concise.
2. There are many aspects to communicating besides the writing itself that must be considered. Know them all. And use them wisely.

That's the reason I wrote *How to Write It:* to provide you with easy-to-use, total answers for creating effective communications.

INTRODUCTION

What will you be putting into writing over the next several months?

Maybe you'll write a personal invitation to a wedding anniversary party, a letter describing why you expect a manufacturer to replace your broken dishwasher, a resume, or a request to the neighborhood architectural committee asking the committee to approve your use of a new siding for your home. You may write an employee newsletter, a production report, a sales forecast for next quarter, a press release announcing a subordinate's promotion, a letter of condolence, a letter of recommendation, or a response to a letter from an attorney concerning your rights in a property-line dispute. And maybe you'll want an error on your credit record corrected, or you'll respond to a notice of audit by the IRS.

Every day the demands to produce well-written business and personal communications grow in number and complexity, so the ability to write easily and effectively will both add value to and make your life easier.

How to Write It is a *complete* writing reference. It was designed to equip you to take on all the writing tasks you will face: personal and professional.

A quick review of the table of contents shows you just how easy this book is to use. The first chapter provides a solid start, focusing on writing principles. Browse and select a specific written communication you find tough—if not impossible—to write. Turn to that chapter, and note how it is organized. It gives you visual examples—*models*—you can adapt for your own communication. And each chapter gives you guidelines to get you to a successfully completed communication. You may use the lists of sentences and paragraphs to get you started or to help you eliminate stilted words or phrases. Review several chapters and you'll see that this book is organized to help make all your writing tasks easy, quick, and efficient. But more than that, each chapter is designed to help you produce an effective written communication.

Chapter 2 gives you some additional help with layout and design, and illustrates how to create show-don't-tell visuals, like tables and charts. For sticky questions about forms of address, check the appendices.

This book will help take the fear out of any writing project. Using it will save you time and will help you prune your communications down to their essential, effective best. It will help you check what you've written, and it will help you eliminate lethal, stilted prose. And, as you continue to use it, *How to Write It* will help you develop the skills of clear, powerful, writing.

I. PRINCIPLES

1
GETTING STARTED

If language is not correct,
then what is said is not what is meant;
If what is said is not what is meant,
Then what ought to be done remains undone.

—CONFUCIUS

We write to be understood. And the fastest and best route to that goal is clear and concise language. It sounds easy enough, and it is, if we will embrace a few simple principles. Learn these, and enjoy the rewards of effective communication.

KNOW YOUR MESSAGE

The first element in getting your audience to understand you is knowing what you want to communicate. It sounds easy enough, but this is where most messages get derailed.

Before you begin to write, think your message all the way through. No matter how complex it is, this step will make your job much easier and produce a much better result. It's the best investment of time you'll make in any writing or communicating exercise. And the practice of taking the time to do this will help you develop skills of analysis and organization. Distill your message into a single, simple sentence.

Once you have your message statement in mind, use the rest of the steps in this chapter to develop, order, refine, and effectively express it.

WRITE FOR YOUR AUDIENCE

Since the *reader* is your reason for writing, ask yourself some basic questions:
- Who is my reader?
- What does my reader already know about this subject?
- What does the reader need to know?
- How will the reader respond?
    - Will he or she be receptive?
    - Will he or she object?
    - Will he or she be hostile?
    - Will he or she be indifferent?

Make some notes about your reader, as a guide. This will help ensure that you have your reader firmly in mind, which will, in turn, give your writing the proper focus.

Example: You are going to announce a company open house to department employees and to the general public. For your department employee readers, the focus and content of what you will communicate will be very different from the focus and content of the announcement for the general public. Think about who your two groups of readers are, what they already know, and then what each group needs to know. Your notes about what to include in the announcement to each group might look something like this:

	General Public	Department Employees
What:	Occasion/ Open house	Open house
Why:	New product/ background, development, benefits, etc.	New product launch
Where:	Address and directions	Specific instructions about areas to be open and those to be closed to visitors
When:	Date, time	Date, time, complete schedule of employees on duty for specific time slots
Who:	Open to public	Detailed assignments for each employee

Obviously, since you have two very different groups of readers, the best approach will be to complete two written communications.

Knowing your reader before you begin writing is vital to effective communication.

DEVELOP YOUR MESSAGE

The secret to effective writing is knowing *precisely* what you want to say to the reader before you start. This means getting down to the main elements of your message.

To do this, the next step is to ask yourself some basic questions:

* What do I need/want to tell the reader?
* What do I want to accomplish with this message?
* How do I want the reader to respond?
* What do I want the reader to do after reading my communication?

Then crystallize the intent of your message by looking more closely at your own motive in writing. Ask yourself what you want your message to accomplish. Do you want to inform the reader? What information do you want to give? Do you want to persuade the reader? Of what? Motivate the reader to take some

action? Apologize to the reader? For what? Or, is the purpose to follow up on or confirm a verbal discussion, or to simply create a written record?

Most of your messages will be to inform and/or persuade; sometimes you will want to motivate.

A little work here will help to ensure that your message hits the bull's-eye. So, be very precise. Here are some examples of well-thought-out message statements written in a single sentence:

* You can save $525.00 each month if you use our accounting services.
* The meeting is at 10:00 A.M., Tuesday, in my office.
* Buy our Model 104B Analyzer.
* Please send me complete information on the Model L15 Wicker Whacker.
* We must reorganize our distribution system to be profitable.
* I cannot attend the values seminar.
* I recommend we invest $5.2 million in the new analyzer product line.
* I was so sorry to hear about the loss of your spouse.
* I need 12 volunteers for the dance.
* This plane won't fly!
* I want your suggestions on our lunchtime policy changes.
* We need to hire 40 assembly-line workers.
* You overcharged me $376.50.
* Our Model 650B machining station will help your company make $3.4 million next year.

Distilling your message into a single, precise sentence gives you a head start. It means you'll be taking the next writing step from a secure position. Your message, when complete, will be strong and clear and undoubtedly shorter than it would have been without this step.

For practice, read through several communications on your desk. What, in a sentence, is the message statement of each? What should it have been? Is the message of each clear? Garbled? Off base? Complete?

Now you know (1) what you want to communicate, (2) who you are communicating with, (3) the main points of what you want to say, and (4) what you want to accomplish with your communication. If you view writing as a two-way conversation, your job will be easier, and the end result will be better. It will also help you to use the correct voice and tone.

The Alphanumeric Outline

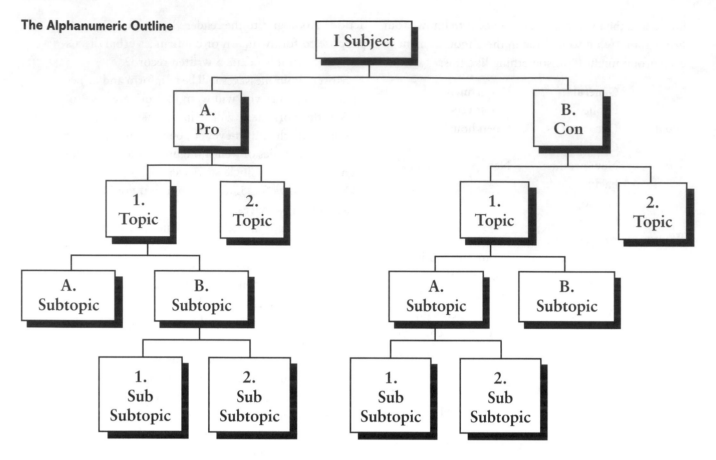

This traditional outlining method works best for material that follows a logical progression.

The Stream of Consciousness Outline

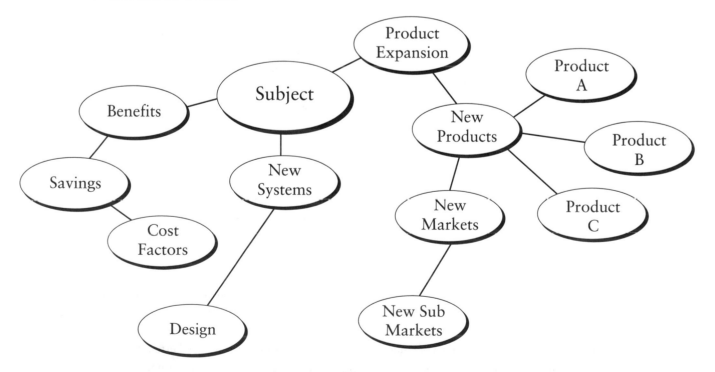

This outlining method works best for material that doesn't follow a logical progression.

USE CLEAR, LOGICAL PROGRESSION

When you began thinking about writing, you had some ideas in mind. Maybe you even made some notes—a very good practice.

Write down the main points, or parts, of your communication in the most logical order. You can do this in the traditional alphanumeric system (I., A., 1., a.), or in a more stream-of-consciousness form often depicted by a series of connected circles, as shown in the two figures. You can put your ideas into your computer, or you can use index cards and write them out by hand. But start to think about organization, and form your headings in as logical an order as possible. Then list subpoints: (1) Be consistent with the information and background of your reader, (2) order your outline the way your reader most likely thinks about the subject, or (3) order it chronologically or developmentally.

By organizing your thoughts on the basis of what the reader needs to know about the subject and what you want the reader to do after reading your communication, you will make your task much easier. And keep going back to your message statement. It will help you stay on track.

Your points should be lining up under these sections:

Introduction/Statement of Purpose
Why you are writing and/or what you are writing about.

Background/Explanation
Outline the body of your communication under the subpoints you have organized, keeping your reader in mind.

Summary/Conclusion
Summarize your points.

Call for Action/Response
Call for action and/or request the reader's response.

As you write down your points, think of them in terms of occurrence or chronology. This will give order to your ideas. If you are going to define a procedure like running laboratory tests, your ideas will need to be sequential. If you are writing about sales growth over the past five years, your order may be chronological. If your subject naturally orders itself in one of these ways, go with it. Your choices for developing your writing are many:

- Chronological
- Sequential
- Spatial
- Comparisons
- Analysis
- Division and classification
- Deduction (general to specific)
- Induction (specific to general)
- Cause and effect
- Increasing order of importance
- Decreasing order of importance

Think while you write, too, about whether illustrations will make your message clearer and more interesting.

FLESH OUT YOUR OUTLINE

Remember, a strong outline releases you to begin writing. It's like a road map. The complexity of your message, your reader, and your own work methods will dictate when your outline is complete. And remember, too, that the steps are not necessarily sequential: Some of the important steps in the writing process cross over and cross back. For example, during the outlining process, you will probably write some parts of your message, go to the next step, and then return to a previously written portion of your communication.

COMPLETE ANY NECESSARY RESEARCH

You may need a number of kinds of research. At a minimum, you will go to the notes you made during outlining. You may also have to interview others for facts and input, research published sources, and read through special unpublished papers and facts. Or, you may have to do a survey or develop a questionnaire to get your facts and information. Make sure your research is thorough, and if you develop a research instrument such as a survey, use care to create one that will give you valid, objective data (see "Questionnaires and Surveys," page 219).

Although often this decision is prescribed by your industry or discipline, you will need to fit your message into one of these general categories:

- Formal report
- Informal report
- Memorandum
- Proposal
- Letter

After selecting the format, follow the instructions given in the correct chapter and the conventions of your own organization, industry, or discipline.

WRITE YOUR DRAFT

Let yourself go. Using your outline, notes, written passages, and gathered information, give yourself over to the act of writing. Most writers should concentrate on getting all the writing done first, without trying to polish. If you have completed all the other steps, you will be clear on your point of view, methodology, and content. For many writers, the draft is written in a very concentrated work session, writing without rereading. Let your ideas flow, and get them all recorded.

REVISE

Although writing is hard work, revising is the most difficult task. Clear, precise writing that appears to have been written with ease, usually requires hard, intense labor. Here are a few guidelines:

- Be sure you have written a topic sentence for each paragraph, and then pay off in the paragraph by producing the content this sentence has promised.
- Insert headings and subheadings to keep and direct the reader's attention and to make your message clear, easy to grasp, and visually appealing.

- Know that revising is usually a several-times-over process. Be diligent.
- Check for accuracy and completeness. Put on the reader's hat here: What does the reader need to know, and in how much detail?
- Go back to your message statement and write your opening and introduction.
- Keep sentences short, between 12 to 15 words.
- Keep paragraphs at about eight lines.
- Vary sentence length and structure to add interest.
- Think about visual appeal and arrangement as you proceed.
- Check for continuity and create transitions. Does each paragraph build on the one before it?
- Be sure your message is clear. Have others read it and give you input.
- Check for any word or paragraph problems outlined in the following sections.

EDIT, EDIT, EDIT

Writing is really talking on paper, so make your communications talk. Sometimes reading aloud what you've written turns on a light. Listen for stilted words, remoteness, obscurity. You want your communication to sound conversational, more like speaking face-to-face than a speech. That means, of course, that you should look for any hint of talking down to your reader.

There is a place for formal writing, but formal writing isn't pompous, wordy, remote, stilted, or stuffed with polysyllabic words.

Be Clear and Be Brief

It's very easy to get attached to what you write, but in revising, you must be ruthless. Ask yourself whether each word has real meaning, a necessary function. If the answer is no, cut it. Getting rid of all the deadwood takes real effort and professional detachment.

Simplify for the General Reader

Use a simple word if it works. Use technical words when they are the best choice—when their meaning is known to your reader and when technical words are the most direct and precise. This doesn't mean that your writing will be dull or simplistic. It will be clear, strong, and easy to understand. Check the examples at the end of this chapter for using direct, simple words instead of pompous, stuffy ones to make your meaning clear.

Make Your Communication Reader-Friendly

Reader-friendly writing means clear and direct writing. It also means an overall visual layout and appearance that invites the reader to read. Use white space so your communication looks open and easy to read, and use headings to catch the reader's attention. Lists, graphs, and charts will make your message visually appealing.

For lists, observe a few rules:

- Start each step with an action verb, but not the same one.
- List each step separately. Don't combine them.
- Make sure each step is in logical sequence.
- Write each step as a full sentence.
- Keep the sentence construction parallel.
- Use an active voice, if possible.

Use Parallel Construction and Consistent Tense

It's amazing how important this principle is. When your ideas are equal, give them equal construction, whether they are items in a list, headings, sentences, or phrases. You can do this by using the same grammatical structure. Like the list statements we just did, each is constructed as a complete sentence, and each begins with an action verb.

Use Powerful Words

Verbs are your friends. They will happily carry your meaning if you select the correct ones. Verbs enliven your writing and turn passive statements into active

ones, if your pick your verbs from the active side of the family.

And don't stop at active verbs; select colorful, precise, and vibrant verbs. Let's try these comparisons:

The hour passed very slowly.
The hour crept by.
The hour inched by.
The hour crawled by.
Time stood still.

None of these sentences is wrong. Some verbs just do more precise work than others. Some create a more vivid picture, and some are more appealing because they don't suffer from overuse. If you write in an active voice, using active verbs, and select them for their precise meaning, you will enliven your communications. Your message will come to life. So, put your subjects to work with active verbs.

The most listless verbs, and often worst offenders, are those in the "nominals" category—verbs turned into nouns by added endings: *-ing, -tion, -ment, -ance, -ing, -al,* or *-ure.* Here are a few of those verbs that usually appear with *to* in front of them:

Verb	Nominal	Verb	Nominal
conclude	conclusion	inflate	inflation
direct	direction	assess	assessment
fail	failure	submit	submission
provide	provision	attend	attendance

You can see how important it is to use active verbs whenever possible.

Check the lists in this chapter while writing. The charts that follow provide some more guidelines to help you select simple, powerful words.

To help the flow of your ideas, use words and phrases that work as road signs for your readers.

Use Transition Words to Help the Reader Understand

To show	Use		To show	Use
sequence	then		*an explanation*	for example
	in addition			one such
	to enumerate			for instance
	number __			to illustrate
	first, second, third			also
	next			too
	the next in this series			to demonstrate
	besides these			
contrast	unlike		*cause and effect*	then
	different			as a result
	in spite of			for this reason
	on the other hand			the result was
	on the contrary			what followed
	opposite			in response
	opposing			therefore
	however			thus
	contrary to			because of
	very different			consequently
				the reaction
similarity	like			
	the same			
	similar			
	close			
	likewise			
	also			
	near			

Use Simple, Direct Words

Instead of	Use
10 A.M. in the morning	10 A.M.
a substantial segment of the population	many people
above mentioned	these, this, that, those
absolutely complete	complete
absolutely essential	essential
accounted for by the fact that	caused by
achieve purification	purify
activate	begin
actual experience	experience
add the point that	add that
adequate enough	adequate
advise	tell
along the lines of	like
am in receipt of	have
an example of this is the fact that	for example
analyses were made	analyzed
answer in the affirmative	yes
any and all	any, all
are of the opinion that	think that, or believe that
as of this date	today
as to whether	whether
assent	agree
assist	help
at a price of $10	at $10
at the present time	now
at the present writing	now
at this point in time	now
attached hereto	attached
attached please find	attached is
attempt	try
attributable	due
basic fundamentals	facts, basics, fundamentals

Instead of	Use
be desirous of	want
blue in color	blue
came to the conclusion	concluded
cancel out	cancel
category	class
cease	stop
circle around	circle
coalesce	join
cognizant	aware
collect together	collect
compensate, compensation	pay
components	parts
concede	admit
conceive	think
conception	idea
conclusion, conclude	end
connect to	connect
consensus of opinion	consensus
consequent results	results
considerable	much
constructive	helpful
deemed it necessary to	[eliminate]
deficiency	lack
delete the most insignificant	delete
deliberation	thought
delineate	outline, draw
demonstrate	show
descend down	descend
despite the fact that	although
determine	find
disappear from sight	disappear
discontinue	stop
during the year of 2008	during 2008
early beginnings	beginnings

Instead of	Use
effect a change in	change
eliminate	cut out
empty out	empty
enclosed herein	enclosed
encounter	meet
endeavor	try
enter in the program	enter
equitable	fair
establish	set up
evince	show
exactly identical	identical
exemplify	show
exhibits a tendency to	tends
facilitate	help
few in number	few
first and foremost	first
following after	following
for the purpose of	for
for the reason that	because
frequently	often
function	use
give a weakness to	weaken
give an indication of	indicate
give encouragement to	encourage
have at hand	have
hold in abeyance	wait
I am of the opinion	I think
I will endeavor to ascertain	I will try to find out
in my opinion I think	in my opinion, or I think
in order of importance	order
in order to	to
in regard to	[eliminate]
in the amount of	for
in the course of	during
in the event of	if

Instead of	Use
in the event that	if
in the interest of time	[eliminate]
in the majority of cases	most, or usually
in the majority of instances	often
in the matter of	about
in the nature of	like
in the near future	soon
in the neighborhood of	about
in the normal course	normally
in the normal course of our procedure	normally
in the opinion of this writer	in my opinion
in the same way as described	as described
in view of the fact that	because
indicate	show
initial	first
initiate	start or begin
institute an improvement in	improve
interpose an objection	object
involve the necessity of	require
is corrective of	corrects
is found to be	is
is indicative of	indicates
is suggestive of	suggests
is suggestive of	suggests
it appears that an oversight has been made	I [or we] overlooked
it has been brought to my attention	I have learned
it has been recognized that	[eliminate]
it is apparent that	therefore, or it seems that
it is incumbent on me	I must
it is noteworthy that	[eliminate]

Instead of	Use
it is the intention of this writer to	[eliminate]
it would not be unreasonable to assume	assume
join together	join
large in sample size	large
make a decision to	decide to
make the acquaintance of	meet
may I call to your attention	[eliminate]
may or may not	may
modifications contained herein	these changes
most complete	complete
multitudinous	many
mutual cooperation	cooperation
my personal opinion	my opinion
new innovation	new
objective	aim
obligation	debt
of a confidential nature	confidential
on behalf of	for
on the basis of	by
on the few occasions	occasionally
on the grounds that	since
on the part of	by
optimum, optimal	best
owing to the fact that	since
perform an analysis of	analyze
perform an examination of	examine
perhaps I should mention that	[eliminate]
permit me to take this opportunity	I want to
pertaining to	about
preparatory to	before
present a conclusion	conclude

Instead of	Use
prior to the time of/that	before
proceed	go
proceed to separate	separate
procure	get
prolong the duration	prolong
provide information about	inform
provided that	if
the purpose of this memo	[eliminate]
range all the way from	range from
reached an agreement	agreed
report back	report
secure	get
similar	like
state the point that	state that
still continue	continue
structure our planning pursuant	make plans
subsequent to	after
subsequently	later
supplement	add
surrounding circumstances	circumstances
take into consideration, taking this factor into consideration, or take under advisement	consider
tangible	real
terminate	end, stop, dismiss
the committee made an agreement	the committee agreed, or we agreed
the committee made the decision	the committee decided, or we decided
the fact that	[eliminate]
the field of photography	photography
the purpose of this memo	[eliminate]
the question as to whether	whether

Instead of	Use
the undersigned	I
the writer	I
there is no doubt	[eliminate]
this report is an offering	this report offers
to be in agreement with	agree
to have a preference for	prefer
to summarize the above	in summary
total effect of	effect of
transact	do
under date of	dated
under no circumstances	never
undertake a study of	study
until such time as	until
utilize, utilization	use
visualize	see

Instead of	Use
we deem it advisable	I suggest
what is believed is	[eliminate]
whereas	but
whereby	which
whether or not	whether
with a view to	to
with reference to	[eliminate]
with regard to	about
with the result that	so that
with this in mind, it is therefore clear	therefore
within the realm of possibility	possible
you will find attached	attached is, or here is

Proofread One Last Time

Put what you've written aside for a while, then take one last objective read through it. When you can answer the following questions with a "yes," you've made your communication as clear as possible:

- Did you write *to* your reader?
- Have you used an active voice whenever possible?
- Have you kept your message simple?
- Have you used specific, not vague, words?
- Have you used present tense whenever possible?
- Have you omitted all the unnecessary and redundant words?

Now, with these principles in mind, turn to the chapter that features the communication you are writing. Each chapter is set up so you can use these steps to make your writing reader-friendly and bulletproof.

2
DESIGN AND LAYOUT

One picture is worth a thousand words.

—FRED R. BARNARD

Design and layout can make your communication come alive and make your message immediately apparent. Now, with so much technology at your fingertips, design becomes much simpler, but you must develop the ability to plan and visualize what you want to convey. Then decide what will appeal to your reader and help his or her understanding of the material.

Plan. Use spacing, indenting, underlining, numbering, boldface type, and different sizes and types of lettering to make your message more understandable and visually appealing. Visual appeal is key not only in its ability to grab the interest of your reader but also to help the reader remember the details of your message. Learn to think in terms of text formats that set off paragraphs; typefaces to denote sections; use of color; and graphs, tables, flowcharts, drawings, and lists that promote your message and reinforce it to your reader. You will need to study basic layout and design elements, and learn a few facts about typefaces and type sizes, but the results will be well worth it.

THINK ABOUT CONTENT

Evaluate your content in terms of the following points:
- Know your audience and decide what precisely they need to know.
- Decide what you want to emphasize to help you focus on how you will create special displays.
- Review the options of the system you will use to produce your communication. Desktop publishing and computer capabilities create many possibilities.
- Begin to think in multiple colors if your communication warrants and you have this capability and budget.

Examine your text for ways to make it visually more appealing:
- Use boldface headings in a larger type size to draw the reader's attention and help him or her focus on the subject.
- Use white space to create the impression that your communication is short and easy to read.

- Use underlining, indenting, and varied but consistent spacing to break up the density of the text and help the reader scan for specific information.
- Decide which elements of your communication should be reinforced by art, graphs, or charts, and create these.
- Determine if much of your information can be distilled into table form for easy, immediate understanding.

Create tables to display large important groups of data:

- Think of general-information tables first, keeping them as simple as possible.
- Use specific-information tables as needed, but don't create tables where simple tabulating within the text works as well.

Design graphics that are understandable at a glance, using these guidelines:

- Reduce graphics to their simplest, clearest elements.
- Make graphics appropriate to their contents in size and arrangement.
- Use complete titles that answer the *who, what, why, when, where,* and *how* questions.

- Number graphics consecutively by type. (For example, Cell Division, Phase I; Cell Division, Phase II; and so on.)
- Locate graphics near the related text.
- Refer to graphics in the text.
- Use footnotes as needed below the graphics.

 Here are a few other things to keep in mind:
- Pay special attention to the layout of text and images.
- Remember, the eye focuses first on the upper outside corner of the left-hand page and the lower outside corner of the right-hand page.
- Create a communication in which all the parts look like a unified whole.
- Reader-test your communication whenever possible and make any necessary changes.

ELIMINATE WRONG MESSAGES

Remember that graphics supplement your written message; they don't replace it. Don't create visual "noise" by using too many, confusing, or too varied illustrations, charts, or graphs, and don't make the visuals too complex. This defeats the purpose.

Selecting Type Arrangement

Design and layout can make your communication come alive and make your message immediately apparent. Now, with so much technology at your fingertips, design becomes much simpler, but you must develop the ability. Design and layout can make your communication come alive and make your message immediately apparent. Now, with so much technology at your fingertips, design becomes much simpler, but you must develop the ability Design and

Long lines, double-spaced.

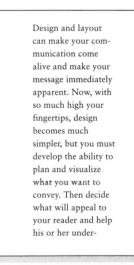

Design and layout can make your communication come alive and make your message immediately apparent. Now, with so much high your fingertips, design becomes much simpler, but you must develop the ability to plan and visualize what you want to convey. Then decide what will appeal to your reader and help his or her under-

Short single-spaced lines, which make use of white space.

Design and layout can make your communication come alive and make your message immediately apparent. Now, with so much technology at your fingertips, design becomes much simpler, but you must develop the style, want to convey. Then decide what will appeal to your reader and help his or her understanding of the material.

Design and layout can make your communication come alive and make your message immediately apparent. Now, with so much technology at your fingertips, design becomes much simpler, but you must develop the style, want to convey. Then decide what will appeal to your reader and help his or her understanding of the material.

Type on facing pages should align at top, left, and bottom.

Justified Copy

Design and layout can make your communication come alive and make your message immediately apparent. Now, with so much technology at your fingertips, design becomes much simpler, but you must develop the ability to plan and visualize what you want to convey. Then decide what will appeal to your reader and help his or her understanding of the material.
   Design and layout can make your communication come alive and make your message immediately apparent. Now, with so much technology

Design and layout can make your communication come alive and make your message immediately apparent. Now, with so much technology at your fingertips, design becomes much simpler, but you must develop the ability to plan and visualize what you want to convey. Then decide what will appeal to your reader and help his or her understanding of the material.
   Design and layout can make your communication come alive and make your message immediately apparent. Now, with so much technology

Design and layout can make your communication come alive and make your message immediately apparent. Now, with so much technology at your fingertips, design becomes much simpler, but you must develop the ability to plan and visualize what you want to convey. Then decide what will appeal to your reader and help his or her understanding of the material.
   Design and layout can make your communication come alive and make your message immediately apparent. Now, with so much technology

Left justified: *Lines start at the same position at left.*

Fully justified: *Lines start and end at the same position on the left and right, respectively.*

Right justified: *Lines end at the same position at right.*

Setting Type in Columns

Design and Layout

Design and layout can make your communication come alive and make your message immediately apparent. Now, with so much technology at

your fingertips, design becomes much simpler, but you must develop the ability to plan and visualize what you want to convey.

Then decide what will appeal to your reader and help his or her understanding of the material. Design

Two-column grid

Design and Layout

Graphic design and layout can make your communication come alive and make your message immediately apparent. Design and layout can make your communication come alive and make your message immediately apparent.
Now, with so much technology at your fingertips, design

becomes much simpler, but you must develop the ability to plan and visualize what you want to convey. Then decide what will appeal to your reader and help his or her understanding of the material.
Design and layout can make your communication come alive and make your message immediately apparent.
Now, with so much technology at your fingertips, design becomes much simpler, but you

must develop the ability to plan and visualize what you
Design and layout can make your communication come alive and make your message immediately apparent. Now, with so much technology at your fingertips, design becomes much simpler, but you must develop the ability to plan and visualize what you want to convey.
Then decide what will appeal to your reader and help his or

Three-column grid

Six-column grid:
This design consists of two text blocks, the first with four columns of space, and the second with two.

Table

Types	Samples		
	Column 1	Column 2	Column 3
A	xxx	xxx	xxx
B	xxx	xxx	xxx
C	xxx	xxx	xxx
D	xxx	xxx	xxx
Total	xxx	xxx	xxx

Use tables to display groups of data.

Flowchart

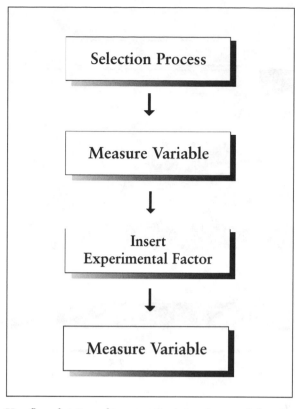

Use flowcharts to show progression or sequential steps.

Line Chart

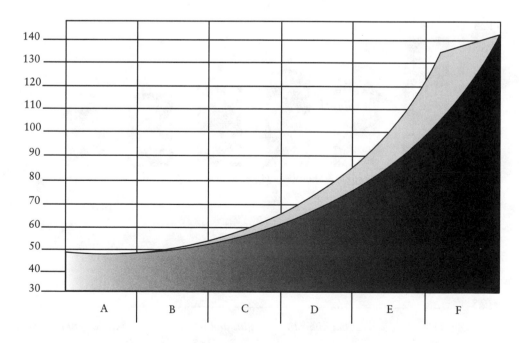

Use a line chart to show quantity change.

Horizontal Bar Chart

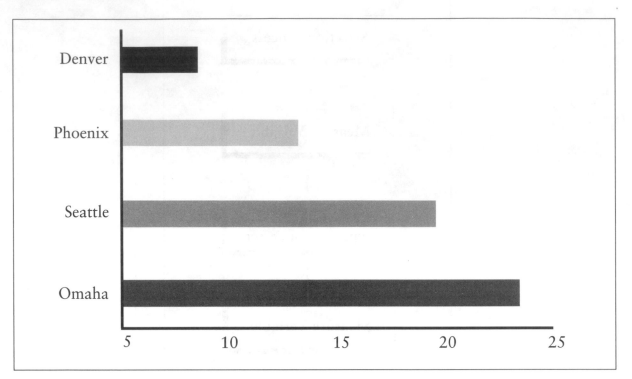

Use a simple horizontal bar chart to show quantity change over time or distance. Use a multiple bar chart to show up to several kinds of quantities. Different colors add visual interest and show comparative values.

Bilateral Bar Chart

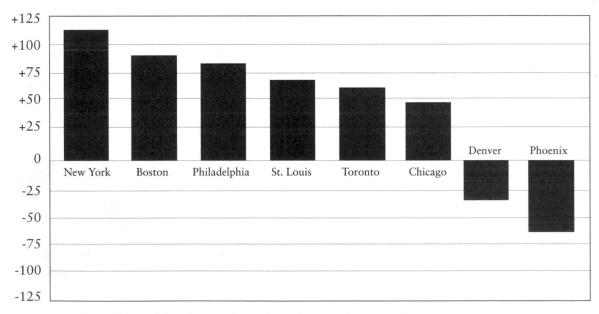

Use the bilateral bar chart to show plus and minus changes and percentage changes.

Pie Chart

Use the pie chart to show how the whole is divided.

Statistical Map

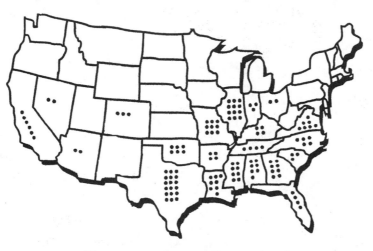

Use a statistical map to illustrate distribution.

Pictogram

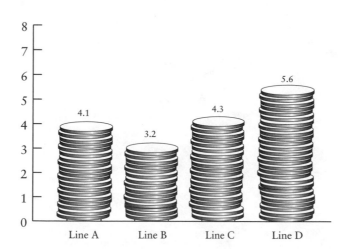

Use the pictogram to show quantitative differences in picture form.

II. SOCIAL

3

ANNOUNCEMENT

The difference between the right word and almost the right word is the difference between lightning and the lightning bug.

—MARK TWAIN

An announcement may be good news or bad news, but the form itself is consistent: Get the reader's attention, then give him or her the single message you want to communicate. Be direct, focused, brief, and *timely*.

DECIDE TO WRITE

Announcements are suitable for many of the events and changes in our lives:

- Change of address
- Anniversary: wedding or business
- Birth or adoption
- Personal life event: graduation, wedding, marital separation, divorce, retirement, or death
- Employee change: resignation, promotion, transfer, special achievement, new employees, job opening
- Opening a business, branch office, or store
- Business changes: new business name, price changes, product recall, new programs, products, policies, hours, practices, contracts, organization buyout, merger, bankruptcy, expansion, acquisition, company layoff, downsizing, closing, or record sales
- Seminars, workshops, or conferences
- Open house for home, business, or school

THINK ABOUT CONTENT

- Ask yourself *who, what, when, where, why,* and *how* to help focus the information you want to communicate.
- State the information in order of importance.
- Be direct, brief, and concise.
- Check the prescribed format of different kinds of announcements.
- Emphasize the goodwill aspects of your news. If your company is changing working hours, for example, emphasize the greater convenience for employees and customers.
- Use the "need-to-know" guideline in making your announcement. Who needs to know your news?
- When it's appropriate, emphasize the reasons for your news to promote understanding and goodwill.

ELIMINATE WRONG MESSAGES

- An announcement should supply complete, basic information. Leave out lengthy explanations or extraneous facts. Even when the announcement is a hybrid—combined with a sales message, for example—the format and style should strengthen the single message.

- Don't let employees hear or read your information from an outside source first.
- Don't put off a bad news announcement. It is usually best that your bad news be received directly from you rather than from another source. If nothing else, announce the basic news and state that full information will follow.

CONSIDER ANNOUNCEMENT TYPES

- A personal name change is announced by stating that, as of (date) the person formerly known as (name) will be known as (name). No explanation is needed, but written notes to friends and colleagues are desirable.
- Graduation announcements are usually formal and printed but certainly may be handwritten. This announcement has evolved because space at graduation ceremonies is now restricted to only a few invitations per graduate. Send only to close family members and friends. This announcement may be sent with an invitation to a graduation party. "No gifts, please" may be written in the lower left-hand corner.
- Engagement announcements can be handwritten or printed and should be sent to relatives and friends. Because of the rich tradition of this announcement in our culture, a special section has been devoted to it (see page 28).
- Wedding announcements are often printed in a prescribed format. They may also be personal letters or notes (see "Invitations," page 65).
- Birth or adoption announcements are usually made by both parents to friends and relatives. The announcements may be selected either before the birth, and then the final information phoned in after the birth, or commercial cards with blanks may be purchased and then filled in and sent out. Include the infant's sex; birth date (and time, if you wish) or age (if adopted); parents' full names; siblings' names (if you like); and an expression of happiness. Parents may also send an announcement to newspapers and other publications that print this information. Example:

"Roger and Brenda Dell of 344 South Parker Road, Littleton, are delighted to announce the birth of a son, Jared, on August 12, 2007, at Littleton Hospital. They have one daughter, Meredith, four. Mrs. Dell is the former Miss Brenda Sales."

When the couple has been divorced before the birth, the announcement is made by the mother, in the name she now uses. Widowed women may use "Sally and the late Paul Davidson." A single mother should use her chosen title and name. In all cases, personal announcements are in the best taste. Personal birth and adoption announcements should also be sent to close colleagues and work associates.

- Retirement announcements are especially important when the retiree is a doctor, dentist, or other professional. These announcements are usually combined with the announcement of the person taking over the practice or any other changing business information. Printed announcements with a good-news emphasis are important here.
- A death in the family is difficult at best. The immediate family must notify other relatives and friends by telephone and ask that they notify others. If funeral arrangements have been made, this information can be given, eliminating the need for another round of calls. The next step is notifying the attorney of the deceased. Written announcements generally take a number of forms:

1. An announcement may be arranged by the funeral home, or a paid newspaper notice may be placed.
2. An obituary may be written by newspaper staff. Usually the information is verified by a close family member. Information generally included is the complete name of the deceased (including the original family name), date of death, date of birth or age at the time of death, address at the time of death, names of immediate family members and place of residence, hours and location where friends may call on the family, place and time of the funeral, whether the funeral is private, and frequently a request that any contributions be given to a charity (often designated) instead of flowers being sent to the funeral home.

3. A news article describing the achievements and contributions of the deceased may be written by newspaper staff and/or a family representative.

4. Printed announcements may be sent to colleagues and/or out-of-town acquaintances.

5. Handwritten notes may be sent to out-of-town relatives, friends, and acquaintances.

- Legal announcements or announcements with legal implications should be made in conjunction with the proper attorney. Plans to remarry where there are legal agreements in place, adoption of children, change in payment of debts incurred, all come under this category.

- Annulments are very private matters and should be handled with the utmost confidentiality. Generally, only immediate family and close friends are told, and then only on a need-to-know basis. They may be told informally and verbally, or in a personal note.

- Divorce is also the private business of the two people involved and a printed announcement is in very poor taste. Informal notes may be sent as necessary to those who have a need to know. A statement and no explanation is best.

- Good business news is best announced by using a press release. Sending the release to newspapers and other media is a good way to get the word out. Be sure to include a contact person and complete contact information: telephone and fax numbers and an email address (see "Press Release," page 350).

- Business announcements (opening a branch, moving to a new location, introducing a new product, and the like) offer the opportunity to stage an open house. Printed announcements or invitations, a newspaper announcement, and perhaps announcements by other media are the best ways to get the word out.

- Bad business news—if the news is of major public concern—may best be handled by calling a press conference to make a statement. Letting people hear directly from you first gives the organization points for being forthright, open, and honest. This approach also preempts cover-up rumors and/or an unfavorable spin, which can follow when a story originates from the media.

- Board of directors' meeting announcements should follow corporate bylaws, state requirements, and federal laws. Include the date, time, place, reason for the meeting, and who is invited. A waiver of notice or proxy card is enclosed with a postage-paid, addressed return envelope.

- A change of address, status, or mode of doing business should be sent, with only the pertinent information, to the businesses or people who need to know. If this change has legal ramifications, check the particular requirements for making such an announcement or notification.

- A business change should put the information in its best light. State the change; why it's being made; the benefits for employees, customers, clients, and others affected by the change; and any expressions of appreciation to those involved.

SELECT A FORMAT

- Formal personal announcements for such things as an engagement (see page 28), open house, new business, retirement, and the like are often printed or engraved on a white or off-white card and mailed directly to the recipients in matching envelopes.

- Birth or adoption announcements may be hand-designed, printed, or the blanks of commercially available cards filled in and sent in matching envelopes to friends and relatives.

- Interoffice announcements are usually best done in memo format, and may be sent by email.

- Meetings, changes of address, sales, new business openings, and reminder-type announcements are often sent by email, or may be printed on postcards and mailed.

- Newspaper announcements are best completed after contacting the correct editor and learning exactly how he or she wants the announcement submitted. Most will be by email.

- Business letterhead, typewritten, with generous margins all around, is the best choice for disseminating information to a general readership. It is also sometimes still used when submitting information to the media. Media announcements (see "Press Release") must include a contact name and telephone number.

SELECT STRONG WORDS

announce	inform
appointed	introduce
call	notice
celebrate	open
change	pleased
delighted	promoted
happy	report
honor	start
immediate	welcome

CONSTRUCT EFFECTIVE PHRASES

change in hours

effective immediately

give notice that

located at a new address

open for business

please join us

pleased to announce

to inform you

will open soon

WRITE STRONG SENTENCES

Start with a key verb. Then construct information in concise order of importance:

We welcome Brian Lee Turner, born August 20, 2006, at 3:36 P.M., weighing seven pounds and six ounces, measuring twenty-two inches, to the family of James and Janice Turner.

Greg and Alice Albright are proud to announce the adoption of a baby boy, Alexander Lee, age seven months, on September 15, 2006.

Our new sales policy will allow you to extend the billing period fifteen additional days for new orders.

We are pleased to announce that Mr. George F. Frommer has accepted the position of Chairman of the Board of Directors at Chances effective June 1, 2006.

We must increase the price of the Model A-455 Diluter from $566 to $625 effective July 1, 2006.

Robert R. O'Malley of Pittsburgh, formerly of Denver, died of leukemia September 12, 2006.

John H. Hadley, formerly of Danberry, a physician and program director at St. Mary's Hospital, died August 30, 2006, in St. Louis.

The "Race for the Cure" breast-cancer benefit 5K run will take place at Washington Park's Pavilion on September 29, at 8:00 A.M.

BUILD EFFECTIVE PARAGRAPHS

Focus on an action verb and the essential facts to build strong and effective paragraphs. For example:

We rejoice at the birth of our beautiful new daughter, Kathleen Kate McNeilly, born at 2:34 A.M., Thursday, May 10, 2006, measuring twenty-one inches and weighing eight pounds, four ounces. Her parents, Ben and Mary McNeilly, and sister, Jennifer, two, welcome her into their hearts and home.

Baby Boom will open its doors in the Tamarac Square Center (next to Lloyd's Jewelry, main floor) Friday, July 15. Bring in this card for your free T-shirt. Store hours will be 10:00 A.M. till 9:00 P.M., Monday through Saturday. Open noon till 6:00 P.M. on Sunday. Sign up to win our $500 shopping spree!

Cooper's sales grew 33 percent this quarter over last quarter. The growth, said CEO Bradley Sandler, was due to the introduction of the new Model Z-560, which sold over 3,000 units.

Quick Lube offers you a full oil change—including filters—for just $24.95 at our new full-service garage on Evans and Orchard. We'll do it in just 20 minutes, while you wait. Bring in this card to receive your free sun visor.

Davis and Company Manufacturing announces the recall of their Model A-7655 Air Conditioner due to defective gaskets found in some units. Leaks from these units may cause nausea due to gases that are not properly sealed in the compressor. Please return all Model A-7655 Air Conditioner units to the place of purchase for a replacement.

Barker, Taylor, and McKenzie are pleased to announce that Harold P. Garon has joined the law firm as a partner. Mr. Garon, who has spent the past five years at Yale and Gates, will head the firm's corporate practice.

Jake Walker Pierce, formerly of Denver, a physician and program director at St. Mary's Hospital, died August 23 in St. Louis. He was 35.

The opening of the Burn Unit at St. Joseph's Hospital will take place Thursday, April 10, at 2:00 P.M. The dedication ceremony will include a speech by the governor and music by the Utah Children's Choir.

New production hours for Plant D are 6:00 A.M. to 3:00 P.M. for Shift A, and 3:00 P.M. to 12:00 midnight for Shift B. The Shift C schedules, special assignments, and shift changeover policies will be handled in each department. This new policy has been set in response to employee requests and to coordinate with suppliers' schedules.

Sandra F. Frank, formerly of Schenley Advertising, has joined Marks, Inc. as creative vice president. She will handle all the conceptional aspects of the new Brewer campaign.

Dr. Richard Lewin announces his retirement, effective April 30. His practice will be taken over by his associate, Dr. Stanley Dever.

EDIT, EDIT, EDIT

Pay attention to precise detail to insure that your reader gets the message you want to send.

Adoption

*Roger, Delores, Jonathan, and Allyson Carver
are proud and happy to announce the adoption of*

a daughter and a sister, Jessica Rae, born January 12, 2006	*a son and a brother, Michael Roger, born November 13, 2005*

who arrived from China on December 10, 2005.

Divorce

*[Handwritten]
(Date)*

Dear Eleanor,

Regrettably, Dan and I are divorcing.

My temporary address for the next six months will be my parents' home, 144 East Walnut, Detroit 49332. I will stay on at Becker and Becker, and Dan plans to take a position in Los Angeles. I'm sure he will let you know where he settles.

I cherish your friendship, and will be in touch again as soon as I get things settled.

With love,

Jennifer

Birth

Larry and Lucy Melville welcome a beautiful baby girl,

Melanie Louise,

who arrived August 12, at 2:30 P.M. weighing 7 pounds, 8 ounces; and measuring 20 inches.

State the good news.

Make sure the information is complete.

Divorce

[Handwritten]
(Date)

Dear Alice,

For reasons I don't wish to discuss, Patrick and I are divorcing after five years. Since we both value your friendship, it makes this separation even more difficult. (Who gets the friends in these situations is always a dilemma, but I hope in our case it will be both of us.)

I will be living with Susan Blake for the next six months, 167 Downing Street, Denver 80233. When we get moved in and the telephone is connected, I'll give you a ring.

I'm sure Patrick would welcome a call from you. He will be staying in the house.

Talk to you soon.

Yours truly,

Jennie

Formal Professional Announcement

French and French
is pleased to announce
that

Susan A. Banes

has joined the firm
as a partner.
She will be in charge of
Southern Spain Operations.

New Employee

Be precise and complete.

State information in order of importance.

MEMO

DATE: (Date)
TO: All Employees
FROM: Cleo Barker
SUBJECT: Mr. William A. Carey Joins Glucks as System Sales Vice President

We are pleased to announce that Mr. William A. Carey will join Glucks as vice president in charge of system sales, effective June 1. Bill will be in charge of all Model Lines A, B, and C sales activity, which will be consolidated to our offices from our Seattle and New York offices.

Bill was in charge of automated sales at Z-Rocks for the past seven years and was instrumental in that company's outstanding sales growth of 55 percent during that period.

Please drop by the Sales Department, introduce yourself, and welcome Bill to Glucks.

Obituary

CALVIN LEIGH HOLMES, of Denver, a banking director, died September 12 at his home. He was 62. Private funeral services will be held September 15 at Faith Church in Hampden Memorial Gardens.

He was born January 27, 1943, in Ft. Collins. On September 20, 1974, he married Mary Jo Appleton in Colby, Kansas. She preceded him in death.

Holmes was a banking and agricultural director at Commerce State Bank in Littleton, Colorado, and he was a member of the Farm House Fraternity. He was a lieutenant in the Navy during the Vietnam War.

He is survived by two sons, Steven Holmes, of Denver, and Fred Holmes, of Chile, and a daughter, Margaret Anne Holmes, of Phoenix.

Price Increase

Dear Customer:

Beginning May 1, it will be necessary for Lawer and Frisk to raise our consulting rate from $225 to $250 an hour. We regret that this change is necessary, however, this is our first increase in over 10 years. (Please see the recent survey reported in *Denver Business,* which indicates that, at the new rates, Lawer and Frisk will still be about 15 percent below the rate structure of similar firms in the area.)

We value the opportunity to serve you, and welcome your concerns and comments. Please contact Julie Reese at 303-555-0123 with any questions about your account.

Sales Meeting

Memo
DATE: (Date)
TO: All Sales Representatives
FROM: Ted Garcia, National Sales Manager
SUBJECT: National Sales Meeting, April 10, from 10:00 A.M. to 3:00 P.M.

A sales meeting will be held on Tuesday, April 10 from 10:00 A.M. until 3:00 P.M. in the Board Room at Central Headquarters. Lunch will be served.

An agenda will be mailed to you on March 30. If you have any agenda items, please send them to me by March 18.

Please let me know immediately if you will be unable to attend. Thanks, I look forward to seeing all of you.

Professional Office Relocation

(Date)

Dear Patients:

I will move my offices to 1400 Clearwater, Suite 540, on July 8. This is what you have been asking for: a new, larger, and more convenient building.

There is free parking under the building and an elevator directly into our lovely, new reception area. The new office telephone number is 727-555-0123.

I look forward to seeing you on your next visit.

Yours truly,

Dr. Charles Rose

New Policy

Memo
DATE: (Date)
TO: Department Managers
FROM: Stewart Collins, VP
SUBJECT: New Lunch Policy

To alleviate the congestion and long lines in the cafeteria between noon and 1:30 P.M., we will serve lunch in three shifts by department:

Preparation Department — 11:30 A.M.

Office Personnel and Production
    Department — Noon

Sales and Shipping — 12:30 P.M.

Please try to assign employees who need another time equally over the schedule.

I appreciate your cooperation in making this change. Give me a call if you have any comments or questions.

Be sure to address the *what, why, when, where,* and *how.*

New Product

*John Henry Ford
1335 North Arapahoe Road
is pleased to announce that*

*THE NEW MODELS
HAVE ARRIVED.*

*Come take a test drive.
Bring this card to receive a
free parking lot car locator and
register for our Mustang Give-Away.
September 15–17,
10:00 A.M.–9:30 P.M.*

New Business

*Sole Music
is opening in your neighborhood
at 433 West Prince Street
(across from Joe's Deli).
If your feet don't feel like dancing,
bring those shoes on in
and we guarantee
we'll tune them up!
Bring this card for 25 percent off
your first repair.
10–9 Mon. through Fri.;
noon–9 Sat.
303-555-0123*

ENGAGEMENT ANNOUNCEMENT

Over the past several decades, many factors have influenced the traditional practices of announcing an engagement to be married: the changed role of women in our society; the high rate of divorce and remarriage; same-sex relationships; and the dramatic changes in the ages, career status, mobility, and financial resources of those who are becoming engaged. Although we still cling to some of the traditional, time-honored elements of announcing a couple's engagement, many of the old items of protocol are falling away in favor of announcements that more accurately reflect our changed roles. However, the most important element in the engagement announcement should remain the sharing of the joyous news.

To make the announcement public, it may be printed in newspapers and other publications. Contact the social editor and ask for the desired format. A black-and-white glossy photograph of the engaged couple or just the future bride may appear with the announcement.

Here are some guidelines that are still generally accepted. If a young woman has not been married, her parents usually make the announcement:

"Jack and Julie Bremmer of Cottonwood Manor, Texas, announce the engagement of their daughter, Katherine Anne Bremmer, to Alex James Smerthington, son of John Z. and Lucy Smerthington of Minneapolis, Minnesota. A June wedding is planned.

Ms. Bremmer graduated from Texas A and M and is a communications consultant for Beams and Motes Advertising Agency. Mr. Smerthington graduated from Texas A and M. He is associated with Mickey Advertising Agency in New York City."

If one of the future bride's parents is deceased, the announcement is made by the other:

"Mrs. Barbara Gates announces the engagement of her daughter, Ms. Sandra E. Gates, to Dr. David R. Cole. . . . Ms. Gates is also the daughter of the late Robert Gates."

If a parent of the future groom is deceased:

". . . son of Mrs. Abigail R. Wright and the late Mr. George B. Wright."

When the engaged woman is divorced or widowed, her parents may make the announcement, using her current name.

A mature woman, single, divorced, or widowed, may make her own announcement:

"The engagement of Miss [Ms. or Mrs.] Deana Turner to Mr. Jacob Die has been announced . . ."

When the future bride's parents are divorced, the announcement is usually made by the mother:

"Mrs. Susan Raines announces . . . Ms. Raines is also the daughter of Mr. Julius B. Raines of Boston, Massachusetts."

When the divorced parents are cordial, they may announce the engagement together:

"Mr. John Kelly of Ft. Lauderdale, Florida, and Mrs. Margaret B. Waters of Indianapolis, Indiana, announce . . ."

If a remarried mother makes the announcement, it may read:

"Mr. Richard R. and Glenda F. Gaines announce the engagement of Mrs. Gaines's daughter, Ellen Sue Bates, . . . Ms. Bates is also the daughter of Mr. Robert G. Bates of Riverside, New York."

If the engaged woman is adopted, the family that raised her from infancy has no reason to mention this fact. If she joined the family later and has retained her original surname, the announcement should read:

"Mr. Roy and Mrs. Rose Weinstein announce the engagement of their adopted daughter, Ms. Carla Reid, daughter of the late Mr. Carl and Mrs. Trudy Reid."

If the engaged woman is an orphan, the nearest relative, godparent, or dearest friend may make the announcement as may the woman herself:

"The engagement of Daisey Marlys Gibson (daughter of the late Mr. Darrel and Mrs. Alta Gibson) is announced . . .

The parents of the engaged man may make the announcement when the woman is from another country, has no living relatives, or for some other reason has no contact with her family. The man's parents should not make it in their own names, but in the woman's parents' names:

"The engagement of Miss Sutra Batra of Bombay, India, to Dr. Walker Dennis Tabor, son of Dr. Walter and Gloria Tabor of Kentilworth, Illinois, is announced."

The couple may elect to announce their own engagement, either alone or in concert with their parents:

"Steven Barr and Louise Albright announce their engagement . . ." Or, *"Louise Albright and Steven Barr join with their parents, Mark and Helen Albright, and Albert and Joan Barr, in announcing the couple's engagement."*

If an engagement is canceled, the same persons who received an announcement should also be notified, simply, of this change.

Engagement

Douglas and Anne Wittenberger
announce
the engagement
of Anne Wittenberger's daughter,

Elizabeth Sterling Dunning,
to
Robert Townsend Fielder,

of New York City.

Miss Dunning is also the daughter of
Larry Dunning of Phoenix.

4

CONGRATULATIONS

Whatever kind word thou speakest, the like shalt thou hear.

—ANONYMOUS

Nothing makes our accomplishments sweeter than the compliments and praise of others. We've gotten away from the practice of sending notes and letters of congratulations over the last couple of decades, so if you send one, yours may make a lasting impression. Send congratulations often, making your notes sincere and totally positive. Focus solely on toasting the recipient's achievement or happy event.

DECIDE TO WRITE
Send congratulations for events like these:
- Personal achievements such as graduation, award, promotion, successful speech, publication, winning a competition, receiving a prize, finishing a marathon, completing a course of study, receiving a rating for a hobby or avocation
- Family events like marriage, birth or adoption of a child, anniversary
- Life events like a birthday, retirement, first or new home
- Religious events such as joining a church, baptism, confirmation, first communion, bar or bat mitzvah, ordination, taking vows, becoming elder or deacon

- Business achievements like an award for top or outstanding sales, promotion, new job, new assignment, new title, starting a new business, getting a new contract, having a book published, joining an association, other business success
- Election to office in a club or association, professional society, political post, social club

THINK ABOUT CONTENT
- Write immediately. But if you've heard the news long after the fact, or if you have procrastinated, write anyway, and note briefly why your greeting is late: "Congratulations. I may not be swift, but I'm still delighted that you are now a vice president."
- State the occasion for congratulations in the first sentence or two.
- Use the word *congratulations* early.
- Write conversationally as you'd talk to the person. (A note to a friend will be less formal than one to a business associate.)
- Connect the person to the achievement, occasion, or event.

- If appropriate, relate how you learned the news, include a newspaper clipping, or refer to a shared memory.
- Relate something that bears on the occasion or event, but remember to keep your message focused on the recipient.
- Make sure your message has the ring of sincerity.
- Express your best wishes for the person and your expectation for continued success.
- Make sure your congratulations letter has a single focus.
- Make it short. Three to six sentences is usually just right.

ELIMINATE WRONG MESSAGES

- Don't assume a tone improper to the relationship you have with the recipient.
- Avoid being overly flattering. Effusive, unmerited praise is never appropriate.
- Keep your message focused. A congratulations letter should include only congratulations. Use another letter to address other matters.
- Avoid negative phrases like "Who would have believed it?" (especially for occasions like birthdays and anniversaries).
- Watch your language and phrasing. Avoid words and phrases—like, "How lucky can you get?"— that imply luck, happenchance, or anything other than personal merit.
- Don't be insensitive. Know how the recipient regards the event or occasion. For example, if the recipient prefers not to discuss the fact that this is his 20th year with the company and this promotion should have come 10 years ago, it is insensitive to refer to the fact that he or she had been passed over. If the recipient has very negative feelings about the event or occasion, don't send the letter at all.
- If you can't be sincere in your congratulations, don't write. If a friend is, in your opinion, marrying the wrong person, don't write a hypocritical letter of congratulations. If a business associate gets a promotion you feel belonged to another, don't write.

- Don't overuse the congratulations message for such "public relations" purposes as "Congratulations on opening your new checking account at Fisherman's Bank." A welcome letter is more appropriate.

TAILOR YOUR MESSAGE FOR EXCEPTIONAL SITUATIONS

- Six months after an employee has retired, another congratulations letter that cites some contribution the retiree made to the company, states how the person is missed, and includes continued well wishes will mean a great deal to the recipient. This letter can be signed by all the employees with whom the recipient worked.
- Congratulations on successfully handling a very difficult situation, such as the illness of a family member, divorce, unemployment, or being passed over for promotion, must be handled with great care. Again, such congratulations should reflect a deep personal relationship with the recipient, and if done properly, can be very meaningful.
- Congratulations are often misused as a ploy in sales letters. Be sure your letter doesn't err in intent by mixing these messages.
- Use a public forum to give your greetings when it's appropriate. Many newspapers, for example, have a section for family and friends to print congratulations on an anniversary.
- When using a commercial greeting card to extend congratulations, be sure to make the card personal by writing your own message in addition to the printed one.
- Congratulations on a new family member should be sent immediately. Such greetings have now extended to include even a new pet.
- Tradition no longer dictates that messages to a future bride and groom be different. In this area, at least, we have gained parity. Either the words *best wishes* or *congratulations* apply equally to either person.

SELECT A FORMAT

- Personal congratulations usually take the form of a note handwritten on personal stationery. The commercial fold-over notecards are also fine.
- For a birthday or a specific occasion, commercial cards are often used, but be sure you include a handwritten message.
- For associates from business, clubs, politics, professional associations, and other organizations, a more formal typewritten letter is often better than a handwritten note. Base your choice on the relationship you have with the recipient and the importance of the occasion or good news.
- In an informal or casual work setting, you may send an email to congratulate a colleague on a small accomplishment. Email is becoming the vehicle of choice for many business and personal communications.

SELECT STRONG WORDS

accomplishment	generous
achievement	gift
admire	gratified
applaud	happy
appreciate	honor
asset	imaginative
celebrate	impressive
cheer	incomparable
commend	innovative
compliment	inspiring
congratulate	invaluable
contribution	inventive
create	kudos
debut	leadership
dedicate	legendary
distinguished	meaningful
effort	memorable
enterprising	milestone
esteemed	momentous
excellent	occasion
exceptional	outstanding
exciting	perfect
extraordinary	performance
feat	pleasure
fine	progress
future	proud

recognize	tribute
resourceful	triumph
respected	unforgettable
sensational	unique
skills	unparalleled
special	unsurpassed
success	unrivaled
superb	victory
superior	vision
talented	visible
thrilled	vital
tidings	well-earned (adj.)
tradition	well-wishers
tremendous	winning

BUILD EFFECTIVE PHRASES

always admired your

congratulate you on

continued success in

delighted to hear of your award

deserve adulation

fine accomplishment

held in the highest esteem

how marvelous to hear

impressed with such an accomplishment

join with you in celebration

offer warmest congratulations

outstanding news

received a well-deserved honor

recognize your accomplishment

what an outstanding job

what a wonderful achievement

wish you every happiness

you have achieved

your contribution to

your vision has never faltered

your winning entry

WRITE STRONG SENTENCES

Start with an action verb that expresses your feelings. Put the verb into a phrase, then a sentence:

Congratulations, you did that job perfectly.

I've just heard your good news and am delighted for you.

Congratulations on your well-deserved promotion.

You certainly earned the high praise the reporter gave you.

No one worked harder on the Keene project than you did.

Take a bow for a job done well.

BUILD EFFECTIVE PARAGRAPHS

Remember, the best notes or letters of congratulations are short. This approach adds impact. These paragraphs may constitute most or all of your communication.

Congratulations on a terrific job! I was delighted, but not surprised, to read your piece in the *Wall Street Journal*. I've seldom seen a piece so well thought out, and so extensively and soundly researched.

Congratulations on receiving the Expert Skier Award. It is well deserved. You sliced through that powder on Saturday like a real pro.

Our warmest congratulations on the birth of William III. He has selected two of the most wonderful people we know for parents.

Congratulations on an exceptional job in whipping the St. John's Annual Bazaar together. It bore your expert fingerprints, and profits were the best ever.

EDIT, EDIT, EDIT

Keep your congratulations simple, sincere, and in tune with your relationship to the recipient.

Congratulations on Marriage

[Handwritten]
(Date)

Dear Diane and Kirk,

We were overjoyed to learn you will be married in June. Congratulations. May the love you two now share deepen each day of your lives. Our very best wishes for a wonderful, fulfilling life together.

Love,

Uncle Jasper and
Aunt June Bug

Write immediately.

State congratulations early.

Congratulations on the Birth of Children

[Handwritten]
(Date)

Dear Carolyn,

What wonderful news that the twins were born and are doing well. I've heard they were pronounced "perfect" by the pediatrician, and we rejoice with you.

I'm sure you would much rather have brought them straight home from the hospital, but perhaps this will give you a little time to rest up. I'll call you next week to see what you need. In the meantime, please call me if there's any way I may help.

Lovingly,

Marjorie

Congratulations on a Wedding Anniversary

[Handwritten]
(Date)

Dear Elizabeth,

Congratulations! Of course we'll attend your fiftieth wedding anniversary celebration. Jack and I will be proud to relate the story of the weekend on Lake Witless. It remains a favorite in this family.

You two have achieved a unique level of oneness in your marriage that we've long admired. Our best wishes for many, many more years of even more happiness yet to come.

Affectionately,

Katie and Jack

Congratulations on a Job Well Done

[Handwritten]
(Date)

Dear Bert,

Before you took over Boy Scout Troop IV, the dropout rate was one in two. Over the past year, we have seen our own son, George, go from dread to anticipation in preparing for the next troop meeting. Congratulations. You have truly performed a great service to these boys.

Sincerely,

Melvin Wellington

Congratulations on a Career Achievement

[Handwritten]
(Date)

Dear Jennifer,

Congratulations, Dr. J. E. Jensen. That has a wonderful ring to it. We join you in your happiness; we are so proud of your outstanding achievement. You have demonstrated what determination and hard work can produce, and we know the fruits of your labor will be plentiful.

All the best,

Booker and Alice

Congratulations on Reaching a Personal Goal

[Handwritten]
(Date)

Dear Robert,

Meeting an imposed deadline is difficult, but reaching a self-set goal that no one else believes possible is a feat of determination and extraordinary self-discipline. Congratulations on achieving the AAS designation. I'd like to hear all the details during our Thursday luncheon.

Your friend,

Rich

Congratulations on New Business

[Emailed or handwritten]
(Date)

Jim:

I'm giving you a standing ovation! Congratulations! What a phenomenal accomplishment, winning the Joker account. (I should know; I've bid it three times and lost all three.) I can hardly wait to see your new ideas rolled out over the coming months.

I've always known you have great creativity, and now it will be showcased on the big stage. What a tremendous and well-deserved achievement!

Best wishes for continued success.

Regards,

Adam

Office Congratulations

[Emailed]

Bob:

You've really gotten the Stafford project group off dead center and moving in the right direction. Your approach at the meeting this morning was masterful. Your effective enthusiasm and charm has even gotten the disgruntled members of the group in a very positive frame of mind. Congratulations!

All the best,

Marc

Congratulations on a Promotion

[Typed]
(Date)

Dear David:

I was delighted to hear you will be the First Vice President in charge of creativity. Congratulations. A more deserving or talented partner could not have been selected for the post.

I'm looking forward to seeing many more of the unique ideas that brought you this Gold Pick Award at our agency.

Sincerely,

Winnie Backus

Special Project Congratulations

[Emailed]

Sarah:

Two words: you rock! You created the perfect balance of visual and text in your Power Point presentation. It was outstanding. Congratulations.

Cheers,

Sam

5
CELEBRATIONS OF LIFE

That it will never come again
Is what makes life so sweet.

—EMILY DICKINSON

To share in celebrating a life event of another person increases the joy for both the celebrant and you. Whether it's a christening, confirmation, communion, bar or bat mitzvah, coming out, graduation, anniversary, or retirement—a rite of maturation or a religious rite of passage—this is a unique opportunity to add your voice of support and best wishes. Don't miss it! Notes to those reaching a new phase of life are best infused with personal anecdotes and even quotes from the masters of life. Focus carefully on the person to whom you're writing, and do some research to make sure you've hit the exact, right tone.

DECIDE TO WRITE
Send a personal note with good wishes for the future for:
- A baptism, christening, or dedication of an infant or child
- Ceremonies of faith, such as first communion or confirmation
- Bar mitzvah and bat mitzvahs
- Celebrations and occasions of maturation and entering a new stage of life like coming-out parties, sweet sixteen parties, *quinceañeras,* debutante events, and similar occasions
- Family events like reunions, wedding anniversaries (also see chapter 4, "Congratulations")

THINK ABOUT CONTENT
- Focus on the person.
- Reflect on his or her positive growth and development.
- Write a brief, personal, warm, and positive anecdote or story about the person, if possible.
- Conclude with best wishes for the future.
- Include a picture that will add to the celebration (but not be embarrassing), if possible.

ELIMINATE WRONG MESSAGES
- Learn something about the occasion, event, or rite before writing your message, if you're unsure. This will help you avoid writing something inappropriate or offensive.
- Don't let your message go beyond your personal knowledge and true feelings, or it will ring false or insincere.
- Avoid anything that could embarrass the celebrant. Check first, if in doubt.
- Don't mix messages. Keep the message focused on the celebrant and the occasion or event and its importance to him or her. Reserve questions and other subjects for another time.
- Be careful not to refer to others' accomplishments or make comparisons: "When I turned sixteen . . ." Keep the focus on the celebrant.

CONSIDER SPECIAL SITUATIONS

- Do something special for the celebrant. A treasured photo or a handmade bookmark could easily be included in your note.
- Offer to do something that will make the occasion even more special: Include a "love coupon" that features some benefit of the new status being celebrated. Check with a parent or other responsible adult about an appropriate gift: a roadtrip for a now driving-age person or a tea for a young woman coming out.

SELECT A FORMAT

- A handwritten note on your own personal notecard is the first choice.
- An appropriate greeting card—handmade, computer-generated and printed, or commercial—with your written message included is appropriate.
- If you're sending a gift, write your personal message on a gift card and attach it to the gift.
- You may also want to send an emailed greeting (even an animated one), but don't let it replace the mailed greeting with a special handwritten message for someone you share a close relationship with.

SELECT STRONG WORDS

accomplished	memories
achieved	notice
celebrate	occasion
delighted	praise
feat	record
grand	rejoice
happy	remember
honor	special
impressive	success
innovative	thrilled
join	tradition
joyful	triumph

BUILD EFFECTIVE PHRASES

accomplished so much
achievements like yours
delighted to hear
join with the well-wishers
ready for great things
shall always remember
we are all so proud
we rejoice with you
what a wonderful thing
with solemn respect

WRITE STRONG SENTENCES

Your whole family is so proud of you as you embark on a whole, new phase of your life.

You've turned every life change into an opportunity, and we can hardly wait to see what you do with retirement!

You have demonstrated that you are fully equipped to step up to this next great life adventure and turn it into something spectacular!

BUILD EFFECTIVE PARAGRAPHS

Congratulations on making your first communion. It's a day you will always remember and cherish, as your entire family does, as you take this holy step.

We rejoice with you as you take this giant step into adulthood. You'll be terrific at all you do; you've already demonstrated that you have all the skills.

I'm sure all those things I appreciated about David, the boy, will be some of the same characteristics that will make David, the man, very, very special. Best wishes as you set out on this new adventure called adulthood.

EDIT, EDIT, EDIT

Read your message aloud when you've finished to be sure it sounds just right.

A Young Man's Bar Mitzvah

[Handwritten]
(Date)

Jacob,

Mazel tov! I remember your grandfather's and your father's bar mitzvahs, and now I am fortunate enough to witness yours. Such a wonderful time and such a wonderful family you have. I know you will become one of the next generation of leaders in our community. You have already demonstrated that you are equal to the challenge, with all the excellent study you've completed to reach this day.

I look forward to sharing some special stories with everyone at your party.

Congratulations, and welcome to this bold, new world.

Uncle Max

Upon Entering High School

[Handwritten]
(Date)

Dear Jolie,

I know they say Travis High is riddled with temptations and all sorts of things that parents know are bad for you. But I also know you will find a way to make your high school career one of great accomplishment and distinction. You've proven that already in your accomplishments in grade and middle school.

Awesome possibilities lie ahead of you, and we're confident that you'll make the most of them. Know that we're always here for you.

Congratulations! What a grown-up person you're becoming. All the best for a spectacular freshman year!

Love,

Aunt Jennie and Uncle Ream

Reaching Sweet Sixteen

[Handwritten]
(Date)

Dear Maria,

Add to the joy.

Your world overflows with new possibilities, and we know you have the wisdom and maturity to spin them into gold. We've seen you do it many, many times: that first-grade stage performance; on the soccer field; in the swimming pool; in your vocal trio.

Make it personal and special.

We will watch in amazement to see what you'll do next; and stand ready to help in any way we can. Best wishes for a wonderful sixteenth year.

Aunt Rosa and
Uncle Simon

An Uncle Retires

[Handwritten]
(Date)

Dear Uncle Hermie,

What a perfect day you must have had on Friday. All your dreams about the years to come are now within your grasp, as you set out on this wonderful new and exciting chapter of your life.

I know all the inventiveness and genius you brought to bear in your workplace at Dinger will now be focused on building that sailboat, New Horizons. I look forward to working with you on Saturdays. I've got the champagne ready for the christening! Congratulations and best wishes for smooth sailing in retirement!

Love,
Randy

6

HOLIDAY GREETINGS

Welcome is the best cheer.

—THOMAS FULLER

Add to the celebration! That's what makes the seasons of our lives sweeter: celebrating and cherishing them with others. Don't miss an opportunity to extend special greetings to those in your life. Send a personal communication that can add to their holiday joy and celebration.

Businesses, too, can make very good use of holidays to build relationships with their customers, employees, and colleagues. Care should be taken, of course, to keep your communications in tune with the spirit of the season or day. (An overly commercial theme or message for a sacred or religious day will offend many.)

DECIDE TO WRITE

Before the year begins, record all the holidays you will celebrate and make a list of birthdays, anniversaries, and other special days. Businesses need an annual plan and budget for holiday promotions, and four to six months of lead time to get special items prepared and ready. You may want to note some of the following holidays and seasons observed in the United States (US), Canada (C), Mexico (M), and the United Kingdom (UK). Individual country celebrations may not be on the same date.

- New Year's
- Martin Luther King Jr. Day (US)
- Chinese New Year
- Anniversary of the Constitution (M)
- Lincoln's Birthday (US)
- Valentine's Day (C, UK, US)
- Presidents' Day (US)
- Washington's Birthday (US)
- Flag Day (M, US)
- First of Muharram
- Ash Wednesday
- Ashura
- St. Patrick's Day (C, US)
- Beginning of spring
- Benita Juarez's Birthday (M)
- Mothering Sunday (UK)
- Palm Sunday
- Passover
- Good Friday
- Easter
- Easter Monday (C, UK)
- Holocaust Remembrance Day
- Battle of Puebla (M)
- May Day Bank Holiday (UK)
- Father's Day

- First day of summer
- St. Jean Baptiste (Quebec)
- Canada Day
- Civic Day (C)
- Summer Bank Holiday (UK)
- Labor Day (C, US, M)
- Declaration of Independence (M)
- Independence Day (M, US)
- First day of autumn
- Rosh Hashanah
- Yom Kippur
- Purim (Feast of Lots)
- Day of the Race (M)
- Columbus Day (US)
- Thanksgiving (C, US)
- United Nations Day
- First of Ramadan
- Halloween
- All Saints Day (M)
- Day of the Dead (M)
- Election Day (US)
- Veterans' Day (US)
- Remembrance Day (C)
- Revolution Day (M)
- Pearl Harbor Remembrance Day (US)
- Virgin of Guadalupe (M)
- Hanukkah
- First day of winter
- Christmas
- Boxing Day (C, UK)
- Kwanzaa

THINK ABOUT CONTENT

- Start by mentioning the holiday you are celebrating.
- Connect the holiday to the recipient.
- Give information or the news element of your message.
- End with a statement of best wishes for the recipient(s).

ELIMINATE WRONG MESSAGES

- Don't send a commercial greeting card with only your signature. Be sure to include a personal, handwritten message.
- Don't mix messages or use a holiday as a reason to deliver another kind of message. Use a separate, appropriate communication for the second message.
- In personal messages, like holiday family newsletters, avoid bragging or self-congratulation.
- Be sensitive to your audience. Don't send a letter filled with news about your wonderful new job and great success to a relative who has suffered long unemployment, for example. And don't send religious messages to a general audience or to those of another faith.

CONSIDER SPECIAL SITUATIONS

Holiday Family Newsletter

A wonderful way to keep up with people you aren't able to visit regularly is an annual holiday newsletter. They have become a tradition for many. Here are a few ways to make yours a welcome part of the holidays:

- Organize your newsletter well: chronologically, by topic, or by person.
- Edit it by subaudiences, if possible.
- Keep it short.
- Include ideas and important information as well as a brief list of family achievements and activities.
- Use a single statement and a detail or two to make your newsletter interesting, humorous, and celebratory: "Mindy's Waterford vase was previewed by 43 airport security people before we got it home from Ireland. Here's what we learned . . ."
- Make it "artsy" and more interesting by including a few photos and copying it on colorful, holiday-themed paper.
- If you print or photocopy your newsletter, still add a handwritten personal message to each recipient.

Year-End Business Newsletter

At the end of the year, share important information about your business with employees, customers, and colleagues. Keep these possibilities in mind as you write:

- Consider what you want to say to each audience. You may decide to send one newsletter to all or may find that it's more appropriate to create a different newsletter for each audience.
- Include information about employee achievements, charitable events in which you've been involved, and fund-raisers that you've sponsored.
- Announce new products and spell out any noteworthy financial success or new directions your business is taking.

Holiday Sales Notice to Customers

Writing your customers during the holiday season can help them remember you. Consider these possibilities:

- Use the holiday sales notice as a very important business tool to help create a loyal customer base.
- Consider a notice advertising a "Before Christmas Preferred Customer Sale." If done annually, the sale may become part of customers' regular pre-holiday shopping routine.

Fund-Raiser Notices

The holidays offer an unlimited number of ways to draw attention to your organization. Here are a few:

- Create a wonderful newsletter that features people who've been helped by your organization throughout the year, or who receive special assistance during the holidays.
- Announce a special upcoming event.
- Share information on an annual drive with target amounts of donations to be raised.

SELECT A FORMAT

- Holiday greeting cards should always include a personal message and a handwritten signature. If you feel at a loss for words, use an appropriate quote to get you started (and properly attribute it) and then connect your personal message to that quote.
- Make your greeting creative. Use a postcard, flat card, brochure, fold-over card, or letter format.
- Always keep your greetings in good taste and in the spirit of the holiday.
- Consider sending animated email greetings, which now have many formatting options. But use this venue wisely. It may, for example, be against corporate policy to create and send official office holiday greetings through email.
- Observe email etiquette. When you communicate with people only through email, it is perfectly proper to send an informal, electronic email holiday greeting. But remember, email is still the equivalent of a very informal memo. For all the people you know "offline," send a greeting by regular mail.

WRITE STRONG SENTENCES

It's a wonderful day for celebrating how very special you are to us.

We can't think about this holiday without realizing the bond we share. Wishing you a wonderful holiday.

Our wish for you is that the spirit and joy of this holiday may be yours for the whole year.

This has been a wonderful year for Harvest House Furniture because of you, our wonderful customers. All of us here join our voices to wish you the very best for the coming year.

As we come again to the end of the year, we realize it is your efforts that have helped us achieve so much. Each and every employee is responsible for our success.

Our best wishes for 365 days of joy and happiness.

Our warmest wishes to you and your dear ones on this very, very special day.

Even though we must be absent on this day, our hearts join with yours as we raise a toast and a wish for blessings in abundance, wisdom, and joy in the coming year.

At this time of year, we count our many blessings, and you—dear, dear friends—are among the most precious.

Near or far away, you are in our hearts and minds as we celebrate this wonderful season.

This day, like every day, we wish you all the best.

Hope you have a joyous holiday season.

It's a great time to count our many blessings of the past year and number one on that list is good customers like you.

May the joy and richness of this season be yours!

Joy and bountiful blessings to you during this holiday season.

In remembering the historical accounts of this day, may the liberating truth be yours to hold and cherish.

One of the delights of this season is reconnecting with those we don't see often, but still remain in our hearts; we think of you often and wish you the best in the coming year.

How we wish we could open the door to our home and see your faces, as the door to our hearts always remains open to you.

Again, we want to celebrate the bounty of this year by offering you, special customer, the opportunity to join us for our Pre-Holiday Special Customer Sale.

We've prepared a very special surprise for you, valued customer, at our year-end celebration sale.

BUILD EFFECTIVE PARAGRAPHS

It's that very special time of year again! Our annual Special Customer Spring Fling wouldn't be the same without you. So, set aside this date to join us for a preview of the very latest in smart women's attire and to take advantage of our preseason prices.

There's absolutely no better time to say how very, very dear you are to us than at this special season. Do you know how much we wish we could be there to celebrate with you and hold you tight?

Our hearts are filled with love for all of you, and this special season just makes it overflow. May you enjoy the most wonderful of holidays.

Inspired by those first days of the celebration of harvest and survival, may that true spirit of thanksgiving be yours on this very special day. We look forward to sharing the bounty with you.

As we celebrate the true meaning of this season, we rejoice at seeing the reality of its precepts in your hearts and lives. And we feel so blessed to be able to share it with you.

From peace in your hearts to peace on earth—what a long journey it seems, yet not too far. Thank you for sharing your peace with us. Our hearts rejoice with yours.

A new year, new goals, new opportunities. May you carry with you into the new year the wisdom and wonder you've demonstrated this year.

It was a perfect delight to receive your newsletter and season's wishes. We're so happy everyone at your house has had such a terrific year. We all send our very best wishes to you.

May your new year sparkle with hope and opportunity. We wish you a year that far exceeds your expectations.

A special person, a special holiday, a special wish. When all of these elements converge, there's bound to be a wonderful celebration! You always make the most of such moments. Add our wishes for a truly wonderful day!

To the traditional wishes for your health and happiness, we'd like to selfishly add our hope of spending some of the holidays with you. (Then, of course, you'll have to add your hope for the more difficult but cherished attributes: long-suffering and patience!) If you're up for the challenge, we'd love to have you join us while you're in town. Do let us know if you might be available for a luncheon, a day, or a weekend.

EDIT, EDIT, EDIT

Reread what you've written to be sure you've expressed yourself the way you intended. Long or short, you'll want to make sure the focus is on the person(s) you're writing to and your heartfelt good wishes for him or her.

Christmas Newsletter

Dear Friends and Kin,

Our year was filled to the brim with the need to be hopeful! Maybe that helps evoke the kind of consciousness it sometimes takes for us to be really thankful for our many blessings. To name a few: We're rejoicing that our son, David, and wife, Diana, became the parents of twins, Mazzie June and Jasmine Augusta, on November 15. Although early, the babies were pronounced "perfect" by the pediatrician. Now we're just trying to get them to grow a bit. We're thankful that our battered and bruised airline employer remains in the skies, and is still sending out those monthly checks. The flu excepted, we're thankful for good health and wonderful family and friends like you. Since this was a "big birthday" year for Carlos, he got a new toy: a candy-red motorcycle. He enjoys riding it with a number of friends who also own cycles. They are even planning a men's cycle odyssey next summer.

Other highlights of the year included our volunteering for the children's reading program. We each tutor a fifth grader once a week, and the rewards are wonderful. Seeing new comprehension and understanding on these faces is probably the most rewarding thing we've ever done.

We're determined to make this new year wonderful, and plan to work on a number of new volunteering efforts, including building a Habitat for Humanity house.

As we continue to pray for peace on earth, we wish you all blessings aplenty this holiday season, and a new year filled with wonderful rewards.

Love,

Carlos and Silvia

Company Year-End Letter

Dear Renolds Family:

We have great reason to rejoice and celebrate as this banner year comes to an end. We surpassed our goal of six million dollars in net profits by $1,565,000! There's only one reason for our great success: the dedication and extraordinary hard work of each and every member of our team. Congratulations!

Each of you, as you know, will share in our financial success. But more important, I believe, is the fact that you have helped to create a supportive atmosphere, a sense of pride in achieving quality workmanship, and a great sense of family. Because of you, Renolds is just a great place to work.

Thank you, each and every one, for making this a banner year.

In appreciation,

William Trasker
President

Family Newsletter at Year's End

Yulia says:

Connect the holiday to the recipient.

The end of December, the beginning of the new year, and it still feels here—as it well may at your home—that our sense of national invincibility is forever lost. I'm sure, like you, it has helped us to hold our families, faith, and country near and dear as never before.

Ah, but this is to be a holiday greeting brimming with good cheer and best wishes!

First, the bittersweet. This fall my father, Ezra, was diagnosed with Alzheimer's disease. Mom, Maria, heroically kept him at home long past the usual dimensions of this disease, until his compulsion to "go home" produced a level of combativeness that required a more secure environment. We miss him. It has been my parents' desire to remain in Mississippi, and the only reasonable choice of facilities for Dad there was the Heritage Home. He still recognizes us, and for this we're thankful, as we are for all the fine examples of how to live an honorable life he provided. He's 75. We're thankful, too, for all the wonderful years he had; and for all the joy and happiness he's brought to those who have known him. He truly enjoyed life and lived it well.

Make it personal, newsy, and brief.

Mom has truly risen to the challenge in every way. She has started driving again after more than a dozen years. She drives 70 miles two or three times a week to visit Dad, taking the dog with her.

Now to the more cheery part. Our three sons are all doing well. We've petitioned to see more of them this year, and remain so thankful to have Peter and Jana still living in Colorado. We keep introducing a contract for their signatures, which commits them to stay here. (No signatures yet.)

Monti says:

Thanks for all your wonderful cards and letters. We really appreciate you keeping us in your hearts.

This year we enjoyed life in our little in-town community of 46 homes. Everything we need or want is conveniently nearby. I especially enjoy living an hour from the best ski areas in the country.

Our visit this year to the beautiful Canadian Rockies (Banff and Lake Louise) was remarkable. The all-day horseback ride, however, created footage fit for *America's Funniest Home Videos*.

Our annual trip took us "down under." Sydney is a beautiful city, with its lush gardens and world-famous opera house. We managed to get tickets to a performance there, and it was a wonderful experience. We cruised the Great Barrier Reef on board the Coral Princess between Townsville and Cairns, and snorkeling among the myriad varieties of marine life, both coral and tropical fish, was the highlight of our trip.

End with best wishes for the recipient.

Our best wishes for a wonderful, healthy, and rewarding new year! Plan to spend a tiny bit of it with us!

With love,

Yulia and Monti

Handwrite a personal message at the end.

P.S. We'd love to set up a weekend get-together in Vail for February. We have so much catching up to do! What do you think?

Year-End Greeting in Poem Form

Dear Friends,

With due apologies to Clement Clarke Moore, 1779–1863, for this abuse of his delightful " 'Twas the Night Before Christmas," a gift for his children in 1822. Ivo gives me permission to share a recent rendition from our family with you, a few select friends, at this time of year.

Our best wishes for wonderful holidays!

Casandra

'Twas the Week Before Christmas

'Twas the week before Christmas, when all through the house
Not a creature was stirring—not even Casandra's mouse (computer, that is);
No stockings were hung by the chimney with care
No ornaments, no glitter, no cheer anywhere! (I had the flu, you see.)
While I lay writhing, feverish, sick in my bed,
Visions of new powder (snow—a base of 50") danced in Ivo's head.
And I with my Kleenex, and he in his cap,
I'd just taken Tylenol and hoped for a five-minute nap,
When out in the garage there arose such a clatter,
What, oh what, I squawked, could be the matter?
Away to the door I staggered—did not flash,
I struggled with the knob,
I tugged weakly at the latch.
The sun was so bright—even without the snow,
In the glare of midday on the objects below,
What to my watering eyes did appear
Was that a sled with a dog or was that a reindeer?
With a perky, midlife driver, gleaming red helmet and quick,
I surmised in a moment that it was *not* old St. Nick.
More rapid than eagles his engine did sing
He whistled and shouted, and named the huge thing: "Isn't she a beauty?"
I knew in that instant things would never be the same.
No, not Dasher, nor Dancer; not Prancer nor Vixen!
Not Comet, nor Cupid, not Donner or Blitzen!
(It's a Honda, "Rice Burner," candy red, and game!)
Ivo's eyes—how they twinkled, enlivened and merry!
His cheeks were like roses (windburn, no doubt), his nose like a cherry!
His droll, chapped lips were drawn up like a bow,
And the beard of his chin was center-parted and shot through with snow.
A wink of his eye and a twist of his head,
Soon gave me to know I had *plenty* to dread;
He spoke not a word, but took off with a whistle
And away he did fly, like the down of the thistle.
(Actually, he says he "tested" the bike at over 100 mph!)
And I heard him exclaim as he vanished from sight,
"Season's Greetings to all, and to all a Good Night!"

Thanksgiving Day Family Reunion

Dear McDermott Tribe,

We're sure you're as giddy as we are about this year's lineup for the family pilgrimage and reunion at David and Regina McDermott's home. We have, you must know, 12 new family members (list enclosed) to welcome. We'll be giving them the McDermott baptism in the traditional way. You know your food assignments, of course, and hopefully each of you has your family history contribution ready to recite. We'll be waiting to hear it.

As a reminder, the program this year is being handled by Tom Wright, and if your family has a special musical or other contribution you want to perform, contact him within the next week, so he can finish his program announcement.

For the family history part of the program, Harry McDermott will read the new genealogy he and his family have researched and assembled; Mary Bench will bring the new, updated family "story"; and Lauren Givens has promised to have the family picture album on display. You may order copies of any of these.

See you on Thanksgiving Day, 1:00 P.M. (For all the ongoing discussions, directions, details, and chatter, go to Harry's website, McDermottsUnite.com.)

McDermotts, a clan together again! May the road rise up to meet you, and may you always be well upwind!

Gavin McDermott

Pre-Christmas Special Family Charity

Dear Christmas Angel,

You know that last year your sharing the spirit of this season resulted in 2,765 children receiving a Christmas gift. And this year we are aiming to make sure that 3,500 children in our area are greeted with a surprise gift on that special day.

This year on December 5, 4:30 P.M., at Summer's Day Preschool, all of us will bring together the gifts we have collected, and we will all wrap gifts and divide them for distribution by the appointed elves. As usual, this will be a very merry workshop experience and celebration for all of us.

Barry McCullom will lead the music, and La Petite, superb caterer, is supplying box lunches for all of us.

We look forward to seeing you again this year for this very special time of celebration.

Patti Reeves

7
CONDOLENCE AND SYMPATHY

*. . . look in thy
heart and write.*

—ASTROPHEL AND STELLA

It is difficult to express your feelings in writing to someone who is suffering a major loss. Empathy for the person, based on care and respect for him or her, is essential. Focus on the person you are writing to, and let your knowledge of the recipient and his or her relationship to the loss guide you.

The letter of condolence or sympathy, while one of the most difficult messages to write, is undoubtedly one of the most important. It may be written to someone who has suffered the death of a relative, friend, or colleague, or to someone who has experienced some other kind of loss (job, home to fire, an unwanted divorce). Your letter should be brief, kind, and offer concrete help, if that is appropriate.

DECIDE TO WRITE
Compose a personal note or letter when:
- Death touches the life of a relative, friend, neighbor, business associate, or employee.
- Illness or injury strikes a relative, friend, business associate, or neighbor.
- Loss of finances, property, business, or well-being affects a friend, employee, organization you do business with, colleague, or client.
- It's the anniversary of the death, or other significant date, to the person who will experience, again, the loss of the deceased.
- Divorce affects a friend or associate.
- Keen disappointment or misfortune—such as not winning an election, loss of a job, or not getting a promotion—occurs in the life of a friend or associate.
- Loss of a pet grieves a friend or family member.
- Relocation of a friend's close relatives or friends creates feelings of sadness and loss.

THINK ABOUT CONTENT
- The first and most essential step is to empathize with the bereaved or distressed recipient.
- Remember the stages of grief: (1) denial and isolation; (2) anger; (3) bargaining or overrationalizing; (4) depression; (5) acceptance and healing. Attune your message accordingly.
- Think about what you really feel.
- Write immediately, but if you have just heard of the grief after weeks or months or have put off the task, still write. It's not too late.
- Use your relationship with the recipient to guide your writing.

- Focus on the recipient, and don't misdirect your message toward your feelings. The bereaved or distressed person will understand that you feel sad, so simply say "I was so sorry to hear of your grief."
- Open with a simple and strong message of sympathy, naming the person, loss, or event for which you are extending condolences: "Lansing and I extend our deepest sympathy to you at the loss of your dear Lindsay."
- Be hopeful. Remember that your message must not stray into pity.
- It may be difficult, but be sure to write employees, clients, associates, and colleagues in times of grief or loss.
- Save long messages that reminisce about a loved one for later, when the recipient is better able to reflect upon those memories without such a keen sense of loss.
- Choose your words carefully, using words that relate to the loss, sorrow, or grief of the bereaved. Avoid cold and harsh words like *dead, killed, deceased,* or *bankrupt, broke, homeless,* and the like.
- Relate a fond memory you have of the deceased, if appropriate.
- Always consider the religious preference, ethnic mores, family wishes, and organizational customs of the bereaved when writing your message.
- Include a message of sympathy to other family members or associates, if appropriate.
- Make a specific offer of help, indicating when and how you will make the next contact to carry through on your offer.
- Close on a warm note.
- Ask the mortuary what the family has requested if you want to send a memento of your feelings in the case of a death, and/or check the obituary column of the newspaper for this information.
- If you send flowers, write a message to accompany them.
- Inquire verbally of a designated relative or friend, or the mortuary, about any immediate needs the bereaved may have and any service or task for which you may wish to volunteer (for example, serving as pallbearer or planning a special commemorative service).

ELIMINATE WRONG MESSAGES

- Don't use overcharged language. "The worst tragedy" or "The most dire news I've ever received" does nothing to comfort the bereaved. The same rule applies to overly sentimental, effusive statements.
- Do not moralize or include statements or clichés meant to be sympathetic. These may be misinterpreted. Remember, this is a time of extreme grief and vulnerability for the bereaved, and language like "He's in a better place now" is not appropriate.
- Don't let your message fall into a pitying or maudlin tone. There's a fine line here. Read your message through several times to ensure you haven't failed on this point. Sometimes it helps to place your letter aside for at least a few hours, then reread it just to be sure.
- Don't give advice. Your sole purpose is to try to give comfort.
- Avoid empty or vague offers of help. Rather, be specific and offer to take the next step: "I will call Joannie tomorrow to see if there are calls I can return on your behalf, or errands you may need to have run."

CONSIDER SPECIAL SITUATIONS

Take special care in these circumstances:

- Divorce of a friend, associate, colleague, or employee requires keen sensitivity. You should know the recipient very well. Make sure your message is timely, brief, and focused on the recipient.
- The death of a child, a stillbirth, or a miscarriage should all be treated the same. Don't fall prey to attempts at "consoling," which tend to diminish the recipient's grief. When multiple births resulted in the loss of a child, offer congratulations on the births of the surviving children first. Then, in a separate paragraph, express your sympathy at the loss of the other child(ren), taking care not to connect the two emotions.
- For loss of a home in a natural disaster, loss of employment, or a financial reversal, it's best to give your message the legs of real assistance. Ask what would be helpful, and present your gift or

offer of help so it does not take on the character of charity. Empty offers of assistance are insulting in the face of crisis.

- The terminally ill person or the person who has suffered a debilitating injury is in a special category. This includes a person who has contracted AIDS. Take your lead from what the recipient has expressed about his or her illness. Don't mention death unless he or she has discussed it openly. It's appropriate to include fond memories you share and/or aspects of your relationship you treasure. Use "Thinking about you," "My thoughts are with you," or other such messages.

- Suicide or a violent crime that results in death or loss is an especially difficult situation. Unless you know the faith and belief system of the bereaved, your message should simply state "I was so sorry to hear of your loss."

- The death of a pet, especially for an elderly person, can be a great loss. A note to such a person at this time, if sincere, will be greatly appreciated.

- In sending flowers to a funeral home, attach a small card addressed to "David M. Meeks," or to "The funeral of David M. Meeks." The plain, single card (available from the florist) should contain a brief message of sympathy, for example, "Sidney, our thoughts are with you and Ann at this time."

- When contributing to a charity in memory of the deceased, include your name and address, in addition to a brief statement such as "This contribution is made in memory of Robert C. Walker, 8100 West Chicago, Appleton, WI." This allows the charity to acknowledge that your contribution was received and inform the family of the deceased of your contribution.

- Anniversary dates shared with a person now gone are a good time to send another thoughtful note of sympathy to a relative, friend, or associate who will again grieve. It will be extremely meaningful if your relationship is close. This is often a good time to share a warm memory of the deceased.

SELECT A FORMAT

- Your message of condolence and/or sympathy must be very personal, and that requires that it be handwritten. Use a commercial card only if it exactly expresses your feelings, and then also include a handwritten message. The most popular stationery is a plain, fold-over card, but plain personal stationery (smaller than 8½ by 11 inches) may also be used.

- For business acquaintances you did not know well or work closely with—this may include an employee who has lost a spouse, a customer, client, or a colleague—either a handwritten note or a typewritten letter of sympathy is appropriate. Use personal business stationery, preferably smaller than the usual 8½ by 11 inches. A 5-by-7-inch size is a good choice.

SELECT THE RIGHT WORD

affection	healing
balm	heartache
bereavement	heartbroken
bitter	heartsick
burden	heavyhearted
care	hope
comfort	lift
compassion	loss
concern	mourn
consolation	overcome
difficult	sad (saddened)
distress	solace
faith	sorrow
gift	suffering
grief	sympathy

CONSTRUCT SENSITIVE PHRASES

a loss for all who knew him

a lovely and true person

a wonderful and rare source of wisdom and wit

deep grief at the loss

extend our sympathies

feelings of loss

he was a very special person

in this time of great sorrow

keep you in our prayers

made so much difference in the world around him

may your wonderful memories add comfort

our deep sympathies are with you

our hearts go out to you

please accept our sincere condolences

saddened to learn

sorry for your loss

there are no words to express

warmest sympathies

we extend our warmest thoughts

well-remembered for his deeds of kindness

will always be remembered

will always have fond thoughts of

will be so missed

WRITE STRONG SENTENCES

Words are very inadequate at such a difficult time.

Our sympathy and warmest thoughts are with you.

Our thoughts are with you at this time of loss and sorrow.

Our hopes are set on a full recovery from your accident.

We were so sorry to learn that Martha's courageous battle with AIDS is over; her life was truly an inspiration to all of us.

I'm sorry to hear that you and Jim are divorcing; I know this is an extremely difficult time and my thoughts are with you.

Not everyone understands the joy and companionship a pet can bring, and how it is missed when it's gone; I was so sorry to hear Smoky died.

We shall miss David's smiling presence.

John's smile and laughter will live on in our hearts, even as we mourn with you his absence from us.

May God's abiding love give you strength and comfort during this time of deep sorrow.

BUILD EFFECTIVE PARAGRAPHS

Words are never adequate to express the proper sense of loss at a time like this. I was so saddened to learn Toby is gone from us.

May the joy of life that was George's sustain you in this dark time of losing him. We will all remember his exuberance in the smallest and simplest pleasures. And we'll all miss him a great deal.

Please don't despair. When we were robbed, the lingering sense of having been violated was the most difficult part of the ordeal. I'll call in a couple of days to see if there's anything we have you may want to use until you replace things.

Divorce often feels like the death of hope, and we know how much pain you must feel at this moment. Please do know that time really does help the healing process. Also know that we are here, and our home and hearts are always open to you. I'll call in a few days to see if you might be up to coming over for dinner.

I felt sick for you when I heard that your position has been eliminated by L. L. Greedy and Company. You're one of the best qualified and most creative people I know, and I'm sure that while it doesn't feel like it today, you'll rise like the phoenix to much greater and better things. I have some ideas about companies that might appreciate a person with your sterling qualifications. I'll call you on Tuesday to see if you're ready to mount a search for a new position.

EDIT, EDIT, EDIT

Use the greatest care to ensure your message is clear and sincere.

Death in a Friend's Family

[Handwritten]
(Date)

Dear Rodney and Kris,

We were stricken to learn of Jordan's death. He was a wonderful person, your son, and we know how very close you were. Words can't touch the depth of sorrow that is yours, but may the joy the three of you shared help to sustain you during such a bleak time.

We will bring the Buick over tomorrow for you to use for as long as you need it. We would like to help by running any errands you may need completed, or answering your telephone if you care to forward your calls here. Please know you may call on us if there's anything else you need.

We will all miss Jordan deeply.

Your friends,

Alice and Art

The Death of a Neighbor

[Handwritten]
(Date)

Dear David,

Ann and I were very saddened to learn of Trudy's death. We respected and admired her contributions to the community, and we will miss her in our neighborhood.

Our heartfelt sympathy to you and the children, James, Rebecca, and Chloe. Please call us immediately if we can be of any help. I'll call next week to see what we may do for you in the weeks ahead.

Sincerely,

Anne and Woody

Choose your words carefully.

Empathize with the bereaved.

Offer help, then follow up.

Death of a Business Associate

[Handwritten or typed]
(Date)

Dear Martha,

I was shocked to learn of Ruth's death. I'm sure this is both a professional and personal loss for you and many others at Banko Corporation.

My staff and I offer our sincerest condolences to you and your entire department.

Regards,

Dudley

Loss of an Infant

[Handwritten]
(Date)

Bebe and Raoul:

How our hearts ache for you at this time when you've lost this long-awaited baby, Collin. Please know our prayers and thoughts are with you each and every day.

If there is any way we can help, please call us— day or night. And when you feel up to a very short visit, we'd love to stop by or have you come over. Just let us know.

Our love and prayers,

Sargh and Soso

Financial Loss

[Handwritten]
(Date)

Dear Lea and Alex,

Please accept this gift to help with anything you may need immediately in this difficult time. Not many people have the courage to follow their dreams as you two have demonstrated that you have. We're sorry for this loss, but we know this great disappointment won't defeat you. It's only a temporary setback.

Our hopes and prayers are with you for a very bright future. We'll call next week to see how we can help.

Sincerely,

Milli and Wick

After a Hurricane

[Handwritten]
(Date)

Dear Doty and Darin:

Who can account for the hurricane making an unexpected right turn? How thankful we are that you weren't injured, yet how we sympathize with you in the loss of your home.

Could we take the children for two weeks so you two can concentrate on all the things you'll need to do to get things back together? We can drive down as early as Wednesday. Or, if there is some other way we can help, you have only to ask.

You remain in our hearts and thoughts.

With love,

Sam and Shorty

Personal Misfortune

[Handwritten]
(Date)

Dear Jill and Jeff,

We were very saddened to hear of your miscarriage. We know how eager you were to have this new member of your wonderful family. There really aren't words at a time like this, but please accept our deepest sympathies. Our thoughts are with you.

With our love,

Ted and Carol

Use your relationship with the bereaved to guide your writing.

Loss of a Pet

[Handwritten]
(Date)

Dear Gerry,

I think Sarge was the smartest dog I've ever known—and the most lovable. We were so sorry to hear about the accident and are sure you are grief-stricken.

I shall never forget the sight of him climbing that ladder to bring back the monkey to you. I know he was more than a friend to you, and you, I'm sure, made him one of the happiest dogs that ever lived.

Affectionately,

Sue

To a Friend Who Was Downsized

[Handwritten]
(Date)

Elizabeth,

Yes, I do feel sad—so very sad that management does this. I've read of some of the turmoil at the parent organization level and know from personal experience that such things create a great deal of stress on all levels within organizations. At times it brings out the very worst in some colleagues (the hanging peril of possible axings—if that's a proper word).

I'm equally sure, like you, that Rory must be put in a position of ultra-anguish. Oh dear!

But, at the same time, I have a bud of joy within that this may be your life blessing in disguise, though I'm sure that at this moment it feels like something very different. A person as wonderful and talented as you will only triumph in new and extraordinary ways. My hope, my most sincere hope, is that this is the opportunity of your lifetime. In fact, I feel very, very sure of it. After all, I'm sure you need the concentrated time to finish the bust of Alexander. And write that novel. (I'm looking into writers' colonies myself at the moment to do that very thing. Might this be something you want to do?)

Whatever you decide to do—after, I hope, taking a well-deserved time off—will come up roses! I've heard a number of writers say (for the record) that getting fired from their editorial jobs was the best thing that ever happened to them. (I'm sure that's equally true of downsizings.)

Bless you. I'll be eagerly waiting to hear of your next great adventure.

All the very, very best,

Sasha

Friend Who Was Raped

[Handwritten]
(Date)

Dearest Victoria,

I've just hung up the telephone after our chat, and I wanted to write down a couple of things we discussed. It's true, unfortunately, that bad, bad things happen to the very best people. And I'm so very sorry that this has happened to as wonderful a person as you. At the same time, I'm equally as certain that you will turn something bad into something very, very good.

I can't imagine what you've gone through—not even close. But I do know that given time you will work your way through this. Please do give yourself time, and use all the support that's available. I'm volunteering for whatever you might need— night or day. You know I'm always available on my cell phone, so please call me. I've also been in contact with some counselors at the Sexual Assault Center (telephone 555-0123), and feel that Denise has a level of humanity and experience you might find helpful. Just tell her you're Sidney's friend.

I value your friendship so much. You are one of the really wonderful people. I'd feel so gratified if you'd allow me to help in any way you may choose.

Love,

Sidney

You Suspect a Friend Is Suffering Physical Abuse

[Handwritten]
(Date)

Dear April,

I'm writing this rather than asking you directly because I feel it's less confrontational and will perhaps allow me to register a concern more adequately. You seem to be distant and to be suffering in some unverbalized way, and I'd like to offer my help.

I won't be shocked, you know, about any type of problem that may exist. My motive for writing you is purely one of a friend who knows, values, and loves you. My door and my heart are always open to you. Please feel you can talk to me about anything that's troubling you. It will remain in complete confidence.

As always,

Krissie

A Friend Who Survived an Automobile Accident

[Handwritten]
(Date)

Dear Elsa,

It was reassuring to hear your voice on the telephone. We are so sorry you've suffered this severe injury, yet so happy you have survived. And now to the process of healing.

I can't imagine what you've gone through. I can only say, again, I've always admired your strength and derring-do, and am 100 percent confident that you will not only survive, but you will emerge triumphant.

I'd just encourage you to allow yourself time to heal, and also to allow those of us who know and love you to pamper and care for you just a little. You could, for example, spend the summer at the lake with us, where the guest cottage sits waiting to welcome you with as much solitude as you desire, and the main house, with as much camaraderie and conversation as you feel up to. You know I'd be thrilled to handle all the physical therapy things, and the cottage is all set up for that.

I'll check in with you next week after you've had an opportunity to reflect on this. Please call me anytime you feel up to chatting. We're all praying for you daily for God's blessing in getting whole again.

Love,

Tessa

Also see GET WELL, page 55; RESPONSE, page 234; and THANK-YOU, page 76.

GET WELL

It is one of the beautiful compensations of this life that no one can sincerely try to help another without helping himself.

—CHARLES DUDLEY WARNER

Offering encouragement when a friend, family member, neighbor, or colleague is ill or convalescing is a wonderful way to build a stronger bond between you and him or her. A "get well" greeting carries with it an element of solace and the hope of recovery, and that's what your message should convey. But this is certainly an area where your communication needs to be in keeping with your knowledge of, and relationship to, the recipient.

DECIDE TO WRITE

Send a greeting card or personal note that includes a personal message of comfort, hope, and encouragement when:

- An accident or injury strikes a relative, friend, business associate, or neighbor.
- The relative of a friend, business associate, or colleague is ill or injured.
- A friend, relative, neighbor, or business associate experiences a long convalescence.

THINK ABOUT CONTENT

Write as soon as you hear and confirm the news.

- First and foremost, think about offering encouragement.
- Rely on your relationship with the recipient to dictate your message.
- If possible, learn something about how the recipient views his or her situation before writing.
- Focus on the recipient and don't misdirect your message toward your own feelings.
- Express simply that you were sorry to hear about the accident or illness.
- Make a statement about your concern.
- Try to relieve any possible anxiety about things other than the recipient's recovery.
- Keep the message sunny and upbeat.
- Be short and concise.
- Consider the religious preferences, ethnic mores, family wishes, and organizational customs of the recipient when writing your message; don't include any conflicting ideologies you may embrace.
- Make a specific offer of help, indicating when and how you will take the next step to carry out your offer, but be sure to offer only that which you can, and are willing, to do.

- Combine your message with a small gift of a book or an activity the recipient can enjoy while recuperating.
- For the recovering child, build anticipation of an upcoming event at a time when he or she will be fully recovered, and include some kind of related activity for now.
- If you send flowers or another gift, include a personal note.
- Close on a warm and positive note.

ELIMINATE WRONG MESSAGES

- Don't moralize or include empty clichés or statements meant to be sympathetic. These can be easily misunderstood, as can such "silver lining" comments as "At least you didn't . . ." or "It could have been much worse."
- Omit any hint of pity.
- This isn't the time to offer unsolicited advice. Think only of offering comfort.
- Avoid insincere or empty offers of help. Put legs on any offer by defining a specific task you will take on and the time you'll follow up.
- Avoid dramatic or tragic words and phrases in referring to either the patient or your own feelings. Phrases like your "tragic accident" or the "worst case" aren't comforting.
- Don't indulge in comparative stories such as "Jim's brother had the same operation . . ."

CONSIDER SPECIAL SITUATIONS

Take special care in these situations:

- The injury or illness will have severe financial repercussions for the recipient. Inquire to learn how best to offer help, but don't let your offer take on the character of charity.
- Don't pry. Be sensitive to the wishes of the recipient and take his or her lead in offering help. If it seems appropriate, you might say something like, "I'd like to help. Would it be helpful if I took over the Rogers project for four weeks?" or "I'd like to organize a carpool to take you to physical therapy, if you'd allow me."

SELECT A FORMAT

- The most frequently used vehicle is a greeting card. Always write a personal message, too.
- Personal stationery in a 5-by-7-inch size is a good choice for a personal note, or a fold-over card may be used.
- For a business associate you do not know well, use a commercial greeting card, personal stationery, or a fold-over note upon which you write a short personal message. You may also elect to use company stationery in the 8½ by 11-inch size, especially if you are including a message about relieving the recipient of his or her workload or other business.

SELECT THE RIGHT WORD

accident	rapid
cheer (cheerful)	recovered
convalesce	recuperate
encourage	reinvigorated
heal	relapse
health (healthy)	robust
hope	support
illness	unexpected
pink	

BUILD SENSITIVE PHRASES

back in healthy form
better than new
completely well again
days of chicken soup and good fiction
encouraging news
fit and robust
good, better, best of health
have every confidence
in our thoughts and prayers
recuperating time will be short
rest and recover
speedy recovery
take time to properly heal
thinking healthy thoughts for you
time to heal
up and about

WRITE STRONG SENTENCES

You are in my thoughts and prayers as you begin your journey toward recovery.

I'm thinking that eight weeks of therapy may put you in fine shape for our annual bird-watching trip to see the sandhill cranes. If it's OK with you, I'm going to put it on my calendar.

I feel certain you'll be dancing the "Electric Cowboy" at the spring cowboy poet's roundup.

We were so sorry to hear about your accident, but were very encouraged to hear that the doctors have put everything back together again.

Recovery seems an innocuous word for all the rehabilitation you have endured.

We shall be ever so happy to hear that you are completely recovered.

There's a fishing trip all planned and ready to go the minute you tell me you are recovered enough to land the big one.

BUILD EFFECTIVE PARAGRAPHS

We were certainly sorry to hear about your accident, but very happy to hear that you are determined to be out of that wheelchair by the holidays. I feel certain you'll be joining us on the slopes next season.

The whole department sends best wishes for a complete and full recovery. I've enclosed a suggested listing of department staff to fill in for you—though no one, of course, can take your place. For the next six weeks, please concentrate on getting up and running at full steam. I'll call and discuss staff substitutes with you next week, if you're up to it.

We know that with your determination you'll make a swift and full recovery. We'd just like to help in some small way. Could we stop by each afternoon at four o'clock and take Toby for an hour?

Your entire fifth grade class is sorry to hear that you will need six weeks to get your leg as good as new. We'd like to organize some visits to help you keep up with your schoolwork. And we'd like to arrange some visits for

letting you keep up on the presidents' game. I'll call your mother next week to see how to work it all out.

I'm sure you'll be so happy you've had this procedure once you're completely recovered. Jim says your doctor has said it'll be five weeks of intensive therapy to get up and walking again. I'd like to volunteer for noon to one o'clock outings, Mondays, Wednesdays, and Fridays. I'm suggesting slow trips around the neighborhood if you're up for it. I'll call in a couple of days to see if that will work.

EDIT, EDIT, EDIT

Set your written message aside for a little while, then re-read it to make sure it sparkles with hope and good cheer.

To an Injured Colleague

[Handwritten on a greeting card signed by everyone in the department]
(Date)

Sarah,

The entire department was distressed to hear your vacation ended with a bone-breaking fall. But we're encouraged that you had excellent medical help so immediately available. — Use your relationship to guide your writing.

We've divvied up your assignments here temporarily, according to your assistant's input, and will try to keep all your balls in the air until you get back. As soon as you feel up to it, give a call, and we'll get your direct input through conference calls and email. — Offer concrete help.

Here are our individual wishes for your complete recovery. We're all sure you'll be in fine shape in time for the summer softball league. We certainly don't want anyone else as our pitcher! — Be sunny and upbeat.

Best,

Todd

A Neighbor's Surgery

[Handwritten on a greeting card]
(Date)

Daisy,

I was sorry to hear that your tumor required surgery, but very relieved to learn you will be returning home on Thursday. I'll put your newspaper inside the front door until I see you're out getting it yourself.

Please let me mow the lawn for you for the next four weeks until we leave for France. And I'll check with Jack to see if you're up to eating one of my chicken delight dinners on Friday.

Our hope is for your return to that robust, competitive gardening good health.

Best wishes,

Jennifer

Medical Tests for a Friend

[Handwritten]
(Date)

Gwyndelyn,

I was so relieved to hear from Hank that the test phase is over, and your doctors are now putting together a treatment plan. I'd like to suggest the Bermuda treatment. We did, after all, plan a two-week dose in those sunny climes before this all started.

I'm just waiting to hear the good news that two weeks of sun and fun is the surefire cure. I'll keep my bags packed, and look forward to seeing you up and practicing that forehand in a few weeks.

Love,

Sissy

A Sick Child

[Handwritten]
(Date)

Robbie,

The Cat in the Hat has asked me to say I hope you'll be up soon, and ready to play.

It's no fun without you, I'm sure that you know. There's no baseball party, no pizza to go!

Hurry, hurry, get well, recover real soon. Baseball starts Thursday, April 20, at noon!

Your pal,

Ben

Keep your message upbeat.

An Injured Employee

[Typed on company letterhead]
(Date)

Dear Jamie:

Maggie Orway has just reported that you had an accident yesterday. We all send our best wishes for your recovery. Maggie has promised to keep everyone here updated on your progress, and she will be checking with your family periodically to learn your preference on the best way to do that.

I have notified AA Medical on your behalf, and Mr. Symons will be in touch with your wife in a day or two. Please don't be concerned about insurance coverage or about your workload here. Maggie will distribute assignments to keep your accounts on schedule until you are able to give your own directives.

Our warmest wishes for your good progress. We will certainly miss you here and will stand ready to help in any way possible. We look forward to your return to work.

All the best,

Hal Volkers

9

WELCOME

True friendship's laws are by this rule express'd.
Welcome the coming, speed the parting guest.

—ALEXANDER POPE

A welcome letter is a great opportunity to start a positive relationship with a new neighbor, a new family member, a new business customer, or a new coworker. Whether business or personal, this letter should be warm and congenial in tone, and it should convey a friendly "glad you're here" message. It may also extend an offer of help—although it's wise to define the limits of your offer.

In business or social correspondence, you may want to tell the reader you are happy in this group (location, social club, work situation, department), and include a suggestion or two about how the person can fit in, learn the ropes, or get oriented.

Your closing statement should reaffirm your welcome.

DECIDE TO WRITE

Use the welcome letter in response to the following:
- New person is about to join the family.
- New neighbor moves in.
- New employee starts work.
- New member joins your club, faculty, school, student association, church, temple, fraternity, or sorority.
- New business starts.
- New employee joins a customer's or client's business.
- New business prospect, customer, client, or associate is added.

THINK ABOUT CONTENT

- Express your enthusiasm and pleasure at making the welcome.
- Keep your message simple and focus on how the other person feels at this time.
- Welcome the person into the organization, family, group, or neighborhood.
- Include, if possible, a complimentary statement about the organization, family, group, or neighborhood.
- Generate some enthusiasm about the future.
- State your best wishes for the person, drawing a relationship between him or her and the organization.
- Be specific and make it as personal as possible.
- Make your offer of help, if appropriate, and suggest a time to meet.
- In the case of an employee, give any details that may be appropriate: work hours, lunch policy and times, parking arrangements, benefits, and so on.

- Close with an encouraging comment.
- Timeliness is very important. You lose the opportunity for the greatest impact if you don't send the letter immediately.
- Your offer of help will never be as valued as it is now, but be sure to set limits you can live with and be concrete in your offer.

ELIMINATE WRONG MESSAGES

- Don't mix messages. This is not the place for a sales message, for example.
- Don't include bad news or negative messages.

CONSIDER SPECIAL SITUATIONS

- A welcome to a new family member should ring with warmth and sincerity, expressing your pleasure at having the person join the family.
- Employee welcome letters are often considered the domain of the human resources or personnel department, and include a packet of information about insurance coverage, company policy, benefits, and other work-related matters. While this may be standard operating procedure, make sure employees are welcomed both verbally by other employees and also with welcome letters. This creates better relationships, allows the new employee to settle in more quickly, and promotes a greater sense of camaraderie and loyalty.
- Neighborhoods are often so insular that it is unusual to welcome a new neighbor with a letter. But we now have so many master-planned communities that the practice of sending a welcome from the homeowners' association should become routine. This can be done very nicely with a welcome basket and a helpful sheet on local shopping, professional services, a directory of families in the neighborhood, and other useful information.
- A personal welcome note to a new neighbor can be helpful in establishing a good relationship. "Welcome to the neighborhood. I look forward to having you over for coffee, so please give me a call when you get settled," says you prefer to be called

first rather than dropped in on. Such a note delivered with homemade cookies is especially welcome.

- Students, attendees, parents, and new faculty members of schools, colleges, and/or special academic programs will benefit from the information and be more at ease if they receive a welcome letter. The letter should include a list of the things they will need for the first class or session, and it should state some of the program benefits, and include an inspiring sentence or two about the session. Naming someone for the new person to contact before the first session is also very helpful.
- With the welcome letter to a potential business customer or client, include a reason for a well-timed follow-up call to help you establish a relationship. "I will call your office next week to arrange a time to stop by briefly and introduce myself, to give you a copy of the Glenwood Directory, and to answer any questions you may have."
- The Welcome Wagon or other new resident service may be a good source of new residents for you to contact if these are potential clients or customers for your business.
- The chamber of commerce, the new business section of the newspaper, and local business publications may be good sources from which to glean the names of new businesses you may wish to contact with a welcome letter.

SELECT A FORMAT

- Business welcome letters, in which you are acting in an official capacity, should be typed on organization letterhead.
- For a welcome letter from you to a new coworker or employee, personal business letterhead may be used, and the letter should be typed.
- New-neighbor welcome messages and those to new members of an informal group or club are usually handwritten on personal stationery or a fold-over card.
- Student and attendee welcomes may best be handled by sending printed or handwritten postcards.

SELECT STRONG WORDS

belong	membership
camaraderie	mutual
community	reception
comrades	share
congratulations	social
conviviality	trust
delighted	welcome
fellowship	

BUILD EFFECTIVE PHRASES

among friends and colleagues

build solid relationships

common goals and purposes

convivial and helpful

cultivate friends here

enjoy the fellowship

extend a warm welcome

find real camaraderie

happy you're aboard

help get you involved

help you build your professional capital

introduce you to members

join our circle of comrades

mutually supportive and helpful

safe and secure place to spread your wings

supportive in so many ways

warm and close circle

wonderful atmosphere for learning

WRITE STRONG SENTENCES

Be focused and concise, then offer a sincere message.

A warm and sincere welcome to you.

I hope you will enjoy your membership as much as I have enjoyed mine over the past 15 years.

A hardy welcome to our project group from each and every one of us.

Welcome to the team! We're all rooting for you and ready to help in any way possible.

We are delighted to have you aboard. Welcome!

We look forward to a long and mutually rewarding relationship.

Welcome to this warm group, where I have found true fellowship and faithful friends.

BUILD EFFECTIVE PARAGRAPHS

Remember, keep it short and sweet.

With great pleasure, I welcome you to the Press Club of Mobile. Your application has been approved by the board and ratified by the members.

Welcome to Bentonville! It's been said that anyone who comes here never wants to leave. My family certainly agrees. We hope yours will too.

Welcome to the Baskerville team. I believe you will find that everyone has the spirit of working together to get the job done. We're very glad to have you, and I invite you to give me a call at any time to discuss questions you may have.

Welcome to West Concord Business Park. I have found this location convenient to all of the metro area, and an ideal location from which to get to the ski slopes on Friday afternoons. I'll call you next week to see if you would care to get together briefly to discuss Park procedures and policies. In the meantime, here's a directory of all the businesses in the area.

Welcome to our entrepreneurial family. I believe one of the greatest benefits of becoming a Small Business Chamber of Commerce member is the Members-of-the-Board sessions, where entrepreneurs help solve each others' problems. I know it's the best business decision I've ever made. Happy to have you aboard!

EDIT, EDIT, EDIT

Be sure your message is brief, warm, and personal.

To a New Family Member

[Handwritten]
(Date)

Dear Jessie,

Welcome to the family!

David is so special to me. He stayed with his Uncle Jack and me during his mother's lengthy illness when he was four and five, and again when he was ten and his mother had surgery. I've loved him like a son since the moment he was born.

So, when I say I'm very pleased you two have decided to get married, it's the sincerest compliment to you, and the truest belief in the possibility of your extraordinary happiness.

I know you'll have a wonderful life together, and I'm thrilled for you both.

Your new aunt,

Bea

To a New Employee

[Emailed]
(Date)

Dear Stacey:

It's a pleasure to welcome you to Doodles and to the marketing department in particular. I believe you'll find this both an exciting company and a challenging department to work in.

I'm sure the human resources folks have given you all the necessary company information you'll need, but I'd like to extend an offer to meet with you for 10 to 15 minutes on the next four Thursdays at 4:00 P.M. to address any questions you may have as you get your footing.

I think you'll find everyone here eager to help you get up to speed. Welcome aboard, and let me know about getting together on Thursdays.

All the best,

Doug

To New In-Laws

[Handwritten]
(Date)

Dear Bebe and Trek,

What could be happier news?

We've said it before, but now that it's official that the two people on the planet we love with all our hearts—Olivia and Ben—are going to get married, we'd like to make a formal declaration: welcome to our family! We adore Olivia, and also happen to believe she has wonderful parents.

We couldn't be more delighted that we'll be seeing a lot more of you two in the years to come. What joy!

Birdie and Edgar

To School Parent-Teachers' Association

[Typed]
(Date)

Dear Ms. Alison:

The PTA at Logan wants to welcome you to our parents and teachers' working group. Our goal is to create a better educational experience for our children.

I feel sure your daughter, Jennifer, will enjoy Ms. Rudy's class. My daughter was one of her students last year, and I found Ms. Rudy to be an extremely skilled and concerned teacher.

Please plan to attend our Thursday social hour, September 18, at 7:30 P.M. in the gym for an informal welcome. I look forward to meeting you.

Sincerely,

June Addison

As a Student

[Handwritten]
(Date)

Susan,

Let me introduce myself and say welcome to the fifth grade at Stanley Academy. My name is Mrs. Moore, and I'll be your homeroom teacher.

I believe you will enjoy our series on "The Birth of Democracy," the four field trips we have planned to the state capitol building and state representatives' offices, and our "Women in US History" project.

It's going to be a wonderful year, and I look forward to meeting you next Thursday in room 43, opposite the administration office. Please bring the items listed in the margin, and wear a big smile!

Your teacher,

Mrs. Moore

To a New Business

[Typed]
(Date)

Dear Mr. Wilson:

Welcome to Wilkerson!

In the past two years we've added 18 businesses to those in town, and the owners all report that they have surpassed their own projections for this time period, some by as much as 40 percent.

Wilkerson has a great atmosphere for growing a service business like yours, and I encourage you to use the many resources of the Business Club, including the Owners' Roundtable, Retired Marketers, and Services for Trade.

Again, welcome. And please call me anytime if I may answer questions.

Yours truly,

Ralph Metor

Reactivated Club Member Welcome

[Typed or emailed]
(Date)

Dear Sarah:

Welcome, again, to the Toronto Womens' Press Society. We are all delighted you have chosen to reactivate your membership after three years. Yes, we have changed our goals and are much more in tune with the needs of women working in the media today.

This year programs include several touring luminaries, a special seminar we're calling "The Future of News," and a series of programs on computer research techniques. Of course we'll also continue our member "Shop Talk" evenings, which are a favorite.

We're so pleased to have you back.

With best wishes,

Enid Lubbick

As a Volunteer

[Typed]
(Date)

Dear Gary:

Welcome to Big Friends Club. In the next two weeks, you will be given three young friend candidates to review before you make your friend choice.

Last year in Cleveland, we were able to match 1,250 boys with Big Friends. On the back of this letter, we've listed some of the boys' comments about the differences their Big Friends have made in their lives. You'll also see some comments from Big Friends.

Being a Big Friend is inspiring, rewarding, and a lot of work. We're so pleased you have decided to help make a difference in a young boy's life.

Remember, we are always here to help.

Sincerely,

Rodney Baker
President

State your welcome.

Offer something positive.

Offer help.

As a Customer

[Handwritten or typed]
(Date)

Dear David:

It was a pleasure serving you at The Regiment today, and I welcome you as a customer of the finest men's custom-made clothing store in the city.

As we discussed, your final fitting for the suits will be Friday the 15th at 4:00 P.M.

I look forward to serving you then. And again, welcome!

Yours truly,

Ted Bunson

To a New Businesswoman

[Typed or emailed]
(Date)

Dear Gwen:

Welcome to Marmet, Missouri!

Since this is the "Show Me State," I'd like to suggest a breakfast meeting on the 15th, 8:00 A.M., at Robins Inn, with a group of new residents and a few of us old-timers. It will be an orientation for important things such as where to buy the best women's suits for the lowest price, where to go when you need to have dinner for 10 in 40 minutes, and where to take your car for a purring tune-up.

We'd also like to give you the opportunity to ask us questions. We have been businesswomen in this town for two to thirty years. (There's a wealth of information here.)

Please call me at 616-555-0123 and tell me you'll attend.

Sincerely,

Joan Slosky

To a New Email-Forum Member

Dallas:

A strong welcome to our little online author community. As you'll quickly see, we offer a brand of help and support here not otherwise available. It's probably the single most beneficial thing I do to help my freelance career. And the members of this group have become true friends.

We have only a few rules written to promote online civility and avoid the problems that this medium has been known to spawn. I've attached a copy for you.

Again, welcome. I look forward to your participation.

All the best,

Cliff

Also see DIRECT MAIL, page 327, and EMPLOYEE CORRESPONDENCE, page 150.

10
INVITATIONS

But all the fun's in how you say a thing.

—ROBERT FROST

Inviting guests to an occasion can be as informal as saying, "Y'all come," or as formal as sending engraved invitations—pieces of art—created and then addressed by a calligrapher. Whether the event is an impromptu pizza party or the 125th Annual Governors' Ball, you'll want your invitee to feel you are expressing a special desire to have him or her attend. Social occasions often cross the lines between personal and business, making distinction between the two impossible. Certainly all such occasions present an opportunity to solidify connections, improve morale, create new relationships, or patch up old ones.

Everyone loves being invited. Create an invitation that makes the recipient eager to attend!

DECIDE TO WRITE
You'll use invitations for many get-togethers:
- Informal parties
- Business events, including such things as trade shows, open houses, exhibitions, new product introductions, and premieres
- New business openings
- Fund-raisers
- Celebrations of a family, religious, or educational nature including showers, rehearsal dinners, weddings, anniversaries, christenings, first communions, baptisms, bar or bat mitzvahs, confirmations, ordinations, graduations, and others
- Hospitality, such as an invitation to be a weekend houseguest
- Educational programs, such as workshops, seminars, conferences, or speeches
- Cultural events, such as concert or theater productions
- Social organization events
- Holiday or commemorative events

THINK ABOUT CONTENT
- Make the form and appearance of your invitation consistent with the formality of the occasion. Invitations to business events may take the form of a business communication, and strictly social events should follow the rules for a social invitation.
- Be sure you include all the essential information: *what, when, why, where, who,* and *how much.*

- Begin with words of personal invitation or state the occasion or event: "You Are Cordially Invited to the Ninth Annual Preferred Customers' Presale Event," "The Fifth Annual Goldminers' Ball," "The Grand Opening of Phinney's."

- List the date and time of the event, including month, day, year, and time, A.M. or P.M. (The day of the week may be listed before the month.)

- The address comes next. A cross street ("at Maple and Main") or brief directions ("turn south off Alameda onto Grant") may be given after the address, or a map may be included with the invitation.

- Supply helpful information for guests, for example, if food and beverages (and possibly which foods) will be served. Giving the time and sequence of events is also helpful. "A light luncheon for out-of-town guests will be served at four o'clock before the six o'clock ceremony."

- Charges and costs, if any, should be listed: "$125 per couple," "Open Bar," "Valet Parking." This information tells the invitees the arrangements and their anticipated expenses involved with attending.

- The RSVP tradition has become very blurred. Since every host needs to know how many, and possibly who, will attend, an *RSVP, Please respond, Please RSVP by (date),* or *Regrets only* should appear in the lower left corner of the formal invitation with a telephone number and an address. Many formal invitations enclose a printed or engraved RSVP card and envelope, addressed and stamped for the invitee's reply.

- You may place information about attire in the lower right corner of a formal invitation. Designations most often used are *informal, semiformal, formal, black tie, white tie, casual, costume,* and *evening attire.* On informal invitations, the host may say something like "Come in slacks."

- When your invitation includes hospitality, multiple activities, or requires guests to make their own overnight or eating arrangements, provide as much information as possible. Making a statement like "Come prepared to enjoy swimming, tennis, and an evening hayride" gives guests an idea of the kind of clothing to bring. If your invitation is to a weekend rally of red 1965 Corvette owners, it will be helpful if you include hotel suggestions and reservation policies, and even information on restaurants in the area.

- The host should not be shy about including the limits of the invitation. For example, "Please plan to arrive Saturday between 3:00 P.M. and 4:00 P.M., and depart Sunday between 2:00 P.M. and 3:00 P.M." "We're a nonsmoking home" will be helpful to host and guests.

- Inform guests, too, about unusual arrangements: "Sleeping arrangements for the Gourmet Cowboy Weekend will be women in the west camp tents and men in the east camp tents. Bring your own sleeping bag, towels, and personal items. There is no electricity. Cots are provided."

- Miscellaneous information can be very important. If guests are to arrange their transportation from the airport, make that clear.

- Parking (and fees), inclement weather information, and notices about alternate plans should all be included. "In the event of rain, we will move inside the Grange Hall."

- Most important, make sure the invitation is warm in tone and leaves readers with the sense you look forward to having them attend: "Please RSVP with an acceptance." "We're so looking forward to seeing you. It's been such a long time. We have some serious catching up to do." "Please confirm by June 15 that you can make it." "It will be so good to see you." "We've arranged some events we think you will especially like."

- Corporate informal and general invitations for such things as an in-office party for a retirement, maternity leave, promotion, service celebration, and the like can be made in memo form, or by email. List the event, time, date, place, and refreshments. Information on contributions for a gift may be included, and if you need a response, a telephone extension number should be given with a time limit: "Call Susan at Ext. 3443 by Thursday at 4:00 P.M. and tell her how many from your department will attend."

- To help ensure a response to your invitation, place RSVP in the lower left-hand section of the invitation and enclose a reply card and envelope which is addressed and stamped. Or, list a telephone number or an address for the response:

    RSVP
    555-0123
    or
    RSVP
    110 Forest Lane
    Rockport, IL 60641

- If you have not heard from invitees by the time you need to make final preparations, telephone them.

- The response card should be simple fill-in-the-blanks. The printer will have several options to select from, but it can simply say:

    M_____
    ___ regrets ___ accepts
    the invitation for
    Friday, January fifth
    at Willow Creek Country Club
    or
    M_____
    will _____ will not _____ attend
    Friday, January fifth

- When you enclose items in the invitation—the response card and response envelope, raffle tickets for a benefit, a separate map, or seating tickets for a performance or graduation—place these items in front of the invitation with the writing side facing the mailing envelope flap so the invitee sees the writing when opening the envelope.

- Dress designations are not as strictly adhered to today, but "white tie" is the most formal, indicating a white tie, wing collar, and tailcoat for men. Women wear formal evening gowns. Today this kind of dress is reserved almost exclusively for official and diplomatic occasions. "Black tie" indicates men are to wear a tuxedo and bow tie. Jackets may be patterned and of almost any color. Women wear gowns or cocktail dresses. "Semi-formal" has come to mean wear shoes, and don't wear T-shirts or jeans.

- The name game can be confusing. When in doubt, call and ask. Issue the invitation in the names of the hosts, for example, "David Greer and Sally Westmore invite you . . ." Address invitations to invitees by their preferred names. Many women now use a business name and another social name. Business invitations may list the titles of the hosts. It's also correct to issue an invitation in the name of a club, friends, a fraternity, or other organization.

- List the times of events in the invitation whenever possible. "Ceremony at six o'clock, reception at half past seven." "Cocktails at six o'clock, dinner at seven-thirty."

- The timetable for sending invitations depends upon the occasion, the distance guests must travel, and everyone's social calendar. Wedding invitations should be sent six to eight weeks ahead. For most formal events and dinner parties, invitations should be sent four to six weeks ahead. For informal get-togethers and casual dinners, two to four weeks is adequate. (Allow an extra ten days to two weeks for getting invitations printed.)

- Include a no-gift statement if appropriate: "Your love and friendship are cherished gifts. We respectfully request no other." "No gifts, please." "Please bring the gift of a favorite recipe." "Please bring the gift of a favorite photo or story to share."

- Fund-raiser invitations will receive a better response rate if you enclose a postage-paid, addressed reply envelope.

- Invitations to guest speakers, panelists, and prospective conference attendees should contain complete information. Speakers need to know the composition of the audience, the goal of the conference or seminar, other presenters and their topics, time allotments, the room size, accommodations, seating style, audiovisual equipment, and other special equipment and connections available for use. Be sure to include the name of a contact person (and contact information) who can answer specific questions. If you are using a hotel for the event, the hotel may offer a complete listing of this information.

THINK ABOUT RESPONDING

- Always respond to a personal invitation—whether it is business or social. Both "RSVP" and "Please reply" require a response. "Regrets only" requires a response only if you will *not* attend. Even if a dinner invitation is in conjunction with an annual sales meeting, board of directors meeting, or special convention, respond as indicated.
- Use the reply-in-kind rule. If the invitation is formal, reply in a like manner. Use the same language as the invitation. Write "Mr. and Mrs. Lewis Curtis accept with pleasure the kind invitation of Mr. and Mrs. Peter Graves for dinner on Monday the tenth of November at eight o'clock." Informal written responses may be made on personal fold-over note stationery. Emailed invitations may be accepted or declined by email.
- A response by either invitee of a married couple is correct. No longer is this considered the domain of women.
- If you must cancel at the last minute after accepting an invitation, both telephone or otherwise notify the host by using email or fax, and immediately write a personal note of regret.

ELIMINATE WRONG MESSAGES

- Informal invitations may contain informal writing, like abbreviations; but formal invitations should avoid abbreviations except *Mr., Mrs., Ms., Dr., Jr., Sr., Lt., Col.,* and other military designations. In formal invitations, do not abbreviate the states in the address. Numbers in the formal invitation should be spelled out, like "eight fifteen Sherman Street" and "seven o'clock." In conjunction with names, use *Second* and *Third* without a comma after the name, instead of II and III. Use a comma before *Jr.* and *Sr.*
- Don't be vague about whom you're inviting. List invited small children by their first name on the envelope under the parents' names. If you are inviting teenagers or older children, each should receive his or her own invitation. If the spouse of an employee is being invited, or if the invitee may bring a friend, make that clear. Use the individual's name whenever possible.

SELECT A FORMAT

- Formal invitations are usually on high-quality white or cream-colored cards with matching envelopes and are engraved. Other choices may be embossed or plain cards with a raised border (plate mark). There is a trend toward hand-crafted invitations for very special occasions. In either case, select cards with proportions of three units by four units. Good choices are 3 by 4 inches to $4^{1}/_{2}$ by 6 inches. Ask the printer for samples.
- Select a typeface or lettering and ink color that are easy to read.
- Printing may be engraved, or, more economically, done in informal style by thermography, which produces raised letters.
- If you create your own invitations, use appropriate artwork or a nice-quality card stock or notepaper and formal wording in the third person: "John and Judith Eisner request the pleasure of your company at a dinner party at their home at Ten Fox Dale Drive on September tenth. Cocktails will be served at seven, dinner at eight. RSVP 555-0123. Black tie."

SELECT THE RIGHT WORD

announce	joy
attend	meet
attention	new
bring	open
celebrate	please
change	pleasure
company	presence
enjoy	receive
greet	rejoice
hope	reply
hospitality	request
inform	welcome
join	

CONSTRUCT EFFECTIVE PHRASES

announce the coming

coming soon

event will be held

happy to announce

introduce the new

open house will

please join us

pleased to introduce

request your presence at

starting at

wish to invite

BUILD STRONG SENTENCES

Start with a key word of invitation and build lean sentences with precise words of welcome. Here are some examples:

We're really hoping Uncle Roy and you will be able to come and have Thanksgiving dinner with us this year.

Will you join Joel Walton and me for lunch on Thursday? It would be so good to see you.

During the Open House, First Bank's loan officers will be available to answer any questions you may have.

This is your special invitation to our Ninth Annual Pre-Sale Celebration.

Our party will be a success, if you'll be here.

Please say you'll come.

Your presence will make it a real celebration.

Our special invitation to you for a very special evening.

It will be wonderful to have a chance to catch up.

BUILD EFFECTIVE PARAGRAPHS

Put precise, complete information in its logical order.

Please stop by our booth #566 at the Chicago Convention Center, Expo 104, September 10–12, and see the new Model 415. Register for a two-week vacation giveaway and a 25 percent discount on the new models.

This is your invitation to a one-month free membership to Valley Racquet Club, 4300 Miners Road, Englewood. This entitles you to full use of the entire health club facilities (with the exception of the indoor tennis courts).

Please bring the enclosed 25 percent off certificate in during our "Madman Special," Thursday, November 5, between 10:00 A.M. and 6:00 P.M. Free hot dogs and sodas for the kids.

The Marketing Department is hosting an after-hours reception to show-and-tell the fall campaign on Friday, August 30, 5:00 P.M. to 6:30 P.M. Please respond with a list of those from your department who will attend.

Monday Night Football happens at my house one hour before kick-off. Won't you and Sally join the rest of the softball team?

EDIT, EDIT, EDIT

The best invitations contain complete, concise information. Ask yourself if you have answered the *what, where, when, how, who,* and *why* of the event. Be sure, too, that you've included details guests will need to know, such as any costs involved, directions, special parking information, and so on.

Invitation to a Formal Dinner

[Printed]

Roosevelt and Suzanne Connors
request the pleasure of your company
at dinner
on Friday, the tenth of September,
at half after seven o'clock
at the Town Club
Heathertown, New York

RSVP
Ten Applewood Lane
Heathertown, New York 10045

Invitation to a Formal Ball

[Printed]

The Governors of Gateside Country Club
invite you to subscribe to
the Annual Springtime Ball
to be held at
The Gateside Country Club
on Saturday, the twenty-fifth of April
Two thousand and six
at eight o'clock
Applewood, Connecticut

RSVP
Georgia Geiger
555-0123

Invitation to an Informal Social Open House

[Printed or typed]

Willow Creek Country Club will hold its
thirty-fifth annual
open house for new members
One o'clock to five o'clock
Saturday the fifth of May
4500 South Willow Creek Drive

Refreshments   Informal Dress
Drawing

Invitation to an Informal Business Open House

[Typed or handwritten]
(Date)

Dear Allyson:

I hope you will come by the hospitality suite, Room 430, at the Westmoreland Hotel on Thursday, April 27, between 7:00 and 9:30 P.M., and introduce yourself to our marketing team attending the Booksellers' Convention. I'd like you to meet Bill Ashton. I believe he will be a great contact for the Grizzly project.

This promises to be our best convention yet. There are already well over 125,000 registered attendees.

Best wishes,

Titus Teeter

Invitation to an Informal Get-Together

[Handwritten]
(Date)

Dear Rachel,

I would be so pleased if you would join us after baby Jennifer's christening on Sunday, the 12th, from 1:30 P.M. to 3:30 P.M. It will just be a small celebration with a few special relatives and friends.

We certainly hope you can make it. Please let us know by calling 555-0123.

Yours truly,

Celeste Castle

Informal Invitation to a Working Business Dinner

[Typed]
(Date)

Dear Jim:

I'm hosting an informal get-together on Thursday, May 12, at 7:00 P.M. for the key players in the Adams restructuring. We will have dinner and then review the proposed elements of the agreement, which I've enclosed. A map is also enclosed.

Please call my secretary at 555-0123 by Wednesday and let her know if you can make it. I'll also need your comments on the enclosed draft by Friday so I can have everyone's feedback distributed to all those coming on the 12th.

Sincerely,

Agatha Jeevers

Acceptance of a Formal Dinner Invitation

[Handwritten]

*Ted and Jane Turnett
accept with pleasure
the kind invitation of
Reginald and Jennifer Trumpet
to dinner
on Friday, the tenth of September
at half after seven o'clock*

Invitation to a Graduation Reception

[Printed]

*Jerald and Olivia Soderholm
request the honor of your company
at a reception to celebrate the college
graduation of their son
Christopher David Solderholm
Sunday afternoon, June twenty-fourth
at three o'clock
in the Crown Room of the Highmoor
420 Eastman Drive
Cleveland Springs, Ohio*

*Please reply to
744 Tamarac Drive
Cleveland Springs, Ohio*

Regrets to an Informal Invitation

[Handwritten]
(Date)

Dear Electra and Warren,

Dede and I are so disappointed we will be unable to accept your kind invitation to dinner at the Metro Club on May 12 for your retirement celebration. We are scheduled to be in France for the entire month.
Have a wonderful time. We'll look forward to getting together when we return. You must tell us all about the event. I'll call when we get back into town to arrange a time.

Best,

Warren

11

APPRECIATION

Apt words have power to suage
The tumors of a troubled mind.

—JOHN MILTON

You will distinguish yourself if you express appreciation in personal and business relationships when another person has performed well. The letter of appreciation is distinctly its own breed, falling within the broad category of goodwill letters. While the distinctions between letters of appreciation, thanks, acknowledgment, and congratulations are often blurred, write a letter of appreciation when someone was just doing his or her job, but in doing so made your life easier, or when you particularly admired the way he or she did the job. It is also appropriate to send a letter of appreciation when someone has performed in a manner that is notable or extraordinary.

DECIDE TO WRITE

Send a note of appreciation in response to:

- Outstanding addresses, speeches, and instruction sessions
- Employees' extraordinary performance
- Pre-, early, or prompt payment by a customer
- Expressions of sympathy
- Letters or acts of congratulations
- An offer of assistance
- Complimentary remarks or acknowledgments in speeches, books, and the like
- Invitations to speak, chair a committee, sing, or sit on a panel
- Salary increase or bonus
- Outstanding or beneficial conduct or act of a teacher, family member, friend, associate, or supervisor
- Financial contributions
- Volunteer's efforts

THINK ABOUT CONTENT

- Begin with the point of appreciation and the rest will flow more easily.
- Make it brief and sincere.
- Express your feelings, naming what you appreciate in natural, sincere terms.
- Explain briefly why you are appreciative.
- If appropriate, offer to reciprocate.
- End with a reference to the future. If appropriate, encourage the recipient to contribute again or express your desire for a future meeting.

ELIMINATE WRONG MESSAGES

- Don't mix messages. Keep news items, meeting announcements, and similar notices for another communication.
- Examine your motives if you are having difficulty writing the letter. It may be that another type of letter is more suitable, or that a letter of appreciation isn't merited.

CONSIDER SPECIAL SITUATIONS

- Hybrid letters with a public relations or sales motive should be carefully thought out. Appreciation should be the primary message or the letter may sound insincere. (See "Sales," page 326.)
- A letter in response to an offer of assistance should express appreciation, accept or reject the offer, and suggest the next step if the offer is being accepted.
- A letter to a team, committee, department, or group of people may address them as a whole. If appropriate, a copy may be sent to each member. Be sure to include everyone.
- Sometimes appreciation must be combined with refusal. If there is an offer to serve on a committee, or a gift is sent that you must refuse, emphasize your appreciation first. (See "Refusal," page 250.)

SELECT A FORMAT

- Handwritten personal notes of appreciation should be your first choice. Use personal stationery or fold-over notes.
- Business letters of appreciation should be typed on letterhead if the recipient is associated with another organization.
- For internal business appreciation, it is usually best to use an interoffice memo or email.
- For routine, quick messages of appreciation for such things as product orders, a postcard may be used, or email. (Also see "Confirmation and Acknowledgment," page 240.)

SELECT STRONG WORDS

admirable	kindness
admire	memorable
aplomb	model
appreciate	noteworthy
aspire	outstanding
commend	pleased
commendable	praiseworthy
entrust	recommend
esteem	remarkable
exemplary	respect
expertise	satisfying
favorite	sensational
finesse	superb
generous	touched
grace	treasure
gracious	triumph
honor	unforgettable
impressive	unique
inspire	valuable
inspiring	

BUILD EFFECTIVE PHRASES

must express my appreciation

how delightful to see

so grateful for your contribution

hold you in high esteem

unequaled in effort

done with such expertise

an exemplary performace

offer my sincere appreciation

I was so impressed by

your performance is noteworthy

such an important contribution

a job well done

held in high esteem by so many

appreciated by so many

set an outstanding example for

demonstrate such dedication

set a high standard

WRITE STRONG SENTENCES

Your contribution to the new plant scheduling policy is one of the best I've seen in 20 years with the company.

I felt your insight helped the committee do a much better job than any of us expected.

Please call on me if I can return the favor.

BUILD EFFECTIVE PARAGRAPHS

It was extremely thoughtful of you to volunteer to be on hand for the courtroom drama. I really appreciate your vote of confidence.

Taking over for Karen Gross when she became ill was way beyond the call of duty. Your extra efforts and dedication to making the organization look good are greatly appreciated.

I really appreciated your demonstrated leadership in last night's meeting. You kept the whole issue from exploding.

EDIT, EDIT, EDIT

Be concise, brief, and sincere.

Response to a Letter of Recommendation

[Handwritten]
(Date)

Bob,

Name what you appreciate. → *I have just received the copy of your letter of recommendation to Begones on my behalf. (Is this me you're talking about?)*

Refer to the future. → *I greatly appreciate your kind words, and I will certainly keep you informed of the progress and outcome as the selection process goes forward.*

Kind regards,

Dave

Response to Help with Work

[Handwritten or typed]
(Date)

John,

It was a real sacrifice for you to change your plans, do double duty on the sales report, and also handle my trip to Atlanta while Anne was ill. I appreciate it more than I can say. There was a critical decision I had to make for her medical care on Thursday afternoon, and matters would have been seriously complicated if I had not been on hand. You're a prince.

Please allow me to do a good deed for you anytime.

Kind regards,

Bill

Response to Prompt Payment

[Typed]
(Date)

Dear Mr. Jepson:

We just received your letter and check for the landscaping of Green Acres. We appreciate your prompt payment.

It was a pleasure working on this lovely project, and we do hope you'll call us for further planning or maintaining the grounds.

We look forward to hearing from you.

Your truly,

Annie Schmidt

Response to Volunteering

[Typewritten]
(Date)

Dear Janice:

It is very thoughtful of you to volunteer to take over three of my class sessions next semester while I attend the workshops. I thought I would have to reschedule the class sessions, and that presented some insurmountable problems. Your offer is a wonderful solution.

I will telephone you next week to set a time to go over the lesson plans. Please allow me to stand in for you next semester.

Best regards,

Nancy Letterer

Response to Extra Effort

[Typed]
(Date)

Dear Mr. Richardson:

I have just received the reworked architectural plans for the addition to the children's wing of St. Joseph's. I know a lot of overtime went into this because of our tight timeframe, but your hard work will enable us to present the plans at the board meeting. We deeply appreciate your efforts. You did a great job.

The board meets in the morning, and I will be back in touch with you tomorrow afternoon to let you know how it went. I truly appreciate your fine work.

Sincerely,

Bill Babson

12

THANK-YOU

There are two ways of spreading light: to be the candle or the mirror that reflects it.

—EDITH WHARTON

Writing a thank-you letter or note in response to an act of kindness or a gift received is both courteous and the civil thing to do. But if you start with that in mind, you'll undoubtedly produce one of those obligatory and lifeless messages that fail to connect with the person you're thanking. Go for a real expression of thanks—one that connects you to the gift and the giver. Make your message brief and write it in a pleasant, conversational tone. Write it promptly because timing sends a very strong message on its own.

DECIDE TO WRITE

Use a thank-you note or letter in response to:

- Gifts of all kinds for such occasions as weddings, showers, birthdays, holidays, anniversaries, and bar or bat mitzvahs, whether these are received personally or in the course of business (also see chapter 13, "Wedding and Engagement Correspondence)
- Acts of kindness and gifts after a death in the family
- Business order or contract
- Job interview, or interview of any kind
- Referrals of clients, customers, or patients

- Reference for a position, whether business or personal
- Hospitality, either business or personal, or both
- Contributions to fund-raising activities, events, and drives
- Membership in a club, association, or professional organization

THINK ABOUT CONTENT

- Focus first on the person who gave you the gift or performed the kindness.
- Think next about what you are thanking the person or company for.
- Reflect on what the gift or deed means to you: how you will use it or how it will help you.
- Connect the dots between the giver, the gift, and yourself.
- Name the gift early, and say thank-you early.
- Use a tone that is pleasant, even enthusiastic, and one that reflects the way you would talk to the giver.
- Mention the appropriateness of the gift or act.
- Add some detail about how the gift or act benefits you, what about it you especially enjoyed, or how you will use it.

- Be brief and sincere.
- Offer something in return if that is appropriate, or optionally, add a sentence or two of compliment to the giver.
- You cannot err in writing sincere thank-yous for acts of kindness or gifts. So, whenever the situation presents itself, use it to show your thankfulness and to make your relationship with the giver stronger.
- For personal thank-yous, don't mix messages. Don't tack on a thank-you in a letter with another purpose.
- For business-social thank-yous, use these guidelines:
  — When a dinner, evening, or weekend outing crosses from business to social at the home of a business associate, send both a written thank-you and a thank-you gift to the host.
  — When you are the guest of honor at an office or business luncheon or dinner, a thank-you note to the host—usually your immediate superior—is in order. If the company president attends, a personal, written thank-you should also be sent to him or her.
  — If you are one of many guests at an office party, or share a meal in the ordinary course of business, a verbal thanks is sufficient. You may also, in this case, want to add a note to your next business correspondence, such as "Thanks for hosting the Thursday luncheon. I look forward to working with you on the Sioux Falls project." This same rule is true for regular luncheons, but for first meetings and infrequent ones, a short thank-you note is called for. This may be either typed or handwritten.
- Send your thank-you note or letter promptly. Here are some general guidelines to follow:
  — Luncheon or dinner, write within one to three days.
  — Stay in someone's home or an act of hospitality, write within several days.
  — For wedding gifts, it's best to send thank-yous as gifts arrive, but all givers should receive thank-yous within three months of the wedding (also see chapter 13, "Wedding and Engagement Correspondence").
  — For "get well" gifts and acts of kindness, there is some latitude, usually until after the receiver recovers. In the case of a serious or terminal illness, another person may certainly send an expression of thanks on the recipient's behalf. It is also generous to write periodic updates to keep friends, family, and colleagues informed. Ask if the giver would like to be included in weekly, monthly, or periodic updates, which you can write and distribute by email.
- Writing promptly makes the task much easier and ensures a much more genuine (and detailed) message.
- Be specific in naming the gift or act of kindness.

ELIMINATE WRONG MESSAGES

- Don't write a thank-you that is really a sales letter.
- Stay away from general statements; make your thank-you specific.
- Don't let your prose go beyond your true feelings. Flowery insincerity defeats your purpose. Instead, simply say "thank you very much."
- The mention of the amount of money received as a gift is sometimes considered tactless. If you know the recipient well, you may be certain that Uncle Joe won't be offended if you write "Thank you, Uncle Joe, for the check for $50." For others you don't know well, simply write "Thank you for the check."
- In the short thank-you, the use of "Thanks again" at the end of the note does not work well. Instead, conclude with a sincere compliment to the recipient. "You've proven again what a generous person you are."

CONSIDER SPECIAL SITUATIONS

- Don't procrastinate. A late thank-you may seem insincere, and your procrastination must be explained. However, don't belabor your tardiness; just get the note written. "I'm so sorry this note is late. The tornado hit just as we were arriving home." Or, "I'm sorry for not having written sooner to tell you how much I love the red sweater. It's a perfect match with my tartan plaid skirt." "The tardiness of my thank-you note reflects poorly on me, but certainly not on the wonderful wallet." "It's taken me a little while to digest the enormity of your generous act."

- Verbal thank-yous for gifts don't substitute for written ones. If you've verbally thanked the giver, still send a personal, written note.

- A written thank-you is required when a "thank-you" gift has been given.

- When a gift was sent collectively by a number of givers, each should be sent a personal, written thank-you. The exceptions here are when the gift is sent by a family, a company department, or a club or association. In these cases, address the family, department, or club, and request that your thank-you note or letter be circulated or posted.

- Thank-yous for flowers, contributions, and acts of kindness in the case of a death in the family must always be sent. Even written letters of sympathy should be acknowledged with a return note of thanks. These thank-yous may be written either by the person closest to the deceased, or by a close family member or friend. At such times, it is wise to have someone make a record to ease the task and make sure no one's kindness is overlooked. There is obviously much leeway in timing here, but generally thank-yous should be sent within six weeks of the funeral.

- Business thank-yous should be sent by regular modes of transmission. To fax or email a thank-you would detract considerably from its personal quality. However, a routine thank-you for a regular business luncheon may be combined with a letter with another main message, or sent by email if this is acceptable within the organization culture.

SELECT A FORMAT

- The form of choice is most often a commercially purchased fold-over notecard or personal stationery.

- Formal printed cards or stationery can be used to express thanks for very large events, like large political campaigns or major fund-raisers. Still, a personal, handwritten note is in order for gifts.

- When the gift was personal or social, the thank-you should be handwritten.

- When hospitality was extended in a business associate's home, the thank-you is addressed to the home address.

- Business-related thank-yous are usually type-written on company letterhead, personal business stationery, or a good-quality paper.

- When there are exceptionally large numbers of people to thank, or there is the possibility of oversight, as in the death of a community leader or when many people have contributed to a political campaign, it is important to wrote a public thank-you to local newspapers and other appropriate publications.

- A formal announcement of thanks does not, of course, substitute for personal ones to people whose efforts or gifts were exceptional.

POWER WORDS

cherish	remember
delighted	right
elegant	satisfied
enjoyed	stunning
excited	thanks
exquisite	thrilled
generous	timely
great	touched
keepsake	treasure
kindness	treat
lovely	unforgettable
noteworthy	useful
overjoyed	wonderful
perfect	

POWER PHRASES

all-star gift

delightful choice

exquisite taste

extraordinary treat

frosting on the cake

generous gift

grace and style

great timing

how generous of you

I will always be thankful for

keepsake to treasure

lovely in the extreme

more than kind

no one else would have done this

offer my personal thanks

perfect choice

perfect in every way

perfect timing

perfect weekend

precious memento

precision and flair

selfless gift

your extreme thoughtfulness

something to always treasure

thrilled to receive

very special

unique

warm hospitality

we so benefited from

what a kind thing to do

who else would have thought

wonderful respite

wonderful selection

you always add panache

you are so thoughtful

you're an exceptional person

you've made my day

WRITE STRONG SENTENCES

Start with the gift and how it will be used. Then connect the giver with the act of giving, and with you.

Thank you for referring Alice Bannock to Adam, and more precisely, to me.

We are touched by your thoughtfulness.

Thanks to all of you at White and White for contributing the time and energy to the Women's Corner project.

Your crew did an outstanding job of answering the phones during the viewers' fund-raiser; due to your efforts, we received $90,000 in pledged contributions.

All of the family was touched by your act of kindness in serving as head pallbearer at Dad's funeral.

I can't tell you how wonderful it was to see you come through that door in such a dark hour.

I can't remember attending a more relaxing and enjoyable dinner party.

It was extremely kind of you to call me about the opening at Formed Container.

Tickets to "Sherman's Forces" were unavailable, and we would have missed the event if it hadn't been for your generosity.

What an absolutely perfect dinner party.

I will always treasure this gift, but especially the fact that it came from you.

It's a perfect gift, and one that makes me feel even closer to you.

EDIT, EDIT, EDIT

Thank-you notes are generally not more than a paragraph or two, so make every word count.

For a Job-Candidate Lead

[Typed]
(Date)

Dear Dennis:

State what you're thankful for.

Thank you for referring your friend Molly Swartz for the computer programmer position we discussed. I have just interviewed Molly and I believe she is an outstanding candidate.

It has almost restored my sense of hope after being burned three times.

State why you are thankful.

It was exceptionally thoughtful of you to follow up after our golf discussion. I'll let you know if this becomes a working relationship. We certainly need the skills and stability Molly possesses.

Offer to reciprocate.

Please let me know, as I said, if you want me to give you a couple of names for the drafting position.

Embrace the relationship.

That was a great putt on the 18th, by the way; I'm determined to give you a greater challenge next week.

Regards,

Lee Ann

For a Party

[Handwritten]
(Date)

Caroline,

I've never been so totally surprised! How did you ever plan a 50-person party of office staff, organize it, and pull it off right under my nose, complete with those fantastic Caribbean decorations, without me getting wind of it? I never suspected. You are truly a wonder, and a very dear friend. Now when exactly is your birthday?

Affectionately,

Karen

For Weekend Hospitality

[Handwritten]
(Date)

Dear Daisy and Duff,

State what you're thankful for.

What an absolutely delightful weekend. Rox and I had just about burned out from four consecutive long, long weeks of back-to-back deadlines. Then this. What a breath of fresh country air!

State why.

It was a wonderful respite and change of pace. The card games were lots of fun, too, though I suspect I'd be even more enthusiastic if I'd have been on the winning team a few more times.

Refer to the future.

A small token of our appreciation should arrive tomorrow. Do remember you've promised to allow us to reciprocate by accepting our brand of hospitality (city, not country) next month. There's a great new production at the community theater and a Broadway musical in town too. Are you game for one or both?

All the best,

Rox and George

For a Gift

[Handwritten]
(Date)

Dear Aunt Jennifer,

I've deposited your very generous check in my college fund. I'll use the money to purchase an alarm clock, so I expect I may experience mixed emotions when I hear it go off. But I'll always think fondly of you for your gift.

Thank you.

Your niece,

Lois

For Serving as a Speaker

[Typed]
(Date)

Dear Gabby:

Thank you for speaking to the Women's Press Club on Wednesday. The turnout was up 20 percent. I'm sure that was due to your popularity and your timely topic: "Blowing Your Own Horn."

Initial response after the meeting was that this was the best program we've had this year. I've also been asked if you would consider conducting a half-day seminar in the spring. We would, of course, pay you your regular fee.

Thank you, Gabby, for creating interest among our members.

Very truly,

Ruth

For Conference Coordination

[Handwritten]
(Date)

Dear Joel,

Thank you for doing such a perfect job in both orchestrating the entire three-day conference and working in all those thoughtful details so every single spouse and family member could have a custom-fit experience. I didn't initially think a dude ranch was a good choice, owning not a single set of spurs, but it was perfect. I've gotten a dozen enthusiastic calls requesting that we do it again next year.

Perhaps the bad news for you is that no one else will ever be able to fill your cowboy boots! You did an absolutely perfect job!

All the best,

Avery

For Dinner

[Handwritten]
(Date)

Dear Millie,

Dinner was ambrosial! Just like every meal I've ever had at your house. Thank you for inviting Dick and me. We always enjoy getting together with you and Franz. It was a lovely, lovely evening, and we were especially "wild" about hearing the details of your African adventure.

Fondly,

Sherry and Ed

For an Interview

[Handwritten]
(Date)

Dear Bea,

Thank you for the well-structured interview. Your planning, coordination, and interview techniques allowed me to both demonstrate my potential fit in terms of skills and expertise and also comprehensively assess what working with all the departments within Crackers is like.

I believe I would make a great fit on the marketing team, especially in contributing to long-range goals. Tom and I—it seemed in our interview segment—could work seamlessly together and challenge the best from each other.

Thank you for such a fine interview experience. I'll look forward to learning your list of finalists. I'm available for any follow-up questions you or other department heads may have.

Sincerely,

Jack

For a Business Luncheon

[Emailed]

Henry:

Thank you for orchestrating such a productive luncheon. The Back Room reservation was a stroke of genius. It allowed the privacy and quiet the Cooks team needed to listen to our proposal, discuss it in detail, and come to the decision to go with us as their project management team.

Well done, well done. And congratulations on this brand new account. I'm looking forward to working with you and your whole group as we put in place this wonderful project.

Best,

Sam

For a Funeral Bouquet

[Handwritten]
(Date)

Dear Lynn and Lester,

   Thank you for sending the beautiful arrangement of sweetheart roses to the mortuary for Mom's funeral. How thoughtful of you to select her favorite. I'm sure you remember her extensive trellis in the backyard from which she supplied the whole neighborhood with bouquets each season.
   We'll all miss her and her rose garden, but what an appropriate and wonderful send-off. It meant a lot to David and me to have roses there.

   Sincerely,

   Susan and David

Also see ACCEPTANCE, page 245; APPRECIATION, page 72; CONFIRMATION AND ACKNOWLEDGMENT, page 240; RESPONSE, page 234; and WEDDING AND ENGAGEMENT CORRESPONDENCE, page 83.

WEDDING AND ENGAGEMENT CORRESPONDENCE

You have opened up the prison gates of my womanhood. And all the passion that was unsatisfied in me for so many years, leaped into a wild reckless storm boundless as the sea . . .

—EMMA GOLDMAN TO BEN REITMAN

Engagement and wedding celebrations can be as varied as the people joining their lives. While many traditional rules have given way to expressions of individuality and creativity, it remains important that engagement and wedding communications reflect both the spirit of the occasion and your desire to have others join in the celebration. There will be many opportunities for both those being honored and those celebrating with them to express joy and good wishes in writing. Join in with a full heart.

DECIDE TO WRITE

- Decide how formal your wedding will be—casual, informal, semiformal, or formal. This will dictate the style, tone, choice of language, typeface, ink, printing method, paper stock, and color that you will use for your correspondence.
- Determine the size of the wedding party and the number of guests to be invited.
- List the communications you'll be sending.
- Compute the total numbers of communications you'll send, then select a common paper stock, typeface(s), layout and design(s), and ink.
- Order some additional blank letter paper and notecards for such things as inviting a friend to

be in the wedding party and thanking the many and various people who will be helping you create your wedding.
- Consider the special situations of those on your list of friends, family, and associates. You may wish to send wedding announcements to some people you know won't attend, along with a personal note that indicates you wanted to include them in the celebration even though you know they won't be able to attend.

WEDDING COMMUNICATION TYPES

Thinking through your entire schedule of events very carefully—from announcing the engagement through sending out the thank-you notes for gifts and participation—will help you decide the types of communications you will need. Wedding consultants can help with many of your decisions, but first be sure to have your event and budget firmly in mind. Consider the following communications and select those you will use:

Sent by the Wedding Couple or Family
— Announcement to close family and friends of the upcoming wedding (informal, personal letters and notes)

— Notifying an ex-spouse, if appropriate (informal, personal letter or note)
— Announcements: newspaper and printed formal or handwritten informal
— Introduction of bride and groom's families (personal letter by family members)
— Invitations to be wedding attendants and participants (personal letter or note)
— Save-the-date cards
— Wedding guest invitations
— Wedding announcements (printed and sent to those not attending)
— Reception or wedding dinner invitations (may be part of the wedding invitation)
— Confirmation of or request for items or services
— Wedding shower invitations
— Bachelor's party invitations
— Postponement or cancellation
— Wedding rehearsal invitations
— RSVP cards (included in the invitations, when used)
— Information on accommodations, maps, and activities
— Thank-you notes for gifts, assistance, special help, contributions
— Letter paper and notecards for related wedding correspondence

Sent to the Wedding Couple and Family
— Congratulations notes
— Acceptance notes for wedding party participation
— Refusal notes, or notes declining invitation to participate in the wedding
— RSVPs to invitations (cards filled out, when included; or personal note RSVPing or declining)

THINK ABOUT CONTENT

The busy days between an engagement announcement and a wedding include planning, printing or writing, and conveying much happy information. The following lists will help you with your pre- and post-wedding activities:

Engagement Communications

• *Informing the children.* When there are children involved, it's usually best for the marrying parent to first tell the children. The well-being of young children, of course, should be the first and foremost consideration. When the engaged couple has adult children, this may be done verbally, or with a written letter.

• *Informing close family and friends.* Even if you use the telephone to first make the announcement, it's still wonderful to send a written message. Order these letters so those who are dearest and nearest—parents, brothers and sisters, special aunts, grandmothers and grandfathers, close friends—are told before anyone else. You may want to include some brief information about the couple: where each grew up; the college each attended; their degrees and career fields; when and where the couple met; where the couple plans to live; and when the wedding is to be (approximately, if the date has not been set).

• *Notifying an ex-spouse* can be done with a personal note or letter. (Legal restrictions may dictate how notification is carried out.) Where there's acrimony between divorced, childless people, the communication may best be made immediately after the ceremony.

• *Introduction of bride and groom's families* may be done with a personal letter—traditionally the groom's family contacts the bride's family and the bride's family responds. The letters generally express delight and welcome the soon-to-be in-laws into the family. Today, when the parents live a great distance from each other, the introduction is sometimes first done by a telephone conversation or even a conference call where the couple introduces everyone. Sometimes further contact is made by email to arrange a meeting and carry out other arrangements.

• *Engagement announcements* can be made in many ways, from very informal to formal. A formal, printed engagement announcement is usually made by the parents, for example: "Mr. and Mrs. George Stomp of Maryville, Maryland, announce the engagement of their daughter, Diedre, to Bernard Dehm, son of Dr. and Mrs.

Richard Bard of Newcomb, Maine. A November wedding is planned." Older couples may make the announcement themselves, as may couples without close family members. Announcements, too, are often made public in newspapers and special publications.

- A *newspaper announcement of the engagement* will involve submitting information in the paper's prescribed form. This may be in writing (on any type of business stationery) or by email. Study the newspaper to determine the kind of information they will include, the preferred order, and whether they will use a photograph. Normally this will be (1) parents' names and place of residence(s) or hometowns; (2) complete names of the engaged couple; (3) colleges from which each graduated and/or current places of employment; (4) date of wedding, or general plans.

- The *official engagement announcement,* which may include the formal introduction of the families, is often made at an engagement-announcement dinner or party hosted by the bride's parents, family, or friends. Sometimes the groom's family, when they live at a distance, will also host an engagement party or a party after the wedding to honor and introduce the bride to family and friends. The engagement announcement is traditionally made by the father of the bride, and a toast is made, whether or not the engagement is a surprise.

- Invitations to the engagement-announcement dinner or party may be informal or formal, handwritten or printed.

- *Invitations to wedding attendants and participants* are often made in person or by telephone, even by email; but it is also nice to write a personal letter or note expressing why the invitee is being asked to participate. (The same is true, of course, of the person sending a note of acceptance.)

- Be sure all basic information is included: what the total costs will be and who is paying for what. (Obviously, there may be a number of lengthy verbal discussions, but a handwritten note is a fine way to make this very clear.) It's very important to consider this carefully, of course, because such an invitation usually means a substantial expense for the invitee, and acknowledging this and allowing for a graceful way to decline are necessary.

- *Save-the-date cards* are used when a destination wedding is planned, or for a wedding planned for a particularly busy time of year. These will usually be sent 12 weeks before the wedding.

Wedding Communications

- *Bridal shower invitations* are usually sent to small, intimate groups of close friends and relatives who want to wish the bride well. Invitations are usually preprinted, fill-in-the-blanks notecards with matching or coordinating envelopes. Sometimes inviting guests is done in person or by telephone, or, in the case of coworkers, by email. Be sure to inform guests if it's to be a surprise, if there's a theme (kitchen gifts, etc.), and/or if there will be gifts at all. Usually a close friend, bridal attendant, or relative sends the invitations and hosts the party.

- *Wedding guest invitations* reflect the style of wedding. For a small, informal wedding, you may choose to write a simple, informal invitation. Include complete information on a high-quality notecard or fold-over note. This is best written in black or dark ink with a good pen. Be sure to include complete information, including to whom an RSVP should be directed. Begin writing your invitation with an informal phrase:

  — *Theresa Trompe and Brendon Whittle invite you to celebrate their marriage . . .*
  — *Joy Royce and James Beaver would be honored to have you share the joy of the marriage of their daughter . . .*
  — *Our joy will be more complete if you will share in the marriage of our daughter . . .*
  — *Sandra Spencer and Alex Bromm invite you to their wedding . . .*
  — *Our daughter, Jennifer Rowe, will be married to Grunnar Hyatt, on Saturday. . . . They will speak their vows at. . . . We invite you to join us to witness their vows, and be our guest at a reception that follows. . . .*

- A *formal invitation* uses more formal language, is printed or engraved in a formal typeface, and uses high-quality card stock that is formal in both paper type and ink color. The invitation will have two envelopes, and the outer one should be hand-addressed—often lettered by a professional calligrapher. The inner envelope is not sealed and may be addressed to the invitees. Slipped into the inner envelope is the invitation, face up when the envelope is opened. A sheet of tissue or other decorative paper, traditionally to help preserve the engraving, may be placed in front of the invitation.

- There may be other enclosures as well: a pew card (for a large wedding), an invitation to a reception, admission cards for the service, maps, a listing of accommodations, and other information about the area where the wedding is to be held. An RSVP card (required by the US Postal Service to be at least 5 by 3½ inches) with its own addressed and stamped envelope will also be included. An at-home card that gives the couple's home address may also be included. The invitation text is written in the first person, and should include the formal names of parents, if they are extending the invitation; the formal names of each of the wedding couple; date, time, and place; and reception, if any. The invitation should include an expression of the couple's wish for the invitees' attendance. Formal or semiformal wording includes the phrase "request the honour [honor] of your presence."
  - The full date, including the year, is always used in the wedding announcement.
  - *Words spelled out.* On the wedding invitations, spell out the year: "two thousand and seven." Also spell out the date—"Saturday, the eleventh of June" or "the twenty-fifth of July"—and the time—"at three o'clock" or "at half after two." Names should be spelled out in full. If someone prefers not to use his or her full middle name, omit it altogether.
  - *Numerals.* Addresses with more than one number are expressed in numerals—"345 East Washington Street"—while single numbers are written out—"Number two Chester Lane."
  - *Abbreviations.* Periods may be used after Mr., Mrs., and Ms. to abbreviate; but write out in full titles such as Doctor, and military ranks,

such as Colonel. (See Appendix I, page 387, for a listing of titles.)
  - *Punctuation.* Use commas only when phrases on a single line require them: "Saturday, the tenth of June."
  - Include the proper phrasing for special religious wedding ceremonies; for example, when a Roman Catholic mass is part of the ceremony, include the phrase "and your participation in the offering of the Nuptial Mass" on a line below the groom's name.
  - When you send an invitation to only the wedding service, do not include an RSVP.
  - When a reception invitation is included, request an RSVP.

- *Reception or wedding dinner invitations* may be part of the wedding invitation, and may simply state, "and afterward at a reception at the College Club . . . ," or may be a separate invitation inserted in the wedding invitation. An invitation to a separate reception may be worded, "Mr. and Mrs. Donald Stikes request the pleasure of your company at the wedding reception for their daughter Georgia Rose and Mr. Elmer Quest . . ." When only a small group will be invited to the wedding, invitations may be given by telephone or in person, or with a ceremony card. It may be worded, "The honour of your presence is requested at the marriage ceremony . . ." It is mailed with the invitation to the reception. If the invitation is to the reception only, less formal wording may be used: "request the pleasure of your company . . ."

- *Wedding rehearsal party invitations* are the traditional territory of the groom's family, although many couples who've been working for some time host this event themselves. Sometimes the rehearsal party is hosted by someone else. This event need not be a dinner, but may be a brunch after a morning rehearsal, or an afternoon get-together.

- The invitations should be sent by those hosting the event. Wedding participants and close family members, and their spouses or fiancés/fiancées, are usually invited. Others who should be invited are the officiant and spouse, and any children in the wedding party and their parents. Out-of-town friends and relatives who've arrived for the wedding are often invited to attend, but it is certainly not expected. The guest list may also include a few other select relatives and close friends, but too many guests may detract from this intimate and special occasion for the wedding party.

- The invitations may be handwritten, printed, or engraved, and should include time, place, and information about dress that is appropriate. Include a request for RSVPs, and give name, telephone number, and/or other contact information.

- *Bachelor's/bachelorette's party invitations* are usually informal, and may even be made by telephone and/or email. These events may be as simple as an evening get-together, or as elaborate as a long weekend of celebration for the wedding attendants and a few close friends. Sometimes the bachelor's party is arranged by the best man and the bachelorette party by the maid of honor.

- *Wedding announcements for the newspaper or other publications* have different requirements and rules for publication, so check early with the publications in which you want to publish your news. Often the information must be submitted several weeks before the wedding so it can appear immediately after the ceremony. Follow the newspaper's format, but check to be sure the following information is included: the full names of the bride and groom; date, time and place of the wedding; name of the clergy or officiant presiding over the ceremony; names of the members of the wedding party, including their relationship to the couple, if related; names, hometowns, and occupations or achievements of the parents of the couple (occasionally even grandparents and/or distinguished other relatives are included); and degrees and other titles or accomplishments of the couple. Descriptions of the wedding, including such items as flowers, the bride's dress, the attendants' attire, music, special ceremony notes, and the place of the reception, may be included. The general or specific address of the couple may also be included.

Other Communications

- *Thank-you notes for gifts and good wishes* are usually sent on notecards created from the same paper as your wedding invitations. Send your notes no later than three months after the wedding. Also send a personal note to each person who has sent special good wishes in lieu of a gift. Though once the responsibility of the bride, writing thank-yous is now shared by both the bride and groom. If gifts are received before the wedding, thank-you notes may be written then, though it is nicer to include information about how the gift is being used. However, a telephone call confirming the gift has been delivered or sending a printed acknowledgment that the gift arrived is appropriate.

- In your thank-you note, name the gift, and make the connection between it and you, whenever possible. You may be able to tell the gift giver how you have used or will use it, and some nice detail about the gift and your appreciation for it.

- *Confirmation letters* are needed to document arrangements for engagement announcement dinners, rehearsal dinner, and other events (such as a bridal shower at a restaurant) as well as wedding arrangements: your reservation of a church, chapel, or temple; organist, instrumentalists, or soloist; restaurant; photographer and/or videographer; bakery; caterer; and any other arrangements specific to your wedding. In all correspondence, be specific and include all the details of the agreement. Always confirm all the conditions and the charges involved.

- *Congratulations cards* or notes may be sent to family members, as well as the couple, after the engagement announcement and/or after the wedding.

- *Broken engagement or wedding postponement announcements* aren't required if no formal announcement was made. If personal letters or notes were sent out in announcing the engagement, use the same means to briefly inform the same people of the change. No explanation is needed.

ELIMINATE WRONG MESSAGES

- While email responses are fine for emailed congratulations, they should not be used for responses to gifts or acts of kindness or service.
- Don't write collective thank-you notes to cohosts of a shower or other special events. Each person deserves an individual note of thanks.
- Keep a detailed list of all those who helped in some way, including those who offered hospitality to out-of-town guests, the clergy who performed the ceremony, the organist, the soloist, and others. Your list will help eliminate the possibility that someone is overlooked when you write your thank-you notes.
- Money gifts are usually very welcome. Don't forget to include how you plan to use the money in your thank-you note.
- Don't ask where a gift may be returned if an unwanted or duplicate gift is received.
- Creating a web page for your wedding with a general welcome and note of general thanks is fine, but it's not a substitute for sending individual, handwritten notes of thanks.
- Avoid a one-size-fits-all approach when writing thank-you notes. Make each note personal and sincere.

SELECT A FORMAT

- Many options are now available for wedding stationery. Make your selections with the complete family of engagement and wedding communications in mind. Coordinating these pieces can go as far as being consistent with the colors and formality of the wedding itself.
- Be sure to select a typeface, paper stock, and ink color that can be easily read, and that will work well for all the pieces you will send. Remember that some colors (such as blue) don't copy well, if you will need to make copies of any piece.

SELECT STRONG WORDS

celebrate	observe
company	pleasure
exchange	presence
favour (or favor),	rejoice
formal or semiformal	request
happiness	save
honour (or honor),	share
formal or semiformal	union
joy	vows
keep	wishes
nuptials	

EDIT, EDIT, EDIT

Be sure to proof and proof again each piece of your printed wedding correspondence before printing. (It's helpful to have more than one person proofread.) Errors result in costly reprinting and much lost time.

Formal and Semiformal Wedding Invitation

[Printed, though invitees' names may be handwritten in provided blanks]

*Doctor and Mrs. George Foremost
request the honour of the presence of
<u>Mr. and Mrs. Nigel Holmes</u>
at the marriage of their daughter
Melody Renee
to
Mr. Cecil Strong
Saturday, the tenth of June
two thousand and seven
at half after four o'clock
First Presbyterian Church
Indianapolis, Indiana*

Formal Engraved Invitation from Bride's Parents

Mr. and Mrs. Worthington James
request the honour of your presence
at the marriage of their daughter
Judith Anne
to
Mr. Kirk Von Russell
Saturday, the ninth of February
two thousand and seven
at half after the hour of three o'clock
Second Baptist Church
Summerfield, Ohio

Ceremony Card

[Printed and enclosed in the envelope with the reception invitation; used when the ceremony list of invitees is shorter than the list of invitees to the reception, but too long for handwritten invitations.]

The honour of your presence
is requested at the marriage ceremony
Saturday, the seventh of December
at seven o'clock
Redford Congregational Church

Reception Card

[Printed and enclosed in wedding invitation]

Reception
immediately following the ceremony
[or at four o'clock]
University Club
342 Central Avenue
Riverside, New York

The favor of a reply is requested [or RSVP].

Informal Invitation from the Couple for a Home Wedding and Reception

[Typed or handwritten]

Esther Spoon and Victor Davidson
hope that you will join us in celebration
for our wedding and reception brunch
Saturday, June twenty-seventh
at half past twelve o'clock
220 East Walker Street
Spokane

RSVP

Informal Invitation to a Small Wedding

[Handwritten]

Dear Mr. and Mrs. James Royce,

Richard Cleft and I will be married on June eleventh at three o'clock at the University Club. We do hope that you will join us for the ceremony and for a reception immediately afterward.

With love,

Jennifer Beale

Acceptance to Be Bridesmaid

[Handwritten]
(Date)

Jasmine,

What joy! Yes, I'm delighted to accept your invitation. I shall be honored to serve as a bridesmaid at your wedding. I'll wait for your note with all the details, then I'll be in touch. What a happy day June 18 will be.

Best wishes,

Paula

Invitation to Be Matron of Honor

[Handwritten]
(Date)

Ginny,

I know we agreed as kids that we would be in each other's weddings, and no one else can really fill your sisterly role as my matron of honor. But I also know that your college expenses have been extremely high, and that Rob's unemployment has caused a huge strain on your finances. I estimate that the dress and accessories will total about $400, and then there's transportation across the country, time away from your job, babysitting, etc. Airfare roundtrip will be about $1,500 if no special rates are available. Mom and Dad said they could underwrite $500 of the expenses, and I can come up with $250, but that still leaves a huge sum of well over $1,000.

I also realize May 15 is undoubtedly finals time for you, but we couldn't set any other date because of Jared's overseas assignment.

I won't hold you to your promise, Sis. I'll completely understand if you must decline. In fact, I propose a first anniversary dinner together instead. Jared and I will come to San Francisco, and we can make it a very special occasion. What do you think?

Sisters forever,

Laura

Confirmation of Matron of Honor Acceptance

[Handwritten]
(Date)

Chelsea,

I'm so delighted you'll be my matron of honor. I really can't imagine walking down the aisle and not seeing you ahead of me as you have been all my life, Big Sister. You've made my joy complete with your acceptance!

Your little sis,

Melody

Note to Ex-Spouse Informing Him of Marriage

[Handwritten]
(Date)

Isaiah:

I wanted to let you know that on Saturday I married Jeremy Stone. I will now be legally Stephanie Stone, and will reside at 345 Adams, Berkeley, California. Please send any communications to this address.

Stephanie

Informal Note of Broken Engagement

[Handwritten]
(Date)

Pam,

I'm so sorry to have to tell you that Richard and I have broken our engagement. I am, therefore, returning the lovely linen tablecloth and napkins you were so thoughtful to send us.

Love,

Eleanor

Letter to Ex-Spouse and Mother of Groom's Children

[Handwritten]
(Date)

Tina:

I want you to hear this first and directly from me: Ingrid and I have decided to marry. I know you may have concerns about how this will affect the children, shared custody arrangements, and schedules, so I'd like for the three of us to sit down and try to amicably work this out in the best possible manner for the kids. We suggest a Saturday meeting in two weeks at Friskies. Say 10:30 A.M. Will that work for you?

We haven't made any public announcement, but we will tell the children just before the three of us meet, letting them know that we will all work very hard to be sure they will have all their needs met.

Although our differences are many at this point, and our relationship is long fractured, we share a huge interest in the welfare of three little people, and I believe for their sakes we can commit to put aside all our personal conflicts and structure the best future possible for them.

Please let Ingrid and me know if you will be able to meet as suggested. If not, please suggest a workable time and place.

Adam

Canceled Engagement

[Printed]
(Date)

Mr. and Mrs. Justin Overton announce that the marriage of their daughter, Rachel, to Stephen Wells, will not take place.

Informal Wedding Rehearsal Invitation

[Handwritten]
(Date)

Dear Janet and Jack,

David and I are hosting a rehearsal dinner for Jennifer and Rafe, Saturday, July 7, at 7:00 P.M. at Long Putts Country Club. We hope you will be able to join us.

We look forward to hearing that you will be able to make it.

Sincerely,

Deanna and David

Personal Note Informing Close Family and Friends of the Wedding: Save the Date

[Printed]
(Date)

To Our Dearest Family and Friends,

Yes, dear ones, we are finally getting married. Our happy day will be September eighth, and it is with full and hopeful hearts that we'd like to ask you to save the date to be present with us and help us make our public declaration of love and commitment complete by your presence.

A formal invitation and all the details will follow.

Sarah and Ben

Personal Note Informing Special Aunt of Wedding

[Handwritten]
(Date)

Dearest Aunt Susan,

I'm delighted to tell you that Booker and I will be getting married sometime in the spring. No date as yet, since he only asked me Saturday, on the second anniversary of our meeting, at a little gathering at Gotsford Park where our dogs were responsible for introducing us. Funny story: we finally introduced ourselves two years ago in this San Francisco dog park after our dogs, Molly (my Airedale) and Ace (his "kennel mix" happy dog), had become such romping friends. Well, our dogs, and those of all our friends were there to surprise me on Saturday morning at six! (Does this tell you something about the wonderful character Booker is?)

I'm ecstatic! Many, many more details over a lifetime of happy dog tales to come!

Your niece,

Madison

Letter to Parents of the Bride

[Handwritten]
(Date)

Alice and Bruce,

What a wonderful wedding service you orchestrated for your beautiful Kerry. I've never witnessed vows so rich in meaning as those exchanged by Kerry and Kendal.

Never has a bride looked more radiant, or gorgeous. Now I certainly appreciate what you have been going through all these months. Knowing you these twenty years, I appreciate that you are a perfectionist, but on the occasion of your daughter's wedding, you succeeded at the highest level. Not one tiny detail was overlooked. I couldn't believe that every table for the sit-down dinner for the entire 300 guests was festooned with scallops of tiny rose buds, and that each table had a pedestal of the loveliest arrangement of roses and ivy I've ever seen.

My, this wedding was a once-in-a-lifetime royal event, and one Newton and I will never forget.

We look forward to having you and the newlyweds over for a dinner party after they settle in. We'll be so happy to see the wedding photos, and hear all the behind-the-scenes stories.

Affectionately,

Newton and Adelle

After-the-Wedding Letter to the Bride

[Handwritten]
(Date)

Dallas,

Yours is only the second wedding I've ever attended where the bride and groom sang their wedding vows. It was truly angelic, and brought tears to my eyes. I appreciate now more fully what an absolutely perfect fit Egan is for your family. When your mother told me how you two are a match made in heaven, she didn't mention you were a heavenly duet; but now that I've heard it for myself I know that it's true.

What a bright and glorious future lies in store for your musical careers together. How happy I am for you, and how I look forward to embracing you as a couple.

With love always,

Aunt Erma

After-the-Wedding Note to the Bride from Her Grandmother

[Handwritten]
(Date)

Avia,

You have made your mother and grandma very proud today. You're all grown up into a fine and strong woman, and today have taken a wonderful husband we all adore. What a happy, happy day. I'm full of joy to overflowing, and I just want you to know how much the two of you, Mr. and Mrs. Bond, are loved.

Grandma

After-the-Wedding Note to the Groom

[Handwritten]
(Date)

Isaiah,

What wonderful choices you and Hannah have made in selecting each other. What a blessing that you will have each other, and what a blessing you two will be to the whole family.

Aunt Esther

Wedding Gift Thank-You Note

[Handwritten]
(Date)

Janette and Derrick,

We love the waffle maker and have, in three mornings, had buttermilk, walnut, and golden waffles. How did you possibly know that the color is spectacular in our kitchen? Here's Rick on his morning operating the maker. See what a great match it is with the toaster, and even the wallpaper. Thank you both so much. We'll think of you with every waffle. Your thoughtfulness, gift, card, and all your best wishes touched our hearts. Stomachs too!

Sophie and Ricardo

Also see ANNOUNCEMENT, page 21; CONFIRMATION AND ACKNOWLEDGMENT, page 240; CONGRATULATIONS, page 30; INVITATIONS, page 65; REFUSAL, page 250; and THANK-YOU, page 76.

14
PERSONAL LETTERS

We are because we write.

—SANDRA E. LAMB

A personal letter is a wonderful way to spread your good news, offer comfort and solace, pass on information, create a special bond, and share a mutual sense of belonging. The time-honored method of sending messages—penned, addressed, stamped, and sent through the mail—has been a staple of our civilized society.

We cherish those penned personal letters, and marvel at those collections kept over time, tied with a silk ribbon, and passed from generation to generation. Stored in lined and scented boxes, preserved in a climate-controlled atmosphere under glass, or even stuffed into a shoebox, these missives are very special. They offer the power to bind families and friendships together—perhaps in great part because they offer us a path to discovering who we are. They help define us.

There will always be a place for your personally penned, heartfelt message sent to a friend or family member. It will be treasured because it contains something of yourself in your own penned words.

DECIDE TO WRITE

When your message is very personal or you want to create a special connection to the person you are writing to, the best choice is a personal handwritten letter.

The following are examples of types of personal letters you may wish to write:

- Happy-news letters sent for birthdays, anniversaries, graduations, life achievements, and all sorts of occasions.
- Correspondence that keeps you in touch with friends and relatives.
- Letters of introduction, initiating a relationship, or observing the etiquette of introduction may have the character of a personal letter. An example of this is the traditional use of these letters between the parents of an engaged couple.
- Personal letters of appreciation following a death in the family or sent in response to acts of kindness, cards, and other deeds.

THINK ABOUT CONTENT

- Construct a light, humorous, and positive opening, or begin with a point of mutual interest.
- Get to the point of your letter, keeping the tone conversational.
- Think in terms of entertaining and storytelling.
- Include newsy bits and topics of interest to the reader, such as shared memories.
- Offer your opinions and ideas, but do it in an open manner.
- Keep the conversation going by asking your reader questions about topics of mutual interest. (But don't turn it into a questionnaire, and be sure not to include questions that could be interpreted as overstepping the bounds of privacy.)
- Include a definite invitation or statement that requests a response or further contact.
- Close with a warm greeting of affection and anticipation of hearing from or seeing the person to whom you're writing.

ELIMINATE WRONG MESSAGES

- Don't write in a time crunch or you're likely to produce a letter that sounds terse and incomplete.
- Starting with an apology or question for the reader sets the wrong tone.
- Don't just respond to questions asked in your reader's last letter; introduce news and stories of interest to the recipient. Eliminate negativity.
- Avoid conflicts, misunderstandings, and regrets by reflecting on your letter after you've written it and proofreading it thoroughly before you mail it.

TIPS THAT WILL HELP

- Develop a personal letter writing habit to create special connections with relatives and friends. Establish a place and time for writing personal letters so it becomes an enjoyable part of your schedule rather than a chore. Use a laptop letter-writing desk or a special, equipped desk, and choose a day and time that are just for writing letters. This will allow you to write in a comfortable, regular, and organized way.

- Keep a well-stocked inventory of personal stationery, notecards, postcards, and perhaps even something like the tools to create your own photo postcards from photographs you take yourself.
- Don't wait too long between writing letters. This can become a barrier to writing.
- Review the last letter from your friend or relative, and be sure to respond to the questions asked and comment on the ideas contained in it.
- Develop a "voice" or storytelling quality in your letter writing by including rich details that help draw verbal pictures.
- Make it a habit to collect things you know friends and relatives will enjoy. Keep them in your laptop desk or another assigned place. It's a wonderful surprise to open a personal letter and find something special—canceled stamps for a stamp collector, a special bookmark for a bibliophile, a newspaper clipping containing information of interest, art or school work from a child in the family to a grandparent or other relative, a photograph taken the last time you were together. Your reader will appreciate your thoughtfulness.
- The weather report can be obtained by anyone who tunes in to the media. If you include weather news, tell a story about it, how the weather affected you, or someone or something of mutual interest.
- If you include something of a sensitive or emotional nature in your letter, leave it on the desk for a day or at least a few hours. Reread it when you can do so objectively, and try to think like your intended reader. Even read it aloud to hear how it sounds. Giving your personal letter this test will help ensure that you don't send something you will later regret.

CONSIDER SPECIAL SITUATIONS

- Establishing a letter-writing habit with a small child can create a very special bond. Think of Beatrix Potter's wonderful stories and the sketches she drew and included with her notes to her little friends. You don't need to be an artist to include some drawings to illustrate your stories. Stories that include the child you're writing to are especially welcome. Ask questions the child will want to answer. Even enclose a self-addressed, stamped envelope to encourage a reply.

- Parents may teach children early to write letters, first by encouraging them to dictate very short ones while you record the words. A thank-you note is a wonderful place to start; and the child may write on the note or draw a picture. When a child is still small, establish a place and supplies for the child's own letter writing.

- The need for empathy can't be overstated. Write with your reader in mind. This will help you to avoid writing something offensive or something that can be misunderstood. Still, even though you take reasonable precautions, misunderstandings can occur. If you don't receive a reply to your letter after several weeks, send a short note or letter asking lightly or humorously, "Was it something I said?"

- Writing special letters and even short notes to family members in your household can be very special: a letter explaining calmly how you feel about a conflict; a love note tucked into the suitcase as a spouse is leaving on a trip; or an "I love you" tucked under a pillow. For a child who's apprehensive about an afternoon test, a short note of "You'll do great" in his or her lunchbox will be very meaningful.

- When people are away from home—friends and relatives on extended business assignments, people serving in the armed services stationed overseas, or children attending summer camp— mail takes on added importance. Use your powers of empathy. Avoid emotionally charged statements or comments that may unduly create homesickness or sadness. Keep it thoughtful and cheerful.

- Sensitivity is needed, too, in writing a letter to someone who is suffering an extended illness, or who's received an unfavorable diagnosis and/or prognosis. If you can easily learn from someone very close to the patient how he or she is feeling emotionally as well as physically, this can guide you in writing. When you don't know, it's better to simply state you were sorry to hear the news, you care, and you want to offer help. (This should not be an empty offer. Mention something you've learned that may be helpful, and suggest a way you would carry it out. Also, outline how you'll follow up to learn the patient's wishes.) When possible, include something positive about the person, perhaps his or her accomplishments, character, importance to others, contributions to a cause, or valued qualities. End on as positive a note as possible.

- Personal letters are legal documents when they contain items that would normally be included in a will or document concerning medical or end-of-life care. For example, stating that you want your niece to have your china may legally entitle her to it. The same is true in authorizing such things as medical care for a dependent child or adult. Use a personal letter to make known your wishes about medical care of a dependent person. If a child is being cared for while you are out of town, for example, you may wish to write a personal letter stating, "I hereby authorize [caregiver's name] to act on my behalf in the case of a medical emergency for the welfare of my daughter/son [child's name] during my absence." Sign the letter, stating your relationship as parent. If you are the legal guardian for an elderly relative who would not want his or her life prolonged in the event of natural death (loss of heartbeat or breathing), a letter stating such and including the order "Do not resuscitate" should be written and signed by you, with the notation "legal guardian." Check with local legal counsel to ensure the proper procedure in your area.

SELECT A FORMAT

- Develop your own signature style of personal letters and notes.
- Select a family of coordinating stationery and notecards to create visual continuity.
- While you'll use a slightly more formal presentation and language in a personal letter of introduction to potential new in-laws, for example, use language that sounds conversational.

WRITE STRONG SENTENCES

It was wonderful getting to visit with you today, and learning all about the new puppy.

I've just read a wonderful book that I believe you'll enjoy.

I saw a special on the medical channel last night that gave information I believe you'll want to have.

Here's the recipe I used for that soup you liked.

How wonderful to open the mailbox and find that ivory envelope with your handwriting on it.

It's a ritual here: we talk about you at breakfast, lunch, and dinner.

We're sure you must be totally unpacked at this point and ready to start your new East Coast life.

Just when I thought Rafe was totally potty trained, he decided that he didn't want to be a "Big Boy."

I'm sending special thoughts to you because I know that your chemistry final is day after tomorrow.

I know how tough it is to be recuperating from a loss of mobility, and I thought I'd send on a few ideas I'd love to have your input on.

Here's something I know you're dying to know.

BUILD EFFECTIVE PARAGRAPHS

It's a great day of rejoicing at this house! Daisy returned from her military tour of duty on Saturday. We spend every minute we can just looking at her and marveling that we have her back with us, safe and sound.

Let me tell you what I've learned about the workshop series and answer your question: is it worth the investment of time and money? If you are weak in the areas of real estate law you need to know, I'd say the course is definitely worthwhile.

This year's reunion is one you won't want to miss. As of today, I have yeses from all the original "Smarties." Here's the lineup so far . . .

I've started a list of items our homeless families need. Next to the list are the items we have collected so far. Please check your closets and storage areas, see what you have that you can spare, and give me a call.

I've been away from home now for sixteen days, five hours, and nine minutes, but who's counting? No one is calling "Mommie, where's my red sweater?" "Mom, he's hitting me," or "Who's got my baseball glove?" Why do I miss those questions so?

Here's my fish report, Dad, just in case you forgot you challenged me to surpass the family record set by you when you and Gramps went to Watchitaw: big-mouth bass, 13; walleyes, 17; and northern pike, 28. I'm thinking someone (that would be you) is going to owe someone (that would be me) a new fishing rod when someone (me) gets home. There are seven days left of fishing. Can you imagine what kind of totals someone (me) will have by then?

EDIT, EDIT, EDIT

Don't send your letter without rereading it to make sure you've eliminated all errors of spelling, grammar, clarity, or omission. To many of those you'll write, a correction here or there isn't critical, but you'll still want your letter to have a neat and polished look.

In Response to Class Reunion Invitation

[Handwritten]
(Date)

Dear Sue Ellen,

What a delightful surprise to see your announcement about a class reunion ten years after you were elected class reunion secretary by 249 rosy-cheeked, naive, 18-year-olds. Ten years ago on that day before high school graduation, I doubt I had any interest in a reunion in the "distant" future. But a reunion certainly appeals to me now, so here's my eager "yes" with my reservation and check.

I look forward to hearing all about your outstanding college career, and your soaring music career. I applaud your idea about sharing news before the reunion on the website, and I will do that. Maybe the old "In Tunes" could even perform that number we did for the spring concert our senior year. What do you think? Count me in on that too.

All the best,

Mary Dale

Sharing Ideas for Fund-Raiser

[Handwritten]
(Date)

Dear Lizzie,

Thank you for volunteering to help with this year's fund-raiser. I find that I'm not bubbling with fresh ideas, as I'd hoped. The only things that come quickly to mind are using the old standbys of donated items to be auctioned off in a silent auction before the gourmet dinner, and asking a couple dozen celebs to donate a lottery "lunch with" to the highest bidder. Or, we could sell raffle tickets and select winners by drawing.

You are my secret winning-ideas weapon, so if you'd give these, and any ideas you have, a spin in that marvelous ideas section of your super brain and let me know what you'd think, I'd greatly appreciate it. I know your ingenuity has no bounds, and I can hardly wait to hear what you come up with.

I'll need to have something together to present to the committee by the 15th. How about a lunch next week to brainstorm?

As always,

JoBeth

99
PERSONAL LETTERS

Resolving a Family Rift

[Handwritten]
(Date)

Dear Jody,

I have a matter of family fractured relations I believe we may be able to resolve, and I've decided the best way to handle it is for me to write to you and ask for your input and cooperation. Here it is. As you know, my parents have recently been estranged from your parents, and I feel sure that this break in the wonderful relationship they once enjoyed may be as much a mystery to you and your parents as it was to me until last week.

Though this may be difficult to understand, my parents are also estranged from Uncle Arnie and Aunt Sue, and for the very same reason. It seems that during a series of family get-togethers last year, both your parents and Uncle Arnie and Aunt Sue asked numerous times about my brother, Sam. Jody, this is a very painful situation for my parents because Sam has separated himself from our family, and we hear nothing from him.

The last time this happened, Mom says, all four relatives asked repeatedly about Sam and pressed my parents for details about why we don't hear from him. This questioning, unfortunately, resulted in my dad feeling that your parents as well as Uncle Arnie and Aunt Sue had overstepped their bounds, or were deliberately trying to be hurtful and make him and my mother feel bad.

I've told my parents that I'm sure the questions were simply intended to demonstrate interest and concern. Their response is that I wasn't there, didn't hear them, and, therefore, don't know (which, of course, is true).

Here's my suggestion: If you're willing, would you please talk to your parents—I'm also writing to Aunt Sue and Uncle Arnie—and ask them to write to my parents. If they feel they can, I'd suggest that they simply explain they didn't intend to make my parents feel bad and they won't bring this painful subject up again.

Hopefully this will allow my parents to reestablish their treasured connection with yours, and with Aunt Sue and Uncle Arnie. I hope I'm not labeled a meddler here—I did tell Mom I was going to write—but I just don't want this family rift to continue.

Thank you, Jody. Please do contact me if you have any further suggestions or questions. I look forward to all of us getting together again in July for the Albert reunion—once again one big, happy family—with our fathers sharing fishing and hunting stories, and our moms reminiscing about their lives as sisters in the big city.

With love,

Susan

Welcome to the Minor League

[Handwritten]
(Date)

Dear Randy,

Your mom is busting at the seams with pride at the announcement of your arrival to the minor league. We're all hopeful, of course, that you'll be the first in this family to wear the insignia of a major league team on your uniform. I know you've heard the stories (until you can recite them in your sleep), but I don't think anyone has shown you a picture of Uncle Will when he was in the minors back in 1933. In fact, I don't think anyone knew this picture existed. I just found it in the library with several stories about the team. I'm sending copies of them along too.

We'll be glued to our TV and newspaper waiting for news that you're being sent up. Actually, I don't think we need worry about missing the announcement. Your mom just wouldn't let that happen.

Congratulations! We're all on your team, Kid.

Love,

Aunt Bea

Surgery Update

[Copied and mailed and emailed]
(Date)

Dear Family and Friends:

Thank you all for your wonderful cards, emails, telephone calls, and other expressions of care and concern. I'll use this copied note until I get the opportunity to sit down and write each of you individually.

Jack did get through the surgery fine, and we will now wait for the postsurgery test results to learn if the cancer has all been removed.

Yesterday, as you can imagine, was not one of our better days. While Jack felt very ill, the biggest weight on us was the waiting to learn if and when the surgery would take place.

There isn't any more news at this minute, but I'll send it as soon as we receive it. I've created an email list, and I'll send out emails of update as news becomes available.

Do keep your messages coming. Jack is cheered and encouraged by your care and concern.

All the best,

Jenna (jenna@email.com)

Information You Requested

[Handwritten]
(Date)

Dear Anna,

Here's my business card as you requested. It was a pleasure meeting you at the Bears' reception. Cary Regan is the senior editor to whom you would submit a query on the topic you mentioned. She's in charge of the lifestyle area, and querying her by email is fine. I've worked with her and find her to be a skilled and able editor.

If you'd like a better idea of what The Simpsons is looking for in new features, take a look at their editorial calendar at www.simpsons.com.

Best,

Ginger

Also see APPRECIATION, page 72; CONDOLENCE AND SYMPATHY, page 47; CONGRATULATIONS, page 30; INVITATIONS, page 65; and THANK-YOU, page 76.

III. JOB SEARCH

15
NETWORKING

*There is nothing to writing. All you have to do
is sit down at a typewriter and open a vein.*

—RED SMITH

Networking is the process of getting connected. Someone you know links you to someone you don't know so that both you and your new contact can exchange and gain information. In the case of job hunting, networking can give you a great advantage in receiving consideration for a particular position. Successful networking is reciprocal: you provide information and contacts for others, and they (or someone else will) do the same for you.

You need to know several important points about networking: (1) it is best done as an ongoing exercise of friendship and professionalism; (2) it involves being positive and helpful; (3) it is best approached as an exercise of giving as much or more information than you receive; (4) it is credited with being responsible for the majority of successful job acquisitions; and (5) it will be far easier to do if you create a system of sources and a method of follow-up that keeps you in touch with your contacts.

So, when you know that an effort to find new employment is in your future, your first step is to hone your networking skills—long before you begin your search for a specific job. Honing your networking skills is just as important as keeping up with informa-

tion and skill changes in your career field. Networking has never been easier than in this time of instantaneous communication.

Creating an effective networking letter is your next step. This serves both as a letter of introduction and as a personal sales letter when you use it to introduce yourself as a candidate for a job. It should contain your best persuasive writing. It is used to locate job openings or even to be the stimulus for creating them, and it must include enough crisp, powerful statements about your abilities to entice the reader to want to learn more. In our present job culture, where the dynamics of employee and employer are changing rapidly, this letter is becoming an increasingly important tool.

A networking letter should be sent out as an essential part of a job-search campaign to specifically identified individuals within carefully targeted organizations. It is the most positive, effective, and time-saving way to conduct a job search. In many cases it may be emailed.

Do not include your resume, but rather end your letter by requesting an exploratory or "informational" interview. If you're mailing your letter, enclose a self-addressed, stamped envelope or include your email address for the reply to increase your response rate.

If you have gotten no response after four weeks, send a slightly different networking letter to the same executive or another carefully selected executive within the organization. The response rate for second mailings is as good as that for first mailings.

Networking letters are most successfully used by mature, established professionals. In addition to being used when you are searching for a job in your current field, they also are often used when you seek to use your skills in a new field.

DECIDE TO WRITE

Send this letter to:

- Request a personal interview in your present career field
- Investigate career-change possibilities
- Gather job or career information
- Get noticed by a number of people within a company
- Follow up after your first letter hasn't gotten a response
- Get the interest of headhunters

RESEARCH

Building your network must start with the people you know. Personal and professional associates can help identify organizations and key people to contact.

The most common starting places are school and college associates, and fellow members of professional associations. Researching these to locate people has never been easier. Now with extensive online resources, you can easily network without leaving your office. Be sure to check the following:

- Corporate listings
- University websites
- Professional and industry directories
- Online job boards
- Association websites
- Career websites
- Online search engines
- Newspaper ads and articles
- Yellow Pages (make a telephone call and personal contact before sending a networking letter)
- Headhunters

THINK ABOUT CONTENT

Write so the reader will want to learn more about you. The reader needs to see something in your letter that identifies closely with a problem he or she is having at the moment that needs to be solved. All businesses, no matter how smoothly they run, experience one problem after another. Your letter must include actual deeds you have accomplished and problems you have solved. Here are some general rules to think about as you begin writing:

- Use action words, verbs instead of nouns, whenever possible.
- Be sure your statements convey a sense of power.
- Be specific, not general. Remember, you are asking about a specific kind of position.
- Address your letter to the person with the power to hire: the company president, chief operating officer, chief executive officer, or appropriate department head. Remember, in organizations things move much better from top to bottom than bottom to top.

More specifically, there are two types of openings in a networking letter: topical and accomplishment.

Topical Openings

Topical openings capitalize on current trends, current events, and identified industry needs. Timing and circumstances play a very important role here, making this opening difficult. A topical opening is, however, the most electrifying if used properly.

If New Horizons Airlines is buying lots of TV time for their wild animal ads and you have extensive specialized experience in this, you might start your letter like this:

I filmed charging rhinos in Nairobi last week as the ad director for the Sweetie account. I am responsible for all phases of the $36.2 million dollar campaign.

Here is another example:

I believe there are still many practices of Japanese manufacturing we need to use in this country. I have just returned from Japan after five years of living and working there. I am now home to stay in Dallas.

Here are two examples written by an advertising account executive:

Yes, Harry Smith is right. I did sell Californians orange juice from Florida.

Bill Yeats is wrong: I didn't sell snow cones in Anchorage. But I did sell bathing suits and water skis.

Accomplishment Openings

Accomplishment openings are much more useful than topical openings simply because they are more adaptable. Where the topical opening depends on the right timing and particular circumstances, the accomplishment opening can be easily adapted from your resume. Use an example that fits the business situation or cycle at the moment, and, if possible, include the name of the contact from your network who is known to the person to whom you're writing. Here are examples:

Sam Evert suggested that I contact you about your need for a new advertising manager. I developed the new-home ads that produced more than 455 visitors a day every Saturday and Sunday in Sam's new community, Lone Star Estates.

As Bobbi Boxer may have told you, as marketing manager for a consumer product, I helped increase sales 32 percent by creating and implementing a new marketing policy.

Janet Stearns was my assistant when I managed five multimedia continuing medical education programs that resulted in net profits of 24 percent over estimates.

As controller and treasurer of Teddie Greene's manufacturing company, I turned an operating loss into a net profit of 21 percent of sales before taxes.

Paragraph Two

Your second paragraph should tell the reader why you are writing:

Janet thought your marketing department may need a person with my skills and experience. If so, you may be interested in some of my other accomplishments.

Or, try some of these transitional second paragraphs:

Your company may need a marketing manager. My experience, therefore, may interest you.

I understand you're looking for a marketing manager with home-building training, experience, and expertise. I'd like to review some of my other accomplishments for you.

Teddie suggested I contact you and discuss your need for an advertising manager with my experience.

I understand you are expanding your marketing program and need someone with my experience and background.

Show Me

Then come the "for instances." Lift three, four, or even five short and relevant examples from your resume and transplant them into your networking letter.

Don't overload your letter. Less is more. Let your examples stand out as if you'd thrown shocking red paint on a canvas.

Try to use no more than ten to twelve words per sentence, keeping paragraphs between three and six lines each. This will take effort, but it will be well worth your editing time. You may want to throw in the name of your school, but not necessarily your specific degree. Name the school and degree if they say in an understated fashion: quality product. For example, if you earned an MBA from one of the country's top MBA programs, list it. Also, if you know the addressee graduated from your alma mater, list it. Many such items have been real door openers.

The Ending

In closing, ask or suggest action within the power of the reader. Don't be shy. Ask for the exploratory, or informational, interview. With as much zing as possible, say something like, "I'd like to discuss details of my experience with you in a personal interview."

Or, "I'll call you Thursday to arrange a time for a personal interview." You want to make sure that the ending will be the beginning.

Again, do not include a resume, and don't mention it in your closing paragraph.

ELIMINATE WRONG MESSAGES

- Don't write ". . . discuss any possible positions that you might have to offer." This statement weakens your letter.
- Don't mention your resume. If you do, the reader will ask you to send it, and you may have lost the interview opportunity.
- Never write "I would like to show you how I can help increase your profits." The reader may consider this presumptuous from an outsider.
- Don't mention any specific kind of training that could affect the intended direction of your letter. Do mention your educational background. This usually adds to the reader's receptivity.

GET THE WORD OUT

- Develop your own mailing list. Keep notes about your contacts and their responses to your letters.
- Always verify the correct spelling of your contact's name and his or her current title.
- Regard all your contacts as a community, and keep in touch with them.
- Send out new letters every week.
- Continue the campaign until you have accepted a position and have started work.

SELECT A FORMAT

- Letters should be typed on personal letterhead or stationery, or emailed if you have received an okay to do so.
- When emailing, carefully create your point of contact for your subject line—for example, "Bill Bly's friend" or "Fellow AGMA member."
- The visual appearance of the completed letter should be open and inviting. Indent points and create wide margins to produce a lot of white space.

THINK ABOUT TIMING

- Four weeks after your first mailing, send a slightly different letter to those who haven't responded.
- After a personal or meeting introduction, follow up within a day.

SELECT ACTION VERBS

activated	launched
built	obtained
changed	organized
completed	reduced
created	reorganized
cut	restructured
demonstrated	revamped
doubled (tripled, quadrupled)	saved
	sold
enabled	solved (resolved)
engineered	stopped
envisioned	succeeded
increased	transformed
instituted	won

BUILD POWER PHRASES

completely revamped

created a new plan

created a new product

cut costs by

demonstrated the new

developed a solution

increased production by

increased profits by

increased sales by

initiated the cost-saving plan

instituted cost-cutting measures

reduced overhead

reduced waste by

reorganized the department

restructured the deal

restructured the debt

saved the company

solved the overhead problem

succeeded in building

won approval of

WRITE STRONG SENTENCES

Use action words. Replace nouns with power verbs whenever possible.

Reduced waste by 43 percent with a single, no-cost production change.

Doubled sales in 18 months.

While chief engineer, I expanded the market for the Model X-123 by improving the product and designing four attachments.

BUILD EFFECTIVE PARAGRAPHS

I'd like to discuss further details of my experience in a personal interview. I will call you next Wednesday to arrange a time and place.

As marketing manager for Reholdt, Inc., I increased sales 18 percent in 12 months by instituting a new marketing policy. I believe you would find the details of this policy very interesting. The ads we developed launched the new product in great style. In the first year, it captured a 23 percent market share.

As a department manager in the largest department store in the state, I doubled the sales volume of the ready-to-wear merchandise in three years. Profits were 13 percent above the store's previous average.

EDIT, EDIT, EDIT

After finishing your letter, shelve it for a day or two so you can reread it with a fresh perspective. You may also want to ask people whose opinions you respect to read it and comment before you write the final letter.

First Contact Offering Information to Colleague

[Emailed]

SUBJECT: Webmaster Info You Requested

Hello Jennifer,

Yes, I have an excellent webmaster (mistress?) I'd recommend. Her name is Josie Bails. She is swift in making changes to my website, listens carefully to my input, has a great eye for layout and innovation, and is very reasonable: $65/hour.

When I was in Europe without access to a printer, she even printed out a book proposal I emailed her and mailed it to my agent. All at a very nominal fee.

Josie's website is www.rightaway.com; her email address is josie@rightaway.com; and her telephone number is 650-555-0123.

I've told Josie you may call. Please mention my name.

All the best,

Gertie

First Contact Offering Job Lead

[Emailed]

SUBJECT: A Manager Position Opening

Dear Rita:

My friend Dan Glover at Spikes needs a high-powered saleswoman like you. I know you've been wanting to make a change, and I believe this may be an ideal fit for you.

I've taken the liberty of mentioning your skills (not your name, or that you're looking), telling him I've been very impressed with your outstanding accomplishments. He'd really like to talk to you, I believe. Quote: "Now that's the kind of sales professional I'm looking for."

Please give him a call at 503-555-0123, if you're interested. And, of course, mention my name.

Best wishes,

Millie

First Contact Job Opening

[Emailed]

SUBJECT: Your Next Job?

Hi Lizzie,

When I returned to the office last week after the conference, I learned from the university president that he's reorganizing the student loan department. He wants a take-charge professional like you to come in from the outside because of the politics involved.

I responded that I just happened to have been talking to a very qualified person at the conference, and I would ask you if you're interested.

He'd like to talk with you.

If, indeed you are interested, please email him at sml@phillips.edu, and put my name in the subject line. I, of course, didn't offer your name or any details, only said that you were, in my opinion, the sort of person who could do an excellent job with the reorganization he has in mind.

I'll keep my fingers crossed. Please let me know if this works out. Or, if you'd like the other scant details I have, please give a call. I'll be in this afternoon.

All the best,

Rose

Seeking Sales Manager Opportunity

[Typed and mailed]
(Date)

Mr. Ruben Sternberg, President

Dear Mr. Sternberg:

Mr. Len Lesser suggested I contact you about your need for a sales manager. As national sales manager of RemKo, I increased sales volume 32 percent in an industry that was growing at the rate of 4 percent a year. If your company faces growth challenges, you may be interested in how I accomplished this. I created a multifaceted plan which, when implemented:

- combined five sales regions into two,
- reduced manpower costs by 17 percent, and
- increased profits by 22 percent.

Achieving this level of performance required recruiting and developing a top team of sales professionals, instituting a sales incentive program, and dramatically increasing—by 19 percent—the sales in two product lines. We were awarded the National Sales Association's "Top Performers" award four out of the past five years.

I'd like to talk to you about several of my ideas that might benefit your company. I'll call your office next Thursday to see about arranging a time.

Cordially,

Calvin R. Clements

Second Phase Follow-Up Letter After Meeting at Association Conference

[Emailed]

Dear Mr. Abbott:

Nice talking with you, if ever so briefly, at the MMA meeting yesterday. Here's a recap of what we discussed, concerning my four years at Critters Manufacturing:

- As marketing manager, I increased sales by 42 percent in 18 months.
- Launched three new products in one year that triggered first-year sales of $4.2 million in new markets.
- Recruited and trained 25 salespeople who, within one year, were the top producers for the company.

I graduated from the Wharton Business School, where I specialized in sales management and marketing.

I would be happy to discuss many other details of my experience with you in a personal interview, including some of the ideas I've instituted that are working well here for a situation very similar to the one we discussed. I will call your office on Thursday morning to arrange a time.

Sincerely,

Daisy L. Sluggs

Seeking Engineer Position

[Typed and mailed]
(Date)

Mr. Ivan Prather
Vice President, Engineering

Dear Mr. Prather:

As chief engineer I expanded the market for the Ryan Model 880 by improving the tolerances by 34 percent. This improved product has secured new sales in high temperature and high-load applications not previously possible.

I believe Ramsburg's Model 4000 has similar product-application potential, and I would like the opportunity to discuss my engineering approach with you. I shall call your office next week to arrange a time and place.

Sincerely,

Lydia S. Squares

Seeking Accounting Opening

[Typed and mailed]
(Date)

Mr. Todd Ryder, President

Dear Mr. Ryder:

My long-time prison friend, Larry Grieves, suggested I contact you. I have been in Dawes Prison 37 times. Each time I performed a professional audit as a public accountant examining accounts, costs, and the management records of the prison. I've also been in Blinder Mental Hospital a few dozen times—for the same reason.

Larry said Evergreen may need a diversified, well-seasoned professional to assume accounting responsibilities. If so, you may be interested in my background and achievements.

I have completed general audit work for
• 24 government entities,
• 76 different business enterprises,
• 53 industrial manufacturers, and
• more than 135 other types of public and private institutions.

I also designed the accounting system, which became a model statewide, used for the townships of Marek County. I would welcome the opportunity to discuss with you how my skills can benefit Evergreen, and I will call you next week to arrange a time.

Yours truly,

Jamie S. Small

Seeking Sales Manager Opening

[Typed and mailed]
(Date)

Mr. Buck Rogers, President

Dear Mr. Rogers:

I just read about your plans to expand into manufacturing an upscale line of furniture, and I'd like the opportunity to discuss with you my experience in this area.
• As sales manager for a small Midwest manufacturer of fine furniture, I increased sales over 225 percent in two years.
• While managing a sales force of 22, I added two dealers and a manufacturer's representative to expand sales to 42 states.
• I developed and instituted inventory procedures that reduced inventory by 16 percent.

I will be in Columbus on April 10 for the National Furniture Convention, and I'm hoping we can get together for a detailed discussion. I will contact you next week to arrange a time and place.

Sincerely,

Frederika R. Fink

Seeking Public Relations Opening

[Emailed]

SUBJECT: Wonderful "Hot Rox" Piece in *Creative*

Dear Mr. Barker:

I just read the Hot Rox piece in *Creative* magazine, and I'm impressed by your dynamic organization's commitment to finding new creative talent. I believe some of my accomplishments fit your desired employee profile:
• Created and established a department that drew strong support from 85 percent of employees and the community
• Recruited, trained, and motivated a highly diverse group of personnel from six departments into an effective team
• Developed and executed a community relations program that has won national recognition
• Administered a department program that reduced costs by 22 percent and increased production by 17 percent

Perhaps my search for a growth opportunity will fit with your search for an innovative, creative, and productive public relations leader. I would like to discuss the possibilities with you. I will call later this week to arrange for an appointment.

Sincerely yours,

Dumar Q. Tyler

Seeking Entry Marketing Opening

[Typed and mailed]
(Date)

Ms. Jeannine Trump
President

Dear Ms. Trump:

I just graduated from Duke University where I majored in marketing and graduated cum laude. I was the first African-American student to receive the coveted Student of the Year award. Perhaps your marketing department would be interested in someone with my enthusiasm and capabilities. During the four years I worked before returning to college for my final year, I:
• Organized direct-mail campaigns of over 20 million letters and brochures that received an 11 percent response rate.
• Completed market research and sales forecasting that sold our services to four accounts over $500,000.
• Created a promotional package that established sales distribution in a 23-state area and gained a 67 percent label recognition for a start-up mineral water.

I would like to discuss my education and experience with you. I will call you next week to arrange a time and place.

Very truly yours,

Juliet S. Guest

Also see RESUME, page 118, and RESUME COVER LETTER, page 109.

16
RESUME COVER LETTER

A clear statement is the strongest argument.

—ENGLISH PROVERB

The resume cover letter, also known as the application or broadcast letter, is a sales letter—one of the most important sales letters you will ever write.

While the cover letter or transmittal letter (see "Cover Letter," page 230) for reports and proposals is primarily a laundry list of the "covered," or enclosed, documents, the resume cover letter has three distinct functions: (1) get the reader's favorable attention, (2) clearly and quickly identify the job or position for which you are applying, and (3) create enough interest in your qualifications to compel the reader to read your resume.

The goal of the resume cover letter is to get the reader to delve into your enclosed resume and then call you to arrange an interview. Focus on one or two precise skills the employer needs. Highlight your achievements in those areas—with numbers whenever possible. Make your letter brief.

DECIDE TO WRITE

- Find out who is responsible for hiring for the position you want. Learn as much about the position and the hiring person as possible. Address your letter to that person. Personalize your letter, if possible, to demonstrate that you have done your homework. Beginning with "Dear Sir," "Gentlemen," or "Madam" does not convey the kind of message you wish to convey. There are many ways you can obtain the name of a particular person. Certainly calling the organization and asking for the person's name is one of the most direct.

- Organize your letter under three or four short paragraphs: (1) An *opening paragraph* that states the job, introduces you as a qualified candidate, and refers to your prior contact or network connection, if you have one; (2) a *second paragraph* with highlights of your experience and/or qualifications that make you uniquely right for the position; (3) an *optional paragraph* that offers a constructive idea about the solution(s) you can offer; and (4) a *closing paragraph* that is a call for action on the part of the reader and indicates when you will contact the reader to follow up on your letter.

- Begin to draft your letter, and fill in details within the paragraphs.
- Identify the specific job immediately.
- Write something unique. It's important to convey your skills and even your personality, which eliminates the flavor of a form letter.
- Take a few risks. You must tell the reader why you are uniquely qualified for the position. Describe the value you can bring to the organization. Be sure to communicate your achievements and capabilities in a way that suggests assistance and support, but be careful that your tone doesn't smack of being boastful.
- Speak the language. Every specialty has a culture and its own particular vocabulary. Use it, but be sure not to overdue it. At the same time, keep your language conversational and friendly.
- Keep your sentences short.
- Demonstrate energy and enthusiasm.
- Lead the reader to examine your resume. Consider using two corresponding dots: one in the margin marking the statement in your letter, and the other marking the explanatory reference in your resume.
- Give full information on how, when, and where you can be contacted.
- Be innovative to get extra attention. A colored dot or a star adhered to one corner of your letter and resume (but not if you use the dot described above), a unique design approach, or even an audiovisual presentation (if applicable within your business culture) can work to bring extra attention to your qualifications. But be sure not to sacrifice readability or clarity, or to otherwise cloud your message.
- Close with a friendly but proactive statement that promises or requests further contact. Ask for the next step: a meeting or conversation with the reader. Be as specific as you can. For example, "I will be in San Francisco next week, and would like to meet with you at that time. I will call your office on Thursday morning to set a date and time."
- Make sure your letter is short. Rarely should it be more than a single page.
- Edit to give your letter punch.
- Reread and polish it until your letter sings.
- Consider handwriting a postscript statement, like your call to action, at the bottom of your letter.

ELIMINATING WRONG MESSAGES

- Avoid formal, dry, and/or vague words and terms.
- Use specialized technical terms unique to your field to show you are an insider, but don't overload it.
- Don't go on and on; be concise.
- Eliminate general statements. Be specific.
- Don't lift statements directly from your resume.
- Avoid addressing your letter to the human resources or personnel departments, unless absolutely necessary.
- Avoid an arrogant tone. Read aloud to check for flow and tone.
- Delete passive verbs; substitute action ones.
- Don't send a letter with typos or errors of any kind; double- and triple-check everything.

CONSIDER SPECIAL SITUATIONS

- Send a networking letter (see "Networking," page 102) when it's more appropriate.
- Remember that each resume cover letter and resume should be tailored to the specific position. Think of your resume as a toolbox of skills, and each position as requiring a specific tool from within that box. This will help you craft a better letter and resume and realize better results.
- When you request an exploratory interview and/or there is no present opening, a networking letter or a referral letter will offer a better first communication option. Use a resume and possibly a resume cover letter as a second step, preferably as a follow-up to a face-to-face meeting.
- Be sure to include all your marketable skills, especially if you're returning to the job market after a long absence or if you are seeking your first job. Volunteer activities, achievements in scouts and other organizations, and experience in athletics and other endeavors are all things you may use in creating your resume and resume cover letter.

- If you are applying for a new position while still employed, be sure to state the fact in your resume cover letter to avoid any possible breach of confidentiality.
- If you know all the specifications of a job opening, you may want to use a comparative listing of your qualifications, sometimes called "executive summary," "briefing," or "skill summary." You can use two columns to create a visual comparison:

Job Specification	My Skill Summary
_____	_____
_____	_____
_____	_____

- When sending your letter to a third party, head-hunter, or other employment service, you may be more informal. Concentrate on the kind of job you are seeking and your qualifications for it.
- When application forms are required, especially when you are using email, the employer usually won't accept a resume and resume cover letter as a substitute. In these cases, you will need to complete the application form, but you may also want to submit your resume cover letter and resume by either email or regular mail (or both) to the specific person(s) responsible for hiring.

SELECT A FORMAT

- White or open space creates the pleasing impression that your letter can be quickly and easily read. When your letter is emailed, keep the length to one screen, if possible. Check your word count: it should be no more than 250 words in 12-point type.
- Be creative. In the very competitive job market, make your letter distinctive but still within the realm of what is acceptable in your field. People in the arts, advertising, and public relations professions usually have more latitude than those in banking and publishing, for example.
- Sign your letter boldly and with confidence.
- A thoughtful and clear handwritten postscript statement on the letter will be read first. Make good use of this fact.
- Select a high-quality paper stock that matches your resume stock. A cream or ivory paper, or even a very light color may work well to distinguish your letter from others. Be sure to use something acceptable within the business culture.
- Use a typeface that's clear and easy to read, and is consistent with the business industry. Also, use one that copies well, in a case a reader wants to share it. Make sure your type is at least 10 picas in size for ease of reading.
- Leave at least a $1\frac{1}{4}$ to $1\frac{1}{2}$ inch border all the way around your letter to create inviting white space.
- Consider placing a red dot or some distinguishing eye-catcher on your resume and cover letter, if this is acceptable within your industry.
- Hand-addressing the envelope to a specific person may increase the chance that the person will read it.

POWER WORDS

Start with a power verb. Use the first person and present tense whenever possible; use past tense—words ending in -ed—for action in the past. Avoid using adverbs—words ending in -y and -ly. They can dilute your message.

accept(ed)	arbitrate(d)
accomplish(ed)	arrange(d)
ace(d)	articulate(d)
achieve(d)	assemble(d)
act(ed)	assess(ed)
actuate(d)	assign(ed)
adapt(ed)	assist(ed)
add(ed)	attain(ed)
address(ed)	augment(ed)
adjust(ed)	author(ed)
administer(ed)	authorize(d)
adopt(ed)	award(ed)
advance(d)	balance(d)
advise(d)	bought
allocate(d)	built
amend(ed)	catalog(ed)
analyze(d)	classify(ied)
anticipate(d)	compete(d)
apply(ied)	complete(d)
appoint(ed)	conceive(d)
appraise(d)	conduct(ed)
appropriate(d)	consolidate(d)
approve(d)	contract(ed)

control(led)
coordinate(d)
create(d)
decrease(d)
deliver(ed)
demonstrate(d)
designate(d)
design(ed)
develop(ed)
devise(d)
direct(ed)
dissolve(d)
distribute(d)
double(d)
eliminate(d)
energize(d)
enlarge(d)
establish(ed)
examine(d)
expand(ed)
facilitate(d)
govern(ed)
group(ed)
guide(d)
hire(d)
implement(ed)
improve(d)
increase(d)
index(ed)
interview(ed)
introduce(d)
invent(ed)
investigate(d)
launch(ed)
maintain(ed)
manage(d)
moderate(d)
monitor(ed)
negotiate(d)
orchestrate(d)
organize(d)
originate(d)
outperform(ed)
persist(ed)
persuade(d)

perform(ed)
pioneer(ed)
plan(ned)
prepare(d)
present(ed)
privatize(d)
problem-solve(d)
produce(d)
program(med)
progress(ed)
promote(d)
propose(d)
purchase(d)
realize(d)
recharge(d)
recommend(ed)
reconstitute(d)
recover(ed)
recruit(ed)
rectify(ied)
redesign(ed)
reduce(d)
regulate(d)
reinstitute(d)
render(ed)
renew(ed)
reorganize(d)
repair(ed)
replace(d)
replicate(d)
represent(ed)
reprogram(med)
research(ed)
reshape(d)
restart(ed)
restructure(d)
retool(ed)
revamp(ed)
reverse(d)
revise(d)
revitalize(d)
revive(d)
revolutionize(d)
rotate(d)
route(d)

schedule(d)
service(d)
simplify(ied)
slash(ed)
sort(ed)
specialize(d)
specify(ied)
start(ed)
streamline(d)
strengthen(ed)
structure(d)
succeed(ed)
summarize(d)
supervise(d)

systemize(d)
train(ed)
transact(ed)
translate(d)
trim(med)
triple(d)
trump(ed)
turn(ed) around
uncover(ed)
unify(ied)
unravel(ed)
widen(ed)
won
wrote

POWER PHRASES

Select precise action statements that convey your achievements and skills using results and solid examples.

completed 8,000 flight hours without a safety infraction

created employee benefit program with 94 percent satisfaction rate

implemented 25 new standards in 14 months

improved plant safety record by 23 percent

increased production by 15 percent

increased profits by 34 percent in 24 months

outperformed competitors by 11 percent

outsold a field of 55 salespeople for five consecutive quarters by at least 19 percent

qualified the organization for accreditation in seven months

reduced waste by 22 percent in six months

wrote reports that received 89 percent positive reviews

WRITE STRONG SENTENCES

Start with a power verb to properly focus your sentences. *Created, restructured, initiated, launched, conducted, controlled, administered, constructed, managed, interceded, established, enacted,* and *marketed* are some examples. The sentences below include other examples:

Please review my journeyman skills demonstrated at Beck: I consistently—94 percent of the time—solved customer problems, on time, under budget, and with high rates of customer satisfaction.

I believe my skills, especially as demonstrated at Crystal's, could create the right solutions to your production crisis.

My award-winning writing at Golman was instrumental in increasing sales by 17 percent.

I haven't missed a deadline in seven years.

On my watch, production at Demming increased 18 percent and absenteeism fell 22 percent in five months.

My team revamped the inventory system in five months, reducing stock overhead costs by 23 percent.

I request 15 minutes of your time to show you my PowerPoint "New Goals" marketing approach that helped turn around Kramer Corporation.

Using my complete manager skills, I've organized and supervised inventory and shipping at Grace.

I will call your office on Thursday to inquire about arranging an appointment.

There are three things in my resume, I believe, that you may want to review.

I look forward to discussing some specific ideas with you.

I'd like to explain in a personal interview details of my experience that I believe could benefit Arco Corporation.

I thrive on challenges such as the one you described in Sunday's *Post* ad.

I'm ready to step up to the position of director from associate director, and I'd like the opportunity to tell you why.

Theodore Sturgeon recommended I talk to you about your office manager opening.

I have a solid electrical engineering background and education, as well as award-winning design experience.

BUILD EFFECTIVE PARAGRAPHS

Be brief. Your letter should be no more than three or four paragraphs in length. Remember, shorter letters get read quickly and first. With this approach, you'll increase your chances of making a positive and lasting impression.

I believe my complete reorganization of Pester and Company's legal department—see the highlighted area on my resume—demonstrates the skills you seek in a person to head up your legal department. I'd like to discuss with you details of my experience.

I believe my marketing skills, as illustrated on my resume, can add value to the position of controller at Crinkles. I was able to increase Black's market position while controlling the budget.

I worked very hard to reduce overhead at Gator Corporation by 24 percent in five months. The expertise I gained in that position, I believe, uniquely prepared me to take on the challenge of your operations manager position. Please review the details of my responsibilities on my resume enclosed. I look forward to discussing with you how I implemented this change.

I was excited to learn you are looking for an account executive with award-winning experience in the home-building industry. I've won state, regional, and national awards (see marks on my resume) for creating the best marketing, ad, and public relations campaigns for my clients. I'd like to discuss with you how I believe these approaches could help create award-winning campaigns to help Sanders, Inc.

Please note that although I'm a lightweight in copywriting experience—as you'll see on my resume—I'm a heavyweight in the areas of fresh ideas, enthusiasm, and real ability. I've won four academic ad-writing awards, including one for cell phones. May I show you these ads from my portfolio in a 10-minute interview?

I've been preparing for the role of department head for 10 years. I'd like to discuss with you details of how I could be effective as your director of nurses.

EDIT, EDIT, EDIT

Give your letter some shelf time before you go back for final editing. This gives you the opportunity to see it objectively and allows you to remove excess words or phrases and weak statements. Place action words front and center, be concise, and check to ensure your tone is conversational. Most of all, be sure your enthusiasm shines through.

If possible, ask another professional whose advice you value to review your letter before sending it.

Make one final check to be sure your letter is visually pleasing and free of typos.

Referral Follow-Up for Sales Manager Position

[Typed]
(Date)

Ms. Audree Divers
Systems Manager

Dear Audree:

As we discussed on the telephone, Sarah Beele, your friend and mine, was insistent that my successes as sale manager are the perfect solution to your present sales force problems. I'm sure she has told you that here at Wickers I created a bonus program for our salespeople, which has produced a sales increase of 28 percent in eight months, and has improved sales staff satisfaction over 54 percent.

I'm intrigued by your opportunity, and would like to discuss details of my work here and at Beekins. As you requested, I've enclosed a resume describing my role at both companies. I believe my solutions may work well for you.

Please call me at 323-555-0123 to arrange an interview time. Or, if we haven't met, I'll introduce myself next week at the trade show in Las Vegas.

Sincerely,

Hazel Hubbard

Response to a Newspaper Ad

[Typed on 8½ by 11-inch stationery]
(Date)

Ms. Abigal Appleton
Deputy Editor

Dear Ms. Appleton:

Tom Uphill, your photographer at Baker and my friend, told me you are responsible for hiring the new senior editor, the spot advertised in Sunday's *Post*. He suggested I write directly to you.

Here's how I believe several of my skills match up with your advertised requirements:

Ad Requirements	My Skills
College journalism degree	Graduated cum laude, University of Chicago, BS in journalism
3–5 yrs. editorial experience	3 yrs. assistant editor at Holbrook's
Works well under pressure	Met all deadlines, under budget, in the past eighteen months.

Details of my experience are listed on the enclosed resume.

I'd like the opportunity to show you my portfolio, and will call your office on Thursday to arrange a convenient time.

Sincerely yours,

John Que

Follow-Up After Chance Meeting

[Typed]
(Date)

Mr. Frank Brown
Chief Executive Officer

Dear Mr. Brown:

It was a pleasure meeting you at the National Home Builders Association convention in Dallas last week. I especially enjoyed the opportunity to see the operation of your electronic skylights.

I'm following up our discussion, as you suggested, with this letter. Over the last six months with Wilson Windows, I have
- successfully introduced a new product line,
- trained 45 sales representatives, and
- realized substantial market penetration already, with profits for the year estimated to be in excess of $3.4 million (compared with $2.2 million last year).

You can see by my enclosed resume that I also have other skills that could benefit Atulac.

I'd like to discuss details of my experience with you. Wednesday morning I'll contact your office to see about arranging a meeting for the week of January 21.

Sincerely,

Germaine Q. Ruddick

Referral for Summer Job

[Typed]
(Date)

Jennifer Beales
Head Librarian

Dear Ms. Beales:

My friend on your staff, Mr. Rob Anderson, suggested I send you my resume and request an interview for the position of summer clerk. I am pursuing a library science degree at the University of Michigan and am a lifelong lover of books.

I have held several volunteer positions working with children and young adults, including ones with the Girl Scouts, the Literacy League, and Children at Risk. I have also volunteered at Vulcan Library as a children's hour storyteller.

I will call you next week to request an interview time convenient to your schedule.

Sincerely,

Joan Diddly

Sending Resume After Telephone Contact

[Typed on 8 ½ by 11-inch stationery]
(Date)

Philip Tinsdale
Vice President

Dear Mr. Tinsdale:

Thank you for the invitation to submit my resume for your international sales manager position. As I mentioned during our telephone discussion, Jack Belzer was enthusiastic about my contacting you. He did, in fact, cover many of the requirements of the position.

For the past five years, I have headed the international sales efforts at Manchester, a position that included:
- creating sales offices in Belgium, France, Germany, and Great Britain;
- recruiting and managing a group of 34 independent sales representatives;
- providing full training of all European representatives;
- securing 43 percent, 34 percent, 28 percent, and 37 percent of the Belgian, French, German, and Great Britain markets, respectively; and
- surpassing $45 million in annual sales with excellent margins.

I look forward to discussing details of my experience with you, including how I feel I can add value at Smith. I will call your office Monday morning about 10:00 a.m. to arrange a time and place for a meeting.

Sincerely,

Jacob Seles

Comparison Letter—Responding to a Newspaper Ad

[Typed on 8 ½ by 11-inch stationery]
(Date)

Celeste Vickers, Vice President

Dear Ms. Vickers:

I noted with interest your opening for an accounting manager in Sunday's *Tribune*. I am looking for just such a growth opportunity.

I believe my skills and experience closely align with the qualifications you are seeking:

Applegate Requirements	My Skills and Experience
Accounting degree and several years accounting experience.	C.A. degree, 1999, from DePaul; and over five years of experience.
Demonstrated ability to manage and motivate staff.	Effectively managed staff of 14, including two senior accountants.
Strong analytical and administrative skills.	Developed a base reference library for 350 clients.
Outstanding oral and written communication skills.	Initiated department staff meetings. Created skill training classes for four personnel levels with 95 percent participant "excellent" rating.

Some of my other achievements are outlined on the enclosed resume.

I would welcome the opportunity for an interview, and will call your office next week to arrange a convenient time.

Yours truly,

Jamie Baxter

Response to Blind Ad with Employment Agency

[Typed]
(Date)

Chairman of the Board

Dear Chairman of the Board:

I was dubbed the "turn-around king" by the North Chicago Chapter of the A.M.A. in the *C.M.A. Journal,* issue IV, June 15. Over the past ten years, I've taken three companies from the bankruptcy court to profits of $500,000, $2.1 million, and $1.8 million. One of these companies is Plastic Forms in Hollywood, Florida.

I would like the opportunity to discuss with you the details of what I've done and how my skills might work for your organization. I'm enclosing a resume for your review.

I will call your office next week to arrange a time convenient for a brief meeting.

Sincerely,

Cornelius M. Conover

Response to Ad for Controller

[Typed]
(Date)

Jeremy R. Levitts, CFO

Dear Mr. Levitts:

Your ad in the Sunday *Journal* for a controller especially interests me because I just sold my own business—Small Wonders, a children's toy company— for a profit, and I want to continue my career with a progressive company. I've enclosed my resume for your review.

I look forward to discussing with you how my qualifications, integrity, and seasoned experience might benefit Miracles.

Yours truly,

Jack Beams

**Applying for a Teaching Position
After a Telephone Introduction**

[Typed on 8½ by 11-inch stationary]
(Date)

Dear Mrs. Grimm:

As we discussed on the telephone today, I'd like to teach at Buck Elementary on the third- or fourth-grade level. I will graduate from Anvil College this spring, and plan to move to your area immediately afterward.

I've had student teaching experience in the third- to sixth-grade levels in suburban, urban, and inner-city school districts.

During summer vacations I've taught "at risk" preschool children in the Head Start Program, and fifth-grade "at risk" inner-city children. I've learned to be creative, nurturing, and, most important, patient.

My goal is to continue to develop as a compassionate, enthusiastic, and intelligent teacher. I believe I can make a positive contribution to your school, and would like the opportunity for an introductory interview. I plan to be in Buck County next week, and would like to come in at that time if you could spare 15 minutes.

I'll call you on Friday to learn if you're able to arrange a time, or you may reach me until then at 503-555-0123.

Sincerely,

Pay D. Piper

Emailed Response to Association Website Ad

[Emailed]

SUBJECT: Director of Marketing Communications Position

Dear Mr. Webster:

I'd like the opportunity to show you my portfolio, which illustrates exactly how I planned and executed a complete turnaround of the Adams Master-Planned Community, located just twenty-five miles from Harvey. In ten months, we took Adams from near foreclosure to profits estimated at more than $50 million. The community went from no sales in six months to 15 sales in a single weekend. (See my enclosed resume and list of clients.)

If you'd like, please review other examples of my creative approach and products on my website—marketingmasters.com—under projects.

Please contact me at 401-555-0123 to arrange an interview.

Sincerely,

Cecil Caster

Response to Website Ad for Director, Media Relations

[Emailed]

SUBJECT: Director, Media Relations

Dear Kay:

I'd like the opportunity to discuss with you how my local, regional, and national media skills, in addition to my ability to serve as spokesperson and to create and direct a media relationship plan, may be the combination of skills you're looking for to fill your director of media relations position.

Please take a look at my website, iamsavvy.com, and click on "Media Projects" to see just a few of the media programs I've developed from inception through execution of the actual event. I'm also including below a complete resume and a client list for your review.

Please contact me to arrange an interview time. I am in the city this week, but not next, and I could meet with you either tomorrow at 2:00 P.M., or Thursday at 2:30 P.M.

Sincerely,

Melody Chimes

17

RESUME

*By a small sample we may judge
of the whole piece.*

—MIGUEL DE CERVANTES

 Your resume is a synopsis of what you have to offer. It should include what you have done, what you know, and who you are. It must have the meat and muscle of facts and figures, and it should have a certain flair and pizzazz. The proper balance of these elements equals the power and impact you'll need to sell yourself as a worthy candidate.

The secret to writing a great resume is knowing the audience—the person doing the hiring—and the organization. The key, then, is writing your resume to show that you are the best person for a specific job.

DECIDE TO WRITE

Send your resume:

- In response to newspaper and other media ads
- In response to an invitation from an organization
- As part of your job-search campaign
- To accompany and support a proposal, report, or other document that is based on your qualifications and experience
- In connection with running for political, club, or association office
- To document your qualifications as a speaker, author, expert witness, or other type of authority

DECIDE ON RESUME TYPE

There are three basic styles of resumes: the chronological, the functional, and the creative. Select the style that showcases you the best and is best matched to your target audience. There is no "correct" or "incorrect" form. You may even want to use one style for one audience and another style for a different audience. And sometimes you may want to combine styles to best illustrate why you are the best person for the position.

Chronological Resume

The chronological resume is the most traditional. It uses a time sequence to list work experience and education, usually appearing in reverse order beginning with the present.

Use the chronological resume when:

- You are pursuing traditional fields (government, education, banking).
- Your work history shows a strong growth pattern or direction.
- Your title progression is impressive.
- You're continuing on the same career path.
- Your present or last employer is important.

The chronological resume is *not* the best form for everyone. If any of the list below applies to you, it is probably better to use one of the other styles.

Don't use a chronological resume when:

- You are just entering the job market (a recent graduate).
- You're changing career direction or goals.
- You have holes in your work experience (periods of unemployment).
- Your career has plateaued and remained there for some time.
- You are returning to the job market after a long absence.
- You do not wish to divulge your age.
- You've changed employers frequently.

Functional Resume

The functional resume focuses on capabilities and skills. Usually these are listed by areas, and may or may not include dates.

Use a functional resume when:

- You are changing careers.
- You are entering the job market.
- You are reentering the job market.
- Your experience lacks a demonstrated career path.
- You are a consultant, freelancer, or have completed temporary work.
- Your latest job appears to be a demotion over previous ones.
- Your work experience seems somewhat unconnected to the position for which you are applying.

Don't use a functional resume when:

- You have not targeted your resume toward a certain position.
- You do not have well-defined accomplishments and capabilities.
- You do not have enough experience to demonstrate functions performed.

Creative Resume

The creative resume is a free-form style and can be extremely effective in showcasing your skills and capabilities—particularly for artists, writers, actors, public relations personnel, and people in the media. An account executive looking for a new position in an advertising agency effectively used a resume with cartoons to land a high-powered position, for example. A CEO of a public relations agency was elected to an important association president post by preparing audio tapes of voice impersonations touting the various attributes that made him the best person for the job. He played it for association members at a campaign luncheon.

Executives of various disciplines, as well as actors, spokespersons, freelance photographers, and illustrators, have used audiovisual resumes of all types to land sales jobs, manager jobs, acting roles, and all sorts of other types of jobs.

And computer experts, graphic designers, actors, and photographers have created interactive resumes that they put on Internet systems or emailed to employers.

Use a creative resume when:

- The target of your resume is a creative or specialized audience who will appreciate it.
- You decide it is the only medium that can adequately express who you are.
- You especially want to showcase your creative talents.

Don't use a creative resume when:

- You are seeking a position in a traditional field, such as government.
- You are not well-grounded in your own creativity.
- It won't be otherwise "acceptable" to your audience.

THINK ABOUT CONTENT

Learn as much as possible about the employer and target audience. Assess the position you are seeking—preferably a specific position within a specific organization—and the key ingredients needed to fill it.

Then work through the following steps of assessing and writing out your skills, personal characteristics, and experience, keeping in mind the resume style you have selected. Use the following steps as a working guide. Create separate categories of information in your computer file or on index cards—skills, characteristics, results of your efforts at work or elsewhere—for ease in completing your final draft.

STEP 1

Make an inventory of your personal information, focusing on your skills, abilities, and strong points. There are really two types of skills: general and specific.

General skills, like analyzing, communicating, and writing, are often taken for granted because they seem like things everyone can do. List the general skills you use in your work, because every job requires them. The inventory on page 121 can help you identify your general skills and their job applications.

STEP 2

Select your twelve strongest general skills from the list, and translate them into specific technical skills that produce measurable results. These are job-related skills like inputting on a keyboard, which produces a piece of correspondence. Here are a couple of examples:

General skill

Related activities

Specific skills

Organizing

Making order out of chaos, establishing physical order, categorizing facts.
Setting up a filing system, creating a systematic way to categorize inventory in a warehouse, and rewriting and editing reports.

General skill

Related activities

Specific skills

Negotiating

Bartering, holding a position, convincing others, arranging terms, establishing standards.
Setting up conferences with hotels, establishing sales prices for products, developing contract terms, arranging details of sales, establishing salaries.

General skill: _____

Related activities: _____

_____

_____

Specific skills: _____

_____

_____

STEP 3

Factor into your skill statements those things that express your personal characteristics, and select those that best describe you. The following words may not appear in your completed resume, but they will help you in forming your final statements.

____ Able	____ Intense
____ Ambitious	____ Intuitive
____ Assertive	____ Loyal
____ Careful	____ Masterful
____ Caring	____ Open-minded
____ Communicative	____ Organized
____ Creative	____ Persistent
____ Decisive	____ Persuasive
____ Dedicated	____ Political
____ Determined	____ Precise
____ Diligent	____ Quick
____ Easygoing	____ Responsible
____ Energetic	____ Results-oriented
____ Flexible	____ Rigid
____ Forthright	____ Sensitive
____ Friendly	____ Strong
____ Hardworking	____ Supportive
____ Helpful	____ Tactful
____ Honest	____ Thorough
____ Humorous	____ Trustworthy
____ Imaginative	____ Warm
____ Intellectual	____ Willing
____ Intelligent	

STEP 4

List your accomplishments in the most powerful terms.

STEP 5

Include any pertinent special-interest areas and any results (accomplishments) from your experience in school, training, sports and hobbies, military and service, community activities, home, and, of course, work experience.

General Skill Inventory

General Skill	Related Activity	Specific Job Skill
Acknowledging others		
Acting		
Analyzing		
Building		
Classifying		
Communicating		
Conceptualizing		
Convincing others		
Cooking		
Counseling		
Dancing		
Drawing		
Driving		
Entertaining		
Following instructions		
Growing things		
Innovating		
Interior decorating		
Keeping records		
Learning new material		
Managing people		
Manual dexterity		
Meeting deadlines		
Meeting new people		
Negotiating		
Nurturing		
Organizing		
Painting		
Planning		
Reading		
Remembering		
Repairing things		
Researching		
Running		
Supervising others		
Supporting others		
Teaching		
Traveling		
Understanding new material		
Using mechanical tools		
Visualizing		
Walking		
Working with numbers		
Writing		

Education Examples

Achieved a 3.8 GPA while working 20 hours a week and participating in two extracurricular sports.

Established the Women's Republican Club and solicited membership from 1,320 undergraduates.

Served as editor of the class yearbook.

Initiated an Easter Seal spring frolic, which raised $5,240 for the Kids' Summer Camp program.

Special Interest Examples

Organized a tennis tournament for 520 participants.

Read the complete Great Books of the Western World.

Designed and created three new, complicated quilt patterns.

Improved my USTA tennis ability level from a 2.0 to a 4.5 in three months.

Training Examples

Graduated number two from the effective sales program.

Completed the AMA marketing-for-profit workshop.

Completed the Xerox sales training program.

Graduated from a women-in-business-managing-your-time seminar.

Sport/Hobby Examples

Organized and initiated a fiction-writing group of 10 members.

Organized a tennis league and tournament for 54 participants.

Designed and built a seven-room vacation house in fourteen months.

Military Examples

Completed airborne training second in my group of 76.

Learned conversational German in five months.

Mastered an AS-11 guidance system in five months.

Community Activity Examples

Organized a group gubernatorial campaign for leading candidates in four months.

Implemented a Meal-on-Wheels program for the aged for 1,500 participants.

Initiated, organized, and conducted seven healthcare programs for 5,000 participants.

Successfully petitioned—obtaining 5,500 signatures—against irresponsible mining operations.

Family and Household Examples

Remodeled a seven-room house in my spare time in eight months.

Established a family trust fund for seven siblings.

Managed an annual family budget of $56,000 for nine.

Rebuilt five, small home appliances.

STEP 6

List your last four jobs, starting with the most recent, and work backward. Carefully sort through your experience, enumerating five distinct results for each position you held. Think in terms of results you can express in concrete terms of facts and figures. Make your results as action oriented as possible.

Here are a few examples:
- Organized a company library of 5,000 volumes.
- Prepared a career-advancement plan for five entry-level careers.
- Increased production by 20 percent by eliminating four clerical steps.
- Planned and administrated the orientation program for 35 employees.

Position: _____

Dates: _____

Employer: _____

Five results: _____

_____

_____

_____

_____

STEP 7

Focus on how the results you have listed relate to your career future. Go back over the items you have selected, and use a three-number rating system to indicate their relevance to your future career: a *1* represents very career-oriented results, a *2* represents somewhat career-oriented results, and a *3* represents results that are not relevant to your career.

Organization and Wording

- Think in terms of your career objective. Divide information into areas: objective, special skills, work history, education, training, and licenses.
- Arrange the elements within each area to showcase the best of what you bring to a particular position.
- Make your most powerful statements first. Place those less powerful in diminishing order.
- Keep it simple.
- List experience in a straightforward manner, with the employer's name, but not address, recorded.
- Emphasize action words and hard results.
- Keep statements to 15 words or less. Less is more.
- Use power phrases and use "bulleted" statements.
- Be specific.

Experience

- Think in terms of value to the reader. Emphasize what you can do for him or her.
- State what you did, not what the reader should think about you. For example, "I am an excellent writer" is an evaluation. "I wrote four marketing analyses rated excellent by six department heads" exemplifies your expertise.
- Part-time jobs may be used by recent graduates looking for their first job.
- Personal references should not appear, but have them available in the event they are requested.
- Limit personal information to only that which is pertinent to the position or the demonstration of your character.
- Include personal awards or achievements if they are pertinent.

Education, Professional Training, and Affiliations

- Education, for anyone who has more than three years work experience, should appear at the bottom of the resume.

- Pertinent licenses, certificates, and other qualifications should be listed.
- Professional associations can be very important to your career, especially if you held a prominent office. List those that apply to the position you are targeting.

ELIMINATE WRONG MESSAGES

In a resume, it's crucial to communicate the message you want. It is just as crucial to avoid sending the wrong message. Keep these things in mind as you write:

Content

- Do not exaggerate, distort the facts, embellish, or lie.
- Don't be shy. State clearly and succinctly your best attributes without a braggart or flippant tone.
- Get rid of statements that do not stress results.
- Check to be sure all errors have been removed.
- Do not include an "Objective" that states your individual goals. Focus, instead, on what you can do for the organization.
- Never state the salary you are seeking.
- Don't overload your resume. It should not include everything you have ever done.
- Unless it is relevant to the position, don't include personal information like age, weight, height, marital status, religion, or political affiliation; salary information; references or statements like "references will be furnished upon request"; or a picture of yourself.

Style

- Use sentences with fifteen or less words and paragraphs of three to four lines.
- Eliminate articles—*the, a, an*—whenever possible and select strong verbs to convey the meaning you want.
- Eliminate unnecessary descriptive words: "creative, innovative, hard-working, futuristic, dedicated, bottom-line oriented." Dull resumes contain lots of descriptive statements that look like they were copied right out of corporate personnel manuals.
- Eliminate vagueness and jargon.
- Don't be wimpy. Use power verbs and precise, hard facts and figures. (See examples in table on page 124.)

Wimpy	Powerful
1. Responsible for all sales activities for the year.	1. Increased sales 41 percent over the previous year.
2. Wrote employee-procedures manual.	2. Authored a 98-page employee-procedures manual, which received rave reviews from 92 percent of department head reviewers.
3. Improved department efficiency.	3. Increased department efficiency by 35 percent (measured by time-and-quantity parameters).
4. Recruited and trained technical personnel.	4. Recruited and trained 75 technical personnel who performed at 94 percent efficiency after one year of employment.
5. Expanded laboratory operations.	5. Expanded laboratory staff from 85 to 425 technicians functioning at an overall efficiency rate of 94.5 percent.
6. Conducted in-college and university interviews.	6. Developed a new supply source of 195 top technical candidates by interviewing at 50 colleges and universities.
7. Handled company's advertising.	7. Increased inquiries from 65 to 97 a week by means of effective advertising.
8. Opened new sales offices in five cities.	8. Conducted feasibility research and established five new sales offices. Each operated at 24 percent above sales quotas in the first year and a half (seven months ahead of schedule).
9. Substantially lowered operating costs in division.	9. Initiated cost-reducing plans in the division, which resulted in 45 percent ($47,000) cost reduction. There was no negative effect on production or future capabilities.
10. Handled all bookings for travel and accommodations.	10. Negotiated travel accommodations for 35 executives that resulted in savings of $220,000 a year.
11. Put on training sessions for department supervisors.	11. Conducted leadership training for 54 supervisors, 89 percent of whom expressed a "high level of satisfaction."
12. Managed personnel department.	12. Headed personnel department of 46 professionals with annual budget accountability of $1.75 million.
13. Developed equipment that resulted in substantial company savings.	13. Developed electrostatic production spray equipment that resulted in $3 million in company savings in 14 months.
14. Initiated new employee programs.	14. Created and implemented two new employee-relations programs that reduced employee turnover by 32 percent.
15. Raised a family of six for the past 10 years.	15. Managed and organized a six-member household on an annual budget of $42,000.
16. Wrote a procedural manual for Museum of Natural History.	16. Conceptualized, organized, and authored an 80-page volunteer procedural manual for the Museum of Natural History.
17. Reduced operating costs in my division by $42,000.	17. Initiated cost-reducing plan in my division that resulted in a 42 percent ($42,000) cost reduction. There was no negative effect on production.

CHECK YOUR FINAL DRAFT

- The employment section of your resume should include a maximum of four or five positions held. If you use the chronological listing, do not leave periods of time unaccounted for.
- Document your pertinent education, association memberships, pertinent personal information, if any, and skills or training.
- Enlist the help of friends and professional associates whose judgment you trust. Ask them to critique your resume, using the following checklist:

	Yes	No
1. Are statements clear and concise?	___	___
2. Are there any superfluous or unnecessary words?	___	___
3. Have I included what should be eliminated?	___	___
4. Is it easy to follow?	___	___
5. Are my accomplishments well showcased?	___	___
6. Have I accounted for all the time covered?	___	___
7. Have I included my address, phone number, and a place where I can be easily reached?	___	___

SELECT A FORMAT

- Computers make it possible for you to target each resume. Select professional-looking type-faces (fonts).
- Use a high-quality printer to print your resume.
- Try to put all your information on a single sheet.

- Position your name, address, and contact numbers in the center, flush left, or in a manner so your resume looks balanced.
- When choosing a typeface, consider Helvetica, Times Roman, Schoolbook, or New Century. Don't combine styles unless you're an expert. Use boldface type, strong italics (many are too weak), large type, and attention-getting spacing, to make your point. You may want to use boldface type on your subheads and/or other items like name and telephone number, job titles, job objective (if used), education, and special skills and licenses. These are items you may want to stand out.
- Use 11 point or larger fonts for easy reading. You may want to use larger type for your most important information.
- Print in black ink for ease of reading and copying.
- Balance your material vertically and horizontally on the page so that it looks open and clean. Use the white space to get the reader's attention.
- Select a quality paper. If you're answering an ad, your resume may be one of hundreds. Isn't it worth the risk of color (buff or cream) to get extra attention? Using pastels and "shocking" colors is taking considerably more risk, however, so use these only if you know the target reader well and are sure your choice of paper won't be labeled "unprofessional." Test your paper selection to be sure it copies well. (Some heavy papers jam copiers.) Select envelopes that match your resume paper.
- Check to ensure you have no typos. Use the computer spell checker, but also go over the resume to catch correctly spelled words that are incorrectly used, like *to* for *too.*)
- Give the resume a little breathing time before your final proofing. It's amazing how much difference just a little time can make in your ability to have a completely fresh, objective look.

Myra Loomis
3444 Fuller Avenue, Phoenix, AZ 85283
Phone: 480-555-0123
Email: bigbird@willis.net

Objective: Senior-level consultant or contract position for media relations and/or public relations.

Areas of expertise: National, local, and trade media placement; and writing for clients in consumer products, energy, financial service, food, healthcare, restaurants, and travel fields.

EXPERIENCE

Principal
MDM Communications | Chicago, IL | 2001–Present
Provide media relations and writing service to 15 to 20 organizations nationwide. In one month, secured commitments for four feature placements among targeted media; placed feature stories in three local business magazines for national manufacturer seeking to improve national visibility; and secured positive news coverage for publicly traded companies among leading business media, including the *Wall Street Journal, Barron's,* Bloomberg Television, *Business Week, Financial Times, Forbes, Fortune, Investor's Business Daily,* CNBC, and CNN/fn.

Vice President
Scream Advertising | Dallas, TX | 1999–2001
Second in command for Client Services of public relations division at $50 million per year agency. Responsible for new business development, staff recruitment, and supervision. Spearheaded launch of Jolly Looney Tunes Meals for Kids that became Jolly's second largest brand within six months. Expanded Jolly account to include two additional product lines.

Senior Group Manager
Just Right Advertising | Austin, TX | 1996–1999
Supervised three of the full-service public relations agency's top five billing accounts. Consistent winner of monthly agency award for outstanding media placements. Promoted five times during tenure.

SKILLS
Consulting: business development, media relations, media training
Media relations: product introductions, targeted media placements, media tours
Project management: publications, special events, vendors, and freelance talent management
Research: product/category/competitor, soft soundings
Writing: advertorials, brochures, articles, collateral, case histories, marketing materials, newsletters, press kits, press releases, proposals, reports, scripts

AWARDS AND RECOGNITION
PRSA Award of Excellence (Silver Anvil finalist), 2005

EDUCATION
Bachelor of arts, journalism (with honors), University of Texas, Austin
Certificate of business administration, DePaul, Chicago
Graduate business courses, University of Texas, Austin

Chronological Resumes—Financial Analyst Resume

Conrad Cunningham Manchester
25 Outrigger Street
Marina Del Rey, CA 90292
310-555-0123

PROFESSIONAL EXPERIENCE

Senior Financial Analyst
Houlihan Lokey Howard and Zukin | Los Angeles, CA
1998–Present

- Manage all facets of securities analyses. Completed over 30 mid-sized corporation due diligence pro formas in 12 months, including quantitative financial analyses, debt restructuring, and offering memoranda for principal investment groups.
- Conducted over 20 separate real estate investment services, including in-depth debt restructuring, quantitative financial analyses, and due diligence on 30 deals.
- Completed merger and acquisition services on up to seven deals at a time, including 24 private placement and 23 exclusive sales of middle-market companies. Purchased and placed $125 million in corporate business debt. Executed 24 business valuations, including fairness and solvency opinions.
- Developed 35 new business opportunities with middle-market companies for purchase and corporate bond reissues.

Member, Board of Governors
University of San Francisco | San Francisco, CA
1996–Present

- Propose alternative fiscal plans to the Board of Directors. Establish student scholarship criteria. Represent Southern California alumni in fund-raising activities and public relations.

Analyst, Restructuring/Litigation Group
Price Waterhouse | Los Angeles, CA
1994–98

- Provided restructuring and bankruptcy advice to 45 creditor corporations. Included due diligence and debt restructuring analyses.
- Prepared internal financials for 45 client corporations and evaluated alternative strategic plans for 37 restructured companies.
- Designed financial models for 36 distressed companies.

EDUCATION

Honor Student
University of San Francisco | San Francisco, CA
Bachelor of Arts, Economics/Philosophy, 1994

Chronological Resumes—Middle Manager Resume

Jennifer Maynard Boyles
1765 West Island Way
St. Charles, VA 29741
803-555-0123

PROFILE

Middle manager in healthcare setting with excellent communication skills and a keen eye for detail and accuracy. Self-starter with strong customer-service skills and the ability to work effectively in a high-pressure environment. Possess fine ability for accuracy in accounting, bookkeeping, and math.

EXPERIENCE

Resource Coordinator, MERCY HOSPITAL, Charleston, SC | 2003–Present
Work closely with physicians to identify and evaluate patients who need extended care. Attend all medical/surgery rounds to conduct patient psychosocial assessments. Consult with families to advise on extended care placement. Consult with physicians and social workers to implement patient-care programs. Organize and implement two healthcare teams that serve more than 200 patients per day. Coordinate all patient discharge, transfer, and referral records. Create statistical reports for extended care placement using spreadsheet software. Design and create database file system to update extended care and rehabilitation facility resources.

Patient Care Coordinator, ST. FRANCIS HOSPITAL, Charleston, SC | 2001–03
Coordinated and supervised all patient floor records and services. Received admissions and arranged discharges. Kept medical records current. Ordered and compiled lab work records. Inventoried, maintained, and ordered supplies as needed with 98 percent accuracy.

Program Coordinator, ST. FRANCIS HOSPICE, Charleston, SC | 1999–2001
Created and implemented new budget, which cut costs by 15 percent while increasing patient satisfaction by 17 percent. Prepared payroll for 65 employees and performed and/or oversaw accounting functions.

EDUCATION

Clemson University, Clemson, SC, 1999
BS in Human Services Management

Funcational Resumes—Assistant Restaurant Manager Resume

Emma Cornell Worthington
1145 Evert Street
Cleveland, OH 44101
440-555-0123

OBJECTIVE: Restaurant Assistant Manager Trainee

RESTAURANT EXPERIENCE

<u>Management</u>

Prepared payroll for staff of 25

Completed light bookkeeping, made bank deposits, and maintained records for taxes

Opened, balanced, and closed cash registers

Ordered supplies and arranged for equipment maintenance

Decorated restaurant

Arranged special events for reservations of 15 or more

<u>Personnel Supervision and Training</u>

Trained and supervised 20 waitresses and 12 hostesses

Hired and terminated staff

Successfully mediated dozens of employee disputes

Completed work schedules for 25 employees

<u>Menus, Food Preparation, and Presentation</u>

Ordered over $50,000 per month in food and liquor supplies

Maintained inventory and organized stockroom, which resulted in savings of 15 percent

Oversaw sanitation and preparation of food, which consistently received the highest health departing rating

Planned menus and oversaw quality and accuracy of deliveries, which resulted in savings of 7 percent each month

Supervised food presentation, which resulted in 22 percent higher customer satisfaction

EDUCATION

Associate of Culinary Arts, New York College of Culinary Arts, 1994

Funcational Resumes—Crisis Counselor Resume

Jennifer M. Bateman, RN
3212 East Burlington Street
Wilmette, IL 60651
312-555-0123

QUALIFICATION HIGHLIGHTS

- Skilled in working with people in crisis.

- Work well independently or as a team member.

- Ten years successful research and collection of data as clinical nurse.

PROFESSIONAL EXPERIENCE

Counseling

- Crisis intervention and long-term counseling with individuals of diverse backgrounds and problems, including confinement, terminal illness, and institutional group living.

- Advised study group volunteers of positive test results including venereal disease, TB, high blood pressure, and other abnormal blood values.

- Directed and coordinated the medical follow-up for 300 individuals with problems.

Research

- Completed 40 human nutrition research studies.

- Established critical test procedures.

- Prepared samples for analysis and transport.

Management/Supervision

- Head nurse in charge of supervising support staff, research volunteers, and graduate students for a Northwestern University nutritional study.

- Authored two 80-page procedural manuals and delivered in-service training talks to 300 staff members.

- Taught data-collection and handling techniques to 75 research participants.

- Assembled data and wrote 42 reports of studies. (See bibliography.)

EMPLOYMENT

2001–Present | Research/Clinical Nurse II, Northwestern University/USDA
2002–Present | Health Consultant, Chicago School District

EDUCATION

BA, Journalism, DePaul, 1986
RN, Northwestern, 1989

Creative/Combination Resumes—Health Education Administrator

Denise Leah Golightly
2345 West Highline Drive
Leadville, CO 80461
719-555-0123

OBJECTIVE
Community Health Education Administrator

QUALIFICATIONS

- Award-winning assessment and communication skills.
- Proficiency in program development, presentation, and group facilitation.
- Over 10 years experience in varied and complex human-relations responsibilities.
- MSW degree with fieldwork experience in medical and psychiatric settings.
- Proven ability to work independently and with multidisciplinary team.

PROFESSIONAL EXPERIENCE

Community Relations and Education

- Agency liaison to 24 secondary, high school, and college classes; lectured on health and education issues.
- Recruited 45 adoptive couples for hard-to-place children. Developed, organized, and coordinated 12 training sessions and 10 support groups.
- Developed and presented 32 special community education programs.
- Organized 18 community school workshop programs for parents.

Administration

- Established 10 in-house and interagency planning programs on extended medical care and adoptions.
- Prepared 15 comprehensive, expert reports, and recommendations for agency and court use.
- Contributed to establishing $2.5 million in budgets, and worked with financial officer to authorize monthly disbursements of $9,000 to $25,000 for monthly budgets.
- Supervised 17 caseworkers and technicians.

Counseling

- Achieved 87 percent improvement rate with individuals and families through use of crisis-intervention techniques and long-term counseling. Those counseled came from diverse backgrounds and status, and the presenting problems including life stress, illness and disability, and life transitions.
- Performed in-depth investigative interviewing and personal assessments.

EMPLOYMENT
1992–Present | Kaiser Hospitals, San Francisco, CA
Medical Social Worker

1990–92 | Marin Human Resources Agency, San Rafael, CA
Counselor for AdoptionChild Abuse

1986–90 | San Francisco Social Services
Caseworker—Low-Income Families

EDUCATION
BA, *cum laude,* Sociology—University of San Francisco
MSW University of San Francisco

Creative/Combination Resumes—Computer Service Manager Resume

Franklin Q. O'Day
13245 Osprey Drive
Wadsworth, Florida 33597
352-555-0123

OBJECTIVE

Computer Service Manager

QUALIFICATIONS

- Diagnose and repair at a 97 percent accuracy rate.

- Skilled in all major computer equipment types.

- Experienced both in working independently and supervising others.

EXPERIENCE

- Used diagnostic programs to locate defective components on all types of PET computers.

- Found and solved problems beyond the scope of diagnostic programs, such as thermal integrated circuit failure and unstripped wire in keyboard connector.

- Kept electronic equipment, including microcomputers, operating at 96 percent efficiency.

EMPLOYMENT

1992–Present | Senior Electronics Technician
University of California, Berkeley, CA
Radio Astronomy Laboratory
Test and install sensitive receivers and computer-control equipment for radio and optical telescopes, working from engineer sketches and diagrams.

1988–92 | Electronics Technician
Beckman Instruments, Richmond, CA
Developed, tested, and repaired prototypes for high-speed electronic counters.

EDUCATION

- Santa Monica City College. Engineering major, three years.

- University of California, Berkeley. Electrical Engineering major, two years.

Also see BIOGRAPHY, page 358; NETWORKING, page 102; and RESUME COVER LETTER, page 109.

APPLYING ONLINE AND BY EMAIL

I have come to believe that if anything will bring about the downfall of a company, or maybe even a country, it is blind copies of emails that should never have been sent in the first place.

—MICHAEL EISNER, FORMER DISNEY CHAIRMAN AND CEO

Job searching has been revolutionized by the Internet.

Certainly in the computer, computer software, and related industries applying for jobs by posting a resume online or sending it by email is the rule and not the exception. In most other fields, as well, email is the vehicle most often used to introduce yourself as a position candidate.

But, because of its informality, anonymity, and immediacy, it's very important to use this medium carefully, and to be sure you've created the proper balance in your approach and tone.

Email is usually the casual Friday of the interoffice memo. However, when you are introducing yourself and your skills to a potential employer, your tone should be conversational, but not *too* casual. You want to be sure to communicate that you understand this is, after all, business.

With a press of the "Send" key, your application, resume cover letter, resume, and/or networking letter will instantly appear on the computer screen of the person who has the power to hire you. You'll want everything you send to promote you for the position.

DECIDE TO WRITE

Post your resume:
- On your website
- On job-search websites, such as Monster.com
- On association, alumni, or other organization websites and/or in directories

Email your resume:
- In response to an online ad
- When an email address is offered in a newspaper, magazine, or other publication ad
- To a person who has requested it

THINK ABOUT CONTENT

For your website resume and your resume to post:
- Study the principles of good web design, and examine lots of posted resumes before you decide how you want your resume to appear.
- Install a counter on your website (not visible to visitors) so you will know how many visits your website receives
- Consider confidentiality. You may wish to use only an email address and/or cell phone number as contacts.

- Research employer ads and develop a list of "designator" nouns (interior designer, electrician, Lotus CLS) so your resume will be viewed when employers search for your qualifications. The more precise your designators, the more pre-qualified the search results.
- Study websites where you want to post your resume for any special requirements.

For your email resume:

- Format as a plain text file (.txt), or use ASCII-compatible characters so it will appear accurately across most systems and applications.
  — Omit word-processing elements like boxes, bullets, underlining, graphic lines, italics, or boldface type.
  — Use a simple font, like courier, of 11 points to 14 points.
  — Use hyphens or asterisks (up to 60 characters per line including spaces) to create horizontal lines.
  — Margins can't exceed 65 characters per line, including spaces.
- If special design features are included or required, scan your resume as a PDF file.

BEFORE YOU START

- Complete as much research as possible. Tailor your letter and resume to the specific position, and the specific person who has the power to hire you.
- Find out if the person receiving your email application prefers that you supply your resume as an attachment or inclusion in the body of the email.
- Review the rules in the appropriate chapter(s) of this book for the type of message you are sending.
- Focus on your reader: evaluate your message in terms of telling the reader what he or she needs or wants to know.
- Create your letter and/or resume first as a word processing document for ease of editing.

THINK ABOUT CONTENT

- Start with an informal greeting if you know the reader, slightly more formal if you don't.
- Communicate enthusiastically your motivation and skill strengths, and how they fit the position requirements.
- Present your skills as a solution to the reader's problem(s) whenever possible.
- Refer the reader to the details in your resume, if it's included or attached.
- In your letter, make a connection between the reader and yourself in the *first paragraph,* and immediately introduce the reason you are writing. Name any existing point of reference: a referring person, an ad, or the like. If you've been referred to the reader, use the referring person's name only if you have permission to do so.
- Give details of what you have to offer—preferably a solution to the reader's problem—in the *second paragraph.*
- The *third paragraph* should be a strong close, and it should state how you'll follow up. Ask for the interview. Be sure to include your contact information.
- Use the inverted-pyramid structure in composing your message: most important information first, details later. Be concise.
- Use the subject line wisely. Think carefully about a concise, definitive, and attention-capturing line. For example, if you've been referred to the person, you may want to include the referring person's name in the subject line; or, if you are a member of an association to which the person belongs, you may want to include this in the subject line as an identifying point.
- Include a hyperlink to your website, if you have one, where you have more extensive resume information and appropriate visual and text work samples.

ELIMINATE WRONG MESSAGES

- Don't put ALL CAPS in the subject line. This is the equivalent of shouting. While this may get attention, it usually won't be positive.
- Wait to fill in the TO: line until *last,* when you're completely confident you've input exactly what you want to say. That way you won't accidentally send a message you're not ready to send.
- Don't lift statements directly from your resume and put them in your letter. Duplication is boring and unoriginal. Your reader won't be impressed.
- Avoid the use of acronyms or emoticons in any of your business messages. They are too casual.

19

LETTER OF RECOMMENDATION

He who says there's no such thing as an honest man, you may be sure is himself a knave.

—GEORGE BERKELEY

The terms reference letter, letter of evaluation, letter of verification, and letter of recommendation are often used interchangeably. By strict definition, the *verification letter* is the most general of the four, and is used to document very general points of personal history: confirmation of employment (dates and position), credit status, and schooling.

The *reference letter* also includes general information such as dates of employment, position, credit status, place of schooling and/or employment. This letter often includes a general recommendation about character, and was once used very routinely in the "To Whom It May Concern" format when an employee left an organization's employment.

This is not a general practice in today's business world, but there are often times when employers, prospective employers, or other organizations want verification of employment, scholarship, character, and/or credit status, so a letter of reference is requested. In response, send this letter specifically to the person requesting it and supply only the information requested that conforms with your organization's reference policy.

The *letter of evaluation* gives a more thorough accounting of both the negative and positive aspects of a person's history, although in our litigious society, negative points are often very limited or omitted entirely. This letter is often routinely completed as part of an employee's review process and is placed in his or her confidential personnel file.

The *letter of recommendation* promotes one person to another. It is generally written by a former supervisor in the workplace or a professor or teacher when requested by a former employee or student.

The organization and content of all these letters are very similar, but this chapter will concentrate on the letter of recommendation as it is the most commonly used. Most everything here applies to the other letters as well. (See samples at the end of the chapter for specific examples of the reference letter and the letter of evaluation.)

For your letter of recommendation to be effective, you must be familiar enough with the person's abilities, skills, and performance to offer specific information.

Before you start, review your organization's policy. It may prohibit you from answering a request for information on a former employee or associate. Many organizations have a policy that limits reporting to only certain broad, verifiable facts. If you do respond, stay away from information about the person's age, race, religion, sex, marital status, pregnancy, criminal record, citizenship, organization memberships, and mental and physical handicaps, unless—in an unusual case—the information is clearly related to the position. If you are not very familiar with the person, or you cannot recommend him or her, decline. (Remember, in most instances the person will be able to read your letter under the provisions of the Privacy Act.)

DECIDE TO WRITE

Compose this letter to:

- Respond to a request about a former employee or company you have been associated with.
- Promote a candidate for club, sorority, fraternity, association, or honor society membership.
- Recommend a candidate for a job, grant, scholarship, or special award.

THINK ABOUT CONTENT

- Identify and verify the request.
- Be sure you know the position for which the person is applying, and write the recommendation in light of that knowledge.
- Explain your relationship to the person, stating your position, title, and any other pertinent information.
- State the person or company's full name, position, or status. Include dates of employment or association, position titles, primary responsibilities, and professional or honorary associations.
- Respond directly to the inquiry, addressing the specific questions asked.
- Give a general recommendation that sets up the organization of the letter. Use a tone that is businesslike but friendly, warm, and informal. A cold or overly formal letter will not help the person being recommended.
- Organize the details in a decreasing order of importance.

- Be explicit and substantive. Vague and general statements distance you from the person you are recommending and are not persuasive.
- Be honest and truthful, and give every fact the emphasis it deserves. If you report a negative point, for instance, give only enough emphasis to convey an accurate picture. Because negative facts are usually given more weight in the reader's mind, it will be best to subordinate any given, or omit them.
- Detail two or three characteristics in their order of importance. Instead of "Julie has excellent skills," write "Julie consistently inputs 110 words a minute using WordPerfect, Paradox, or Harvard Graphics software." Listing more than three examples diffuses their impact.
- Verify the reason for the resignation or termination of an employee or relationship, as appropriate.
- Reaffirm and summarize your recommendation, and invite the reader to write or call for more information.
- End on a note of goodwill or best wishes.

ELIMINATE WRONG MESSAGES

- Don't go overboard or make statements you cannot prove.
- Avoid the "To Whom It May Concern" approach; address your letter to a specific person. If this isn't possible, use the memo format of "DATE, TO, FROM, RE (with regard to): Introducing Dana Ledbetter" or another suitable heading that indicates the memo topic.
- Don't advise the reader. Statements like "You should hire her fast" or "Don't let him get away" could work against the person being recommended.
- Don't give the information without checking out the request. Refuse to supply a recommendation, or give information only verbally.

CONSIDER SPECIAL SITUATIONS

When Someone Asks You to Write a Recommendation

- Using a subject line, which identifies the request and the person, helps get your letter off to a direct start.
- When recommending a company or product, use only direct examples from your personal experience to state your case, citing, too, the exact application and method of use. It is wise to frame your recommendation in terms of your "opinion" based on this experience.
- Because we live in a litigious society, caution must be used in deciding the contents of your letter of recommendation, reference, or evaluation. Some organizations do not give this information either over the telephone or in writing. Many organizations will only confirm the person was employed, the dates of employment, and the person's title. Litigation charging negligence has ensued, too, where the former employer did not disclose the former employee had been charged with theft or other problems.
- Assume that anything you write may end up in a court of law, and if you do not want to defend it, don't write it. If there is any question about your statements being actionable, consult legal counsel before sending.
- Do not write a letter of reference if you can't honestly recommend the person.

When You Ask Someone to Write a Letter of Recommendation

- Be sure to give that person specific information that will help in tailoring the recommendation to your specific needs. For example, "Jim, I'm a candidate for the new-product manager position at the start-up company, Waddle's. In your recommendation letter for me, it would be most appropriate if you would review my position and work on the Model F-56 (development through getting it to market)."
- After the letter of reference has been sent, be sure to thank the person who wrote it. (See "Thank-You," page 76.)

SELECT A FORMAT

- Type on letterhead, personal stationery, or quality bond paper. The appearance should be professional.
- Interoffice recommendations, references, and evaluations may be done in memo form.

SELECT STRONG WORDS

capable	honest
character	impeccable
commendable	integrity
competent	invaluable
congenial	irreplaceable
conscientious	irreproachable
considerate	loyal
cooperative	meritorious
decorated	noteworthy
dedicated	outstanding
distinguished	productive
dynamic	professional
effective	reliable
efficient	remarkable
energetic	resourceful
ethical	respectable
excellent	trustworthy
exemplary	valuable

BUILD STRONG PHRASES

can confidently recommend

could always be counted on

dedicated to doing an outstanding job

discharged his duties professionally

enthusiastic in taking on new responsibilities

entirely trustworthy

exceeded the job description

excelled in going beyond the required

exerted extraordinary efforts

extended himself to complete the work

first-class employee in every regard

I highly recommend

initiated new approaches to problems

organized and efficient

outstanding contributions

performed beyond the requirements

performed in an outstanding manner

recommend without reservation
set an outstanding example
solution oriented in facing problems
take-charge person
team player
took initiative
well-respected by coworkers
wholeheartedly recommend

WRITE STRONG SENTENCES

Start with a powerful verb, and then construct strong, concise sentences like these:

Julia Barnes earned the respect of her coworkers.

Jennifer Bose had $11 million in unpaid royalties sorted out and deposited in the correct accounts in four months.

Carla Grieves increased production by 17 percent in seven months.

Employee satisfaction increased over 30 percent during Myron Fee's first year as director of personnel.

It was a sad day at Koelbel when Chico Martinez tendered his resignation.

BUILD EFFECTIVE PARAGRAPHS

I felt a great loss when Elsie Walkio resigned to move to Phoenix with her husband. For over 10 years she kept me prepared and on time. I don't expect I'll ever find another secretary as fine or as efficient as Elsie.

Here are just a couple of examples. Josie worked an entire weekend preparing separate project packets for a national sales meeting because our copy equipment had failed the week before, and no one else knew how to assemble the packets. She saved our company hundreds of thousands of dollars by revising the manual-review procedures; and she never missed an administrative employee's birthday.

Let me know if you need any additional information, and please give Robert my best regards.

EDIT, EDIT, EDIT

Make your recommendation clear, concise, and detailed enough to be credible.

Letter of Verification

[Typed and mailed]
(Date)

Dear Ms. Griswald:

I hereby confirm that Roscoe Wallace was employed by Ditty's in the shipping department as a processor on April 5, 2001. Mr. Wallace's employment continued for five years until he tendered his resignation on June 10, 2006, at which time he was a process supervisor.

Mr. Wallace's record indicates no disciplinary action during his employment, and he left Ditty's voluntarily.

Sincerely,

Mildred Owens
Human Resources

Letter of Reference

[Typed and mailed]
(Date)

Ellen Dorms

Dear Ms. Dorms:

I'm responding to your request for an employment reference letter for Alex Tributes. Our policy is to provide the following information: Mr. Tributes was employed by Shakers from June 5, 1999, through March 10, 2003, as a machinist. His employment was entirely satisfactory, and he left Shakers to move out of the area.

We do not provide salary information or other details of employment.

If I can be of further assistance, please contact me by telephone: 574-555-0123.

Sincerely,

Hazel Nutt
Human Resources

Letter of Reference—College Student

[Typed on 8½ by 11-inch stationery and mailed]
(Date)

Mr. Bradley Turnnet
Director of Human Resources
Prommet Enterprises
43 Spring
Springfield, OH 45502

Re: Kelly Vassel Reference

Dear Mr. Turnnet:

As Kelly Vassel's former professor and employer, I am pleased to recommend her for your position of controller. I've known Kelly Vassel for four years, first as a student in two of my economics classes, and then as an intern and research assistant on my Fuller Project.

Kelly was an excellent student, with far above-average grades. She consistently maintained a GPA of over 3.8 (A = 4.0). It was on the basis of her applied scholarship as well as her initiative and participation in class that I offered her the position of intern and research assistant. In this role, Kelly performed independently (after my approval), and was a very worthy employee, demonstrating maturity, creative thought, and the ability to take responsibility. Her work succeeded in helping to secure two grants for the Fuller Project. Her reports and grant applications were well written and comprehensive.

I enthusiastically recommend Kelly to you. She has demonstrated that she is very capable of doing an outstanding job as controller.

Please let me know if I can offer any additional information.

Sincerely,

James Broyles
Professor of Economics

Personal Reference for a Friend

[Typed and mailed]
(Date)

Dear Mr. Archibald:

I'm writing in response to your May 18 letter requesting a personal reference for Saul Bellweather. I have known Saul for 11 years. His father and I are partners in the same law firm, and his mother has been my wife's CPA for 15 years. Our families have gotten together socially over the years of our affiliation, and Saul and my son, Teddy, are best friends.

Saul possesses fine character traits. He has always pursued his own path, excelled in what he set out to do, and carried through on assigned tasks.

If you need further information, please call me. Obviously, I give Saul the highest recommendation.

Sincerely,

Barclay Withers

Recommendation for Promotion Within the Company

[Typed and mailed]
MEMO

DATE: September 5, 2005

TO: Derek Woodward

FROM: Maria Whitmore, VP of Sales

SUBJECT: Leah Harvey Promotion

Leah Harvey has completed her tour here in the fast-track program. Although the youngest in the sales department, Leah has performed well in decision making, problem solving, and negotiating. In fact, she is our number one performer. She closes at the highest rate (76 percent) and in the shortest time (31.5 minutes) of anyone in the department.

Leah desires to be a district sales manager, and I believe she possesses the skills to be one of the best. I recommend we place her in the opening for Region 13.

Recommendation for New Law School Graduate by Professor

[Typed and mailed]
(Date)

Reference: <u>Your Letter of May 12 Requesting a Recommendation for a First-Year Lawyer</u>

Dear George:

Yes, I have an exceptional recommendation for the position at Krause and Krause. I was fortunate enough to have Neil R. Reynolds in three of my classes at Stanford Law School. He is a breath of fresh air. Not only did he finish in the top of his class, he demonstrated rare leadership skills on special team projects. Neil has an intuitive sense of justice—real justice—and came up with completely innovative ways to carry it out to the advantage of all involved on three occasions I recall in detail. I've never seen another student with this ability. I could go on and on.

I tried to get Neil in at Stanton and Gregg, but we took three new graduates last year, and our practice is presently undergoing some changes in scope and direction.

Neil comes with my highest recommendation. If I can offer any additional information, please call.

Sincerely,

Bernardo Blackburn

Recommendation for a Former Employee

[Typed and mailed]
(Date)

Dear Mr. Bellows:

I highly recommend Robert Levine. He worked as my secretary in the office of the president, and as statistical clerk for five years. He had a confident, take-charge manner, which was, at the same time, cordial. His statistical work was accurate and thorough.

In five years, Robert missed three work days. He was always eager to see a project through to completion, even if it meant staying after hours. I don't believe Robert ever angered a customer calling over the telephone (even though there were a few who angered me). In fact, Robert's skills in dealing with clients and callers in this office were outstanding.

Obviously, I recommend Robert. If you'd like any additional information, please call.

Sincerely,

Nathan Neustetter

Recommendation for a Long-Time Customer

[Typed and mailed]
(Date)

Reference: <u>Your Request of April 15 to Supply a Reference for Sidney Wales</u>

Mr. Ray Karnes:

We have done business with Mr. Sidney Wales for 12 years. We are pleased to refer him as an outstanding customer who conducts his business in a conscientious and satisfactory manner.

There has never been an unresolved dispute or an overdue notice in all these years. Oh, that all our customers were so prompt and honest!

If you have any further questions, please call.

Cordially,

Samuel Wise

Recommendation for a General Contractor for Home Remodeling

[Typed and mailed]
(Date)

Dear Mr. and Mrs. Beem:

I'm pleased to recommend Conceptions General Contracting for your custom home remodel. I hired Ted and Alice Reilly, Conceptions owners and principals, eight months ago to complete three bathrooms, kitchen, den, and foyer—a complete redesign through reconstruction. The Reillys scheduled subcontractors so we could continue to inhabit our home while the remodel took place, and they orchestrated every detail exactly as they had promised.

The entire remodel was completed on time and on budget, and we are delighted with the workmanship and quality of every detail. I also found the Reillys' suggestions and recommendations to be invaluable, and they saved us both many dollars and undue frustration.

If there are any other details you'd like to discuss, or if you would like to see the work they completed in our home, please contact us to arrange a time (775-555-0123).

Sincerely,

Dee Yates

Recommendation of Former Graduate Student

[Typed on 8½ by 11-inch stationery and mailed]
(Date)

Dear Dean Callan:

Edward A. Meyer, PhD, is an outstanding scholar, a capable teacher, and a diligent and tireless worker.

Dr. Meyer's scholarship is demonstrated by his 3.8 GPA (out of 4.0) here at Marquette, as well as his performance in undergraduate work at MOO U. He was in two of my human resources classes and did excellent work, making As in both. He demonstrated a keen, scholarly inquisitiveness, and worked diligently to excel. I expect that trait will help him make a great contribution in the field.

I believe he has already begun on that course with the publication of portions of his dissertation in *HR Magazine* and *Administrators' Digest*.

I have heard three of Edward Meyer's speeches, and he did an excellent job in all of them. I have also observed many of his classroom sessions while he served as my graduate assistant for two years. He entered the classroom well prepared, maintained a thoughtful learning atmosphere, and challenged the students to stretch a bit.

In summary, I recommend Dr. Edward Meyer as a teacher of behavioral management. I'll be pleased to discuss any of this information in greater detail if you care to call me.

Sincerely,

Herbert K. Kline, PhD

Offering a Neutral Recommendation

[Typed and mailed]
(Date)

Dear Otto:

Star Reising held the position of customer service representative with Stitches from May 10, 2005, to March 15, 2006. During this period of time she was promoted twice within the department with appropriate salary increases.

Star left Stitches to return to college.

Sincerely,

Melvin Whales

Declining to Give Recommendation

[Typed and mailed]
(Date)

Dear Jackson:

My secretary relayed the message that you called and asked for a recommendation to Breakers for the position of manager you have applied for.

Reflecting on the years we worked together, I do not feel I worked closely enough with you to offer a meaningful evaluation and recommendation on the factors that Breakers will want. I certainly will confirm your employment and salary history if you would like to have someone contact me for that information.

Best wishes in your job future.

Sincerely,

Stanley Blacker

Also see INTRODUCTION, page 154; REFUSING AN APPLICANT, page 143; REPRIMAND, page 172; REQUESTS AND INQUIRIES, page 224; CREDIT DENIAL, page 309; and THANK-YOU, page 76.

20

REFUSING AN APPLICANT

A powerful agent is the right word.

—MARK TWAIN

Since this letter is bad news given to a recipient who may already be under stress, the utmost tact is needed in constructing it. The objective is to maintain a spirit of goodwill, if possible, and to avoid antagonizing the recipient of the letter. At the same time, it's necessary to state your decision conclusively. You need not justify it; doing so may invite the recipient to try to get you to change your mind. (Also see "Declining a Position," page 146, and "Refusal," page 250.)

THINK ABOUT CONTENT
- Start with a positive, neutral statement.
- Thank the applicant for applying, using a positive statement about his or her skills or qualifications, if possible.
- Set up the explanation for refusal, stating only the organization requirements.
- Make a clear statement of refusal.
- Tell the applicant what will happen to his or her application and future prospects with the organization.

- Close with a goodwill statement, offer suggestions or alternatives, or compliment the reader. Any good suggestions, referrals, or compliments will enhance your goodwill efforts.

ELIMINATE WRONG MESSAGES
- Do not make negative statements.
- Make no comparisons with the winning candidate.
- Offer no excuses, and leave no question about the finality of your decision.
- Never blame others for the refusal.

CONSIDER SPECIAL SITUATIONS
- Respond quickly to minimize disappointment.
- Cast your response in terms of your company's needs, and don't reflect on the applicant's lack of qualifications. For example, don't write "You don't meet the requirements" but rather "The position requires at least 10 years experience."
- Applications and resumes received by email may also be refused by email.

SELECT A FORMAT
- Business refusals should be typed on letterhead when your response is by mail.
- Email responses may be sent to those who applied by email.

USE STRONG WORDS

consider	match
consistent	qualifications
decline	respond
experience	review
future	seasoned

BUILD EFFECTIVE PHRASES
after the committee's review

appreciate your application for

appreciate your time and effort

can assure you careful consideration was given

cannot offer you

carefully considered

do not have other openings at this time

evaluations were exacting and thorough

final candidate has been selected

have selected a finalist

many excellent candidates

our decision was made difficult by

please contact us again

require extensive experience

reviewed your excellent qualifications

thank you for applying

the selection process was difficult

will keep your resume on file

WRITE STRONG SENTENCES

Thank you for applying for the office manager position.

The selection committee has selected a candidate with extensive experience in this exact research.

It was a pleasure meeting you.

We will keep your resume on file for six months in case an opening suitable for your qualifications should present itself.

BUILD EFFECTIVE PARAGRAPHS

It was apparent to our selection committee that you have a very bright future in genetics engineering. They were especially impressed with your ideas on cell division.

Thank you for your resume in response to our opening for a marketing director (April *Marketing News*). Your experience is impressive, but this senior position requires at least 15 years in the field.

I would like to suggest you contact Mr. Ray Miller of IN-PLANT Placement. He provides an extraordinary service in connecting candidates with positions in this field.

With your permission, we will keep your resume on file so we may consider you for future openings. Our procedure is to review resumes on file first when a position opens up or is created. If an appropriate position becomes available at Carlisle, we will be pleased to consider you for it.

EDIT, EDIT, EDIT
Make your message as positive, brief, and concise as possible.

Refusing a Production Management Applicant

[Typed]
(Date)

Dear Jack:

Thank you for applying for the production management position at Castle. Both Mr. Reynolds and I were very impressed with your accomplishments over the past five years. The production management position requires, however, extensive experience in the Roberts equipment.

Your inquiry will, of course, be kept confidential, and we will keep your resume in the engineering file should something else open up in the next six months. I wish you continued success in your career.

Yours truly,

Jack Buboinis

Refusing an Underqualified Candidate

[Typed]
(Date)

Dear Ms. Curtis:

Thank you for considering Mason and Mason Engineering as a place of employment. You made a very positive impression here with your outstanding work history and interview skills. As we discussed, however, the present status of our design department and the projects we have in-house demand that we hire a candidate with skills and experience in these specialized areas.

We would like to keep your resume and copies of your work samples on file. We anticipate that six to eight months down the road we may be expanding the design department. At that time, we'll reevaluate our needs. Should you meet them, we will contact you to arrange an interview.

Best wishes for what we know will be a brilliant career.

Sincerely,

Kim Sanders

Refusing a Freelance Submission

[Emailed]

SUBJECT: Picnics Query Response

Dear Jody:

Thank you for submitting "Picnics" for our consideration. It has been read here by several editors, and it is our determination that it doesn't meet our current editorial needs.

"Picnics" shows great promise, and we do hope you'll submit another piece to us in the near future.

All the best,

Ed Getty

Senior Editor

Refusing a Candidate Due to Internal Delay

[Typed]
(Date)

Dear Ms. Schneider:

I was pleased to meet you and discuss the position at General Television for an administrative assistant to the executive director.

I was very favorably impressed with your skills and poise.

Since your interview, we have had other changes in the organization, which have required that we delay hiring an administrative assistant for at least five months.

I would like to keep your resume on file to reconsider at that time, and I invite you to contact us in four months about the position. Again, thank you for coming in. Perhaps we will have the opportunity to discuss this position or another one at a future time.

Sincerely,

Sally Weinstein

Refusal of Submitted Resume

[Emailed]

SUBJECT: Resume Response

Dear Mr. Bellows:

Thanks for sending me your resume. We presently have no temporary openings that match your qualifications, and we are freezing all hiring for permanent positions for the next five months.

If you are seeking a position in June, please watch our website for our posted openings, and resubmit your resume if there should be one that matches your qualifications.

Sincerely,

Lenny Lever

Also see REFUSAL, page 250.

21

DECLINING A POSITION

Tact consists in knowing how far to go too far.

—JEAN COCTEAU

The letter used to decline a job offer is a refusal letter with the central theme of good-will. While you'll want to leave no uncertainty about your decision, your refusal should be stated tactfully. (See "Refusal," page 250.)

DECIDE TO WRITE
- Open with a friendly or neutral "buffer" statement.
- Thank the employer for the job offer.
- Review the facts and give an explanation, if applicable, for declining the offer.
- State in definite, clear, and positive terms that you must decline the offer based on the explanation you presented.
- End the letter on a cordial note, one that establishes or reestablishes a positive relationship.

THINK ABOUT CONTENT
- Make sure you understand the timeframe and respond within it.
- Always leave a situation on good terms. Keep the option for future contact open.
- Keep the lines of communication open even after you have declined the job offer.

ELIMINATE WRONG MESSAGES
- Do not leave your decision open to debate.
- Don't belabor the bad news.
- Don't leave the impression that you will reconsider a modified offer.

SELECT A FORMAT
- The letter should be typewritten on personal stationery.
- Email a response if the application process was conducted through emailing.

SELECT POWER WORDS

appreciate	generous
choice	goals
consider	offer
consideration	opportunity
decision	options
decline	pleasure
description	recognize
difficult	reply
enjoyed	respond
flattered	

BUILD EFFECTIVE PHRASES

a difficult decision

after careful consideration and deliberation

after weighing all the factors

I am flattered, of course, but

I cannot accept the position

I do appreciate the offer

I do sincerely regret

I have concluded that it isn't a proper fit

I have, of course, considered it carefully

I must say no

my final answer is

my final decision must be

thank you for offering

WRITE STRONG SENTENCES

It was a pleasure meeting your fine staff of engineers yesterday.

I was very impressed with the efficiency of the quality-control operation.

Thank you for orchestrating the interview process, and for the offer of the marketing manager position.

BUILD EFFECTIVE PARAGRAPHS

I have enjoyed the past month of interviews and screening for the position of plant manager at Wickliff. I believe you, Brad Williams, and Dennis Bradley make an outstanding team.

I am flattered by the offer of vice president of client affairs at Metcalf and Metcalf. It's an exceptional opportunity; but after careful consideration, I must decline.

Your generous offer of a partnership at Lockhart and Wendell is everything I've worked for these past 12 years. I'm honored that you, David, Lance, and Jacob feel confident in my abilities to fill the position. Ironically, after two days of soul searching and lengthy discussions with Carol and the boys, I must decline.

Meeting you and the other people at Cruthers was a pleasure. I was very impressed with the attention to detail the entire department exhibited in doing their work. And I was, of course, pleased to receive the generous job offer that followed the interviews.

EDIT, EDIT, EDIT

Your ultimate job is to say a concise "no" with a written smile.

Declining Position Due to Accepting a More Suitable Position

[Typed]
(Date)

Dear Mr. Harrison:

I was pleased to receive your offer of employment as a systems analyst for Smathers. I was very impressed with the teamwork that characterizes your staff, and the pride in workmanship that is demonstrated in the products you produce.

However, since the interviews with Smathers, I have been offered another position, which is more closely aligned with my career goals, and I have accepted it.

Thank you for your time and the vote of confidence in selecting me. Please give my thanks to Paul Westbrook and David Winters. I enjoyed meeting all of you and the rest of the Smathers team. I sincerely hope our paths connect again in the future.

Yours truly,

Rick Watters

Declining Employment Due to Accepting a More Suitable Job That Fits Family Goals

[Typed]
(Date)

Dear Mr. Broward:

Yes, I did receive your second offer. It was very generous of you to increase the benefit package.

I appreciated the courtesies extended to me during the interview process, and certainly the after-hours interview arrangements.

I enjoyed meeting the therapy team, too, and feel your program is a very important one. I'm sure it will do very well over the next several years with the goals you have set.

All this made it extremely difficult for me to come to the decision to accept another position in Los Angeles that fits not only my career goals but also allows complete coordination with my wife's career.

Thank you for all your efforts on my behalf. I greatly appreciate your thoughtfulness, and hope we will be able to serve together on one of the various professional committees in the future.

Sincerely,

Reginald McDonald, MD

Declining an Inadequate Offer

[Typed]
(Date)

Dear Ben:

Thank you for the offer to head up the public relations operation at Skaggs. I've reviewed all the aspects of the position, and have tried to make the numbers work, but there's simply not a common ground here. I must decline.

I wish you well, and hope you will find someone with the skills you're looking for to fill the post.

Sincerely,

Gerri Grover

IV. EMPLOYMENT, BUSINESS, AND EMPLOYEE COMMUNICATIONS

22

EMPLOYEE CORRESPONDENCE

The only agreements that ever caused me trouble were the ones I wrote with a handshake.

—ANONYMOUS

Employment correspondence is a category rather than a specific type of letter. Many of the letters and memos in this category are actually types covered elsewhere in this book, but it's important to think of these as a group of communications that details the history of the relationship between the employer and the employee.

Both the employee's and the employer's perspectives are reflected here because all this correspondence should become part of the employee's personnel file reflecting his or her relationship with the organization.

Starting when an applicant tries to secure a position, there may be a number of letters written between the potential employee and employer. Obviously it's in the applicant's best interest to make as many appropriate contacts with a potential employer as possible. During each telephone conversation and each face-to-face meeting, for example, the applicant may create the opportunity to follow up with a letter. These letters can be pivotal in demonstrating his or her writing skills. If this applicant is hired, it is likely that copies of these communications will make their way into the employee's personnel file. During the course of employment, written communications between the employer and the employee become even more important in documenting the history of the relationship.

Because of our litigious society, some of the most important communications to document are difficult or negative messages, such as a reprimand, termination, or resignation. Because they are so important, they need special consideration. (See "Reprimand," page 172, "Employee Termination," page 179, and "Letter of Resignation," page 176.)

DECIDE TO WRITE

This group of letters, memos, and other documents may be used to:
- Respond to a job applicant or candidate
- Apply for a job
- Communicate with an employee
- Communicate with an employer
- Become part of the record for and between employee and employer

THINK ABOUT CONTENT
- Keep job applicants informed in order to create a positive impression of the organization.
- Make it a practice to tell people when they are doing a good job. It does wonders for goodwill and usually improves work quality.
- It is important to maintain a written record of letters of employment; any and all agreements

between the organization and the employee; changes of status with titles and financial agreements; and other decisions made between employer and employee. Make sure you commit these to writing, and keep copies in the appropriate personnel and personal records.

- In addition to following the instructions for the type of letter being written, make sure your letter is clear and to the point.
- Introduce the subject of the letter; state it clearly and concisely.
- Offer the explanation, backing it up with facts.
- Close with a statement of goodwill, or on an upbeat note, if possible.
- In our litigious society, it's important to document all corrective actions that are taken and make these a part of the employee record. (See "Reprimand," page 172.)
- Keep current on legal requirements in relationships with employees, and keep all related records.

ELIMINATE WRONG MESSAGES

- Review pertinent laws, regulations, and policies before writing to avoid any statements that could result in a legal battle.
- Don't write negative messages if you can avoid it. Almost anything you have to say can be said positively. If you are angry, process your anger privately, not in a letter that can be made public.
- Don't use a written message to avoid a verbal exchange. The written employee message, for example, should usually be used to document what has been said in a face-to-face meeting.
- Don't communicate personnel matters through email exchange unless you have an established organizational policy to do so, and a secure computer system.

SELECT A FORMAT

- The interoffice memo is the most commonly used vehicle for employer and employee communications. The exceptions are the letters of employment, termination, and resignation. In these instances a formal typewritten letter on personal or organization letterhead is appropriate.

WRITE STRONG SENTENCES

Two invoices marked "original" were sent for October, November, and December to the Baker Grand Rapids and Sioux City offices.

There was no safety officer on duty from midnight to 8:00 A.M. on February 17 through 25.

Your scheduled date for the complete physical examination is July 5.

You are being promoted to Corbett Vice President of Finances, effective July 1, 2007.

You have used all of your allocated sick days for the employment year of April 1, 2006, to March 31, 2007.

Thank you for your request to go on a flextime work schedule.

BUILD EFFECTIVE PARAGRAPHS

As I discussed with you, the vacation schedule you designed for your department for July and August of this year, 2006, impaired business operations and resulted in extra expenditures, and possibly the loss of two accounts. We had 23 customer complaints of double billing, for example, because payments had not been entered in the computer, and there were about two dozen complaints from our personnel that there was no one in your department to answer questions.

I've reviewed your request for a leave of absence from March 1 through July 31, 2006. Please be in my office in the morning at 10:00 A.M. to discuss this. Bring with you a copy of your physician's recommendation for this leave.

I'm sorry to learn of the interpersonal conflict within the marketing department. I have reviewed possible transfers for you, as you requested. There are three options open. Please be in my office at 10:00 A.M. on Friday to discuss them.

EDIT, EDIT, EDIT

Cut out unnecessary words, and arrange paragraphs so the reader may easily understand the message. Even with difficult communications, end on as positive a note as possible.

Report of Unsatisfactory Performance

[Typed]
MEMO

TO: Richard Parks

FROM: Jim Fuchs

DATE: October 5, 2006

SUBJECT: Rick Hanson's Unsatisfactory Performance

I have just received the fourth customer call this month that Rick Hanson has made a substantial error in analyzing a customer account. Dick, these errors occurred on four of our top accounts. (See attached reports.)

All of these customers have requested a change of analysts. Would you please handle this and let me know by Friday who the new analyst will be?

Warning About Intoxication

[Typed]
(Date)

Dear Lars:

Following up on our discussion of this morning, this is your second and final warning that McGraw does not tolerate intoxication on the job. Your first warning was issued on May 15, 2006, for the incident on May 12, 2006, when you were found to be intoxicated. (Report copies are attached.)

Please be in my office at 9:30 A.M. tomorrow to tell the employee committee why you should not be terminated effective June 15, 2006. The committee will give you their decision on Thursday. As you know, there is a required treatment plan to follow to remain employed here.

Lars, we all want to see you turn this around. We don't want to lose you.

Sincerely,

Joseph Dutton

Sexual Harassment Claim

[Typed]
(Date)

Dear Lisa:

I have reviewed your complaint of sexual harassment by your supervisor, Allan Reek. Again, as we discussed in my office, Dimensions wants to provide a positive work environment for all employees, and that means we will not tolerate sexual harassment.

I have initiated a full investigation by Mort Jansen, plant manager, and Jennifer Swan, vice president, Human Relations. One or both of them will contact you in the manner you requested within the next couple of days.

We will make every effort to resolve this situation swiftly and justly. Please contact Jennifer Swan or me if you have any other questions or comments.

Sincerely,

Marla Drapples

Maternity Leave

[Typed]
(Date)

Dear Julie:

Congratulations on the anticipated birth of your baby! We are extremely happy for you. I have arranged for you to take a leave of absence, as you requested, from July 1, 2006, through December 1, 2006. Jayne Dorsett of personnel will contact you to complete the paperwork.

What an extremely exciting time for you and Bill. We all wish you and your family the very best.

Sincerely,

Alexandria LaSasso

Promotion Denied

[Typed]
(Date)

Dear Alex:

Thank you for your bid for the job opening number 9-9821. It was an extremely difficult decision, and you were well in the running. But after final evaluation of all of the 21 final applicants, Mel Berger was awarded the position.

I was sorry to deliver this disappointing news in our meeting this morning, but I'm sure that your skills and outstanding record will allow you to obtain an equal position in one of the openings coming up in the next few months.

Sincerely,

Martina McPhee

Resolving Favoritism Complaint

[Typed]
MEMO

TO: Nicole Lazar, Manager

FROM: Sandra Lewis, Director of Personnel

DATE: May 10, 2007

SUBJECT: Employee Complaints

As I discussed with you this morning, we have had four complaints alleging favoritism in your treatment of subordinates.

I believe you can resolve this problem by holding a department meeting and explaining the criteria and the selection process that resulted in JoAnn Beales being promoted to assistant manager.

Please let me know by October 12 whether you feel this is satisfactorily resolved without intervention from Personnel. We will have someone from this department attend the meeting and give the job description and qualifications, if you like.

The subordinates involved have also been asked to indicate their response to Personnel, if they wish.

I will get back to you on October 17 to discuss the resolution of this complaint.

Recommendation for Employee Promotion

[Typed on 8½ by 11-inch stationery]
MEMO

TO: Jackson Davis

FROM: Vivian Long

DATE: January 10, 2006

SUBJECT: Daniel Vider's Promotion

I recommend Daniel Vider for the Region Four sales manager position, effective July 1, 2006. His performance over the past 18 months meets the criteria, even surpasses it in some areas:

- His <u>sales</u> are the highest in Region Four. Dan sold 11 percent over his own projected goals, 17 percent over mine.
- His <u>management</u> skills, as demonstrated in his customer correspondence and during customer interviews, rank at a 98 percent "very satisfied." He is also held in high esteem by all the other salespeople.
- Dan's <u>planning</u> and other <u>activity levels</u> I must rate very high also. He set a goal of 45 new customers this year and he has 57. He planned the mail out of four new direct-mail pieces, and met that goal with a 12 percent response rate. His follow-up converted all these respondents to customers, and he brought in another 10 percent from his original mailing list. He has also demonstrated the ability to change directions and adjust his planning to company changes.
- As far as <u>product knowledge</u> and <u>new product applications</u> are concerned, Dan has performed far above average and demonstrates a willingness to work on this area.

I conclude that Dan rates very high in our criteria for both can-do and will-do, and even though he is junior in seniority, we should reward him with this promotion.

See also ACCEPTANCE, page 245; CONFIRMATION AND ACKNOWLEDGMENT, page 240; CONGRATULATIONS, page 30; EMPLOYEE TERMINATION, page 179; LETTER OF RESIGNATION, page 176; REFUSAL, page 250; REFUSING AN APPLICANT, page 143; REPRIMAND, page 172; REQUESTS AND INQUIRIES, page 224; RESUME, page 118; RESUME COVER LETTER, page 109; THANK-YOU, page 76; and WELCOME, page 67.

23

INTRODUCTION

In this world, you must be a little too kind in order to be kind enough.

—PIERRE MARIVAUX

The letter of introduction was created for a much different society, to introduce one person to another for social or business purposes. Today, we live in a very mobile society, equipped with many forms of instant communication, and in a business and social climate of assertiveness. Therefore, the written letter of introduction is seldom used as it once was. When it *is* used for business introduction, it carries little obligation; the social introduction carries more.

The letter of introduction is more often used today to introduce yourself, in situations like that of a professor teaching a class online. It is also used to introduce a new employee or organization representative such as a product manager or sales representative. And it is used to introduce new products or services.

Today the purpose of the letter of introduction is a combination of reference, recommendation, and explanation. For example, the professor teaching an online course will introduce him- or herself with a short personal biography, a listing of course materials (and/or a reference as to where these will be posted to the course website), an introduction to the course, what the class will cover, and what will be expected of students.

DECIDE TO WRITE

Use this letter when you want to introduce:
- One person to another
- A new employee
- A new product or service
- One service or organization to another
- Yourself to subordinates, clients, students, or others with whom you are initiating a business or social relationship

THINK ABOUT CONTENT

- Since the letter of introduction implies the approval of the person being introduced, agree to write it only if you can do so wholeheartedly.
- Give the full name of the person you're introducing and some of his or her background. For a new employee, state the person's position, effective date of employment, and, if appropriate, the person to whom he or she has reporting responsibility. List the pertinent information: new employee's experience, education, expertise, past employers, major clients, special projects, and awards. Ask other employees to welcome the new employee.

- State *why* you want to introduce the two people. Give any characteristics, points of interest the person and the reader may have in common, and any other helpful information.
- Make your letter cordial and brief.
- Offer more than one or two points of commonality, if possible.
- Suggest a meeting time, place, and an arrangement that does not obligate the recipient to entertain the person you are introducing.
- Tell the reader the possible benefits of meeting the person, using the service, or joining the organization.
- Give the reader an opportunity to decline.
- Thank the reader.

ELIMINATE WRONG MESSAGES

- Don't write the introduction casually. Don't, for example, agree to write for a person you do not believe merits it.
- Do not presume the reader will be anxious to meet the person, and don't make statements like "I know you'll be glad to meet him" in your letter.
- Don't just plunge in. Give full consideration to the reader, even though you may be making the introduction as a favor to the person you are introducing.
- The letter of introduction should not obligate the reader to socially entertain the person you are introducing. Be sure not to imply or suggest this.

CONSIDER SPECIAL SITUATIONS

- When you use a letter of introduction to introduce a new sales employee to customers or clients, all the same rules apply. In addition, it's important to affirm your support to both parties.

SELECT A FORMAT

- Unless the recipient is a personal friend to whom you send handwritten letters, the letter of introduction should be typewritten on letterhead or on business, personal, or plain stationery.
- A form letter may be used when the message is being conveyed to a number of recipients, such as the introduction of a new sales representative or a salesperson to customers or clients.

- Introductions to clubs, groups, or associations are best typewritten on personal stationery or the appropriate letterhead, but certainly may be handwritten.

USE WORDS OF CORDIALITY

admire	favor
advocate	introduce
associate	meet
benefit	mutual
character	pleasure
colleague	recommend
endorse	suggest
enjoy	

USE EFFECTIVE PHRASES

benefit from discussing with her

don't feel obligated

great fit, a

greatly appreciate

I admire her very much

I believe you will enjoy

if you have time

introduce to you

I respect very much

may I suggest

much in common

my dear friend and colleague

my pleasure to introduce

recommend you meet

WRITE STRONG SENTENCES

I believe you will enjoy meeting with her.

I think your time will be well spent if you can spare 30 minutes to meet her.

I've heard you mention you would like to meet Dr. Allan Beard.

I'm sure both you and Jennifer will benefit from a brief meeting.

One of my dearest friends, Alex Rivers, will be in Los Angeles next week.

You have heard me mention Joan Brookstone in reference to the new theory on disease control.

BUILD EFFECTIVE PARAGRAPHS

One of my dearest friends, Jenny Creighton, will be in Los Angeles the week of the 21st for the National Advertising Convention. I believe her graphic designs are just what you are looking for to use in the Cooler campaign.

As I said on the telephone, Alice Bradford will be staying at the downtown Empire Hotel, and a message may be left for her anytime after the evening of the 20th. She said she has no plans for lunch on the 22nd or 23rd, and, as we discussed, I told her you may call her.

In addition to her great campaign work, Tink is a fine person with interests in several areas similar to your own: quarter horses and hang gliding. And I believe you could use her skills on future projects. I hope—if you can manage a meeting—that this works out.

EDIT, EDIT, EDIT

Your job is only to create an opportunity. Make sure your information is direct, clear, concise, and bears the tone of cordiality.

Introducing Friends

[Handwritten]
(Date)

Dear Claire:

As I mentioned to you on the telephone, Adeline McDougell is a designer for Limone's. She will be in Baltimore next week for the Women's Forum, and will be staying at the downtown Fairmount Hotel. I believe the two of you would enjoy each other's company. Since you will both be attending the Forum, what better time to meet?

Well, I'll leave the rest up to you. Adeline and I will understand if prior commitments—producing the Forum must be a huge task—make it impossible for you to schedule a time to get together.

My best wishes for the success of this important event.

Sincerely,

Stella Dare

Introducing a Sales Representative to a Customer

[Typed]
(Date)

Dear Bernie:

This will introduce Ned Remick, Smith and French's new Region IV representative. He will be calling on Rx Inc. on Wednesday, next week.

After graduating from Victoria College, Ned spent seven years with Johns and Johns sterile products' division in New Jersey. He distinguished himself for five years as sales representative of the year for their medical instrumentation division.

I think you will find him extremely knowledgeable about our entire product line. He has a well-earned reputation as one of the finest and most conscientious salespersons around.

I think you'll be delighted to know, too, that Ned's a stock-car driver and huge Buff's fan.

Please take a few extra minutes to talk to Ned. I hope you will think as highly of him as I do.

Cordially,

George Cordiss

Introducing Friends to a Club

[Typed]
(Date)

Dear Delmar:

It is a pleasure for Sandra and me to introduce Winn and Gloria Stickler to the Greenwood Country Club. The Sticklers have been distinguished members of the Shaker Heights Country Club in Omaha for over 15 years, and have just moved to Denver in the past three months.

It has been our privilege to have been both business associates and personal friends of the Sticklers for over 17 years. They are truly two of the finest people we know, and people who have contributed greatly to the community in terms of fund-raising for lung disease.

If the Sticklers desire to join Greenwood, Sandra and I would be honored to sponsor them. (They could help us win that elusive mixed doubles tennis championship.)

Sincerely,

Dexter Dowd

Introducing a New Personal Trainer

[Emailed]

Dear Amy and Jake:

I'd like to introduce Roger Bilks, who will serve as your new personal trainer. He replaces Jennifer Watkins, who is presently on maternity leave.

Roger has been with Fit as a Fiddle for seven years, starting as a receptionist in May 2005, and working his way up to personal trainer this past June. He has distinguished himself as an outstanding body-builder and certified trainer.

I believe you will find Roger very skilled in helping you make sure every aspect of your fitness is achieved. Please email him at rbilks@fitasafiddle.com, or call him at 555-0123 to introduce yourselves.

Sincerely,

Joe Banks
President

Introducing a Business Associate

[Typed]
(Date)

Dear Conchita:

It's my pleasure to introduce Margaret Merritt, who served as vice president in charge of book buying for Bookworms for over 15 years. Since a family move takes her from us to Bakersville, our considerable loss may be your gain.

Margaret is fully capable to stepping directly into the management of your store, so you may start that carefree retirement you so deserve.

Margaret and her husband, Jim, are in Bakersville until the 25th, and I'm sure she would be happy to arrange an appointment. You can reach her at 555-0123.

So nice to hear from you. Give my best to Ralph, and I look forward to receiving those postcards from remote and exotic places. You've earned it!

Best,

Jo Roberts

Introducing a Graduate Student

[Emailed]
(Date)

Dear Dr. Rodham:

This will introduce Kevin B. Doerr, PhD candidate in our department here at the University of Minnesota. As we discussed, I greatly appreciate your willingness to show Kevin your work on the absorption experiments. I'm sure you will find him a brilliant student. He is also prepared to discuss with you our related work here.

Please let me know if I may return the favor for one of your associates. I'd be happy to consider a candidate you would recommend for our program here.

Kevin will, incidentally, call your office on Wednesday morning to set an appointment time.

With regards,

Giles Newbuck

Introducing a Business Associate

[Emailed]
(Date)

Dear Ben:

I'd like to introduce Roger Eggbert from the *Chicago Herald*. As I mentioned on the telephone, Roger is doing a special series on small business practices that work, including marketing techniques that make a real difference in sales volumes. Yes, I can tell you with confidence that Roger has never misquoted me, nor presented a one-sided or biased report.

As part of Roger's research, he is putting similar companies from different geographical locations together in a long-distance, teleconferencing program. I've sat in on several of these groupings, which meet through the miracle of telecommunications, and it's amazing what they are accomplishing. I think you would find it very helpful. They also continue communication through an online forum.

Roger will call you next week and set a time to meet with you. If you decide to participate, I'll be eager to hear what you think about it.

Sincerely,

Bea Ross

Introducing Yourself as Professor

[Emailed]

Dear Students:

I'd like to introduce myself. My name is Daniel Q. Rogett, PhD, and I'll be your professor for the online creative writing class 402.A: "Writing for the Big Screen."

I graduated from the University of Iowa's MFA program in 1988, and then attended the University of Colorado's law school, graduating with a JD in 1991. After seven years in the fantasy world of law practice at Herbert, Jacobs, and Hazelnutt, I returned to the reality of my true passion, writing lifelike characters for film. I also continue to practice part-time as an attorney in the area of literary law. Over the past seven years, I've written seven screenplays, four of which sold to Dreamfield Productions. These were produced, and have appeared on the big screen as the films *Just Desserts, April Fools, Warlords,* and *Celebration.* (If you have any criticisms of these films, you'll get an opportunity to state them in class.)

All the details for the class are listed on the website I've set up, www.isu.edu/screenwriting. The class text, assignments, and schedule are also listed there. Online chatroom discussions, which you are required to attend, will be held on Tuesday evenings from 7:00 P.M. to 9:30 P.M. Forum questions and comments may be posted on cwlists@isu.edu.

You may reach me or my assistant, Dana Smith, with any additional questions at 805-555-0123 or by email at drogett@isu.edu.

Welcome to "Writing for the Big Screen." You will work very hard in this class, but by the end of the semester, you will have finished your first complete draft of an actual screenplay.

Sincerely,

Daniel Q. Rogett, PhD

Introducing a Business Service

[Emailed]

Dear Maggie:

We talked a number of months ago about finding an accounting firm for auditing and other financial services we both needed. I'd like to introduce you to Arthur Q. Small and Associates, a full-service, small-business accounting services firm, located in the southeast part of town near my business.

Maggie, this man is excellent. He comes to my office, picks up my records (or examines them on the spot), and gets back to me with the results and completed audits or whatever else I need the next day. I couldn't be happier with the quality of his service, his charges (well, maybe if they were free!), or the ease of having him complete the work. I must also say he has already saved me a considerable amount of money by creating a new billing process, which he also administers on my behalf. Take a look at his website, www.small.com, for a complete listing of services and charges.

If you are still looking for this service, you may want to contact him at 555-0123.

Best wishes,

Elena Boots

Also see LETTER OF RECOMMENDATION, page 136.

MEMO

At the speed of business today, if you wait two days to get something printed and sent out, it is dated.

—JAY R. SCROGGINS

The memo or memorandum is the lifeblood of any organization. It is the informal, written communication used within the organization among its members. A memo may be a short note, a report, or a much longer document such as a plan, analysis, or proposal. The memo is also used to communicate with outside organizations and individuals with whom you have an ongoing relationship. Today memos are often, if not always, sent by email.

While memos vary in formality and length, the quality of writing should be conversational in tone and tailored to the reader. A few organizations still call these memos *internal letters, interoffice letters,* or *intraorganizational reports,* though more often, when they are sent electronically, they are simply referred to as "emails."

Effective memos are essential to the success of any organization because they provide a clear record of decisions made and actions taken. They also inform, delegate, instruct, announce, request, and transmit documents. It's important to know that careers are made and broken on memo writing power or the lack of it. Remember, each good memo you write will help your reputation and promotability.

DECIDE TO WRITE

Use the memo wisely to:

- Distribute information across organizational lines.
- Communicate policy and procedures up and down organizational ranks.
- Create a permanent, organizational record of plans, decisions, instructions, and actions.
- Confirm verbal discussions and decisions.

THINK ABOUT CONTENT

Before You Write

- Understand your organization's memo policies and protocol, particularly reporting responsibilities, etiquette, and the filing system for storing memos. Follow protocol when you decide whom to address and whom to copy. Here's an example: in many organizations, if a middle manager addresses the memo to his supervisor *and* a vice president, this indicates the manager has a direct reporting relationship to both. Sending a copy to the vice president, in this example, may indicate a direct reporting responsibility to the supervisor and a reporting access to the vice president. In some organizations, sending the memo directly to the vice president would be considered circumventing the proper chain of command.

- Determine the need for your memo. (Creating a blizzard of paper or electronic messages should not be your objective.)
- Be sure you have all the information you need. Do more research if in doubt.
- Consider consulting the people affected to get their input before writing a memo.
- Do the necessary research to make sure you have all the background facts and information.
- Apply the principles in chapter 1, "Getting Started," to ensure your best writing.
- Remember, one message equals one memo. Two messages equal two memos.
- If you find yourself unable to take a clear position, reexamine the need to write the memo.

As You Write

- Begin by distilling the subject matter into a concise, core statement.
- Have your reader firmly in mind, and select the most appropriate language. Keep it conversational yet businesslike and easy to understand.
- Outline the memo points, dividing your information into introduction, body, conclusion, summary, and recommendations. You may select the time sequence pattern or the cause-and-effect pattern, whichever is more logical. For clarity and ease of reading, use subheadings, lists, and numbers when appropriate.
- Use the subject line to tell the reader the specific topic of your memo. For example: "Subject: New Newton copier (model 150) will be installed Friday." Remember, the subject line will also be

used to file the memo. Here are several examples:

Change This	To This
Subject: Performance Evaluation	Subject: Robert Kurtz, Performance Evaluation
Reference: Vacation Schedule for July and August	Reference: Shipping Department Vacation Schedule for July and August
Subject: Sales Training Seminars	Subject: Sales Assistant Sales Training Seminar May 10–25

- Write concisely, using positive statements and action words whenever possible.

Editing What You've Written

- Reread, delete, rearrange more logically, and edit out the non-essential.
- Ask yourself:
  — Have I included all the facts the reader needs to know?
  — Have I answered *who, what, why, where, when,* and *how?*
  — Do the points in my memo progress logically?
  — Have I used section headings and numbers where they could add clarity?
  — Does it flow?
  — Have I used transitions to carry the reader from one paragraph to the next?
  — Does my memo have a conclusion, and/or a call to action?
- Set the memo aside for a period of time, even an hour, if possible. This allows you a "fresh" look and new objectivity when you go back for a final edit.

- Be sure you have summarized or concluded your memo properly and have made a recommendation or outlined the next step of action.
- Finally, read it aloud to yourself. "Hearing" your memo will reveal overused words, unnatural tone, and/or stilted words or phrases. Refer to the lists in this chapter and those in chapter 1, "Getting Started" for examples of words to substitute or cut.

ELIMINATE WRONG MESSAGES

- Don't transmit legal, accounting, or private personnel information through email without insuring there's a secure system in place, and fully understanding Sarbanes-Oxley Act compliance and your organization's email policy.
- Don't copy and/or paste someone's material into a memo without first getting permission and properly crediting the person.
- Don't be ambiguous or vague; be direct, specific, and concrete.
- Don't use an autocratic tone (for example, "I demand," "You must," "It has been decided," and so on). It is unacceptable in most organizations today.
- Don't assign blame or whine.
- Don't pad. Keep your memo to the point.
- Don't deliver a "me-too message" just to have input unless you have been asked for an opinion or vote. Then only "I agree" or "I disagree" is appropriate if you don't have new material to add.
- Don't use officious, stuffy, or formal words when simpler words will work better. Do use the correct technical word when that's the most precise and acceptable.
- Avoid negative, accusatory, demanding, or harsh words and phrases. Negative emotions should not be expressed in your memo. If necessary, have someone else write it. Here are some examples of words and phrases you may want to replace:
  — I cannot understand why you
  — you have failed to
  — I insist
  — I require
  — compelled
  — ignore
  — remit promptly

  — unsatisfactory
  — failure on your part
  — you made an inexcusable error
  — delinquent
  — I must demand
  — no excuse will be accepted
  — a wrong action has been taken
  — cancel the order
  — tardy for work
  — unsatisfactory performance
- Avoid superlatives. Facts, numbers, and statistics are much better.

CONSIDER SPECIAL SITUATIONS

- In our litigious society, it's important to avoid memo content that could be actionable. One way to avoid problems is to keep your memo free of race and gender references. If you have any questions about the content of your memo, consult an attorney.
- Know that anything you write can come back to haunt you in a very public way, even if you've labeled it "confidential." Your memo could one day be published right after your name.
- Always give yourself "think time." Tomorrow you may not want to send that negative memo. In fact, try to put every memo in positive form.
- Give the reader visual clues. The layout of your memo helps your message.
- Measure the words you've used; don't go to extremes. "Never" and "always" aren't good choices, nor are accusing names or characterizations. (Incidentally, make sure you destroy what you've thought better of. The contents of wastebaskets can show up in embarrassing places.)
- Don't generalize. Be sure to document what you've written.
- Use the proper organizational channels. Don't circumvent the lines of authority.
- Memos not only cover tails; they also document sources. Your good ideas should be put into memo form and copies kept in your files. If *your* organization allows it, copy up the organizational line to superiors.
- If you state a problem, offer a solution, or at least alternatives and/or a plan for further action.

- For memos about upcoming *meetings,* do the following:
  — State your objective.
  — Outline the plan of action.
  — Assign tasks to people to ensure they are involved and come prepared to participate.
  — Ask yourself *who, what, when,* and *where* to check for complete content.
  — Give reasons and credit. For example, if the meeting is in response to staff requests, point that out.
- For meeting *agendas:*
  — Give your agenda an action bias.
  — List the *who, what, when,* and *where.* (The *how* and *why* may be the goals of the meeting.)
- For *progress reports:*
  — Use significant action headings.
  — Use action words.
  — Make the report succinct but complete.
  — Summarize the action.
- For *announcements:*
  — Make organization members feel involved. Major changes should be discussed, comments and feedback considered, and alternatives weighed before decisions are made. This eliminates the possibility of people feeling insulted and/or left out of the process.
  — Promotions, resignations, and transfers should be given verbally and followed up with a written announcement.
  — For personnel appointments, it is helpful to include a statement or two about the person's interests and hobbies.
- For *bad news memos:*
  — Make sure members of your organization hear it from you first, not from an outside source.
  — Start out with a positive statement, whenever possible.
  — State specifically what the problem or bad news is, and what the organization is doing about it.
  — Take responsibility for any errors or misjudgments you've made: state them clearly, but don't grovel.
  — Relate the impact on the organization and its members.
  — Ask for specific cooperation and/or action.
  — Promise to keep members informed and keep that promise.
- For *policies and procedures memos:*
  — Be specific about *why* changes are being implemented, and be sure to give the *who, what, where, when,* and *how.*
  — Explain the nature of the changes in terms of what exists now.
  — Make a response as easy as possible.
  — Use bullets, numbers, and headings to help readers absorb points more easily.
- For *recommendations:*
  — Put recommendations up front. Let your readers know why they are important.
  — Give the reasons for the recommendations.
  — State the benefits briefly.
  — End by restating your recommendation and telling the reader the next action step to be taken.

NOTE SOME EXCEPTIONS

* Some organizations use memos to communicate with other organizations. One example is public relations or advertising agencies, which often use memos to communicate with client organizations. A "Client Memo" or "Contact Report" from the agency to the client organization records decisions and supplies information for accounting purposes. (See other appropriate chapters in this section.)
* A few organizations still use form memos so hand-written messages to customers are quick and easy. The forms have several sheets and a copy of the original message stays with copies of responses.
* Subsidiary organizations under one corporate umbrella may use interorganizational memos.

SELECT A FORMAT

* Online email forms make replies very easy. Fill in the "TO:" line last to make sure you don't send a memo before you're completely satisfied with how it reads.
* For printed, paper memos, use internal memo formats. When financial and personnel memos are done on paper, because of confidentiality issues, first sheets are usually printed:

Memo
To:
From:
Date:
Subject:

* Sometimes "confidential" forms are available for restricted-distribution memos. Some organizations print:

__ for your information
__ for your action
__ for your reply

on message-and-reply "speedy messages." (Replies may be handwritten.) Forms may be printed in half sheets ($8\frac{1}{2}$ by $5\frac{1}{2}$ inches) or regular letter size ($8\frac{1}{2}$ by 11 inches). These memos may be color-coded, triplicate perforated forms with well-established distribution lines.

* The subject line functions like a title and aids in filing and later retrieval. Make sure it is topical and complete, not vague and nondescript. Capi-talize all major words in the subject line except articles, conjunctions, or prepositions of fewer than four letters, unless the word is first or last. Don't use all caps in the email subject line unless the subject is worthy of a "shout."

* Signing or initialing a memo is a matter of choice. It usually signifies you approve of the contents. (Corporate policy may require an encrypted digital signature on email.) Initials or signature usually go beside your typed name, and may be installed on your email as well.

USE POWER WORDS

action	order
analysis	outlines
announce	policy
assign	procedure
attached	progress
conclude	proposal
confirm	propose
deadlines	reminder
guidelines	renew
information	report
initiate	review
input	revise
instructions	start
list	status
meet	summary
notice	

BUILD EFFECTIVE PHRASES

all our in-depth research and discussion indicate
all the facts aren't in, but here's what we
all the facts indicate that
I believe this will clear up the confusion
I'd appreciate your input by
our preliminary conclusion is
plan to start using this procedure
please confirm you will be able to attend
please distribute this information
the effective change date will be
this plan of action is proposed
this summarizes yesterday's meeting
we're all pleased to announce
you will be pleased to learn that
you'll see why these conclusions were reached

WRITE STRONG SENTENCES

Use simple, strong words and eliminate unnecessary ones.

Thank you for recommending Jim Baker for the assistant director position.

I'm impressed with your recommendation to start a flextime policy.

Unfortunately I can't approve your July 1 to 15 vacation request.

April production figures slipped 4 percent below present levels.

I just want you to know you are a candidate for the position; the selection process will start December 7.

For the first time, production figures surpassed estimates.

A special sexual harassment seminar will be held for all manufacturing supervisors, Level II or above, May 16–17, 9:30 A.M. to 4:00 P.M. (lunch will be served) at the Regency Hotel.

At the suggestion of Dick Power, I'm requesting a copy of your memo dated February 7 on the Model P-14 performance.

BUILD EFFECTIVE PARAGRAPHS

Subject: New Flextime Increases Production and Reduces Absenteeism at Drexel

Drexel Systems reports a 16 percent increase in production and a 15 percent reduction in absenteeism over six months after converting Level II personnel to flextime. I believe we can adapt Drexel's flextime changeover plan to work well at Lexington. Here's the background information, a discussion of the advantages and disadvantages (including impact on other divisions), a fiscal impact statement, and recommendations for implementation.

Subject: Final Fisher Contract Attached

Attached is the final Fisher contract as amended during our conference call today. Please review it. If you find items not in compliance with the necessary safety requirements, contact me by 4:00 P.M. today. Here's a list of the changes:

Page 7
Line 4 changed from "to all those involved" to "assembly-line personnel."

Page 9
Line 12 changed from "The contract shall be in effect for 7 months" to "The contract shall be in effect for 9 months."

Subject: Graystone Hotel Collateral Pieces Status Report

I met with Joe Adams to complete the review of the insert sheets for the new sales brochure. Everything was approved. I am waiting for his final figures so we can finish the typesetting and complete the printing. The folders are now being printed.

EDIT, EDIT, EDIT

Use simple, clear, powerful words. In addition to the list below, see the list in chapter 1, "Getting Started," page 2.

Use	*Instead of*
about	pertaining to
about	with regard to, with reference to
because	inasmuch as
before	prior to
by	on the basis of
by	on the part of
consider	take under advisement
during	in the course of
for	in the amount of
for	on behalf of
has	in a satisfactory manner
if	in the event that
if	provided that
like	along the lines of
like	in the nature of
may	may, or may not
never	under no circumstances
now	at this point in time
occasionally	on the few occasions
since	on the grounds that, owing to the fact that
soon	in the near future
to	with a view to
today	as of this date
want	be desirous of
whether	whether or not

Board of Directors Meeting Assignments

[Emailed]

SUBJECT: Assignments for the Board of Directors Meeting

The meeting will be held on October 10 at 2:00 p.m. in the Main Boardroom.

Presenter	Agenda Item	Purpose	Time Allotted	Background Reading
K. C.	Production	Information	10 mins.	Mfg. Report
E. E.	Cost analysis	Information	10 mins.	Financial Reports
A. M.	Market report	Discussion	45 mins.	Market Research Report
S. B.	Facilities	Information	15 mins.	Operations Report
M. M.	Long-term plan	Decision	45 mins.	Annual and Planning Reports

Appointment Announcement

[Emailed]

Subject: Aimee Spicer Named Vice President of Marketing

I'm pleased to announce that Aimee Spicer will become our Vice President of Marketing on April 1. Aimee has been with Adams Electronic Systems as Assistant Marketing Director for the past five years, and has helped Adams grow from $21 million in gross annual sales to over $35 million. She knows our business extremely well and has already begun to formulate plans for the expansion of the Circuit Board Division.

A graduate of MIT, Aimee spent the first three years of her career on the West Coast with Pacific Systems, where she served as regional chairperson for the United Way.

Outside the office Aimee's interests were varied and goal-oriented. In both Walnut Creek and Boston, Aimee coached Little League teams. Several won the city championship under her guidance. She has also played co-ed softball for six years; in three of those years her teams won the state championship.

Let the recruiting for our softball teams officially begin! And please make Aimee feel welcome.

Request for Recommendations

[Emailed on a secure system]

Subject: Personnel Manual Recommendations Due Feb. 10

February 10 is the deadline for recommended changes to our personnel manual. Here's how we will handle the revision process:

1. Please review the present manual, discuss recommended changes with your department personnel, and make notations on policies your people feel need to be changed.
2. Submit these recommendations to me in writing by February 10.
3. I will prepare and return to you a complete set of all recommendations, "Employee Manual Recommendations," by April 25.
4. Please discuss these recommendations in your department and return any further comments to me by May 1.
5. Department heads will meet May 10 at 9:30 a.m. in the boardroom to make final revision decisions.

Client Memo

[Emailed on a secure system]

Subject: Chateaux Advertising/Sponsorship in the Steve Watson Golf Classic

I talked with the producers of the Steve Watson Golf Classic Program this morning and reserved the 1/4-page black-and-white ad in the Classic Program magazine. This makes us a "Hole Sponsor," which includes two tickets to play the golf tournament and two tickets each to the banquet, breakfast, and luncheon. We may now elect one (or none) of three options:

1. Upgrade the Hole Sponsorship to a full page, four-color ad (instead of the 1/4-page black-and-white ad) for $1,600.
2. Add one golf player to the Hole Sponsorship for an additional $250.
3. Select a "Corporate Sponsorship"—we could enter three golf players—for $2,250. For this price, we would not get the bells and whistles—the banquet, the breakfast, and the luncheon—but we could host a table in the hospitality tent.

I recommend we select item #1. This is the best value because it allows us to narrowcast our advertising in this publication (10,000 are being printed), which will be kept as a memento.

Please let me know your decision by May 26.

Establishing a New Program

[Emailed]

Subject: Establishing a Residential and Commercial Real Estate Education/ Internship Program

I would like to discuss with you the possibility of establishing a residential and commercial real estate education/internship program here at Woods, using NACREE members as guest lecturers. Can you meet Friday, April 23 at 2:00 P.M. in the boardroom for a 30-minute discussion of program topics, specific people, and dates?

Please respond by 4:00 P.M. tomorrow.

Recommendation

[Emailed on a secure system]

Subject: Mary Turney Recommended for Media Relations Spokesperson

I recommend we appoint Mary Turney to act as media representative for Action Toys. This will eliminate the media problems that have arisen since the introduction of our new Buffalo Bill miniature. The media has been interviewing anyone leaving the plant, and this has resulted in inaccurate information being disseminated to the public. It has also portrayed an inconsistent and sometimes negative image of Action Toys.

Mary's experience in media relations and newscasting qualifies her for this job. I believe her appointment will correct our image problem and help get our Buffalo Bill promotion back on track.

I recommend we vote on the appointment Friday, January 15, 2:30 P.M., at the board of directors' meeting. Please put it on the agenda.

Loss of Account

[Emailed on a secure system]

Subject: Loss of US Army Telephone Services Account

I am sorry to announce that the new US Army Telephone Services contract, which represented 35 percent of our business this year, was awarded to Action Systems, beginning November 1. This will slice our gross income at TTI by approximately 42 percent.

This, of course, will impact all departments. I will have complete information on the details of that impact after Jim Harrison, CFO, finishes his computations on November 4.

It is important to say that TTI personnel performed well on the US Army account and the change in services contractor is routine. It does not reflect any customer dissatisfaction.

It is also important to tell you that our Sales and Marketing Department is in final negotiations on $24 M in bids to three potential customers for contracts that will begin January 1. The department has another $45 M in bids in process with contract dates to begin between February and May. (The Sales and Marketing Department has secured nearly 65 percent of the accounts bid over the past two years.)

Immediately, the loss of the Army account has made it necessary to furlough eight service technicians, four home office accounting personnel, and eight part-time clerks. These people have all been notified. Also, the position of Assistant Marketing Director held by Henry Madison has been eliminated and Henry will leave TTI on Friday. I do not believe any additional staff reductions will be necessary.

I will keep you informed of new developments, and I request your best efforts to help TTI pull together in these transitional weeks ahead.

New Procedure

[Emailed on a secure system]

Subject: New Computer Disk Backup Procedure

Friday's fire in the reception area resulted in our insurance carrier, Stateside Inc., insisting on a procedural change in computer files backup. While McGaw didn't lose any files in the fire, we could have because we have not been consistent in requiring that every department back up computer files.

After much discussion and input from all of you, here is the new policy, which begins today:

- Those working on computers will be responsible to make and update backups every hour. Specific assignments will be made in each department.
- If you are working off-site, be sure you back up on corporate systems.
- Every week, Margaret Willis will check on all the essential data backup off-site storage. Coordinate this information from your department with her.

Please reply to me, indicating you have made all the assignments in your department, by 4:00 p.m. today. If you have any questions or comments, please call me.

Meeting Announcement

[Emailed]

To: All Department Heads

From: Joan Alexander

Date: May 10, 2007

Subject: Weekly Department Head Meeting, May 17, 2007, 9:30 a.m., Boardroom

Agenda:

1. Vote on the vacation policy.

2. Elect a media spokesperson.

3. Introduce the new vice president of marketing, Mark Halpern.

Also see ANNOUNCEMENT, page 21; INFORMAL REPORT, page 200; INTRODUCTION, page 154; LETTER OF RECOMMENDATION, page 136; and TECHNICAL REPORT AND TECHNICAL WRITING, page 204.

25

MEETING NOTICES, AGENDAS, AND MINUTES

To drift is to be in hell,
to be in heaven is to steer.

—GEORGE BERNARD SHAW

 Organizations are powered by meetings. And meetings operate best if there are a stated purpose and a plan known to those who will participate. It's important to create a permanent record and to let those who don't attend know what happened at a meeting. For these reasons, meeting notices, agendas, and minutes were created.

The meeting notice gives the place, date, time, and purpose of the meeting. It usually asks for a response concerning attendance, and sometimes a vote.

The agenda also includes the place, date, and time of the meeting, but its primary function is to list topics that will be covered.

Meeting minutes provide a chronological, written, and accurate record of what happened at the meeting. Minutes may be a brief outline or a very detailed and prescribed form, depending on the audience. Besides providing a record, the process of taking minutes helps direct the group to take action. Minutes also inform absent members and a larger audience (if circulated) about what went on.

The meeting report, unlike the minutes, is not comprehensive. The report (see "Informal Report," page 200) presents conclusions, recommendations, and sometimes a summary of the points and discussion.

THINK ABOUT CONTENT

Notice of Meeting

- Meeting notices are sometimes given long in advance and sometimes on the spur of the moment. In either case, it is necessary to inform enough participants to make sure there will be the attendance needed to conduct business. (The number of qualified participants needed to vote on issues and whether absentee or proxy voting can be used must be checked with the organization bylaws.)

- The written notice must include date, place, time, and the business to be conducted. Remember to cover the *who, where, when, what,* and *why.*

- Ask for confirmation of attendance. If possible, include the meeting agenda, and make any pre-meeting assignments or requests.

- Include all materials necessary so that participants will understand the issues to be discussed.

- Enclose an absentee ballot or a proxy voting form if provided for in the organization bylaws.

- Ask those who won't attend for their input before the meeting.

Attendance Response

- To confirm attendance, state you will attend; confirm the place, date, time, and any travel arrangements; confirm you will complete any premeeting assignment; and give input on any agenda items.
- To decline attendance, identify the meeting; state why you can't attend; mention how you plan to follow up (reading minutes, sending someone in your place, telephoning an attendee, etc.); give any input, approvals, voting power, comments, suggestions, etc. that will be helpful or necessary to the success of the meeting.

Agenda

- Identify the date, place, and time of the meeting. When a speaker, meal, or other item is included, the agenda may be called a program. (*Robert's Rules of Order* covers procedures for the agenda.)
- Arrange items of business in a logical order. Times may be listed for each of the items. The order is usually a call to order, reading of approved minutes from the last meeting, reports from the officers and committees, old business, new business, announcements, and adjournment.

Minutes

- Minutes are difficult to write. The recorder must thoroughly understand the dynamics of the group as well as the history of the subject. The recorder, usually the secretary, must summarize the reasoning of the group without being subjective. Select the recording person carefully.
- List the date, time, place, and kind of meeting; the name of the group; those in attendance; and those absent.
- Produce minutes in abbreviated or full form, depending upon the organization bylaws. But do include the following information:
  - List any substitutes or guests present.
  - List whether the minutes of the last meeting were approved and any corrections made.
  - Include a mention or summaries of any reports. Copies may be attached.
  - All main motions in their final form with the names of the sponsor and seconds must be listed. Give the decision made concerning each motion.
  - Record all the action as it happened.
  - List the date the minutes were written and the name and signature of the writer under "Respectfully submitted."
- Complete the writing and approval of the minutes effectively:
  - Tape-record meetings if formal minutes are required.
  - Write minutes as soon as possible after the meeting.
  - Make sure dates, days, names, and actions are accurate.
  - Have others review minutes and make any corrections before they are finally edited if possible.
  - Proofread and incorporate any reviewer changes.
  - Distribute copies.
  - Approve and accept minutes of previous meeting.
  - Keep a copy of the minutes in a permanent file.

ELIMINATE WRONG MESSAGES

- Omit summarizing discussions and routine announcements.
- Never include personal comments or opinions. Make sure the minutes are completely objective.

SELECT A FORMAT

- Format is dictated by the organization. If minutes are printed out and not just submitted by email, they should be done on organization letterhead, typed, single-spaced, and arranged with a minimum of one inch of white space on all sides.
- Use headings, subheads, numbers, and indentation to make the minutes visually appealing and easier to understand.

Announcing a Meeting

[Emailed]

Dear Dylan:

I have scheduled a producers' meeting for 2:00 to 4:00 P.M., July 7, in conference room 4B on the lot. Can you make it?

We need to decide on final details, cost factors, and the final supporting cast members for the *Last Knight* production. We also need to fill the remaining production openings. (See my list of issues and candidates attached.)

Let me know immediately if you have a conflict, or to confirm your attendance. Come with your choices and recommendations. We need your input to get this wrapped up.

Sincerely,

Jeff Spellbinder

New Organization Meeting Announcement

[Emailed]

Dear Audrey:

I finally have some news about the meeting of the ARRF alumni in the Savanna area. We will meet on August 6 from 6 to 8 P.M. in the Brown Palace Regency Room.

The purpose of the meeting is to get acquainted with other alumni and to decide if we will form a local chapter. Mr. Edward Keivers, executive director of the alumni organization in Los Angeles, will give a 30-minute presentation on what their chapter is doing. He'll also answer any questions about local activities.

There are over 30 local ARRF alumni organizations across the country, and Ralph Weiner will take about 15 minutes to give us an overview of what those organizations have accomplished for members and their communities.

Please respond, letting me know if you will attend and indicating your level of interest in this organization. If you have any questions, call Myron Meeker at 818-555-0123.

I look forward to seeing you on the 6th. Please come early and get acquainted.

Sincerely,

Byron Bennett

Meeting Notice and Agenda Letter

[Emailed]

Dear Ellen:

The Regional Sales Representative Quarterly Meeting is set for March 12 at the Executive Inn (I-25 and Belleview) in the Orchids Room from 9 A.M. to 5 P.M. (Please print out the following agenda for your reference.) Unless I get an email telling me differently, I will expect you to attend.

We will have full details on the new product lines with complete training sessions.

9:00–10:30 A.M.	Customer Profile	*Darlene Darling*
10:30 A.M.–12:30 P.M.	You, the Salesperson	*Logan Greene*
12:30–2:30 P.M.	Luncheon	
2:30–6:30 P.M.	Big Sales Country	*Cleo Pengass*
	Seminar Breakout Sessions	*Frank Dickens, Alex Saunders, Jennifer Fenders, Marilyn Dougherty*

See you there.

Sincerely,

Robertson Givens

Email Confirmation of Attendance

[Emailed]

Dear Dexter:

Of course I'll be at the September 15 meeting at the Broadmoor in Colorado Springs. I agree, the four mornings will be very heavy.

Yes, I'd be pleased to make my "Marketing Blunders" presentation. Given the schedule, I'll make it interactive. I'll need a blackboard, an overhead projector, and a portable microphone. Will you please have your department coordinator arrange these items?

Please confirm my hotel late arrival on the 14th. I can't get in until 10:45 P.M.

I look forward to the meeting. It sounds like an outstanding lineup.

Sincerely,

Sidney Bartles

Meeting Agenda

[Emailed]

GREEN ACRES HOMEOWNERS' ASSOCIATION
BOARD OF DIRECTORS' MEETING

January 11, 2007
7 P.M.–9 P.M., Clubhouse

Residents Welcome

Agenda
Call to Order
Minutes of the Last Meeting
Management Report, Harry Stropp and David Piper
Financial Report, Jeff Swindler
Old Business
  Surveys, Bill Waverly
  Recycling, Bill Waverly
New Business
  Landscaping/Gardening Recommendation, Kathy Klein
Financial Committee Proposal, Jeff Drummer
  Audit
  Cash Management Policies
  Reserves/Dues Increase
Management Contract Bids Review
Misc.

Adjournment

Meeting Minutes (Abbreviated Form)

[Emailed]

AARD Meeting
Minutes

Meeting was September 14, 2007

Commission Members Present: Jerry Holder, Janice Johnson, Bill Wesson, David Wrestler

Staff Members Present: David Weaver, Daphne Justice, Warner Stiles

Staff Members Absent: June Cummings

A regular meeting of the AARD Commission was called to order at 7:05 P.M. on Wednesday, September 14, 2007, at the headquarters conference room, 3400 Riverfront Drive, Phoenix, AZ. The president was in the chair, and the secretary was present.

The minutes of the August meeting were read and approved upon a motion by Jerry Holder.

The treasurer's report was a financial statement with a balance on hand, as of September 1, of $455,655.76.

New business included a proposed motion by David Weaver "that we appoint a subcommittee to review the possibility of investing Commission funds for greater financial return."

A motion was made by Daphne Justice "to hold the annual picnic as we did last year." The commission voted to hold a picnic, and Janice Johnson was appointed to head a picnic committee.

After a review of the new approval procedure, the meeting adjourned at 9:35 P.M.

Respectfully submitted:

Janice Johnson
Secretary

26

REPRIMAND

*Make everything as simple as possible,
but not simpler.*

—ALBERT EINSTEIN

The letter of reprimand is used by a person in a supervisory role when an employee or associate has committed an error or a willful breach of policy, procedure, or practice. The effective reprimand separates the act from the person, and deals only with the act to be corrected. The objective is to produce compliance and/or a positive result.

An indirect or direct approach may be used. (See "Refusal," page 250.) You must decide, based on your knowledge of the person involved. In the case of a direct subordinate in the workplace, a direct approach is usually best.

DECIDE TO WRITE

You may be required to construct this when:
- An employee has committed an error or has willfully broken company rules.
- A member, associate, or student has committed an offense or breach of contract.
- An organization with which you have a relationship or contract has breached the agreement.

THINK ABOUT CONTENT
- Know the laws, regulations, and organization policies that impact the specific issue.
- Remember, your objective is to effect a positive change in behavior.
- To be effective, your anger must first be dealt with so you can be objective.
- Learn all the facts. Conduct any investigation necessary, and record precise details on a time-line. This should be done in an objective way without implicating anyone. And, of course, all the information should be kept confidential.
- Write the reprimand as soon after the offense as possible. The letter should not, however, substitute for a face-to-face meeting. It should be a follow-up record and a notice of corrective action.
- Introduce the reprimand. Set it up with a positive statement about overall or past performance, if this is a first offense.
- Make the letter short. Introduce the problem; state it; give any succinct, constructive criticism; and list any possible action to be taken.

- State the reprimand—be specific—and focus on the act, not the person.
- List any ramifications or any corrective action that will be taken.
- Set realistic, attainable, and measurable goals for improvement or corrective action, and give a time frame.
- Make a positive statement about the person and his or her positive performance, if possible, and list specific goals for improvement.
- Give the person an opportunity to respond.
- Offer encouragement or end on a note of goodwill.
- Have another person well-versed in company policy and the appropriate regulations read your reprimand before you send it to ensure objectivity and compliance with regulations and policy. (Don't violate any confidentiality issues, however.)
- Have legal counsel review the letter, if appropriate.

ELIMINATE WRONG MESSAGES

- Do not make a personal attack; deal with the offense only.
- Omit lengthy explanations, which diminish the impact of your letter.
- Don't belabor the corrective action.
- Don't criticize or use derogatory comments.
- Never send this letter by email.

CONSIDER SPECIAL SITUATIONS

- When the offense is against another employee, such as sexual harassment, consult specialized legal counsel. Both punishment and education may be indicated. Organizations are also advised that legal action against the offender may be indicated. A record should be kept in the organization's central headquarters. The organization must have stepped procedures for corrective action in place and properly documented, and if the behavior isn't corrected, the employee should be terminated. These procedures should be reviewed by an attorney specializing in gender, sexual harassment, and diversity issues.

SELECT A FORMAT

- Most reprimands are typed on organization letterhead since the message is directed to a person.
- Some organizations use a special form.
- Some organizations elect to type reprimands on organization memo forms.
- Some organizations use a handwritten memo format.
- Place a copy in the employee's file.

USE POWERFUL WORDS

action	eliminate
admonish	immediately
cease	infraction
censure	reform
correct	rules
demand	stop

USE EFFECTIVE PHRASES

cease and desist
demonstrate a change in behavior
eliminate such infractions
recommended steps of correction
regret that intervention will be necessary
reverse a negative trend
seek necessary help
take corrective action
violation of company policy

WRITE STRONG SENTENCES

I look forward to a new attitude in your work performance.

Punctuality is vital to the operation of the reception area.

The disregard for safety regulations will not be tolerated.

There is a problem in your work attendance.

Your behavior was out of character, and I am concerned.

Your tardiness is an exception to your otherwise fine performance.

EDIT, EDIT, EDIT

Always allow yourself time to take an objective final look at your letter before sending it. Make any changes needed to produce a letter that will completely resolve an offense, and, hopefully, restore an employee to productivity.

Reprimand for Late Expense Reports

[Typed]
(Date)

Dear Jeraldo:

The accounting department has notified me that your expense reports have been as much as three months late. This is a problem because they cannot finish department expense and overhead reports, and we all need this information to operate efficiently.

If there is an explanation I should know, please get it to me by Friday.

From Friday forward you must submit each month's expenses by the first of the following month, complete with required supporting documentation.

Thank you for complying.

Yours truly,

Sidney Ryder

Reprimand for Tardiness

[Typed]
(Date)

Dear Marie:

On five occasions in the past three weeks you have been from 30 minutes to one hour late in arriving at the office. Marie, the work of your department depends on your being on time, and company policy clearly states that administrative personnel will start work at 8:00 A.M.

If there is something I should know about the facts that created this tardiness, please make an appointment with Alice to discuss it with me before Friday. Otherwise I will expect to see you in your office by 8:00 A.M. each morning.

I will appreciate your cooperation in getting this problem resolved.

Sincerely,

Julie Adams

Reprimand for Rules Violation

[Typed]
(Date)

Dear Jack:

As you know, company policy states that repeated infractions of the sleeping-on-the-job rule receive (1) a verbal reprimand; then (2) a written reprimand; then (3) suspension without pay for three days; and then (4) dismissal. (See page 43 of your employee manual.) On July 10 you were found sleeping at 2:10 A.M. in the employee lounge. The 1:00 A.M. safety checks for your shift had not been made, and the boiler pressures had risen into the caution zone.

On July 21 you were found sleeping at 3:21 A.M. in the cafeteria. The 1:00 A.M. safety checks had not been made, and the boiler pressures were in the caution zone.

This is your written warning before suspension. You know the seriousness of failing to do your job; it creates a safety hazard for other employees, as well as for the surrounding residential area.

Be in my office at 2:00 A.M. Thursday, July 23 to explain your plan of action to correct this problem.

Sincerely,

J. K. Lund

Reprimand for Personal Activities on Company Time

[Typed]
(Date)

Dear Darla:

Your work record until August of this year was outstanding, but since that time I have received four complaints that (1) coworkers have not been getting routine reports from you, (2) there have been six or seven occasions when you were away from the office for several hours without Mr. Jenkins knowing your whereabouts, and (3) there have been at least several meetings in your office during working hours for political campaign committees. Darla, as you know, these are all infractions of company policy. (See 4.15–4.32 in your employee manual.)

I expect you will make the necessary changes in your volunteer work to resume your past fine performance here. Please be in my office on Wednesday, 3:00 P.M. to explain to me your plan of action.

Sincerely,

Sandra Layton

Reprimand for Error

[Typed]
(Date)

Dear Arnie:

Mrs. Anna Gable, age 72, widow for 10 years, was in the laboratory last week for a PB3 test. She just called me saying she received the laboratory test results report, which explain that her "toxicity levels during the third trimester of pregnancy are slightly elevated." Really?

This is the third time within the past five weeks that a patient has received the wrong report. These errors must stop.

Tomorrow at 3:30 P.M., I want a full report that details how these errors in mailing out reports occurred, and the action you are taking to ensure the problem is completely corrected.

Sincerely,

Mike McPhee

Reprimand for Inappropriate Behavior

[Typed]
(Date)

Dear Sassy:

I have received a complaint from Mr. Dennis Simons of ReCoil stating that you, while placing an order on July 11, used abusive language when he told you our shipment scheduled for a July 12 delivery would be delayed. We all share your frustration when commitments aren't kept, but it is not acceptable here to exacerbate a delay by creating a delivery cancellation. This is what Dennis threatened when he called me.

I have resolved the dispute with Dennis, but you are the person who must deal with him if you are going to perform your job. We have a contract with ReCoil for eight more months.

As you know, our relationship with ReCoil is vital to our operation and profitability. Please be in my office tomorrow morning at 8:30 A.M., and give me your proposed solution to the existing friction between you and Dennis Simons.

Sincerely,

Jacob Boiler

Reprimand for Absence

[Typed]

TO: Stan Dever

FROM: Wilbur Scoggins

DATE: May 15, 2007

SUBJECT: Excessive Sick Days

In my memo of April 30, I stated that you have used 12 sick days this year—the allotment for the entire year. This month you have already called in sick an additional four days—May 5, 6, 8, and 10.

Stan, your performance with BackUp has been outstanding, but I must inform you that any additional sick leave this year will be unpaid. In addition, your absence is starting to affect the production of the department. Please come into my office tomorrow at 4:30 P.M., and tell me how you plan to address this problem.

27

LETTER OF RESIGNATION

We'll bid farewell to Cadet grey
and don the Army blue.

—GEORGE T. OLMSTEAD

The letter of resignation is essentially a refusal letter (see "Refusal," page 250). This bad news may be given either indirectly or directly, depending on the situation. In either case, make your letter as positive as possible, using tactful, supportive statements. Assume full responsibility for your resignation and include an acceptable reason for resigning, if possible.

DECIDE TO WRITE
- After you have accepted a position with another organization
- If you are asked to resign by the organization
- When you have decided to retire
- After you have reviewed the organization policy to check timing, procedural, and policy issues
- After you have given your resignation orally

THINK ABOUT CONTENT
- Start with an expression of goodwill to set up your resignation statement.
- Follow your set-up statement with a logical, clear, and positive statement of resignation.
- State that you are resigning your position (use your title) and give an effective date.
- State why you are leaving in an objective, factual tone.
- End with a goodwill statement of appreciation for the experience, training, and/or relationship. You may want to state positive aspects of the company, and/or the people with whom you worked.

ELIMINATE WRONG MESSAGES
- Don't make angry statements. Your letter will remain on file, and this could come back to haunt you.
- Don't forget to include some positive points of your relationship with the organization.

CONSIDER SPECIAL SITUATIONS
- Be sure to check the organization policy concerning resignations carefully, especially in respect to the person to whom you should tender your resignation.
- Consider all the ramifications of your resignation. In an effort to leave under the best of circumstances, you may wish to give your organization more than the standard notice policy requires and offer to train your replacement.
- Most often resignations are given in a face-to-face meeting, and the written resignation is simply a follow-up.

- It is often organizational policy that resignations are made in the form of a memo. Comply with any such requirements.
- Though it may not seem ethical, an organization may wish for an employee tendering his resignation to leave immediately. Be prepared for this possibility.

USE STRONG WORDS

appreciate	new
benefited	opportunity
developed	resign
effective	strong
enjoyed	tender
grown	thank you (thanks)
growth	valuable (invaluable)

BUILD EFFECTIVE PHRASES

benefited from my time here

change career directions

continue to be challenged in new ways

enjoyed working on the team

excellent learning experience

gained valuable skills

move in a new direction

new growth opportunity

provided a growth opportunity

seek a new challenge

special camaraderie

CONSTRUCT STRONG SENTENCES

I gained irreplaceable experience here at Gault.

I shall never forget the great learning opportunity my years at Diddles afforded me.

Shores offered me, a new graduate, an outstanding career-development opportunity.

I'm most thankful for the opportunity you gave me to serve on the Blisters team.

I learned more in my 18 months at Riggers than I did in six years in undergraduate and graduate school.

I shall always cherish my years here, and will always be proud to be a Jitters alumni.

I've experienced three invaluable years of career development in my role here.

BUILD STRONG PARAGRAPHS

I realize I've been fortunate to have been an employee here for three years. This experience has afforded me real career collateral, and I shall always regard my time here fondly.

No more 5:30 A.M. meetings with Jim Greely. No more 5:30 P.M. meetings with Jim Greely. No more 10:30 P.M. meetings with Jim Greely. I must say I will miss each and every one of them, and I'll miss all five engineers in this department who've been such an important part of my cherished memories of working here.

I am very sad to have to end this wonderful working relationship. But I now need to stretch beyond my comfort zone of the great learning experience I enjoyed with the accounting department here.

Thank you for the opportunity to be a Monster employee. There isn't another place I'd have preferred to start my career.

How green I was when I entered the Ortho offices on that bright May morning five years ago. How patient you all were. Thank you for the gentle and terrific seasoning-of-a-rookie experience.

Though I'll be changing organizations, I won't be leaving the many friends I made in this place. I'll be in touch with all of you in shipping.

Though we had marked differences, I appreciate the fact that at Expound each and every employee is given the opportunity to express his ideas. Thank you for the great learning experience.

SELECT A FORMAT

- Usually a resignation is first given verbally, and the written form is a formality that follows.
- Use the standard organizational format. This may be a memo on letterhead, or a letter on letterhead.

EDIT, EDIT, EDIT

Since this provides a final and lasting impression—and is a part of your permanent employee record—make sure every sentence is just right.

Memo—Resigning to Take a New Position

[Typed]

TO: Casey Walters
CC: Doreen Rigors
FROM: Jake Straight
DATE: May 5, 2007
SUBJECT: Resignation from Cool Effective
         June 1, 2007

My four years at Cool Inc. have been the most intense learning experience of my life, and I have undergone a tremendous professional development growth spurt. I arrived here a complete novice, and both you and Doreen Rigors took me under your expert wings. Thanks to both of you for fine-tuning those academic skills, and tutoring me in real business practice done the Cool way.

It's a sad day to announce I am leaving, but I know you appreciate that it's time for me to move into a new area, and develop another set of professional skills.

I will miss each and every one of you, and will always be thankful for the great opportunity offered me to be a Cool employee. My best wishes to each of you, and best wishes for a bright future for Cool.

Letter of Resignation after Reorganization

[Typed]
(Date)

Dean Synder

Dear Dean:

It's a bit like musical chairs, isn't it? And now that I find myself without a chair, I must say it has been both a great experience and a wonderful opportunity to learn.

Thank you for your help in everything, especially your efforts at connecting me with other opportunities. My best wishes to you. I am confident that Quest Corporation will survive and grow.

Sincerely,

Ralph Boggs

Memo—Resigning Because of Loss of Position

[Typed]

TO: R. R. Beams

FROM: Ted West

DATE: March 6, 2008

SUBJECT: Resignation from Choice Matters,
         Effective April 1

The fact that my position here is ending doesn't diminish the great professional experience I have enjoyed. It has been outstanding.

Thank you for the opportunity given me at Choice Matters. I wish the organization great success in the future, and wish the best for each any every one remaining on staff.

Letter of Resignation after Accepting a New Position

[Typed]
(Date)

Alex Chang, Department Head

Dear Alex:

I am tendering my resignation, as I stated. I've accepted a position in Sacramento at Meade. As you know, this was a family decision made to coordinate both Beth's and my professions, and to create the best school environment for our children, Madison and Ben.

Thank you for your understanding. I will certainly miss all of my teammates in this department (and our champion softball team as well). My best wishes to everyone. Best wishes, too, for the continued success of Nerf.

Sincerely,

Dan Withers

28

EMPLOYEE TERMINATION

We live in an age that thinks too little to be wise.

—OLD CHINESE PROVERB

A letter of termination should never come as a bolt out of the blue. This news should first be given verbally in a face-to-face meeting, if at all possible. This letter is then simply the written documentation. If an employee is being terminated because of his actions or failures, other opportunities to correct his performance should first have been given.

Before writing this letter, be sure the criteria of pertinent laws, regulations, and organization policies and procedures have been met. This letter must be direct, stating the reason for the termination; and it should end on as upbeat a note as possible.

DECIDE TO WRITE
- Set the stage by stating your regrets.
- Make a clear statement of termination.
- Give the date termination is effective.
- Give an honest explanation concerning why the decision was made.
- Include any conditions that may apply.
- State any help, such as career counseling, that is being offered.

- Make a statement of goodwill, if possible.
- End with a cordial note or one of encouragement without being false.
- Include the name of someone who will answer any remaining questions, if applicable.

ELIMINATE WRONG MESSAGES
- Avoid being negative or hostile.
- Do not leave any doubt in the reader's mind that he is being fired.
- Don't lay the blame elsewhere.
- Never use email to transmit your letter of termination.

CONSIDER ALL THE FACTS
- Know the pertinent laws and regulations.
- Have a supervisor you trust review the letter before you send it, if appropriate.
- Request legal counsel review, if appropriate.
- Assure the recipient you will not be giving a negative reference, if that is the organization's policy.

179

USE STRONG WORDS

action	final
cancel	immediately
conclude	regret
decision	sever
employment	terminate
end	

USE EFFECTIVE PHRASES

bring to an end
effective immediately
employment will be terminated as of
sever our relationship
terminate your employment
with full consideration

WRITE STRONG SENTENCES

I am sorry to deliver this message, but we must terminate your employment effective immediately.

I'm extremely saddened to have to deliver this news, but due to noncompliance with company policies outlined in letters to you dated March 15 and May 7, we must terminate your employment effective June 1.

Unfortunately, many of the positions at Richmond Instruments will have to be eliminated because of duplication of personnel after the merger.

BUILD EFFECTIVE PARAGRAPHS

There is no good way to say you are being terminated. As of June 15, we must eliminate your position due to the company's present financial crisis.

We must terminate your employment with General Evidence effective July 1. Your hearing with the human resources manager indicated that you were apprehended on June 15, 2006, 7:07 P.M. stealing three computers from the production area.

Copies of all the facts and violations of company policy are attached for your review. These are the same documents that were reviewed during your employee hearing on June 6.

EDIT, EDIT, EDIT

You will, of course, want to remove any ambiguity that might remain; and you'll want to end on as positive a note as possible.

Termination for Poor Performance

[Typed on 8 ½ by 11-inch stationery]
(Date)

Cassidy Lindsay
433 Birch Lane
Rockville, MD 20852

Dear Cassidy:

Regrettably, it is necessary to terminate your employment at Bikers. After several discussions with you (see enclosed memo copies), and three reviews of your work, you have not improved your performance to match the duties of the job description.

Although separation from a company is never easy, it is often the best solution for everyone involved. After a careful review of all the facts, I believe this is true here.

I assure you we will strictly observe Bikers' policy of giving any future references concerning your employment here: we will release only the dates of your employment and your job title, and we will verify your salary with us only if the caller has obtained that salary information from you.

We do wish you every success in your future work.

Sincerely,

Donna Laurent

Termination for Absenteeism

[Typed]
(Date)

Melvin McReynolds
433 Archer Drive
Atlanta, GA 30345

Dear Melvin:

Your absenteeism has prevented you from performing the requirements of the position of assistant plant manager. I had hoped after our last meeting—the third such meeting—on September 15, when you indicated that you would correct this problem, that this action would not be necessary. But as you know, we have reviewed this matter in detail three times.

You employment with Vickers will be terminated effective November 1. Your final check will be mailed to your home, along with other personnel details.

I truly wish you success in the future.

Sincerely,

Marian Leeburg

Termination for Intoxication

[Typed]
(Date)

Martin May
3223 Race Street
Denver, CO 80223

Dear Martin:

Because your intoxication on the job impaired the safety of employees at Jinx, we must terminate your employment effective April 4, 2007. I have attached a copy of the incident report of March 28, 2007, and two other earlier reports.

As you know, when this problem was initially reported you agreed to complete the program outlined in the disciplinary action, but did not. We have no choice, therefore, since your continuing this behavior threatens the safety of other employees.

Your final check will be sent to your home address.

Sincerely,

Kenneth Bacon

Terminate Due to Downsizing

[Typed]
(Date)

Dear Jennifer:

This is the day we all hoped would not arrive, but, due to continuing loss of market share, we must terminate your employment with Cloudy Skies, effective June 15, 2006.

You will have the complete support of our job-locating services, and I've taken the liberty to schedule an interview with Rick Himes in HR to start that process. Rick will also discuss with you the severance package details.

Thank you for your service to Cloudy Skies over these past five years. We wish you well in your future career.

Sincerely,

Alice Bonkers

Position Terminated Due to Downsizing

[Typed]
(Date)

Dear Rachel:

As we discussed, the economic slowdown in the Cleveland market for HighFlyers demands we close the regional office. Sadly, this eliminates your position.

We will terminate your employment with us on July 1, 2006, as agreed, and you will receive severance pay equal to three months' salary. The company will pay your medical insurance for the remainder of the year. In lieu of our bonus program, you have agreed to accept a one-time payment of $26,000. Your retirement benefits will be retained by the company until we receive instructions from you. The personnel department will send you a letter containing all the actual figures.

Rachel, we will all miss you here, but we are confident that your skills will land you an excellent position very soon. Please have any future employer contact me for a reference.

Sincerely,

Marika Lovelace

V. PROPOSALS AND REPORTS

PROExAMPLE POSAL
PROPOSAL

The difficulty is not to write, but to write what you mean, not to affect your reader, but to affect him precisely as you wish.

—ROBERT LOUIS STEVENSON

A proposal is basically a plan to do something. Its purpose is, of course, to persuade. It is usually written in response to an invitation to supply a solution to a need or desire, but not always. Sometimes a proposal is submitted unsolicited or on speculation.

Your proposal may be as short as a sentence, or as long as a number of volumes. It may be as informal as an interoffice memo or verbal presentation, or as formal and complex as a lengthy government document.

A proposal is direct. It must be well-organized, and complete, whether it is unsolicited or requested, informal or formal, short or long. It should start with the reader's needs converted into the writer's purpose. A proposal should include background elements, a full description of the proposed plan, details (time requirements, schedule, costs, alternative factors, performance standards, etc.), ability to deliver, qualifications, benefits, and a summary or conclusion. All this information should point to the writer's recommendations—the focus of the proposal.

UNDERSTAND THE TERMS

- An internal proposal usually recommends change within your organization.
- An external proposal is made to an outside organization.
- A sales proposal, technical proposal, or budget proposal recommends products or services to a customer.
- An unsolicited or speculative proposal is one you submit without an invitation ("submitted on spec"). Inquire first to see if it will be considered.
- A solicited or requested proposal is one you submit after receiving a request for proposal (RFP) or a request for a bid.
- Bid specifications (specs) or guidelines are the rules and requirements proposal writers or bidders receive from the customer and must follow.
- Nonresponsive means the bidder didn't comply with the specifications.

THINK ABOUT CONTENT

Preliminary Actions

- Qualify for the proposal process. Many government, private, and for-profit proposal processes are conducted on an invitation-to-bid basis, or a request for proposal (RFP). You must go through a preliminary qualifying process in order to obtain the opportunity to submit a proposal.

- Research. Complete knowledge of the problem, need, and/or desire of the recipient is the essential first step. Certainly, knowledge of the reader(s) is vital too. If past or similar proposals are available, review them as part of the research process.

- Study and know your reader. This must govern your proposal writing from beginning to end. To persuade the reader you must be able to talk to him or her. That means knowing his or her level of knowledge of the subject, bias, examples he or she will respect, and how he or she can best be persuaded.

Content Order

- Open with a clear and concise *preview* of your message. This will grab the attention of the reader and set the stage.

- Next, craft an *introduction*. Begin with a statement of purpose and a statement of the reader's need or problem. When the proposal is being submitted in response to an invitation, this should be stated here. When the proposal is unsolicited, you must get the reader's attention and overcome any resistance in this section.

- Insert a statement of *background information*, a detailed description of the need or problem. In the case of a proposal to reorganize a corporation, for example, this section would give a historical description of the beginning of the corporation and its development, which explains the need to reorganize.

- Include a need or *problem statement*. The background will naturally flow into a statement of the need or problem. In a very brief proposal, the need statement may appear without a background statement.

- Develop a *plan of action*. This is the core of the proposal: what the writer proposes to do. It must be well organized, clear, and complete. This must be stated as an effective solution that will appeal to the reader.

- Include enough *details* to make your plan clear and appealing. In a long proposal, this section will contain the timetables, materials, costs, requirements, performance standards, quality controls, etc. The writer must anticipate the reader's questions and objections, and answer them in this section.

- List your *qualifications*. The writer must give sound reasons here why he or she (or the organization) is uniquely qualified to perform the proposed plan. This may include giving personal qualifications like resumes, job references, operating procedures, and financial statements. Overall, this section must include evidence that the writer can perform.

- List the *benefits*. Cover the positive results that will result if your proposal is completed. If, for example, a corporation is reorganized, it will be more efficient, be able to expand into new areas, reduce waste, etc.

- Give a *recommendation*. If it hasn't already been stated, this is where your most persuasive statement belongs. It's best to close the circle: refer back to the beginning. "This plan will meet your needs of realizing a 15 percent return by . . ."

- Include a *summary* and *conclusion*. In a long proposal, it is necessary to briefly summarize the proposal points. Any additional information needed will also appear here, and the conclusion must call for action.

Other Considerations

- If the reader's interest is low, put your strongest points first. If the reader's interest is high, put your strongest points last.
- Choose your "testimonials" from people and examples the reader knows, or can relate to.
- Tailor your proposal to the reader's attitudes and beliefs, if you can.
- Use well-organized headings, subheadings, and divisions to make your proposal easy to follow.
- Develop an effective solution that will appeal to the reader.
- Use visuals wherever they will aid understanding.

ELIMINATE WRONG MESSAGES

- Do not use "sensational" claims or facts. Stick to examples within the reader's scope of experience.
- Do not propose elements you cannot back up or deliver, but remember that you will not change the reader's attitude by presenting information alone.
- Eliminate everything that isn't carefully focused.
- Eliminate stilted prose and jargon.
- Never mention people or examples without considering the effect on your reader.

CONSIDER SPECIAL SITUATIONS

- Getting on the qualified list of bidders for government work or some for-profit accounts can be a long and difficult process. Start early.
- Study every related, successful proposal you can get your hands on.

SELECT A FORMAT

- Informal proposals often use the memo form. These are usually simple, routine proposals, and are transmitted by email. An example is proposing the hiring of two new salespeople. The format is simple: introduction (need statement); body or plan; and conclusion, with emphasis on benefits to be gained.
- Formal proposals will be much more complex. Organize your material carefully to make your proposal easy to follow, interesting, and convincing.
- Use enumerations and subheads for impact, understanding, visual interest, and clarity.

A formal proposal format:

I. TABLE OF CONTENTS
II. INTRODUCTION
III. NEED/PROBLEM
   A. Scope
      1. *Objectives.* The overall objective and specific accomplishments. Give the rationale.
      2. *Approach.* Clearly outline the plan of work and the phases.
      3. *Materials, Labor, and Methods.* Details and methodology you will use. Cover your expertise and any difficulties.
      4. *Timetable, Schedule, or Level of Accomplishment.* Break this into relative parts.
   B. Qualifications
      1. *Experience.* General background, specific, and similar experience.
      2. *Personnel.* Qualifications/resumes. Name the responsible person and subcontract sources.

Proposal Features

A proposal may include some or all of these features:

Cover Materials

Cover Letter or Letter of Transmittal
Title Page
Table of Contents
Table of Illustrations or Figures
Abstract or Summary
Introductory Materials
Introduction (Grabber)
Statement of Purpose
(Reference any association with the organization or any association with the problem.)

Problem or Need
Background (of Problem)
Needs Analysis
Solution Statement
Benefits to Be Gained from Solution
Methodology
Feasibility of Solution
Personnel or Staffing Plan
Design and Organization of Personnel Team
Personnel Qualifications
Task Breakdown or Specific Responsibilities
Time and Work Schedule
Testing
Evaluation Procedures
Progress Reports or Checks

Management

Project Organization and Management
Administrative Structure
Management Policies
Cost-Accounting Methods
Payroll and Timekeeping Methods and
*   Procedures*
Credit References and Ratings
Facilities
Quality Control and Assurance Guidelines
Personnel Qualifications and Subcontractors
Experience
Financial Qualifications and Resources
Organizational Support

Budget

Direct Costs
Indirect Costs
Subcontracts
Contract Definition and Terms
Method and Timetable of Payments
Late Penalties

Close

Summary
Conclusion
Call to Action

Appendices

Letters of Reference
Recommendation, Letters of Support, and
*   "Testimonials"*
Resumes of Key Personnel
Applicable Policy Statements, etc.

EDIT, EDIT, EDIT

Before your proposal is finished, it will undoubtedly go through a number of rewriting and editing procedures. Use all your writing skills to make it as clear and persuasive as possible. Get as much input as possible from professionals you admire, and from people qualified to proof the proposal, check facts, critique content, and check for grammatical errors and typos.

Also see COVER LETTER, page 230; REQUESTS AND INQUIRIES, page 224; and RESUME, page 118.

Work Proposal

Rose Design Group
200 West Petunia
Oakland, Missouri 64101

(660) 890-7600

Proposal

(Date)

Crystal Lake Homeowners' Association
5200 East Walker Drive
Oakland, Missouri 64101

Attention: Sawyer Applewood, President

Reference: <u>Landscaping Renovation</u>

      This proposal includes completing the following work by (date). To accept, sign the attached sheet, General Conditions.

	Cost

1. Prepare the site thoroughly, including, but not limited to the following:
   a) remove and dispose of existing junipers
   b) grind out pear tree stumps
   c) remove lowest branches on existing rock mulches
	$ 935

2. Furnish and install 5 yards of compost.	440
3. Furnish and install 110 feet of edging.	145
4. Furnish and install flagstone step stones.	290
5. Rebuild existing rock wall at west side of garage.	430
6. Remove and dispose of existing exposed aggregate.	460

7. Prepare the site, including, but not limited to the following:
   a) remove and dispose of plants.
   b) grind out stumps.
   c) remove and dispose of existing rock mulches.
	1,100

	————
	$3,800

In its simplest form, the proposal communicates to the reader all the information he or she needs to know to make an informed decision. The proposal, when agreed to, can become the contract between the writer and the reader. This requires that the proposal be crystal clear, down to the last detail.

Proposal/Crystal Lake Homeowners' Association/(Date)/page 2 of 2

<u>GENERAL CONDITIONS</u>

UNFORESEEN SITE CONDITIONS

The contractor has made a reasonable effort to accurately estimate the costs for Material and Labor required to complete the project as specified. However, the Contractor may be required to revise this Contract based on "unforeseen" and/or "undetectable" circumstances, which may arise during the completion of the project. Should any "unforeseen" and/or "undetectable" circumstances arise, the Contractor shall notify the Owner of estimated additional costs required to rectify the situation and obtain written authorization to proceed through the use of a Change Order.

MATERIAL QUANTITIES

The Material quantities specified in the Contract are considered to be appropriate quantities, plus or minus 10%. If any additional Materials are necessary to complete the job, the Contractor shall notify the Owner of the additional costs required to rectify the situation and obtain written authorization to proceed through the use of a Change Order. If less Material is needed to complete the job, the cost shall be credited back to the Owner.

CHANGE ORDERS

All additional Work to the conditions of the Contract shall be subject to additional charges and the Contract price adjusted accordingly. No additional Work shall be performed by the Contractor unless written authorization (Change Order) to proceed with such Work, including the price of such Work, shall be issued by the Owner.

UNDERGROUND UTILITIES

The Contractor shall be responsible to have all underground utilities located.

PERMITS, TAXES, REGULATIONS, CODES

The Contractor is obligated to obtain and pay the cost of all permits, licenses, certificates, inspection and other legal fees that are necessary to do the Work, as applicable.

INSURANCES

The Contractor shall be required to carry and keep in force throughout the duration of the Work General Liability and Workers' Compensation Insurances.

CLEAN UP

The contractor shall leave the site free of debris and surplus material at all times and, at the completion of Work, remove all waste, rubbish, excess materials and equipment generated by the Contractor and leave the site in a clean, completed condition ready for Owner's full use and enjoyment.

DISPUTES/ARBITRATION

Any controversy or claim arising out of or relating to this Contract, or the breach thereof, shall be settled by arbitration in accordance with the Construction Industry Arbitration Rules of the American Arbitration Association or the procedures of the Arbitration Committee of the Associated Landscape Contractors of Colorado. Arbitration shall be binding and the decision to enter into such Arbitration shall be initiated by either party of this agreement.

PLANT WARRANTY

All plant material (excluding annuals, bulbs and transplanted materials) shall be guaranteed to be alive and in satisfactory growth one year following the date of installation. Any material that is considered dead shall be replaced, one time only, by the Contractor at no charge to the Owner. The Owner shall notify the Contractor immediately as soon as any plant material begins to show signs of stress (e.g. yellowing, wilting). The Contractor shall not be responsible for plants that have been adversely affected by factors or circumstances beyond the Contractor's control, including, but not limited to, severe winter or unusual temperature fluctuations during any given time of the year, tornado, vandalism, animal damage, improper application of fertilizers or pesticides and lack or excess of moisture.

IRRIGATION SYSTEM WARRANTY

All components of the irrigation system shall be guaranteed to be free of defects and in good working order for one year following the date on installation. This warranty does not cover the system if it has been damaged due to freezing conditions. It is the Owner's responsibility to insure that the system is protected from temperatures below 32 degrees F.

OWNER _____   DATE _____

CONTRACTOR _____   DATE _____

This second page of the proposal, when signed, becomes the legal contract between the writer and the reader.

30
BUSINESS PLAN

*It ain't what you don't know
that gets you in trouble;
it's what you know for sure
that ain't so.*

—MARK TWAIN

The business plan is really a proposal that sets out a new business venture, direction, product, or course of action. Write a business plan in order to gain support for your idea. Like the proposal, it is written to persuade.

Your audience may be potential investors, bankers, and sometimes executives within your organization. You may need to convince a bank or investors to offer financing, or organization executives to offer cooperation, resources, or other types of support, including enthusiasm. You may also want others to offer an evaluation, additional ideas, and counsel. Business plans are generally of limited distribution, and are kept confidential.

THINK ABOUT CONTENT

- Focus your plan on your precise audience, e.g., your bank loan officer. For each audience, you'll want to write a precise plan.
- Research your audience to determine the elements each wants to see. Bankers, for example, will have very prescribed requirements, like a balance sheet, profit-and-loss statement, cash-flow projections, projected expenditures, break-even points, and so on.
- Develop the plan sections:
— The *general business description* will state the business type, products and/or services to be produced, and the market positioning. Start with the legal name of the organization, its location, and status (for example, "X Company is a California Corporation, located at 324 Locust Street, Los Angeles, licensed to do business as . . ."); describe what the organization will do; include a statement about the customer or client base; describe the growth opportunity; explain where the product(s) or service(s) will fit in the competitive field, and what makes the plan viable. Make a brief statement about future growth. This section may be only a sentence or a number of paragraphs in length.
— A *mission statement* briefly defines the purpose and reason for existing. Distill this to a simple statement. For example, "X Company will offer an affordable alternative to Y Company's . . ."
— *Goals* may be segmented into short-term, mid-term, and long-term, but should also be projected precisely on a timetable. Be realistic, offer specific and measurable terms, and be conservative rather than overly optimistic.

— *Management team* members should be identified and their expertise described. Include key support team members, too, like outside consultants, accountants, lawyers, insurance agents, and marketing experts who have committed to work with the organization. Describe their expertise and list some of their references. (You may include resumes in the appendices.) This section may also include a listing of organization positions that will be added in the future, and projections about staging and expansion.

— *Market analysis* is the heart of your plan, because it creates the basis for your plan to succeed. You must demonstrate that you understand the market. This is where you will analyze competitive organizations and products or services, and then show how your product or service can compete and become successful.

— The *marketing plan* must lay out, in concrete terms, what you will do and how you will use various promotional, advertising, and public relations techniques to launch the organization. Include this information for each particular service and product, and for each market segment.

— The *financial analysis* must show, from the beginning of the plan period, how finances will be used to achieve success. Financial statements need to include all investments and starting capital, as well as debt. Projections for financial growth must include a discussion of strengths and weaknesses, cost-control measures, and potential problem areas. Show how you are prepared to deal with them.

Include here a balance sheet, profit-and-loss statements, and cash-flow projections for the short-, mid-, and long-term. Usually projections will go to six months, and one, two, and three years, at least for banks.

— *Appendices* or *supporting documents* will include a number of items to bolster your case. Include resumes of key team members; customer or client contracts or orders; letters of support by experts in the field; marketing studies or focus-group responses; positive reviews of the product or service; patents or licenses; documentation that you have secured incorporation, name rights, and other unique legal documents; and publicity or statements about demand for the product or service. Include anything that helps to make your case, carefully tabbed and correctly referenced in the appropriate plan section.

ELIMINATE WRONG MESSAGES

- Don't think one plan fits all. Be sure you include only the relevant material for your audience, and meticulously focus on and tailor each plan accordingly.
- Don't pad your plan. A winning plan can be as short as a few pages. (The shorter it is the more likely it will be carefully read.)
- Eliminate stilted language. A conversational tone will help warm up your audience.
- Don't mail off your plan without first getting a face-to-face, if at all possible. If a meeting isn't possible, call and discuss your plan with the person who'll evaluate it before submitting it.

CONSIDER SPECIAL SITUATIONS

- Different audiences will dictate the weighting of your plan. Have as much preliminary discussion with the audience (for example, bank loan officer) as possible in the research phase before you start. It's important to make sure you present the information required in the preferred form; submitting a business plan for consideration may be a one-time opportunity.

- Demonstrate that you have a winning plan by using creative resources whenever possible to demonstrate the validity of your plan. Research online the many sources of help available, like the Small Business Administration's group of retired executives, chambers of commerce, and industry-specific counselors.

- Be sure to thoroughly check out any audiences you are considering partnering with. Ask the bank you are considering, for example, for the names of other small businesses they partner with. Check the bank's reserves, and interview similar organizations that partner with the bank. Ask about loan limits, and check the bank's record of calling in loans, extending payment plans, and their willingness and ability to stick with a small business through a difficult period.

- Consider all your options in creating a plan presentation in visual form.

SELECT A FORMAT

- Create a visually appealing printed document by using double-spaced text on $8^1/_2$ by 11-inch quality, white or off-white bond.

- For the printed and bound hard copy (paper) plan, prepare a title page; a table of contents, if needed; and a table of graphs, illustrations, and charts, if appropriate.

- Prepare and print graphs, charts, and illustrations in professional-looking color to illustrate the main points of your plan.

- Use a computer presentation, in person, whenever possible. When your audience can be assembled, think about PowerPoint or another audiovisual format that allows you to "show and tell" to your best advantage. Use actual products and/or service samples whenever possible. Practice your presentation until you can present it flawlessly. Anticipate and prepare answers to key questions.

EDIT, EDIT, EDIT

Fine-tune your plan, have trusted professionals review and critique it, and make any and all corrections and changes until it's perfect.

31

FORMAL REPORT

Whatever we conceive well we express clearly.

—BOILEAU

The formal report collects and interprets data and reports information. Reports are used to inform, analyze, recommend, and persuade. They are usually written in indirect order—presenting information, analyzing it, making conclusions, and making recommendations. The formal report is often very complex and may be bound like a book. (An example is *The 9-11 Commission Report*. See samples at the end of this chapter.) In the business setting, the informal report is usually used for internal distribution, and the formal report is prepared for external distribution to stockholders, customers, and the general public. The formal report is often a written account of a major project. Examples of subject matter include new technologies, the results of a study or experiment, analysis of locations for corporate relocation, an annual report, or a year-end review of developments in the field. Careful planning and meticulous organization are necessary to guide readers through the material.

Three main sections—preliminary, or front, material, body, and back material—help give the report form. Within these sections, there may be a number of subsections as needed:

Preliminary (Front) Material
— *Title Page*
— *Letter of Authorization*
— *Letter of Transmittal*
— *Abstract*
— *Table of Contents*
— *List of Figures*
— *List of Tables*
— *List of Symbols and/or Abbreviations*
— *Statement of Problem, Abstract, Synopsis, or Summary*
— *Foreword*
— *Preface*

Body
— *Executive Summary*
— *Introduction*
— *Text (with Appropriate Headings, Subheadings)*
— *Conclusions or Summary*
— *Recommendations*

Supplemental (Back) Material
— *References*
— *Appendices*
— *Bibliography*
— *Glossary*
— *Index*

PRELIMINARY OR FRONT MATERIAL

Front material describes for the reader the purpose of the report. It provides an overview and lists specific content.

- *The title page* lists the topic or subject, scope, and purpose; lists the writer with title and/or role and affiliate organization; date of issuance (and period, such as quarterly, annual); and the name of the commissioning organization. This page isn't numbered, but is page i; the blank back of the page, also unnumbered, is page ii.
- *Letter of authorization* lists the sponsoring organization (or person) commissioning the work and the report.
- *Letter of transmittal* is a cover letter identifying who the report is sent by, and to whom it is being sent. It may point out special sections or points of interest.
- The *abstract* gives the major points of the report.
- *Table of contents* lists the major sections or headings, in order of appearance, and the page numbers on which they begin.
- *List of figures* (when there are five or more) shows the pages on which they appear.
- *List of tables* is used when five or more of these are used. It gives the page numbers where they appear.
- A *foreword,* when included, contains an introductory statement by someone other than the author(s), giving background and perhaps comparisons to other reports in the field. The writer/author's name appears at the end, along with the date.
- The *preface* is the author's statement about the *what, why, when,* and so on of the report.

BODY

Here's where the methods, procedures, tests, and comparisons used are covered. It also includes the results, analyses, conclusions, and recommendations, if any.

- The *executive summary* is an overview, more detailed than the abstract.
- The *introduction* indicates the report's purpose, scope, and other information.

- The *text* details how the study, investigation, and research were pursued or explored, and the initial findings.
- *Conclusions* or *summary* distills the findings, results, and outcome, and offers deductive conclusions.
- *Recommendations* may be combined with conclusions. This usually states a course of action or results that indicate the need for the next step.

SUPPLEMENTAL (BACK) MATERIAL

The back material lists sources, documentation, and supplemental materials.

- The *appendices* contain supporting information that is either too detailed or would disrupt the flow of the report if inserted in the text.
- The *bibliography* is an alphabetical listing of sources used by the author of the report.
- The *glossary* is an alphabetical listing of terms and definitions.
- The *index* is an alphabetical list of the terms, subjects, or names used in the report, and the pages on which they appear.

THINK ABOUT ORGANIZATION

After determining what sections you'll need to write, start to organize your material in outline form. (Also see chapter 1, "Getting Started," and chapter 2, "Design and Layout.") To organize the report in a conventional outline manner use:

    I. Major or First Level Heading
       A. Minor or Second Level Heading
          1. Subhead or Third Level Heading
            a. Fourth Level
              (1) Fifth Level
                (a) Sixth Level

To arrange the report by the decimal system use:

    1.0 First Level Heading
      1.1 Second Level Heading
        1.2.1 Third Level
          1.2.2.1 Fourth Level

In typing the report, the outline form may be presented in the outline methods mentioned, or in one of the following:

I. MAJOR OR FIRST LEVEL HEADING
   A. Minor or Second Level Heading
      1. Subhead or Third Level Heading
         a. Fourth Level Heading or Paragraph Heading

Headings may be typed without numbers or letters:

MAJOR OR FIRST LEVEL HEADING
Minor or Second Level Heading
Subtopic or Third Level Heading
   Fourth Level Heading or Paragraph Heading

THINK ABOUT CONTENT

- Remember that most *formal* reports use an *indirect* approach. (This is a pattern where the information order is: a "buffer" statement of neutral information or an explanation, followed by a statement of the bad news or the problem, followed by a conclusion statement offering good news or a solution.) This approach introduces the problem, then gives the facts with analyses (when needed), and summarizes the information given.

- The *informal* report often uses the *direct* approach, offering the conclusion or recommendation, followed by the facts often given much more briefly. (See "Informal Report," page 199.)

- Begin by answering why this report is needed, and make your need statement specific. It may be to convey information, to analyze, or to recommend a course of action, or all three.

- The need statement should include the reader. For example, "Our sales representatives need to know why competitive products X, Y, and Z are outselling our product A." Focus your need statement on a specific goal or purpose statement. It can be expressed as a question, a declarative statement, or an infinitive phrase:

  Question: "What do our sales representatives need to know about competitive products X, Y, and Z in order to effectively sell product A?"

  Declarative Statement: "Our sales representatives need to know the features of competitive products X, Y, and Z in order to effectively sell product A."

  Infinitive Phrase: "To sell product A effectively, our sales representatives need to know the features of competitive products X, Y, and Z."

- Divide the task into its component parts. You will want to look at subtopics within the purpose statements.

- If you are reporting information, such as the results of an experiment or a list of books on a topic, the structure will be a straightforward, logical narrative. Make sure your report is objective; base it on facts. This helps free it of opinion and bias.

- If you are making analyses, drawing conclusions, or making recommendations, you probably need to carefully organize some additional elements. Take the case of our product, for example. After defining the broad subtopics—product X, product Y, product Z—you may want to complete some initial observations or surveys of competitive products. You may give these responses to the question "Why are products X, Y, and Z outselling product A?":

1. Products X and Z are cheaper than product A.
2. Products Y and Z are available in designer colors; product A isn't.
3. Products X, Y, and Z are packaged in carrying cases, which buyers seem to prefer over product A's packaging.

You will want to research some facts that can be used as sales points for product A. You may find that:

1. Although product A costs more, it outperforms and outlasts products X and Z.
2. Product A is not a fashion accessory. Designer colors aren't related to performance.
3. Product A is self-contained and has no detachable parts, so it is handsome and more convenient without a carrying case.

At the same time, your observations and surveys may lead you to develop some theories or hypotheses about your product:

1. We should reduce product A's price to be more competitive with products X and Z.
2. We should make product A available in designer colors to compete with products Y and Z.
3. We should develop a useful carrying case for product A to compete favorably with products X, Y, and Z.

- Evaluate your hypotheses by assigning point values to each or by using another test method. They may all be partially true or false. If your hypotheses prove false, you may have to advance some additional hypotheses to evaluate. In the case of product A, research may indicate that price, a wide range of colors, and a carrying case are the three top buyer criteria.
- Break down the subtopics into sub-subtopics, if this is helpful to get at the real solutions to the problem.
- Gather all the information. This can require personal research, data collection, surveys, or experiments. Business problems usually rely on surveys, scientific problems on experiments. Information problems may be solved using library research. Employ objective, proper, and thorough methods here to avoid invalidating your solution.
- Test your gathered data:

  Is it objective? Keep an open mind and consider all aspects to determine if sources are reported fairly and completely. Guard against bias.

  Do others agree? Use the input of others to question and challenge your interpretation.

  Is it reasonable? Check conclusions with logical thinking and make the surrounding facts support them.

  Does it hold up? Play devil's advocate, taking the opposing viewpoint, and see if your conclusions hold up. Represent them fairly in your report, showing supporting evidence.

Statistical data and interpretation are key in many reports. But scientific accuracy and integrity must be used in reporting this information. Check this out thoroughly before including it in your report.

- Organize the information into a report format, keeping precise records of sources.
- Write the rough draft.
- Be consistent in tense. Either present or past works well, but use the same tense throughout.
- Be consistent, too, in personal or impersonal (third person) viewpoint. The personal "I" or "we" can be as effective as the impersonal tests and facts, but different organizations and disciplines prefer one over the other. Often the informal report will use the personal and the formal report will use impersonal. Check your organization's style preference.
- Use effective transition words to begin new paragraphs. This helps keep the reader's attention.
- Make effective use of graphs, illustrations, and charts to make points.
- Enliven your writing by using effective, vigorous action words, but don't overdo it.
- Revise. Cut out nonessential parts, check for stilted words, jargon, inconsistencies, redundancies, and errors in logic. Eliminate any general, abstract, or vague statements. During this process, ask these questions:
  — Does the introduction establish the scope and methods to be used?
  — Are all the points in the introduction fully developed in the body?
  — Is the development of points logical and complete?
  — Are there ideas or sections that should be combined or relocated?
  — Is there a clear solution to, or a complete discussion of, the stated problem?
  — Is there a clear relationship between ideas and facts?
  — Does the report flow logically?
  — Is information complete for reader understanding?
  — Is opinion correctly identified from fact?
  — Have all the facts been double-checked?

—Do headings and subheadings properly reflect content?

—Are all grammar and spelling errors eliminated?

- Review and proofread with as many other people as practical. Consider any pertinent reactions, comments, and changes.
- Edit. It is best to give your report a few days on the shelf so you can become objective again. Then give it a fresh, last look.

ELIMINATE WRONG MESSAGES

- Don't embellish facts, use them out of context, or misinterpret them to support a point.
- Don't use material without giving proper credit.
- Do not make faulty or illogical cause-and-effect conclusions. Use sound reasoning to be sure of a relationship. And remember, conclusions are not always necessary. Some things are inconclusive. Say so.
- Don't make the mistake of assuming a lack of evidence proves the opposite is true. Maybe it isn't.
- Do not compare apples to oranges. Data must be similar in nature for comparisons to be authentic.
- Eliminate digressions or unfocused material. These can easily derail the report.

SELECT A FORMAT

- Establish a consistent format for all you organization's reports.
- Follow an approved and consistent reference system such as shown in the *Chicago Manual of Style* to record footnotes and bibliography listings.
- Create all the necessary graphics in visually appealing form to promote understanding.
- Print and bind the report in a professional manner.

EDIT, EDIT, EDIT

- Employ key content experts to review the report and check all facts included.
- Use a professional proofreader to check for proper grammar, consistent tense, redundancies, and other problems or errors.
- Use a proofreader and the spellchecker to eliminate any typos.

Sample of Report Contents

The 9-11 Commission Report (Listing of Contents):

Front Matter

Table of Contents

List of Illustrations and Tables

Member List

Staff List

Preface

1. "We Have Some Planes"
    * 1.1   Inside the Four Flights
    * 1.2   Improvising a Homeland Defense
    * 1.3   National Crisis Management

2. The Foundation of the New Terrorism
    * 2.1   A Declaration of War
    * 2.2   Bin Ladin's Appeal in the Islamic World
    * 2.3   The Rise of Bin Ladin and al Qaeda (1988–1992)
    * 2.4   Building an Organization, Declaring War on the United States (1992–1996)
    * 2.5   Al Qaeda's Renewal in Afghanistan (1996–1998)

3. Counterterrorism Evolves
    * 3.1   From the Old Terrorism to the New: The First World Trade Center Bombing
    * 3.2   Adaptation—and Nonadaptation—in the Law Enforcement Community
    * 3.3   . . . and in the Federal Aviation Administration
    * 3.4   . . . and in the Intelligence Community
    * 3.5   . . . and in the State Department and the Defense Department
    * 3.6   . . . and in the White House
    * 3.7   . . . and in the Congress

4. Responses to al Qaeda's Initial Assaults
    * 4.1   Before the Bombings in Kenya and Tanzania
    * 4.2   Crisis: August 1998
    * 4.3   Diplomacy
    * 4.4   Covert Action
    * 4.5   Searching for Fresh Options

5. Al Qaeda Aims at the American Homeland
    * 5.1   Terrorist Entrepreneurs
    * 5.2   The "Planes Operation"
    * 5.3   The Hamburg Contingent
    * 5.4   A Money Trail?

6. From Threat to Threat
    * 6.1   The Millennium Crisis
    * 6.2   Post-Crisis Reflection: Agenda for 2000
    * 6.3   The Attack on the USS *Cole*
    * 6.4   Change and Continuity
    * 6.5   The New Administration's Approach

Sample of Report Contents . . . *continued*

32

INFORMAL REPORT

For we write you nothing but what you can read and understand.

—II CORINTHIANS 1:13

The informal report functions to inform, analyze, and recommend. It usually takes the form of a memo, letter, or a very short internal document like a monthly financial report, monthly activities report, research and development report, and the like. This report differs from the formal report in length and formality. It's written according to organization style rules and usually includes an introduction, body, conclusion, and recommendations sections—but usually doesn't include the preliminary (front) and supplemental (back) material (see page 192). The informal report is usually more conversational in tone and typically deals with everyday problems and issues addressed to a narrow readership inside the organization.

Participatory management diminished the role of the informal report, but computers revived it, especially since management team members are frequently in different locations. An informal report is often completed quickly and transmitted electronically.

DECIDE TO WRITE

There are many forms of the informal report:

- Progress report
- Sales activity report
- Financial report
- Feasibility report
- Literature review
- Recommendations and suggestions
- Acceptance or rejection of proposals (see "Acceptance," page 245, and "Refusal," page 250.)

THINK ABOUT CONTENT

- Informal reports usually do not include introductory material, but include it if necessary.
- Start by asking yourself, "What does my reader need to know, precisely, about the subject?" Put this into a purpose statement in a single, explicit sentence. In a memo format, this can be your subject line.

- Use direct order organization. Begin with the most important information, usually the conclusion and a recommendation, for most routine problems. This approach saves your reader time. It offers the important information right up front. Write this down in outline form. For example, if you believe your copy machine should be replaced, you would start with this subject line: Recommend replacing copy machine. In this, you would back up your recommendations with the reasons:
  — Required 12 repairs in the past month.
  — Requires clerk for operation.
  — Produces too few copies per minute.
  — Is out of warranty.
- Or use an indirect approach. Start with general information, review the facts, and end with your recommendation. In the indirect approach, you might start with this subject line: New copy machine offers superior performance.
- Follow this rule for selecting the direct or indirect approach: When your audience favors your conclusion or recommendation, state it directly, then back it up with facts. When your audience resists your conclusion or recommendation, or knows little or nothing about it, give the facts first and state your conclusion and recommendation at the end.
- Organize your information under the subtopics of your report.
- Use a personal writing style—using *I, you, he, they,* and *we*—if your organization allows it.
- Write and rewrite until your report is interesting, concise, and flows well.
- Make a conclusion, summary, or recommendation statement at the end, even if it repeats your subject line.
- Check to be sure you have completely answered or solved your subject problem or statement.
- Have others review it and give input, if possible.
- Give your report a little shelf time, then come back and give it one more fresh review.

ELIMINATE WRONG MESSAGES

- Do not assume a level of knowledge your reader doesn't have.
- Using a direct approach does not relieve you of listing all the facts. Be sure all your backup facts are logically listed.
- Don't fire off a report without giving it an objective, second look. With email and online communications, it's tempting to send something off immediately. Be sure to give yourself reflection time.
- Don't make your report too long. This is usually a sign that it lacks organization. Keep it to under one page for simple subjects.
- Don't automatically begin every report in a direct approach. In our example, for instance, if the facts or evidence is not so clear-cut, you may be considered biased, capricious, or arbitrary. In cases where the subject is not on the top of everyone's mind, an indirect approach may work better.

SELECT A FORMAT

Use memo, letter, or report form. Informal reports are often sent by email.

EDIT, EDIT, EDIT

- Check and recheck your information to be sure it is accurate and complete.
- Have others review and critique your report in draft form, if possible.
- Give your report (and yourself) some breathing time. Go back and read it when you are fresh to make sure you are satisfied with it before sending.

Internal Memo

TO: Employees and physicians
FROM: John Allen, president and CEO
RE: "Give Health a Hand" campaign
DATE: Nov. 22, 2004

With flu season upon us, Good Samaritan Hospital is working to keep central Nebraska healthy through a new campaign called "Give Health a Hand."

Good Samaritan developed Give Health a Hand to remind children and adults that frequent hand washing is the best way to prevent the spread of germs. We have retained Omaha-based Redstone Communications and Hanser & Associates for regional advertising and public relations services surrounding the campaign.

In recognition of National Hand Washing Awareness Week, Dec. 5–11, Good Samaritan will be visiting schools, businesses and restaurants to demonstrate proper hand washing techniques and distribute hand washing kits and posters. The campaign, which has been endorsed by the Nebraska Health and Human Services System, will continue through February.

Highlights of the campaign, to begin Monday, Dec. 6, include:
- TV and radio spots with hand washing theme song
- Hand washing posters and kits (containing hand washing instructions, a bar of soap and a coloring book)
- Announcement of campaign to area news media
- Guest column in the *Kearney Hub*
- Ongoing hand washing events in the community (December through February)

I thank all employees and physicians at Good Samaritan for your ongoing commitment to rigorous hand washing at work, home and in the community. Our community is trusting you, me and all of us at Good Samaritan to Give Health a Hand.

Help us spread the word about Give Health a Hand by sharing information about the campaign with your family, friends, neighbors and others in your community. Key points include:
- Frequent hand washing is the best way to prevent the spread of germs that cause illness;
- It takes vigorous scrubbing with soap and warm water for at least 20 seconds to wash germs away;
- It is especially important to wash your hands before, during and after handling food, as well as before you eat;
- Washing up after using the restroom is imperative. After you've washed your hands, use a paper towel to turn off the faucet and to open the door of a public restroom. Properly dispose of your paper towel; and
- Alcohol-based disposable hand wipes or gel sanitizers are good alternatives if soap and water are not available.
- In addition to frequent hand washing, these four good health habits will help ward of flu and other viral infections:
- Cover your mouth and nose when you sneeze or cough.
- Avoid touching your eyes, nose or mouth.
- Stay home when you are sick.
- Avoid close contact with people who are sick.

Contact the Corporate Communications Department at 555-0123 for more information about the campaign, or if you would like to help conduct hand washing demonstrations or have suggestions on possible venues.

Also see FORMAL REPORT, page 192, and MEMO, page 159.

33

FEASIBILITY REPORT

Come now, let us reason together.

—ISAIAH 1:18

The feasibility report defines a need or proposed idea, then analyzes, compares, and recommends a course of action. When your organization is considering a new location, expansion, or the purchase of new equipment, for example, it's imperative that you look closely to see which course of action is best and if that course of action is likely to succeed. A list of questions should start the process:

- What is the cost?
- Will it be profitable?
- What are the advantages and disadvantages?
- What will the impact be?
- What legal considerations exist?
- Is it practical?
- What are the personnel, training, and skill considerations?

THINK ABOUT ORGANIZATION

This report should contain an introduction, body, summary or conclusion, and recommendation sections. (Review "Business Plan," page 189; "Formal Report," page 192; and "Informal Report," page 199.)

- The *introduction* sets out the the proposal, the purpose of the report, the background, scope, any limitations, and the methods and procedures used in coming to a recommendation.
- The *body* gives detailed evaluation and analysis. It will set out the possible alternative solutions or products, for example, and common criteria used to evaluate them.
- The *conclusion* gives a summary of the results, which will help in making the best decision.
- The *recommendation* is a statement of the writer's opinion of the course of action to take.

THINK ABOUT CONTENT

- Develop a purpose statement. Make this statement as specific as possible. It should include a problem statement if this is part of the reason for the study and report. It must state both the objective and the scope of the report. For example:

  > Our present installation technique is too labor intensive and its service life is too short. This report compares four new installation techniques and recommends one for use by our installers.

- Make a list of all the questions that must be answered. Get the input of all the people involved to develop a complete list. For the example just given, here are some questions you might include:
  — What are the materials costs of each new procedure?
  — What are the training and skills requirements of each new procedure?
  — What are the time and labor requirements of each new procedure?
  — What improvement in serviceability and service life does each new procedure offer?
  — What is the sales impact of each new procedure?
  — What are the equipment costs to complete each of the new procedures?
  — What are the projected savings in service calls for the new procedures?

- Turn these questions into criteria statements by which to measure each alternative, such as
  — The materials cost comparison for Procedures A, B, C, and D.
  — The training and skills requirements comparison for Procedures A, B, C, and D.
  — The time and labor requirements for Procedures A, B, C, and D.
  — The service life comparisons for Procedures A, B, C, and D.
  — The sales impact comparisons for Procedures A, B, C, and D.
  — The equipment cost comparisons for Procedures A, B, C, and D.
  — The comparative savings in service calls for Procedures A, B, C, and D.

- Develop a preliminary study and report outline.
- Complete the information gathering, tests, investigation, and fact finding and collection.
- Develop the final report outline.
- Write the report, using visually effective graphs and comparison charts to make the information interesting and easy to comprehend. The report should include a precise introduction of the problem, purpose, and scope; a body of detailed evaluation of the alternatives; a conclusion which summarizes the evaluation of each alternative; and a final recommendation.
- Rewrite, edit, and review. Use other people to review, making sure the report is complete, polished, and easy to understand.

SELECT A FORMAT

- Use headings, subheadings, and sub-subheadings to clearly guide the reader.
- Use white space to make the report visually inviting to read.

Also see FORMAL REPORT, page 192, and INFORMAL REPORT, page 199.

34

TECHNICAL REPORT AND TECHNICAL WRITING

Fine writing is next to fine doing,
the top thing in the world.

—JOHN KEATS

Good principles of writing—whether the content is technical or not—remain the same for all disciplines. When the subject matter is highly specialized and the report (or other material) is being written for a group of "insiders" who use and understand a special vocabulary of technical terms, the process may be considered "technical writing."

A special language is needed by many disciplines and industries. As in all kinds of writing, the contents should be dictated by the audience, the precise purpose, and the particular discipline or industry. Many organizations have very strict rules and procedures for these reports. Often there are legal requirements for writing them as well.

For example, the research and development department of an equipment manufacturer needs to write troubleshooting reports that list possible causes of precise symptoms or problems. These reports name a symptom or problem, set forth test methods, and then offer possible solutions. They may be written for field-service personnel or technically trained customers who use the equipment. The audience and purpose dictate the content and format.

What technical reports and technical writing have is common are an emphasis on the audience, a well-defined purpose, and a consistent format that reflects the needs and conventions of the discipline or industry the report serves. It is important to know both the "report culture" and organization protocol. Check present and past reports of your organization, industry, and discipline. Also see "Feasibility Report," page 202; "Formal Report," page 192; and "Informal Report," page 199.

DECIDE TO WRITE
Use this communication to report:
- Investigative findings
- Accidents or incidents
- New facts
- Solutions to problems
- Evaluations
- Statement on problems
- Progress
- Status

THINK ABOUT CONTENT

- Review reports used by your organization, industry, and discipline to determine the acceptable form.
- Be sure you understand the audience before you start. Make sure you are writing for a technical audience.
- Obtain or create a glossary of audience-tested, technical terms, and learn them thoroughly.
- Ask detailed questions until you have focused the problem, purpose, and scope of your report.
- Write a preliminary outline, then review it with others involved in the process, if possible.
- Complete the information gathering, investigation, testing, and research, making detailed notes, recording figures, and sources.
- Write a final outline.
- Write your report, focusing the content on completely answering, solving, or fulfilling the promise contained in your beginning problem, purpose, or scope statement.
- Rewrite, edit, and review. Get others to help to ensure objectivity and comprehensiveness.

CONSIDER SPECIAL SITUATIONS

- *Progress* or *contact reports* emphasize what has happened or changed over time since the last report. One of the most common examples of this is the *sales* report. But it is also used extensively—in a very different format—for government projects, political campaigns, advertising campaigns, construction, and many other industries. This report creates a record and keeps others informed. Straight reporting of information with a minimum of comparison is used for this report, which is usually written for a limited audience.

  Use action headings, and make statements concise. Structure the report with an introduction that identifies the project, director, and the project goals. Include a brief summary of the last progress report; a body listing progress, problems, comments, notable features, and budget considerations; a section that previews expected progress for the next reporting period; and a closing section that gives a conclusion about overall progress.

- *Status reports* emphasize the current condition of a project, detailing what exists (rather than what has changed). They are divided into the necessary component parts, and the writer includes detailed observations and some evaluation for a limited audience.
- *Trip reports* and *event reports* are required by organizations to keep other employees informed and establish a permanent record. These reports should be brief, with the emphasis on new information. They are usually done in memo format, addressed to the writer's supervisor, and copied to others. The subject line lists the destination and date. The body gives the purpose of the trip, persons visited, and accomplishments. Include only important events, and use subheads to identify them. End with conclusions and recommendations.
- *Trouble, incident,* or *accident reports* are usually internal memos dealing with accidents, equipment failure, unplanned work stoppage, or other problems. They create an official record and inform a limited audience. Management uses these reports to determine causes and the need for changes to avoid a recurrence. Often these reports are used for insurance and legal purposes, so it is vital that information be factual, accurate, as precise as possible, and complete—without unsolicited opinion statements.
- The subject line should list the precise problem. The body describes the problem. Be sure to answer these questions:
  — Was anyone injured?
  — Where exactly did the problem occur?
  — What happened?
  — What was the exact time?
  — Was there any property damage? What?
  — Was there work stoppage?
  — Who witnessed the problem? (Record complete contact information.)

  Record accurately the time, date, location, treatment for any injuries, damage to property, names and addresses of witnesses, statements of witnesses, equipment damage, and any other important information. Take a photograph record and drawing and/or diagrams of the event whenever possible. Make the tone objective, and place no blame. Conclude with the action taken, and future action that will be taken to ensure that the problem does not occur again.

- *Investigative reports* may give the results of a survey, marketing study, product evaluation, literature search, or procedure investigation. The purpose of this report is to give precise analysis of the subject and offer recommendations.

  Open with a purpose statement. In the body, first completely define the scope of the investigation. If it is a survey, for example, define the number and composition of those surveyed by age, education, geographical location, occupation, income, interest, opinions, and any other information that impacts your information. Define the limits of the survey technique, then report the findings and their significance. Conclude with recommendations. (See "Questionnaires and Surveys," page 219.)

- *Literature reviews* and *annotated bibliographies* are literature or printed-material summaries on specific topics, published in a specific time period. These reviews offer a complete listing with an evaluation, and serve as sources for further in-depth research. For example, a literature review may list all the information published on email over the past five years. A literature review or annotated bibliography may also be part of a larger report.

  Literature reviews help professionals—industrial, medical, academic, and others—keep abreast of new things in their fields.

  Sources may be listed chronologically from the earliest source, or they may be arranged by subtopics covered.

  In the heading or brief introduction, give the scope of the subject to be covered, the sources (books, magazine and journal articles, online sources, etc.), and dates of publication or origination. In the body, give each listing accurately and completely so readers may easily locate listed sources. (Follow a stylebook like the *Chicago Manual of Style*.) For each listing, give the scope of the work and its value to the reader. Be concise.

- An *abstract* gives a very brief synopsis of a longer report or book. A *descriptive abstract* defines the purpose, scope, and methods used; and an *informative abstract* includes this information and the results, conclusions, and recommendations. The abstract should focus on what is important to readers.

- *Staff reports* are written to document and analyze problems, and to recommend solutions. Because this report is usually standardized by the organization, it is easy to develop a macro or merge document on computer software. The report can then be set up in memo format with sections for problem or summary, related factors, facts, discussion, conclusions, and recommendations. Standard responses can be part of the software program so that only particular details must be filled in. Because these reports may play a part in some legal action or employee issue, they must be completed in precise, concise detail. Employees involved are usually asked to review and sign these reports if they will become part of the employee's file. Such reports have serious confidentiality considerations. Therefore, transmission online must be handled by secure systems only.

- The *executive summary* may be a separate, brief document or part of a much longer report. It is similar in structure to the abstract but usually longer. The objective is to briefly cover all the points of a formal report: purpose, scope, methods, results, summary, conclusions, and recommendations. It gives enough concise detail to inform readers of the entire report contents so they will not have to read the full-length version.

  Write this summary to stand alone. Cover the essential information proportionate to the coverage in the full report. Do not refer to tables, charts, or other illustrations not included in the executive summary. Use technical terms understood by the audience. Visuals aren't included unless they are integral to the summary.

Also see FEASIBILITY REPORT, page 202; FORMAL REPORT, page 192; and INFORMAL REPORT, page 199.

35

BOOK PROPOSAL

Inside you there's an artist you don't know.

—JALAI UD-DIN RAMI

The book proposal is a sales tool written to persuade an editor at a publishing house to buy your nonfiction book. Because each book a publishing company takes on represents a substantial financial risk, and because there is so much competition to get a publisher's interest, you need to convince the publisher why your idea is unique, why you are the perfect person to write the book, who will buy the book, and how the book can be successfully marketed to realize the number of sales that will make it a financial success. All these factors define why your book proposal must be very well researched and exceptionally well written.

DECIDE TO WRITE
Use a book proposal to persuade:
- Subject experts to contribute or coauthor a book
- Subject experts to agree to review and "blurb" (a short critique of praise) your book
- A literary agent to represent the book project to a publisher
- An editor to present the book project to his or her publisher's editorial committee
- A book packager to take on the project
- A special sales outlet to carry the book
- An organization to offer a grant or sponsorship for the book project
- A book representative to sell your book to bookstore buyers

THINK ABOUT CONTENT
Your book proposal will need to demonstrate the following elements to be successful:
- A unique idea, uniquely presented
- A distinctive voice that works well with the subject matter
- Writing that is impeccable, clear, and accessible
- Development of the idea that is well organized
- Your outstanding credentials to write on the subject
- A clear and precise definition of your audience and how you will reach them. (Your "platform" or unique qualifications are included here.)
- A sample chapter that demonstrates your writing skills

A book proposal includes several elements. To sell your book to a publisher, you will need to:

- Create a *title page* (see model at end of chapter) that lists the working title of your book; your name, address, and contact information; and/or possibly the name, address, and contact information of your literary agent.

- Develop a *table of contents* for the book proposal, which lists the sections of your proposal and the page number where each section starts.

- Write a brief and compelling *overview, introductory,* or *concept statement* that encapsulates your book idea and names the market for it. This must be your strongest sales statement—usually in 150 words or less. You must convince the editor to read on.

- Draft an *About the Book* section that you can continue to refine as you research and write your book proposal. This section expands upon your first, brief section overview. It answers the *what, why, where, when,* and *how much* questions about your book. Be sure to include any and all of the following to make your proposal complete.
  — Identify the problem or need your book will answer or fill.
  — List the book's additional benefits.
  — Supply supporting statistics or quotes.
  — Give the unique approach that your book will take.
  — List any special features your book will include like photos or illustrations.
  — List the end result for readers, or the greatest benefit readers of your book will enjoy.

- Write an *About the Author* section that details your unique qualifications to author the book. Make a solid case for yourself as the best author choice based upon your education, vocation, profession, experience, research, special connections, knowledge, and/or exclusive information.

- Develop an *About the Market* section that clearly identifies who will buy your book and how you plan to reach these targeted book buyers. If you've carefully set out the need for your book, then defining your targeted readers and how you'll reach them is that much easier. In this section include any direct-sales avenues you plan to use, like speaking engagements at which you will sell books (with number projections based on a proven track record, if possible); special sales ideas you may have; institutional sales you have investigated or arranged; subsidiary sales ideas you have; sales partnerships you have arranged or plan to arrange; and so on. This section is crucial in today's book-selling process. Use concrete numbers, names, and connections, if you can. All these factors, especially your personal record in promoting and your established and ready audience, are called your "platform." This helps the publisher estimate the number of sales your book can immediately command.

- Research the *About the Competition* section thoroughly. It must be complete and current. Gather as many hard facts as possible, reviewing all the competitive (or partially competitive) books and upcoming books. Make accurate comparisons. Your objective here is to illustrate that there is a market for your book. Further, you want to point out why and how your book will outsell competitive titles. Be careful here to include the strong points of other books as well as their shortcomings, pointing out how and why your book, comparatively, will sell.

- Consider including an (optional) *About Book Production* section if you have concrete reasons for wanting the book produced in a certain size, color, or format. The appearance of a book often positions it properly with its competition.

- Include an (optional) *About Publicity and Promotion* section if you are, for example, planning to hire a public relations agent to help create awareness of the book. Name the publicity agent, your precise plans, and the amount of money you plan to invest, if possible. Beyond this, you should list your media connections, and how you plan to publicize and promote the book. The author "platform" information introduced in the *About the Market* section can be expanded upon here.

- Create a *Table of Contents* section that lists the chapter titles in your book.
- Plan a section entitled *About the Chapters, Chapter Summaries,* or *About Book Content* that includes a carefully written synopsis of each chapter. When you have a particularly strong passage, an anecdote, or some other very impressive material written for a chapter, include snippets of text in the synopses to demonstrate your writing skills, voice, tone, and approach.
- Include, if possible, a *sample chapter* or chapters, which are usually, but not always, required or requested by the publisher. Make yours as near to a finished chapter as you can write. This should usually be the first chapter, unless there is a very strong reason to include another chapter.
- Include an (optional) *Appendix, Bibliography,* or *About Sources* section if you have a strong list of authorities and/or sources, permissions, endorsements, or other exclusive agreements. This is more important in scholarly works where your exhaustive approach to researching the subject may be key to a book's success.

CONSIDER SPECIAL SITUATIONS

- Your book title—though the publisher will undoubtedly change it—can be instrumental in selling your proposal. Be sure to study all aspects of titles thoroughly before deciding on one. Study best-seller list titles, the publisher's list of lead titles, and the competitive book titles in the category for which you are writing. Ask yourself: what makes these titles work (or not)? Try brainstorming with other writers, and test your title on a number of writers, book readers, and bookstore personnel to get their feedback. The best titles often come from unlikely sources.
- The average book proposal length is about 25 to 40 pages, though this varies widely.
- Because editors must often read book proposals in their "spare time," make sure yours is inviting and easy to read. For example, the use of bulleted, concise (short) statements that appear in

boldface type, followed by short explanatory paragraphs, in the *About the Book* section can hook the editor into reading more. That, of course, is your objective.
- Videotapes or DVDs of television interviews, copies of related magazine and newspaper articles you've written or been quoted in, and/or examples of unique sales or promotional items you'll use to market your book may be included in your book proposal. The proposal may be packaged in a double-pocketed folder with a die-cut for the insertion of a business card. If you are using an agent, this folder (and your proposal in bound form) is usually supplied by the literary agency.

ELIMINATE WRONG MESSAGES

- Don't be too eager to send off your proposal. An unpolished proposal will be quickly rejected, and you will have lost the opportunity to send an improved version to the same editor or agent. Have a trustworthy expert, or several, review your proposal. But even before you submit it to an expert, set it aside for a while, then reread it with fresh objectivity. Edit it again to make it your very best effort.
- Sending your proposal to the wrong agent or editor will result in both time wasted and rejection. Carefully research the kinds of books an agent and/or editor handles. Then send a simple query letter or call the agent or editor to briefly present your idea and ask if he or she would like to see your proposal.
- Don't overlook or discount small publishers. They often put more promotional effort into the books they publish, and they often keep books in print longer.
- Talk to authors who've published books similar to yours with a publisher you'd like to publish with. Ask key questions like these:
  — Was the publisher willing to negotiate contract terms?
  — How many books were printed in the first printing?

— What kind of promotional efforts did the publisher's publicity department exert? Were they timely? Did they garner interviews and reviews? Were they properly targeted and followed up on? Did the publicity department work with the author to build a really effective publicity campaign?

— Did the publisher get sufficient numbers of books into bookstores and explore other sales avenues?

— Did the publicity department help set up promotional events like speaking engagements in major cities?

• Anticipate the following list of the most common reasons book proposals are rejected, and study your proposal to be sure you've eliminated them:

— "The book doesn't fit our current list," which most likely means you haven't selected the right publisher.

— "The market for this book isn't big enough," which means you haven't demonstrated your proposal is a topic worthy of a book.

— "This type of book doesn't sell" or "The market for this book is too small" may mean that you need to reslant your proposal to demonstrate a larger group of book buyers. Or, it may mean you haven't researched your topic and potential market carefully enough.

— "We don't do well with titles like this" may mean you've picked the wrong publisher, one that doesn't market to the type of book buyer interested in your topic, or you haven't demonstrated why and how your book will sell to book buyers.

— "There's too much competition" means that you haven't demonstrated there's a need in the marketplace for your book.

— "It's too costly to produce" may mean that the publisher isn't prepared to do a book like yours, or it could mean that you need to think about producing the book in a less expensive format.

• Unless you or your agent has a very good reason to exclusively submit to a single publisher, don't limit the submission of your proposal to one publisher at a time. Do simultaneous submissions to a number of carefully chosen publishers. Often it works well to initially submit to three or four publishers (perhaps your second-ranked choices), and examine their responses to determine if there's a common theme that indicates some area where you can improve your proposal. Make any changes indicated, then submit it to your top choice(s).

SELECT A FORMAT

Research competitive and related titles to determine an appropriate size for your book, the number of pages you anticipate your book will run, and whether you believe it should be published in hardcover, as a trade paperback, or in another format. Tell the publisher why you think your book should be published in this particular format if you have a strong reason for it.

CHOOSE STRONG WORDS

appeal	nonfiction
capture	now
current	popular
demand	purpose
discovery	readership
drama	research
examines	resource
exclusive	revolutionary
facts	risk
first	story
idea	style
immediacy	success
market	trend
must-read	untold
need	value
never	voice
new	

CREATE EFFECTIVE PHRASES

best resource

competitive titles

creative plan

dramatic story

draws on life experiences

examines in-depth

find an audience

first-hand experience

first-time release

fresh idea

hidden until now

narrative story

new method

new research findings

newly discovered

offers competitive edge

popular beliefs

powerful examples

proven, yet unknown, facts

revolutionary idea

riveting tale

unique experience

unknown facts

untold story

WRITE STRONG SENTENCES

This book will prove the author's premise.

No competitive title covers this important topic.

Contrary to common belief, this book will prove the opposite is true.

This is an amazing story.

My unique approach to this subject is described in the following chapters.

Book buyers who purchased Strunk and White's *The Elements of Style* will purchase *How to Write It: A Complete Guide to Everything You'll Ever Write,* and they'll place it next to Strunk and White's book on their desks.

This is the perfect reference book for anyone who has suffered a tongue-tied moment.

This is a must-buy book for anyone who will ever be called upon to say a few words.

There is an urgent need in the marketplace for this book.

BUILD EFFECTIVE PARAGRAPHS

Carefully build effective paragraphs, using positive statements. State the idea in the first sentence, and follow it with sentences that explain, expand upon, and/or examine the idea.

Keep your paragraphs short: an average of five or six sentences. And always bear in mind your target reader: the harried editor, who wants to know immediately and exactly what your book idea is, how you will present it, why you are the perfect person to write the book, and how you believe it can be marketed and effectively sold for a profit. Editors, too, will immediately turn to your sample chapter to determine if you have the skills to write the book.

EDIT, EDIT, EDIT

The strength of your proposal may well depend upon the editing. So, don't short-cut this part of your work. It can mean the difference between a sale and a rejection.

It's often beneficial to have one or more subject experts and editors go through your book proposal draft to check for everything from structure, to facts presented, to superfluous words, to typos. Effort and time spent here can pay big dividends.

Title Page and About the Book

Sandra E. Lamb
4567 Street Address
City, State 98701
Telephone: 510-555-0123
Fax: 510-555-0124
Email: sandy123@email.com
Website: www.sandralamb.com

Nonfiction/Gift Book
Approximately 250 Pages

Personal Notes:
How to Write from the Heart for Any Occasion
by
Sandra E. Lamb

A Book Proposal

OVERVIEW

There's a new reality in the whacked-out, frenetic pace of our lives: we're becoming disconnected and isolated. Why?

The biggest response to my book, *How to Write It: A Complete Guide to Everything You'll Ever Write* (Ten Speed Press), has been by people who say, "I love the section on personal notes, but I wanted more. Lots more." This sentiment has come from general users of the book, book reviewers, and "off the book page" reporters. Even radio and television interviewers most often direct their questions at those "sticky problem areas" requiring an outpouring of more than just words. (See attachments: *The Denver Post* interview; my piece for *Family Circle* on apologies; my piece, "When Bad Things Happen to Good Friends," which appeared in *Working Mother*; and my short piece on personal notes in the November issue of *Woman's Day*.)

Typically the comments I receive about the personal notes sections of *How to Write It* range from "This is wonderful," to those like I just received from a *Family Circle* editor when I proposed a new piece on the subject: "This is just what's needed out there, because we never know what to say; what to write, especially in situations of grief. . . . What *do* you say? What *do* you write?"

Personal Notes will help you experience and process your own feelings. Then it will help you connect with the people in your life through writing what's in your heart.

The bonus this book will give you is the opportunity to peek into the personal emotions and notes of historical personalities and contemporary, internationally known figures, because a variety of notes from these people will be included too. This will also reinforce the message that there's great value in writing personal notes, as you see how our heroes have valued them throughout history.

About the Book

WHY THIS BOOK IS TIMELY

* We write 75 to 80 percent fewer thank-you notes, appreciation notes, congratulations notes, thinking-about-you notes, and just-a-note notes than our grandmothers did.

  For the past 20 years, my friend Jenny has created hand-crafted Christmas gifts for her nieces and nephews, and then for them and their children. The number of gifts has escalated from seven to 52. She has *yet* to receive the first thank-you note from even one of these people, aged four months to 42 years old. We need to recapture the art of thanking each other through written, personal notes!

* The latest achievement reports indicate our children are falling far, far behind at reading and writing. They are performing as much as two grade levels below standard. *Why?*

  Because our society isn't writing personal notes like our grandparents did. Even like our parents did. Kids certainly aren't writing them. They don't see us, their parents, doing it, and no one is teaching them to do it. Writing—especially writing personal notes—is becoming a lost art. And this isn't good news. It means our society is losing some of the vital civility and social nuances it has taken us centuries to develop. *We are because we write.*

  We need to reinstitute the value and art of writing. We parents need to start writing, and we need to teach our children why they need to write, and how to express themselves to others on paper.

* Lines between our business and personal lives are disappearing as businesses move into our homes, and more of our business associates become social and personal friends.

  Those "social graces"—and personal notes—we once reserved for a separate category of people, family and personal friends, must now be used equally for business associates.

  These new, multifaceted relationships are more complicated to maintain, and personal note writing is even more important in this new emerging society. (See "When Bad Things Happen to Good Friends," from *Working Mother* enclosed.)

* Electronic advances are dehumanizing. The subtle combination of intimate, immediate, anonymous, and very often truncated communications we now have online is taking the humanity out of our communications.

  There is something very emotional, and very human, that happens to us in the act of taking a pen in hand and writing down our thoughts on paper. This act can't be electronically duplicated. The weight and import of a message are far greater when it comes in handwritten form. Handwritten messages are vital to keeping us connected to each other.

* We've all become too busy to write. In our frenetically paced society, we no longer take the time to really express our emotions.

  Writing by hand is a type of therapy. It can keep us sane and keep us connected to our own inner feelings.

* Ironically, our mobile, electronic society has left us feeling isolated. We are suffering from a universal and growing failure to connect with other humans and to create those "human moments."

  No woman—no matter how she tries—is an island. In fact, most of us do very poorly in isolation. Words like lonely, disconnected, desolate, and depressed come to mind. We need to connect to others, and this book will show you how.

* The new "spiritual awareness" has awakened in us a desire to relate to others.

  Now is exactly the time to provide this wonderful guide to *really* communicating—connecting, communing—with the people in our lives through writing personal notes.

Table of Contents

CONTENTS

INTRODUCTION

36

RESEARCH

Seize the subject and the words will follow.

—CATO THE ELDER

How to write it often depends on knowing how to research it. This can be the most exciting and interesting part of writing. The process of in-depth learning about the subject takes some special skills, and it must not be shortchanged; investigation, or research, is the key to giving what you write the ring of authenticity and authority. Where and how you begin your research will depend upon the subject matter and where you enter the process. Sometimes you'll work from the general to the specific; other times, from the specific to the general.

There are two basic ways to get the information you need: primary, or firsthand research, and secondary, or indirect research. Primary sources include both unpublished and original sources, such as organization records and your own observations, experiments, and surveys. Secondary sources are published works such as encyclopedias, almanacs, directories, various other kinds of publications, periodicals, books, and statistical sources.

START WITH PRIMARY SOURCES

Every writing project will start with primary sources that include your firsthand experience. You'll need to take some or all of the following steps to get this part of your job done:

- Ask yourself what you want your reader to learn from what you write. Be precise.
- Brainstorm with and interview people to determine the need for what you're writing, and to develop your scope and purpose statement.
- Conduct an experiment, take a survey, and gather other firsthand information from expert sources.
- Set up and conduct your own systematic observations and research online by using discussion groups, newsgroups, and/or email queries or requests.
- Test what you've written—information or instructions—on a sampling of your readers before completing your final draft.

CAREFULLY SELECT AND USE SECONDARY SOURCES

Secondary sources are generally more accessible, less costly, and more complete than primary sources. These include published books, articles, reports, Web documents, online discussions, correspondence, memos, brochures, operating manuals, etc. You'll be able to find sources both on the Internet, and directly through libraries.

In today's fast-paced world, making sure your information is "up to the minute" is vital. Often your secondary research will start with limiting sources to the most current and focusing subject matter to precisely what you need.

RESEARCH THE INTERNET

- Use the tools on the search engine to conduct your search. (See the help page.) Enter the term for which you want to search.
- Use qualifiers (Boolean operators)—*and, or, not*—to restrict your search. Also use quotation marks around phrases you want to research (for example "mechanical engineering") to limit results to the phrase as a unit.
- Use the advanced search whenever you need it.
- Try a number and variety of search engines to ensure you've gotten the best results.

INTERNET RESEARCH SOURCES

While public and university libraries now have catalogs and databases available through the Internet, you may first want to use a search engine to locate sources. Here are some basic ones, though the list changes frequently:

- Machine-generated databases that use "spiders" or "bots" to travel the Worldwide Web searching for information include:
    www.google.com
    www.altavista.com
    www.excite.com
    www.webcrawler.com
- Human-generated search engines index fewer pages but offer directory trees that help organize content:
    http://search.yahoo.com
    http://lycos.com
    http://search.msn.com

- Hybrid search engines search the Web and also their own databases of articles to provide indexes not available elsewhere. These include:
    www.northlight.com
    http://dmoz.org (Google powered)
    www.ilor.com (Google powered)
    www.hotbot.lycos.com (Lycos powered)
- For selective, scholarly Web research, try one of the following directories, or check with the governing body at www.icaan.org for new ones:
    www.clearinghouse.net (Argus Clearinghouse)
    http://infomine.ucr.edu (Infomine)
    www.vlib.org (World Wide Web Virtual Library)
- For metasearch engines that search the Web using a number of search engines, try these, but be sure to carefully define and limit your search:
    www.metacrawler.com
    http://dogpile.com
- To locate Web business and government sources, start here:
    http://webbusiness.cio.com (Business Resources on the Web)
    www.pace.edu/library/links/links.html (Business Internet Resources)
    www.inc.com/ibr (Inc. Business Resources on the Web)
    http://dir.yahoo.com/Business_and_Economy (Yahoo's Business Resources)
    www.lib.lsu.edu/gov/fedgov.html (Federal Government Agencies Directory)
    www.fedstats.gov (FedStats)
- Evaluate your sources for authority, accuracy, authorship, bias, and currency. Following are the sponsor website indicators:
  — .aero – aerospace industry
  — .biz – business
  — .com – company or individual
  — .coop – business cooperative
  — .edu – university, college, or educational source
  — .gov – government
  — .int – international organization
  — .mil – US military
  — .museum
  — .name – individual
  — .net – network provider
  — .org – nonprofit organization
  — .pro – professional, such as a lawyer or doctor

RESEARCH THE LIBRARY

- Develop a research strategy and outline of the sources you may need to find.
- You may want to contact a research or reference librarian in a particular area and discuss your goals. This can usually be done by telephone and can help you search more efficiently by directing you to precise sources.
- Go to an online library homepage and access its catalog, databases of articles, and other sources. Libraries license databases, and you will need to be a library cardholder to access these.
- Start your search by subject, author, or title.
- Use the library's online databases to search other sources:
  - *InfoTrac* is a collection of databases containing full text and abstracts of articles in business, health, and general areas.
  - *ProQuest* is a database provider (aggregator), which sells databases to libraries. These include databases specializing in biology, nursing, psychology, historic newspapers, specialized academic indexing, professional indexing, etc.
  - *EBSCOhost* is a database of articles in a wide range of subjects.
  - *FirstSearch* is a collection of specialized databases showing some full text and some abstracts from many library collections (WorldCat and ArticleFirst included).
  - *Lexis/Nexis* is a collection of databases featuring business, legal, congressional, and other articles in both full text and abstracts.

LIBRARY RESOURCES

You may want to start with standard references—online, texts, or microfilm in the library—in your quest to find the best sources. Typically you'll divide these into the following categories and sources:

General Guides

Guide to Reference Books

Encyclopedias

The Encyclopedia Americana
Encyclopaedia Britannica
The Encyclopedia of Careers and Vocational Guidance
Grolier's Academic American Encyclopedia
McGraw-Hill Encyclopedia of Science and Technology

Magazines and Special Publications

Business Periodical Index
Index to the Times (London)
Magazine Index
The New York Times Index
Psychological Abstracts
Reader's Guide to Periodical Literature
Social Science Index
Wall Street Journal Index
Woman Studies Abstracts

More Information

American History Sourcebook
American Statistics Index
Directory of Special Libraries
Encyclopedia of Associations
The Official Museum Directory
The Research Center Directory
Telephone books

Biographical Directories

Dictionary of American Biography (prominent Americans of the past)
Who's Who in America
Who's Who in the East
Who's Who in the Midwest
Who's Who in the World

Almanacs and Atlases

The Business One-Irwin Investor's Handbook
The World Almanac and Book of Facts
Microsoft® Encarta® World Atlas

Trade Directories

America's Corporate Families
Directory of Corporate Affiliation
The Million Dollar Directory
Thomas Register of American Manufacturers

Government Publications

Government Reports Announcements and Index
Monthly Catalog of US Government Publications

Statistical Sources

American Statistics Index
Handbook of Basic Economic Statistics
Predicasts Basebook (also available online through subscription databases such as Gale's Business and Company Resource Center)
Standard & Poor's Statistical Service (also available online through subscription databases such as Gale's Business and Company Resource Center)
Statistical Abstract of the United States

CONSIDER OTHER INDIRECT SOURCES

- Use interlibrary loan services though your library.
- Use association, newspaper, and corporation library sources.
- Use public relations people in corporations, hospitals, and associations.
- Search public records in the courts, prisons, and other public places.
- Research people connections online through www.genealogywebdirectory.com.
- Buy the research services of a reference librarian, private investigator, or search organization.

THINK ABOUT CONTENT

Research is the first step of the writing process:

- *Focus* on the reader to determine the need for writing.
- Prepare a *purpose statement* that defines the scope of what you'll write.
- Perform the needed extra *research*.
- *Organize and draft* the written document.
- *Revise, edit, and polish* what you've written.

37

QUESTIONNAIRES AND SURVEYS

It is not every question that deserves an answer.

—PUBLILIUS SYRUS

Sometimes the best way to get information is to ask questions. But which, and of whom? You will need to establish a survey method and develop a questionnaire, especially if you need information like personal attitudes, opinions, or evaluations.

First, you must identify the information you need and then determine if you need direct research sources for that information. If you do, you must decide how to select a representative sample of the people you need information from, and decide on the format and delivery of your questions. Will you use personal interviews, telephone interviews, or a printed and distributed questionnaire to get the answers you need? Will you interview by email or on the Web? Choose the best format and delivery for your questions to elicit the highest numbers of responses.

The terms questionnaire and survey are often used interchangeably, though surveys are often brief opinion polls, whereas questionnaires often request detailed responses. Either may be an interview on paper, by email, or on the Web. These methods for getting information have the advantage of asking for and getting uniform answers from a large number of people at the same time, thus saving both time and money. They can also allow anonymity, which can be an advantage in getting more and candid responses. Other advantages

can be that those responding to questionnaires are allowed reflective time in which to give more complete answers; and those questioned aren't being influenced by voice inflection or facial expressions.

Possible disadvantages? More opinionated people may respond, whereas others may not; it eliminates nuance in answers; doesn't allow for impromptu follow-up questions; and this method of getting answers can take longer.

Determine the information you need; then eliminate, as better alternatives, direct and secondary research sources for that information (see "Research," page 215).

You will need to establish audience selection and distribution methods, and develop an effective survey instrument or questionnaire, especially if you need information like personal attitudes, opinions, or evaluations.

Be sure the format and delivery of your questions will get the best response. (For some surveys, you may want to use personal interviews, or telephone interviews to get the answers you need.)

DECIDE TO WRITE

Use a survey or questionnaire when you need special information not available through any of the sources you've investigated.

THINK ABOUT CONTENT

- Select a representative sample of the entire audience. You may need to study and employ scientific marketing selection techniques to ensure a valid sample that will produce valid results. Check marketing resources with a reference librarian.
- Write a questionnaire based on what you need to learn.
- Make sure the questions are easy to understand.
- Gear the questions toward facts, and request quantitative responses whenever possible.
- Create a layout that invites readers and allows adequate space for responses.
- Test your questionnaire on a pilot or test group first, get feedback, and incorporate any changes.
- Establish a method for evaluating the results. Remember, you must be able to present the findings clearly and completely, which will require you to objectively interpret answers to questions.

AVOID WRONG MESSAGES

- Avoid leading questions.
- Avoid questions that touch on areas of personal prejudice or bias (unless this is the information you need).

Homeowners' Association Questionnaire

S U N S E T   H O M E O W N E R S

Please complete *one questionnaire per household.* This is to help the new Board of Directors know your desires. Please read entirely before answering.

Name (Optional): _____

House # (Optional): _____

1. *Concerning the process of decision-making at Sunset, we:*
   _____ are pleased with the elective process we have now with the Board interpreting the Covenants and Codes for Community Living.
   _____ would like to see a more direct democratic process, and we pledge to actively participate by voting on decisions.
   Other: _____
   _____

2. *Concerning the interpretation of the Codes for Community Living, 2.3 Unsightly Articles, we believe the following should apply (Y—yes; N—no):*
   _____ Portable basketball hoops should be allowed in front of homes if they are taken in at night.
   _____ Permanent basketball hoops should be allowed to be attached to the front of homes over garage doors if kept in good condition.
   _____ Basketball hoops of any kind should not be allowed in front of homes because they are dangerous so close to the street, as well as "unsightly."
   _____ Basketball play should be restricted to the neighborhood hoop at the clubhouse.

   Other concerns: _____
   _____

3. *Concerning the quality of life at Sunset our family enjoys these amenities (please use O—often, more than once a week; I—infrequently, about once or twice a month; or S—seldom, less than once a month; or N—never):*
   _____ Swimming pool
   _____ Tennis courts
   _____ Jacuzzi
   _____ Clubhouse
   _____ Exercise equipment (in clubhouse)
   _____ Park area
   _____ Enclosed and gated community that eliminates outside traffic during night hours

   Other qualities and services we enjoy and want to preserve: _____
   _____

   Additionally, we would like to see these changes or additions in these items: _____
   _____

4. *We would like to see Sunset expenditures focus on the following areas (numbered in importance 1—top priority, through 5—least important):*
   _____ Extended summer swimming pool hours:
   _____ to _____ Monday through Friday
   _____ to _____ Weekends (Saturday and Sunday)
   _____ Beautifying the park area
   _____ Creation of a baseball area in the park
   _____ Purchase of additional exercise equipment in the clubhouse to include: _____
   _____ Signage and landscaping lighting on Drury Lane at entry

   Other: _____
   _____

Homeowners' Association Questionnaire . . . *continued*

5. *Concerning holiday lighting:*
____ What we have is fine.
____ We would like small white lights on the trees at the entry.

Other: _____

6. *We would like to see these activities (Y—yes; N—no):*
____ holiday community get-together (__ November; __ December)
____ an active Sunset garden club
____ book club meetings in the clubhouse
____ exercise classes at the clubhouse
____ swimming instruction at the pool
____ summer family picnic (__ June; __ July; __ August)

Other: _____

7. *We are willing to organize/volunteer to serve on the following:* _____
_____

We have these additional comments and suggestions for the Board:
_____
_____
_____
_____

Fold your completed survey and place it in the HOA slot to the left of the mailboxes, or mail to Sara E. Faust, 2400 E. Drury Lane, Unit #45, Phoenix, AZ 85001.

VI. INQUIRIES, REQUESTS, AND RESPONSE COMMUNICATIONS

38

REQUESTS AND INQUIRIES

Ask, and ye shall receive,
that your joy may be full.

—JOHN 16:24

At the heart of the request letter is the need to effectively communicate what you want. You must ask that the information you're seeking be sent in response, or that further direction be sent to help in your quest. Your letter should be brief, functional, and gracious in tone. And be sure of the last. You need to make the reader want to help you.

A letter of request or inquiry may be as simple as asking for a price or a free brochure. It may be as complex as requesting the specifications for a product you are including in a bid. The word *inquiry* often has a legal connotation meaning an investigation, and is sometimes used in a more formal letter, "I wish to inquire . . . " or "Referring to your inquiry. . . ." (Erroneously, too, a query letter may be referred to as a request letter. When a writer corresponds with a publisher proposing his composition be published, it is much more a sales than a request letter.)

If you are requesting routine information, make it as precise and brief as possible. But always make it clear and courteous.

This type of letter is, of course, one of the mainstays of business life. And in this, as in all letters, you will leave the reader with an impression about yourself and/or the organization with which you are associated. Business requests should be made on business letterhead. When appropriate, your letter may be faxed or emailed to save time.

DECIDE TO WRITE

When you are seeking one of the following, you'll use a request letter:

- Advice
- Appointments, interviews, meetings
- Business or personal assistance
- Bids, consultations, proposals, estimates
- Change of status: variance or zoning changes, name changes, changes in marital status, etc.
- Contributions, donations
- Information: copies of credit reports, documents, medical records, instructions
- Interviews
- Loan (see "Credit: Offering an Adjustment," page 318; "Credit Inquiry and Providing Credit Information," page 300; and "Credit: Requesting an Adjustment in Payments," page 314)
- Information about job openings

THINK ABOUT CONTENT

- Think through your request before you start writing so that you can clearly state what you want.
- Be sure you understand the protocol of making your request. If you are, for example, requesting a copy of your credit report, you must conform to the particular requirements of the credit company, which usually involve properly identifying yourself, enclosing a statement or copy of credit denial, and enclosing a check for the report. The processes of requesting your military records, medical records, or similar information will have their own special requirements. Find out what these are, and comply in your request to get the results you want.
- When addressing an organization that receives large volumes of requests on a variety of topics, use a subject line to immediately aid the reader in identifying yours: "Subject: Report 1996-B Request."
- If you have several related queries or requests, list them from the most important through the least, so the reader can easily check the items off. Numbering your request items is also helpful to the reader.
- Be sure your request is so detailed that you get precisely the response you want. This is essential when you're requesting bids, for example, because unless your request contains the complete specifications for the work, the reader will be unable to respond. Also include all sources for further information and all deadlines.
- Make responding as easy as possible for the reader. For example, enclose a permission form to use copyrighted materials; a sample of the product you need help with; your email address; your telephone number; a self-addressed, stamped envelope; a postcard; a fax number, etc. Put yourself in the reader's place here, and try to make his or her work as easy as possible. This will also benefit you.
- For long, difficult requests that require much of the reader, and requests that have a response deadline or time frame, telephone and give the recipient advance notice before sending your request.
- Introduce yourself, if yours is anything other than a routine request for prepared information.

MAKE YOUR REQUEST

- Begin with a clear, concise, and courteous statement of your request.
- Be as specific as possible.
- State, if appropriate, the reason for your request and the use you will make of what you are requesting.
- Include a reason why the reader may be interested in responding.
- Let the reader know where (and how) to send the information, or how to contact you with questions.
- Include the invitation to call you collect with questions, if this is appropriate.
- Conclude things in the last sentence or two, restating your request briefly if it is complex and making a statement of appreciation for the reader's cooperation. For example, "All the specifications and references are listed on pages 11 through 18. We appreciate your company's interest in this project, and we look forward to receiving your bid by April 7. We will share with you our decision by April 15, along with any reasons for our decision. Thank you."
- Express your appreciation for the expected cooperation of your reader.

ELIMINATE WRONG MESSAGES

- Do not use a commanding tone: "Send me your report A-510 by return mail" may make the reader bristle.
- Eliminate, too, any apologetic tone, or a tone that does not expect an answer to your letter. "I'm sorry to bother you with this, but I need a copy of the report on early therapy for diabetes" and "If you are unable to send me a copy of the report, I will certainly understand" are too weak.
- Don't bury the items of your request in long paragraphs. Don't write: "Please send me your brochures for Model 75-74; Model 610-66; Model 774-23; Pipettes 566-43; and the Analyzer 511-10." Instead, indent so the reader can easily see what your want. "Please send me your brochures for:
  — Model 75-74
  — Model 610-66
  — Model 774-23
  — Pipettes 566-43
  — Analyzer 511-10"

- Avoid vague requests that may go unanswered or simply be discarded. Do more research in advance so you can make your request specific. If possible, get the name of the person who will be able to help you.
- Don't fail to conclude your letter with a statement of appreciation, which may further energize the reader to help you: "Thank you for handling this request." "I appreciate your help in this matter." "May I receive this information by March 15? Thank you for your help." "I look forward to receiving this material, and thank you." "I thank you in advance for your help in this matter."

CONSIDER SPECIAL SITUATIONS

- Make it a policy to put all requests in writing, and always be explicit. A simple, "This confirms my request for reservations for the Elks meeting at the Boulderado, May 13," won't do. In that example, your request should include the number of guests for whom you are requesting rooms; the number and time of meeting rooms you'll need, and how each will be arranged; the times your guests will arrive; the number of people, time, menus, and service expected for meals. If possible, use a request form from the hotel. You could also ask the hotel or conference center for an example of a request for a similar meeting if you don't do this regularly.
- A request to quote should include a form (in duplicate—one for the reader) with all the pertinent information and a place for the reader's signature. Include in your request a completed form with the exact quote defined—"I request permission to quote the following: . . ." —and list the exact source including book title, author, page number, and the complete information about where you want to use the quotation. Include the title, author, publisher/publication date, price, and the relationship of the quoted material to the whole piece.
- A request to quote should be responded to with a signed permission letter.

- When requesting a change of address, indicate both the old and the new:

    Please change my address in your records

    FROM: 315 South Cherry
              Detroit, MI 49334

    TO: 776 East Alameda
           Denver, CO 80220

- When requesting that copies of your medical records be sent to another physician, you will be required to sign a special consent form. Check on this first to save yourself time. If you're emailing, faxing, or writing your request, it should be stated in the affirmative: "I hereby authorize the transfer [or copies] of my medical records to be sent to . . ."
- If requesting a speaker to make a presentation to your group, use both special tact and precision. You will undoubtedly want to check on the potential speaker's performance record before requesting his or her services. Include complete information about the date, time, location, setting, audience size and composition, focus and subject matter of the meeting, allotted time for the speech, and a list of suggested topics, if appropriate. There's nothing quite as inappropriate as having a "famous" writer as the guest speaker at a writers' banquet, for example, and witness him then use the occasion to vent his unrelated political views, especially if you are promoting the speech as "how you can sell your book."
- In making any request of a government agency, check first to learn the required form and protocol for your request. This will save you considerable effort and help ensure the response you want. If, for example, you are requesting a reevaluation of your property taxes, you will undoubtedly have to include the legal lot number or other location and description information, and detailed information on values of comparative homes in your immediate area. This is usually done by price per square foot.
- In writing to any governmental agency or bureaucracy, use identifying name and numbers to increase the chance of receiving a response:

"Please send me a copy of proposed *Bill Number 555-543: City Crime, May 21, by Senator Q. K. Jackson.*" It's important in requesting government information to state the legal provision under which you are making your request, if applicable. For example, "Under the Federal Freedom of Information Act . . ."

- In requesting changes in governmental policy, designated zones, usage, etc., do your research first. You must understand the history of a particular zoning requirement, for example, because your request must be made in terms of the inappropriateness of that designation and the reasonableness of your request. There may be any number of requirements in getting your request into the right form and obtaining agreement among those concerned. Researching all related matters and complying with form and content requirements will increase the chances of your request being granted.

SELECT A FORMAT

- Simple personal requests for such things as sales literature or a free sample may be requested by email, or handwritten on a postcard, fold-over note, or personal letterhead. For longer, more complex requests, email may be used, or type the request on letterhead.
- Routine business requests to another company may be made through email, by telephone, or on preprinted postcards, preprinted forms, or letterhead. Longer or complex requests should be typed on letterhead. If time is a factor, check with the recipient to see if you can email, telephone, or fax your request.

SELECT STRONG WORDS

aid	inquire
answer	request
appreciate	respond
ask	response
assistance	return
help	thank you
information	time frame

BUILD STRONG PHRASES

as soon as possible

ask for your assistance

by return mail

could you offer your assistance

I need this information by

I need your help in locating

I request the following

I request your information by

I would appreciate your cooperation

I'm writing to inquire

if I may supply any additional information

if there are additional questions

inquire about information

it would be a great help

may I inquire

please call me collect

please respond to this request

request your help

would you be willing to supply

you may email me at

WRITE STRONG SENTENCES

As directed by Mr. R. Roberts, I am requesting a copy of *Patient Care 145: Healthcare Reform.*

I request a double, nonsmoking room (a king-size bed), on the fourth floor, if possible, for Thursday, April 2. I am arriving at 3:10 P.M., on United Airlines on flight #189.

I think we need to have further discussion about our strategy on the Pepper account, and I request that you let me know if you have an hour available on the afternoon of either the 14th or 15th, so I can set it up.

Jack Adams has done some outstanding work on the job descriptions, and I would like to receive a copy of his report at your earliest convenience.

EDIT, EDIT, EDIT

Give your request or inquiry a little time to sit after you're finished writing. Then review it again and ask yourself if you've answered the *what, why, when, where,* and *how much* of your request in precise and concise terms.

Information Request

[Emailed]

Dear Ms. Jackson:

I enjoyed your presentation at the Gates Tennis Club and request specific information on rates at Tennis, Inc.'s camp on the following dates:

April 12 through April 22
June 17 through June 27
August 15 through August 25

Please also give me a listing of the advantages (if any) of being a guest at one time over another. I am a level 5.0 USTA evaluated player, and my objective in attending is to raise my tennis skill level to a 5.5 level. Thank you for your assistance. I look forward to your response.

Sincerely,

Walter Gill

Be specific.

Be cordial.

Make reader want to help.

Report Request

[Emailed]

Dear Mr. Williams:

Ms. Jobs asked me to request a copy of the report passed out at the last meeting of the Atlanta Water Board of Directors. The subject of the report is projections of water usage in the year 2006.

She will appreciate receiving a copy by the 15th. Thank you.

Sincerely yours,

Janet Reems

Request for Order Status Information

[Faxed]
(Date)

REFERENCE: ORDER # 3234

Dear Bob:

There's some confusion here about the status of our order for retainers submitted on April 29. Margie Stich of your office indicated to our Louise Cole that you are out of several of the sizes we need: #4, #6, and #7. Please give me a status report on our order, in writing, by tomorrow. Please fax it to my office: 440-555-0123.

We must have a number of sizes in here by next Wednesday to keep production going.

Yours truly,

Jim Riser

Be specific.

State a time frame if needed.

Give full response information.

State urgency if appropriate.

Request for Job Leads

[Mailed]
(Date)

Dear Jack:

It was nice seeing you at the National Product Managers' Association meeting in New York. I'm happy to hear that the Simmons lead from our meeting resulted in a long-term project.

Jack, confidentially, I am casting about for product manager positions in medical instrumentation corporations with a proactive, employee fast-track philosophy. Since you are in the know with your consulting work, I wonder if you have any recommendations. Obviously, I will treat any information as completely confidential.

I would appreciate any direction you may be able to give here, and will certainly continue to recommend to you any organizations looking for your particular type of consulting services. You may send any such leads to my personal email address: tbottoms@bigbottoms.com.

Regards,

Tim Bottoms

Request for Samples

[Emailed]

Dear Robby,

Please send me eight samples of the AA-345 Gaskets from the production run made on August 8. I also request that you include a copy of the tensile strength tests performed on these.

We plan to run our tests next Wednesday. I will give you a copy of our results the following Friday, so you may incorporate our data into your end-of-the-month report.

Thank you.

Cordially,

Ed Beattle

Request for City Information

[Emailed]

Dear Mr. Taggs:

I have spoken to several residents of Prescott who sing the praises of your city and highly recommend it as a location for retiring. Please send me information on new, low-maintenance housing available, demographics of the city, and information of special interest to newly retired people.

My wife and I will be retiring in 18 months, and we desire to find a suburban location with golf and community resources within walking distance. We are both 55 years old and desire neighbors of all ages. We will be prepared to buy a home in the price range of $250,000 to $300,000, in a one-story, ranch style. We also wish to purchase a new home.

Thank you. Enclosed is a SASE for your reply.

Sincerely yours,

Liam Buyers

Be concise and precise about what you want.

Make it easy for your reader to respond.

Request for Credit Report

[Mailed]
(Date)

Dear Mr. Allen:

As I stated on the telephone, I was denied credit at Crooners Bank on April 10. Enclosed is a copy of that report. Mr. Jesus Garcia, Customer Service Representative, noted that this credit report from your organization indicates a number of late payments and other credit problems. None of these are factual.

I've enclosed a self-addressed, stamped envelope. Please send me a new copy of my current credit record with the corrections we discussed properly indicated. I need this immediately in order to refute and correct this error.

Yours truly,

Lea Grimes

Request for Processing of Employee Records

[Emailed on a secure server or faxed]
(Date)

Dear Mr. Snipple:

As we discussed today, please process the permanent employee paperwork for Jack Jumper, and issue the following:

- Status 2A clearance
- a telephone credit card
- family medical insurance coverage
- an office key to the production department

Mr. Jumper's permanent employment date is August 14, but he will leave on an out-of-town assignment on August 13. I request all his required signatures, etc. be obtained this week, and he be issued his permanent employee packet on August 12.

Please contact me immediately if you are unable to comply. Thank you for your efforts in this matter.

Sincerely,

Denise Diver

Also see CREDIT APPROVAL, page 306; CREDIT DENIAL, page 309; CREDIT INQUIRY AND PROVIDING CREDIT INFORMATION, page 300; COLLECTION, page 321; and RESPONSE, page 234.

39
COVER LETTER

The great artist is the simplifier.

—HENRI-FREDERIC AMIEL

The cover or transmittal letter is a personal message to the reader, accompanying something you are sending him or her and taking the place of what you would say to the reader if you were face to face. It offers pertinent information about the contents and composition of what it is attached to. (When you are sending a report to a group of readers, a foreword or preface may be used instead of the cover letter.) If your cover letter accompanies a report, first tell the reader so, then include the goal of the report, and refer to its authorization.

The resume cover letter is exactly that. It introduces the contents it "covers," or what is enclosed. (See "Resume Cover Letter," page 109.)

DECIDE TO WRITE
Use a cover letter when you send:
- Reports, proposals, contracts, agreements, and other documents
- Applications
- Manuscripts
- Instruction manuals/booklets/sheets
- Contributions
- Samples, prototypes
- Checks unaccompanied by a copy of an invoice or a statement
- Complimentary tickets

THINK ABOUT CONTENT
- State what is enclosed, attached, or has been sent under separate cover. If you are responding to a request, name the requesting person.
- If appropriate, give the number of enclosures, or briefly list the content items.
- State the purpose or goal of the contents and who authorized them.
- If needed, explain how to use the contents.
- End on a note of goodwill.

ELIMINATE WRONG MESSAGES
- Don't be verbose or repeat, verbatim, information from the document. The cover letter should never exceed one-eighth the length of the report. Much shorter is better.
- Do not write a cover letter which is inconsistent with the voice and tone of the report. This applies to the form and format, too.

CONSIDER SPECIAL SITUATIONS

- Report cover letters should name the report, tell why it was written, who authorized it, its contributors, and then briefly summarize it.
- Cover letters for manuscripts sent to a publisher or agent are challenging. Publishers often require authors to describe their manuscripts in one short paragraph that compels editors to read it.
- Routine items are usually self-explanatory and do not require a cover letter. These items include invoices, payments, shipments, or other specialized letters.
- Sample or sales literature cover letters need to be unique and also explanatory. (See "Direct Mail," page 327, and "Sales Follow-Up," page 333.)
- Resume cover letters need to snag the interest of the reader so he or she will read the resume. (See "Resume Cover Letter," page 109.)

SELECT A FORMAT

- The standard format is the typewritten letter on business letterhead.
- An informal email may be used when this is the standard way you communicate with the reader and you are electronically transmitting what is "covered."
- For interoffice use, an email or a company memo is the proper vehicle. Both are used, too, for clients and colleagues in organizations with which you have an ongoing working relationship.
- The form of the cover letter should be consistent with the contents of the mailing. When its function is sales and there is an enclosed sample or "gift," an attention-getting note is usually the best choice.

USE STRONG WORDS

attached	examine
details	included
documents	instructions
enclosed	look

BUILD EFFECTIVE PHRASES

Call your attention to

Details of the experiments

Examine the charts

Here's a listing of what's attached

I'd be happy to answer any additional questions

I'm enclosing a check for

I've attached the report

Please contact me at 555-0123

Thank you for your interest in

This sample is sent

To add your review

You will want to examine

You'll note that

WRITE STRONG SENTENCES

Focus on the contents you're sending and your objective. Concisely describe both.

I've enclosed copies of checks numbered 346, 754, 332, and 987 as you requested.

Your feedback to this initial report will be greatly appreciated.

You may also want copies of our Report #443 on changes in the habitat.

This is your free copy.

The details of the experiment are on page 15.

BUILD EFFECTIVE PARAGRAPHS

I'm returning the spacer prototypes you sent. We tested these on our neoprene Elastomeric roof installation, and found the spacers would not withstand the wind uplift. Our installation details, test conditions, and phased results are included in the final report enclosed.

Here's my proposal, including the chapter outline and sample chapter you requested for *The Owner's Manual for Retirement,* the humor gift book we discussed. I'll be eager to learn your take on it.

This new Employee Manual A-40 was designed to deal with our current issues of diversity at Cobal. Carefully review each section, especially the summaries, and give me your feedback by April 10.

For everything that goes "squeak," now there's Quiet. Try this sample on your biggest noise makers and you'll never go back to wimpy lubricants.

Did you think you'd never find a bandage that would stick? Try this new "Bonzo" on your next boo-boo.

Thank you for your interest in the Gus Grant Program. Complete the enclosed form and return it to us by September 1 to be eligible for grant funds.

EDIT, EDIT, EDIT

Be concise. Many cover letters are only a sentence or two.

Internal Transmittal Memo

[Emailed]

Subject: Annual Report, Draft IV

We have incorporated the changes and comments on Draft III from each of you. In your review of this draft, please pay special attention to the figures on pages 12, 14, and 17. I believe the new company goals statement and the summary on page 25 are now much stronger.

We will need your final comments by Friday at noon. Thank you.

Cover Letter for Franchise Agreement

[Mailed]
(Date)

Dear Mr. Beemer:

Identify contents.

Enclosed is the franchise application, which I have amended according to our discussion. Please carefully review the amendments III, VI, and VIII, as well as the insertions on pages 4, 5, 9, and 11.

I believe this now represents a fair and equitable agreement with the parent company, Pets, and it is my belief this will be an extremely profitable endeavor for Dog Kisses, Inc.

Give precise information.

Please call me if you have any further concerns or questions. If not, please sign all four copies and return them to me. I've enclosed an extra copy for your files.

Thank you.

Yours truly,

Michael Beers

General Cover Letter for Annual Report

[Mailed]
(Date)

Dear Ms. Miller:

I'm enclosing our latest annual report. I hope this contains the kind of information you want on the goals and success of the company, especially in the past two years. You will find those explicit figures and comparisons on pages 5 through 12. but the entire report gives the complete picture of Cantos expansion and growth.

Thank you for your interest in our company, and please call me if you need any further information.

Yours truly,

Victor Weise

Cover Letter for Photograph Negatives

[Mailed]
(Date)

Dear Mr. Mann:

Here are the 12 prints of negatives 24A-C as you requested. We did go back in and touch them up, and I believe the results are excellent.

Thank you for selecting Prints, Inc. for your developing needs. We look forward to serving you in the future. Call on us any time.

Best regards,

Alfred F. Newsman

Cover Letter for Broken Part

[Mailed]
(Date)

Dear Mr. Dean:

As you requested yesterday on the telephone, I've enclosed the broken desk handle. I've also enclosed a photograph of the desk with the broken handle in place.

Be precise and concise.

Please send me a new handle as soon as possible. Thank you.

Sincerely,

Donald Costa

Cover Letter for Shipment

[Mailed]
(Date)

Dear Ms. Betts:

Here's a copy of the new brochure. Under separate cover, I'm sending the additional 450 brochures you requested. The four-color printing is beautiful. It was the right decision to use the fall cover photo; it'll be a very effective promotional tool for you, I'm sure.

All the brochures will be delivered to the central office Tuesday morning. Don't hesitate to call me if you want some taken to the branch offices. We can easily do that.

We look forward to working with you again.

Sincerely,

Stanley Barker

Cover Letter for Report

[Emailed]

Dear Mr. Able:

Here is the Salespeople Report on the survey you asked us to conduct last August 15. As you can see, our observations pointed to some specific needs for new and extensive sales training.

Following the procedures we outlined and you approved in September, we have included these needs in a revised curriculum plan that we will submit to your training director, Jim Bacon, on November 10. We are confident this curriculum will help correct the skill-level deficits of your sales force.

We appreciate the opportunity to serve you. If you want to review any of the details here, please call me.

Sincerely yours,

Robert Berke

Also see RESUME COVER LETTER, page 109.

40

RESPONSE

Writing, when properly managed,
is but a different name for conversation.

—LAURENCE STERNE

A letter of response, whether business or personal, usually takes less time if done immediately. Procrastination is not only a bad habit, it may affect your business and reputation.

Many successful businesses have been built upon the simple principle of a prompt, thorough response. It says to the customer, "I value you, I understand what you want, and your business is important to me." Make sure your response is timely.

DECIDE TO WRITE

Common sense and company protocol are the bywords here. Many companies state that outside correspondence always requires a written response; internal correspondence often requires only a verbal response. Consider writing a response when you receive any of the following:

- An invitation (see "Invitations," page 65, and "Refusal," page 250)
- An announcement
- A gift (see "Thank-You," page 76)
- An inquiry
- A complaint (see "Complaint," page 257)
- A request
- A contribution (see "Thank-You," page 76)

- A payment
- Information
- A note of condolence or sympathy (see "Condolence and Sympathy," page 47)
- An apology

THINK ABOUT CONTENT

- Start with the reason for your response. This is usually a mention of the communication you received: "Thank you for your letter of July 12, requesting the shipping date of the Wickets."
- Make your letter both as complete and as brief as possible.
- Be sure you have responded to all the points of the recipient's correspondence. Sometimes it is best to organize your response in the order of the communication you received. For example, "In paragraph one of your letter . . ."
- Use indenting, bullets, dashes, and the wise use of white space in long or complicated responses to help make your response clear.
- Repeat vital information like the date, time, and location of a meeting.
- Offer other sources of assistance, when appropriate. Make it easier for an inquirer to follow up

by offering additional contact names, numbers, and addresses. For example, "No, we don't carry the Thingys you requested, but Every Product, located at 322 Grace St. in Houston, or at everyproduct.com, has them in all sizes."

- Immediate acknowledgment is the first and best line of action in your response. Often letters of inquiry, requests for information, or complaints require some work before an intelligent and comprehensive response can be given. Acknowledge the letter and tell the reader you are working on a more complete response.

- A response letter to customers should offer value added whenever possible. Many companies have built a strong and loyal customer base by expending that extra effort to include a pertinent research report or send valuable samples of the product. This does not mean stuffing a huge envelope with unrelated sales information, which is never appreciated. It also doesn't mean dodging the point of inquiry.

- A written response to invitations should match the invitation. If the invitation is in third person, for example, respond in third person: "Alex and Mable Wilborough accept with pleasure Frank and Edna Edmond's kind invitation for dinner on Thursday, the twelfth of June at eight o'clock." If there is an RSVP request, you are obliged to respond as promptly as possible; write or call, whichever the invitation indicates. "Regrets only" on an invitation means you are not required to respond if you will attend. However, if two people are invited and one will not attend, if other commitments require you to be late, or if other special circumstances exist, convey this to the host by calling in a timely manner, or by writing a response note (see "Invitations," page 65).

- Invite further correspondence, if appropriate.

ELIMINATE WRONG MESSAGES

- As a rule, do not go beyond the scope of the correspondence you received. (This is a rule sometimes wisely broken.)

- Do not let correspondence go unanswered. A polite response is always in order, even in cases where a rude or unmerited complaint has been received, the wrong company has been contacted, or the request seems ridiculous.

- Rude or insensitive responses are never in order. Don't ever send an insensitive response or one that contains a moral judgment to someone who has had bad news or has suffered a loss.

- Don't let your response start with, "Sorry I didn't respond sooner, but . . ." The proper way to handle this is to respond immediately with something like "I am looking into a solution to your problem . . . and I will be in touch as soon as I . . ."

CONSIDER SPECIAL SITUATIONS

- Complaints require immediate responses. Agree on some point with the writer or thank him or her for writing. Relate the action that has been (or is being) taken, and conclude with a goodwill statement.

- A threatening or abusive letter must be handled very carefully. If litigation is mentioned or implied, it is best to refer the matter to an attorney. If there is a particularly threatening tone, refer the matter to the proper authorities. If it is simply an angry letter, respond as respectfully and objectively as possible, expressing you are sorry the writer is upset.

- Responses to personal requests for contributions should include an opening statement of why you are, or aren't, donating. Enclose the provided form, if any, and request a receipt if you need it for tax purposes. If you do not wish to be on the computerized mailing list for an organization, a note, email, or telephone call stating simply "Please remove me from your mailing list" (or solicitation list) is sufficient.

- Respond to invitations to celebrations like birthday parties, anniversaries, bar or bat mitzvahs, and other events in like manner. A commercial greeting card with a personal message is appropriate, even if you won't attend, and a gift depends upon your relationship to the guest of honor.

- Messages and expressions of condolence and sympathy require a written response. This can take a number of forms: (1) written notes;

(2) printed thank-yous with a handwritten note to those who were close to the deceased, ill, or injured person; and/or (3) a thank-you message placed in the local newspaper for someone who is/was a public figure. Responses certainly may be brief, and may be handled by a designated person outside the immediate family. Responses should be sent within six weeks of the event or, in the case of an injured or ill person, as soon as the person is able (see "Condolence and Sympathy," page 47).

- Responses to an invitation for an interview are usually handled verbally, but there may be the opportunity to send a confirmation. If so, do it. This is an opportunity to impress a potential employer that you are skilled in business etiquette. It can also help you set the stage for a very productive interview. Include a last sentence about "looking forward to discussing my Cropper experience."
- Respond to an apology by acknowledging you received it, accepting the apology (if appropriate), and thanking the sender. If it's appropriate, you may wish to add that you look forward to a future relationship with the sender.
- A response to a note of congratulations should start with "Thank you." A sincere compliment to the sender and a statement about your appreciation for his/her thoughtfulness can be followed by a sentence or two of follow-up news.

SELECT A FORMAT

- Business responses should be typed on company stationery.
- Responses to formal invitations should be done in like manner to the invitation. If you do not use personal printed notecards or stationery, type your response, with the information requested, in the same layout.
- Responding in kind by email is simple. Send a personal, sincere response—although it may be almost entirely "boilerplate."

USE APPROPRIATE WORDS

appreciate	inform
check	investigate
confirm	received
follow up (v)	responding
follow-up (adj.)	thanks

WRITE EFFECTIVE PHRASES

appreciate your consideration
as we continue to research this
as you noted
delighted to hear the news
expect another response from us on
have carefully evaluated
here are the responses in the order of your complaint
here's the current status of the follow-up
I'll be watching this closely
I've enclosed
investigate this immediately
please let us know
responding to your
so pleased to hear from you
thank you for your letter
the next step
value your business
we have received
what great news
will be handling the next step
will follow up on
will keep you informed
your thoughtful note

BUILD STRONG SENTENCES

If I can answer any other questions, please don't hesitate to call or email.

We were sorry to learn that the fishing rod you purchased on October 5 isn't satisfactory, and we are happy to offer you full credit, a refund, or a replacement.

If you have any remaining questions, please call me.

Please accept my apology for the error in your January billing. Your account has been credited with the amount of $45.87.

You are a valued customer, and we will do everything possible to resolve this problem.

As you requested, here is the brochure that describes the greening process.

BUILD EFFECTIVE PARAGRAPHS

Here is the research report on the milk contamination in New York. We will put you on our notification list to receive further reports as they become available.

Your letter concerning a customer-service problem in our Englewood store has reached me for handling. I am presently investigating this incident, and will be in contact with you within the next two weeks to report what I've learned. I am sorry you had an unpleasant experience in our store, and I will do everything I can to try to resolve it to your satisfaction.

I was very surprised to learn you received two Model C-120 Monitors instead of one. Thank you for returning one. Enclosed is reimbursement for the postage and a certificate for you to use in your next purchase of a BillyClub product.

Thank you for detailing your frustration in trying to return the Wacket Thumper. I will investigate the event in the next two weeks, and then I will be in touch with you again. In the meantime, on behalf of Wacket, please accept our most sincere apologies for an unpleasant experience.

We are shipping you two dinner plates today to replace the two you reported arrived broken. I'm sorry this happened. You should have the replacement plates in three days.

Yes, we certainly will honor our guarantee, and I'm glad you brought it to our attention that salespeople in our stores are not aware of the details of this policy. Please return your battery to Steve Watson at Store #31, Yosemite and Arapahoe, and he will take care of it.

Here is the proposal you requested. To meet your Requirements A through K, see the responses below.

I appreciate your apology, and accept it. It does, in fact, restore in me confidence in your customer-service statement.

Thank you for submitting your resume for the manager position. I've forwarded it to the hiring committee, and someone will be in contact with you in the next two weeks.

We're always delighted to hear good news, and yours is especially welcome. How terrific that your book has come out, and you'll be signing at Stutters. We'll be there in the front row.

Just wanted you to know that we received your invitation to the graduation ceremony. We're juggling our schedule in the hope that we will be able to attend. I'll get an answer to you in a couple of days.

We have received your novel, and look forward to reviewing it. Presently, this process is taking eight weeks to complete. Please plan to hear from us by July 1. And thank you for your demonstration of confidence in our literary agency.

Your order has been processed and will ship today. Expect the products to arrive on Tuesday. Thank you for doing business with Slammers, Inc. We look forward to serving you.

EDIT, EDIT, EDIT

Be sure your message is clear and your communication ends on a positive note.

Response to Congratulations

[Mailed]
(Date)

Dear Bobbi,

Thank the reader. Thank you for your kind note of congratulations. Your interest, care, concern, and involvement in my education over the years have helped me get to where I am today: from the distinguished ranks of the PU graduating class of 2005 to the unemployment line!

Offer information. I'm sending out a zillion resumes a day and have listed on 10 online employment job-search websites. And I'm happy to report that I've actually had two interviews: one in Chicago and one in San Francisco. (The jury's still out.) I'll let you know when I move into the gainfully employed mode. Your interest and thoughts of concern are *Close cordially.* greatly appreciated.

Robbie

Response to Customer Dissatisfaction

[Faxed]
(Date)

Dear Mrs. Lincoln:

Emphathize with the reader. I'm sorry the draperies for the yellow room aren't what you envisioned. Of course we'll work with you to come to a satisfactory solution. Our interior decorator did survey the room, and he has three suggestions:

Respond precisely.

1. We can repaint the walls, adding white pigment to the original paint you selected;
Offer value-added solutions if possible.
2. We can add a valance in a Schumacher designer fabric to the draperies that will majestically blend wall and drapery colors and pull the entire room together; or
3. We can refit these draperies for use in another room and start over with another fabric.

Close on a codial note. I will call you on Thursday to arrange a time to bring over a number of samples that will make these *Clarify next step.* alternatives visually clear. Mr. Roberts feels you will be extremely satisfied with any of these solutions.

Sincerely,

Gloria Van der Bloom

Response to Fund-raising Request

[Emailed]

Sam:

Regrettably, I'm not able to make a contribution this year, but I am able to serve on HealthCare Day, and would be delighted to do so.

Please forward this email to the correct person. I can serve from 9:00 A.M. to noon.

Thank you for your valuable contribution to this great service.

Sincerely,

Rob Diner

Response to Job Refusal

[Mailed]
(Date)

Dear Bob:

I don't envy you the difficult decision of selecting the right person to head up the Phoenix operation. Of course I'm disappointed that I wasn't selected for the job, but at the same time I realize the position presents the new manager with some very large challenges that can't be solved without some other key factors being in place.

I appreciate your time and our exchange of ideas during the interview process, and I want to thank you for keeping my resume in your active file. If another manager position opens up with Mizer, I'd like to be considered as a candidate.

I will call you about that golf game too. I think you will enjoy our little course here at Sand Trap.

All the best,

Sam Simmer

Response to Customer for Error

[Mailed]
(Date)

Dear Mrs. Wiley:

I'm sorry your request for a change in your payment plan was mishandled. I'm still looking into how you could have received a form letter for a delinquent account, and I will explain it when I learn the details.

I have resolved the other matter, and the terms of your extension and the amount of future payments are detailed in the faxed contract. Please review it, and call me if you have any questions.

We value your business, and thank you for working with us to resolve this misunderstanding.

Sincerely,

Michael Clinton

Response to Bid Received

[Emailed]

Jack:

Your bid just arrived, and it looks spot on to me after a very quick review. We have five qualified bids coming in, and yours is the first.

Jennie Crumm will be the project engineer on this project, and she'll be in touch with you within the week with additional questions for follow-up.

Thank you for bidding this. It was great seeing you at your presentation on Friday.

Best,

Giddy

Response to Request to Alter Price

[Emailed]

Jimmie and Ruddy:

Thank you for your letter listing the items that need to be repaired on the house at 1010 Statesman Street before you make an offer. This may be handled in one of two ways: (1) you may request the present owner make these repairs, or (2) you may estimate the cost of these repairs, list them, and total them. The total may then be deducted from your formal offer price.

Thank you again for being so alert, and I will be happy to work with you in any way possible—I have sources for bids on repairing these items—so you may complete your computations.

I shall call you tomorrow to learn your decision.

Best,

Ron Moe

Response to Request for Replacement Product

[Emailed]

Dear Mr. Brokett:

Your request for a replacement motor for the Decker Docker saw has been forwarded to our service department at the store where you purchased it. Mr. Fred Mamet, service department manager, will need to see the saw to make a final determination. He asks that you call him between 9 A.M. and 5 P.M., Monday through Friday, to arrange a time to take it in.

I'm sorry you had this problem, and we will work with you to get it resolved.

Regards,

Mike Bolster

Also see COMPLAINT, page 257.

41

CONFIRMATION AND ACKNOWLEDGMENT

The second rule of communicating is to tell 'm that you told 'm.

—ANONYMOUS

The letter of *confirmation* is a tool of business record keeping. Its primary purpose is to retell the reader what action was taken, and to reaffirm the decisions made and terms agreed to. It may have a number of secondary purposes as well. These may include acknowledgment, building goodwill, thank you, appreciation, acceptance, and documentation for legal purposes.

The letter of *acknowledgment* is also a tool of business record keeping (often for legal purposes), but it stops a step short of the letter of confirmation: its job is simply to record receipt and say "Yes, I received what you sent."

DECIDE TO WRITE

Use one of these letters to:
- Acknowledge materials, documents, or items received, or to confirm discussions held
- Reiterate decisions made
- Confirm upcoming meeting information or attendance
- Verify (confirm) reservations
- Create a record

THINK ABOUT CONTENT

- To confirm verbal discussions that change details of an agreement or contract, refer to the original agreement, and define what is changed.
- The confirmation letter may easily become a hybrid. When it confirms the decisions of a meeting between the sender and a client, it may go into explanations of the positions, discussion, and changes involved in reaching a decision.
- Form letters are often used for routine acknowledgments and/or confirmations, and with email this is easily and quickly done. These may be as simple as a boilerplate statement, or prepared list of items that can be checked off and sent with a brief note.
- It is entirely acceptable to include with a letter your own acknowledgment or confirmation form upon which the reader checks an item or pens a brief response. An author may send a self-addressed, stamped postcard, for example, to receive an immediate confirmation from a publisher that his or her manuscript has been received. Grant applications, legal documents, and many other types of notices may be treated

in the same manner. The postal service offers a similar kind of receipt: confirmation of delivery.

- State the points to be confirmed in the context of action taken, discussions, information received, and date, time, place, etc. Brief, complete information is best. Most acknowledgment letters are only a sentence or two; confirmations may be as short or only slightly longer.
- Give any and all pertinent identifying information, including how to contact you, if necessary.
- Close with a friendly comment, and thank the reader for his or her efforts.
- Include a signature line for the recipient if the letter is to become a legal agreement or contract.

ELIMINATE WRONG MESSAGES

- Avoid talking down to the reader: "Be sure to make a note to bring your calendar. . . ." Keep the message brief and objective.
- Don't let a simplistic tone creep in.
- Do not go beyond the bounds of confirming information.
- Don't list future, unrelated action items, or try to persuade.

CONSIDER SPECIAL SITUATIONS

- Confirmations for reservations at hotels, motels, the theater, fund-raisers, etc. may mean that you are agreeing to pay for the reserved item, whether you use it or not. This confirmation is often made by telephone and involves giving a credit card number. When payment is involved, or reservations include special preparation or accommodations, a written confirmation may also be required. In this case, be very specific about date, time of arrival, length of stay, price, accommodations, special arrangements and provisions, specific facilities, and inclusions.
- It is always good to confirm you have received a customer/client order, agreement, change, and/or special request. Keep the acknowledgment letter brief and close in a friendly manner. Acknowledgment letters are required when the intended recipient is not available to respond. In this case, the

designated person should send a brief letter acknowledging receipt, and stating that the intended recipient will respond as soon as possible.

- A confirmation should be sent in response to an invitation, if the host requests it. This is often done on an informal fold-over notecard. (See "Invitations," page 65.)

SELECT A FORMAT

- Email, postcards, form notes, or letters can be used to acknowledge receipt of manuscripts, documents, requests, packages, etc. When you send a manuscript or documents that you want to know arrived safely, you may ask the recipient to send you an email indicating receipt. Or, you may include a self-addressed, stamped postcard with the materials that the recipient can easily return to you. For example,

    Please let me know by completing the following.

    _____ We have received your proposal.
    _____ We will get back to you with a response in approximately _____ weeks.

- Business acknowledgments and confirmations can be made by email or typed on letterhead. Check organization protocol.
- Interoffice acknowledgments and confirmations may be done by email or on simple, printed memo forms that allow the recipient to check the appropriate response.

SELECT THE RIGHT WORDS

accept	indicate
acknowledge	notify
affirm	receipt
agree	received
approve	respond
comply	return
confirm	verify
deliver	

BUILD STRONG PHRASES

as agreed

the agreement will now read

the changes indicated include

these changes reflect our discussion

this updates the contract

we hereby confirm

WRITE STRONG SENTENCES

Start with the action, and write a concise statement.

Thanks for your call. I'm looking forward to our meeting next week.

The five cartons of computer parts were just delivered by air express.

This confirms our agreement that your company will start the renovation on Monday, April 1.

The Jackson Report arrived in our office this morning; we will be meeting to review it on Wednesday.

BUILD EFFECTIVE PARAGRAPHS

As we agreed on the telephone, Rounder and Long will be pleased to represent you in the Webster matter. I have set up a meeting for Thursday, October 7 at 2:00 P.M. with Bill Webster here in my office. I shall be in contact with you immediately after that meeting.

We have received your application to be part of the "Aging Study." We have been overwhelmed with applications, and it will require another two weeks for us to process them and select the participants. Please be patient, and we will contact you in approximately three weeks.

Thank you for your grant application, which we have now received. The winners will be announced on July 15, and all applicants supplying the requested postcard will be immediately notified.

EDIT, EDIT, EDIT

Make sure your communication is simple, clear, and complete.

Confirmation of Bid Changes

[Emailed]

Jan,

Yes, we'll spring for the $3\frac{1}{4}$-inch-wide flooring in Victorian clear maple, an increase of 33 percent over the bid we have.

Best,

Raymond

Confirmation of Receipt of Information

[Emailed]

Dear Mr. Logan:

We have received your mortgage loan application. Because of the number of credit references, employers, and previous lenders on your application, please allow six weeks for loan processing.

If you have any questions, please contact Bonnie McGregor at 555-0123.

Sincerely,

Thirsty Blocker

Acknowledging Receipt of Manuscript

[Self-addressed, stamped postcard mailed by sender for recipient's signature and return]

Yes, Bender and Scrooge has received your manuscript, and will add it to the stack of potential best sellers in waiting.

_____
(Signature)

Please expect a response from us in _____ weeks.

Confirms Verbal Changes in Employment Agreement

[Mailed]
(Date)

Dear Ms. Gupta:

This confirms the changes we made this morning on the telephone to your employment agreement. We will (1) increase the salary to $165,000 per year, (2) increase your vacation after one year of employment to fourteen days, and (3) raise your bonus percentage to seven percent.

Please make these changes in the contract, initial them, and send them back to me for my signature.

We are so pleased to have you coming aboard. Welcome!

I feel sure your relationship with Cunning will be an extremely rewarding one.

Sincerely,

Bebe Gunliffe

Confirms and Documents Agreement

[Emailed]

Dear Mr. Beevis:

This confirms our agreement of this morning's telephone conversation. Yes, you may have access to your pasture land by using my private road, as long as your conduct causes no stress or threat to my livestock grazing in the adjoining pasture.

Your truly,

Bea Holden

Confirmation of Nomination

[Emailed]

Dear Alice:

I will accept the nomination to serve as next year's president of "Hers," as long as you agree to be vice president. (Some might call it blackmail.)

It should be a great opportunity to work together. I look forward to it.

Sincerely,

Valerie Sower

Confirmation and Agreement for Speaker

[Emailed]

Dear Lee:

We at Business Women are so pleased you have agreed to be our premier speaker at this year's convention banquet at the Peachtree Hotel on June 5.

The setting for our meetings will be informal, starting with a cocktail hour at 6:30 P.M. in the Blossom Room. Dinner will be served at 7:30 P.M. You will be introduced by Janet Rewfrow at 8:30 P.M., and we have allowed 30 minutes for your presentation with another 15 minutes for a questions and answers period to follow immediately.

Business Women will pay you an honorarium of $2,500 for your participation, plus we will cover the cost of your flight (coach class), room for two nights, and meals on June 5.

The audience, an expected 400, will be composed of member professionals who will be well versed in sexual harassment issues. Their questions, I expect, will center on cases and verdicts, outcomes in terms of financial settlements to plaintiffs, and future legal trends. We will have an overhead projector and lapel microphone ready for you. Please plan to bring any handouts because getting copies made was a problem last year. As agreed, you may bring copies of your book for participants to purchase. We can furnish a volunteer to handle book sales, if you like.

Rudy Wilkes, who will be carrying a sign with your name on it, will meet your flight: United #221, arriving in Atlanta at 7:30 P.M. on June 4. If there is any change in your plans, please call Rudy at 555-0123.

I will arrive at the Peachtree on June 4 at about 4:00 P.M. I have reserved Room 433. Please leave me a message after you arrive.

If there is any additional equipment you want for your presentation, please contact Sally Dithers at our offices, extension 256, as soon as possible.

We are delighted you will be joining us this year. Please sign below, confirming you agree to these terms, and fax a copy to me at 555-0124.

Yours truly,

Sadie Hawker

Lee Radwitz

_____

Date

_____

42

ACCEPTANCE

All paths lead to the same goal: to convey to others what we are.

—PABLO NERUDA

A note or letter accepting a dinner invitation is easy. Just express your gratitude and anticipation of future enjoyment. The general rule for invitations, at least, is to reply in kind. For formal invitations it may be even simpler because there may be an RSVP card that only has to be filled in and returned.

Accepting a job offer or an invitation to be seminar speaker is more difficult. Your letter may be the only documentation of the agreed-upon terms. Be sure of your decision to accept, then write in a timely manner.

DECIDE TO WRITE

Send an acceptance in response to:
- An invitation to a wedding, dinner, party, meeting, seminar, conference, or hospitality
- A job offer
- Proposal, bid, contract, or a change to these
- A special contribution or donation
- An offer of a favor, help, or recommendation
- Membership approval or invitation to join a club, association, organization, committee, or commission
- Speaking invitation

THINK ABOUT CONTENT

- Consider the person issuing the invitation, especially in the case of a dinner or party, and express your delight and enthusiasm.
- Address your acceptance to the person from whom the invitation, document, etc. came.
- Thank the reader for the invitation.
- State your acceptance, expressing your pleasure at being able to accept.
- Confirm the time, place, and details, if appropriate.
- End with a statement of anticipation or your expectations for the event. (If you find this is something you cannot generate, it may be better to decline the invitation.)

ELIMINATE WRONG MESSAGES

- Don't digress into unrelated business.
- Avoid placing conditions and/or qualifications on your acceptance. Your acceptance should not place conditions or additional demands on a host, for example.

CONSIDER SPECIAL SITUATIONS

- Timing is always important. Send your acceptance within a day or two of receiving it, or as soon after as possible.
- If you have questions, call the host or designated person for clarification.
- When the acceptance is for one of an invited couple, check with the host, if appropriate, to make sure this does not present a problem.
- In accepting a television interview or seminar speaking invitation, be sure you understand all the requirements and details. The first paragraph of your letter—after you state your acceptance—should confirm the details: the time, date, and place, etc., and it should include any questions to be addressed before the event. Be sure the topic is mutually agreed upon in writing. There is no such thing as an "open-ended" interview.
- Teach children early to write acceptances.
- If something comes up after you have accepted, call the host immediately and explain, but remember that your acceptance is a contract—your good word.

SELECT A FORMAT

Reply in the same format as the invitation. If you were invited by email, respond by email. A typed invitation on a business letterhead requires a typed acceptance on a business letterhead; an informal handwritten invitation requires an informal acceptance, usually a telephone call. The exception is if you receive an engraved invitation, and there is no enclosed, engraved reply card. Send a handwritten reply on a card or fold-over note using the same wording and layout as the invitation:

> Mr. Horacio and Ms. Katherine Phinney
> accept with pleasure
> the kind invitation of
> Mr. Peter and Ms. Nancy Kowaleski
> for dinner
> on Saturday, the tenth of December
> at eight o'clock

USE EFFECTIVE WORDS

accept	glad
affirmative	pleased
answer	pleasure
attend	regard
believe	welcome
delighted	will

BUILD STRONG PHRASES

accept with pleasure
accept your gracious invitation
agree to the terms
completely satisfied with your proposal
delighted to be invited
I feel honored
I shall look forward to the opportunity
I will be able
I'm very enthusiastic
it really pleases me to
pleased to accept
we are willing and able
we can satisfy every requirement
what a splendid idea
will comply with your request
yes, I'd be pleased to
yes, indeed, I will
you will be delighted with our

WRITE STRONG SENTENCES

Yes, I'd be happy to accept your invitation.

I believe the conditions you set forth are fine, and I accept your offer.

I'm so pleased to be honored in this way, and I'd be delighted to be your speaker.

I am pleased to accept your offer to be manager of Dusty's Tavern.

We respectfully accept the invitation to attend the State dinner.

Yes, I would be pleased to present the "Stock Watch" portion of the Investors' Program on March 12, 2:30 P.M. at the Bellview.

Please count on me for the Board of Directors Meeting, January 12, at 7:00 P.M. at the Clubhouse.

We certainly wouldn't miss the opening game of the Tigers, and we accept your kind invitation for the tailgate party at 2:00 P.M.

We are looking forward to working with you.

Yes, these changes to the agreement are fine with us.

Yes, we're on board with this all the way.

I do accept your apology for the error in charges.

BUILD EFFECTIVE PARAGRAPHS

I am extremely pleased to be voted into the Business-woman's Hall of Fame. It is truly an honor. I shall look forward to the banquet on February 15, 7:00 P.M. at the Turner Center.

We are pleased to inform you that your bid for the reroofing of the Sports Center has been accepted. The board of directors just met this afternoon. Please call me to arrange a time to sit down and discuss the start date and other details.

Jenny and I will be delighted to come to your costume Halloween party. I bet you won't guess who we are.

EDIT, EDIT, EDIT

Use clear and concise language. Short, enthusiastic, and to the point is the best acceptance.

Accepting a Pickup Game

[Emailed]

Jim:

Count me in. I'll be happy to sub for Jack on Thursday. See you at the park at 4:30 P.M. Cleats on.

Bob

Acceptance to Appear as TV Interviewee

[Emailed]

Dear Anne:

Thank you for your invitation to be a guest on "Business Talks." I am very pleased to be invited and I enthusiastically accept.

I will, as you suggest, arrive at the 4News studios at 1:00 P.M. on Thursday, June 5, for the preparation before taping the segment. I understand the topic is "Starting a New Business," and I will be prepared to go through the basic steps. I shall bring five four-color charts with bulleted items. I will be prepared to answer your questions about accounting, legal counsel, banking, and consultant resources for new entrepreneurs in our community. I would also like to know the names and organizations of the other two guests who will appear on the program, and their exact topic areas.

I have been instructed by my wardrobe people not to wear white or large prints. If there are any other cautions or directions in this area or tips on preparing for the makeup session, please contact my secretary, Biddie Brindle.

Sincerely,

Denise Copperfield

Acceptance of Proposal

[Mailed]
(Date)

Dear Mr. Hill:

Congratulations. Your proposal to provide public relations counsel for the Celebrity Tennis Tournament has been accepted.

We will want to amend the proposal, as discussed, to include the handling of our brochures, press releases, the annual report, and other written communications.

The telephone surveys and letters will be handled by our public affairs department. Mr. Corey Kettle will be in charge of these activities, and he will also be the person to whom you will report.

Please make the above changes in the contract, and call me to arrange a time for all of us to get together. We all look forward to working with you.

Sincerely,

Donahue Bugle

Accepting a Wedding Anniversary Invitation

[Mailed]
(Date)

Dear Satchel:

Rachel and I accept with pleasure your kind invitation to attend the 25th wedding celebration for your parents, James and Demi Whittman, on July 7, at the Grange Hall, 4:00 P.M.

Sincerely,

Darrel Demming

College Acceptance

[Mailed]
(Date)

Dear Byron:

Congratulations! We are happy to announce that you have been accepted to Smuthers for the fall semester. A complete schedule of orientation activities and events is enclosed.

Most of your classmates will arrive here the morning of August 28. We request that all new students go directly to Haver Hall to check in, and there you can set a time to meet with your advisor.

We look forward to having you at Smuthers.

Sincerely,

Jimmie Dithers

Formal Acceptance for One for Dinner

[Mailed]

(Date)

Catherine Bauer
accepts with pleasure
Robert Q. Pompus and Lila Simpson's
kind invitation to a dinner
on Friday, the tenth of August, at seven o'clock
but regrets that
Howard Stern
will be unable to attend.

Accept Request to Write Recommendation

[Mailed]
(Date)

Dear Darin:

I am delighted to accept the invitation to write a letter of recommendation for you to the Dean at Bowens. I shall sit down and do it right now.

I'll be eager to hear how it turns out, and I'll keep my fingers crossed. I could never tell you before, of course, but you were always one of my favorite students.

Cordially,

Bernie Hill

Acceptance of Informal Business Meeting Invitation

[Emailed]

Dear Melvin:

I was pleased to receive your telephone call and invitation to serve on the Germ Inhalant Committee initial luncheon meeting on September 16 at noon at the Regency in Denver. I will fly in the evening before and stay at the Regency overnight. (My secretary will make all those arrangements.)

I will bring 12 copies of the Sneezer's Report and information on conference facilities in Tahoe.

Thank you for arranging this first meeting. I'm pleased and eager to work on this worthwhile project.

Sincerely,

Conrad Greeves

Accepting an Informal Invitation with Substitution

[Emailed]

Dear Nina:

Thank you for extending the invitation for me to represent Nickors at the annual Fireman's Banquet in New York on October 10. However, as I discussed with you, I will need to modify the topic area you requested, "Trends in Inhalation Techniques," to "Equipment for the New Century." I've attached a copy of the presentation I made last week in Los Angeles.

I will be pleased to make the presentation in the 40-minute format, and all the equipment you have listed in your letter of August 12 will be needed. The accommodations you have described are fine.

Please call me with any additional details as they become available. I'm looking forward to attending the banquet and believe the audience will be especially pleased with the new developments I will describe.

Sincerely,

Ezra Newton

Also see INVITATIONS, page 65, and REFUSAL, page 250.

43
REFUSAL

It is not the hand but the understanding of the man that may be said to write.

—MIGUEL DE CERVANTES

The refusal letter has two main goals: to say no and, at the same time, to promote goodwill. This bad news may be preceded by a positive statement, or, if you know the reader prefers directness or will receive the bad news routinely, use a direct approach. In either case, end with a goodwill statement.

DECIDE TO WRITE
Use this letter in responding to:
- Offer of admission to college
- Offer of membership
- Credit applications (see "Credit Inquiry and Providing Credit Information," page 300, and "Credit Denial," page 309)
- Requests for volunteer participation, financial contributions and donations, letters of reference, loans, bids, raises, appointments, meetings, and interviews
- Adjustments (see "Credit: Requesting an Adjustment in Payments," page 314)
- Proposals or bids
- Job offer
- Contractual invitations
- Returns
- Gifts
- Sales
- Invitations to social events, dinner parties, fundraisers, weddings, etc. (see "Invitations," page 65)

THINK ABOUT CONTENT
- First be sure you understand the request or problem.
- Respond as promptly as possible.
- Start by thanking the reader for the offer, invitation, or effort in preparing a proposal, applying, or giving a gift, if that is appropriate. For example, "Thank you for your invitation to participate in sponsoring a fund for young authors."
- Determine the logical explanation or reason for your refusal, making an effort to empathize with the reader during this process.
- Open with a sentence that sets up the explanation. It may be a thank you, it may agree with the reader on some point, or it may combine an agreement and an apology. This helps set a positive tone for the letter and helps to gain the reader's cooperation. Or, begin with a neutral response to the request to help set up your next statement: "Your efforts to establish the Young Authors'

250

Scholarship Fund are very commendable. I wish you success in this worthy endeavor." This is preferable to opening with "We cannot contribute to the Young Authors' Scholarship Fund."

- If you use an indirect approach, the reader is ushered through the logic or reason for your refusal before he or she reads the refusal itself. This allows him or her to gain more understanding of why you are saying no or are responding with bad news: "We at Great Water value promoting young literary talent. That's why we budget five percent of profits each fiscal year to support such causes."
- Stating your case in positive terms can make all the difference:

  We have committed this year's funds, but we will place your request in our file for consideration for next year. Please contact me again in December with updated information about your needs for 2008."

- State your refusal in a clear, unequivocal, and positive statement.
- Always be tactful, even in the face of an outrageous request, and make your refusal devoid of personalities and comparisons.
- Include a counterproposal, compromise, or a suggestion, if possible: "Ms. Susan Sloan is a very qualified speaker who has won several awards for her presentation skills. She would do an excellent job."
- Close with a goodwill statement such as best wishes, or a related compliment. "Best wishes for the success of this year's Young Authors' Fund project. I look forward to hearing from you in December."
- If you have any concerns about possible legal action, consult with an attorney before sending your letter.

ELIMINATE WRONG MESSAGES

- Don't make negative statements.
- Don't offer excuses.
- Avoid unconvincing arguments or opening opportunities for the reader to debate the matter further.

- Don't be harsh.
- Don't leave a question in the reader's mind about your refusal so he thinks he may still persuade you if he tries hard enough.
- Lying is not a good approach.
- Never blame others for your refusal.

CONSIDER SPECIAL SITUATIONS

In the case of an invitation, the refusal letter may also carry the job of making an apology. (See "Invitations," page 65.)

- In refusing an invitation, send your letter or note to the person listed under RSVP, or the first host, and mention any others.
- Explanations for refusing an invitation will depend upon the type of event, the number of attendees, your relationship to the host, and your function at the event. If you are invited to be an attendee at a large convention, seminar, or conference, you may not be obliged to respond, or you may make only a cursory refusal. "I will be unable to attend. . . ." If you are scheduled as the keynote speaker at an international banquet of 2,000 clients, your refusal—especially if you initially accepted and are now refusing—should include a detailed explanation. It should, of course, be made only in the event of a very serious and unexpected situation, not because you got a better offer. You should also make suggestions and/or arrangements for a replacement.
- When you decline to do a favor, such as a letter of reference, an introduction, or set up a meeting, you are not obliged to explain yourself.
- The credit adjustment refusal letter should begin with a neutral statement, which sets up your next statement of strategy but does not give away your decision. The next statement should be positive and factual, and explain your position or reason. You must then refuse clearly and positively, and, if you can, offer a counterproposal. Remember to make your statements in positive terms. Conclude with a complimentary, encouraging, or upbeat message.
- When you use a direct refusal, be sure to start with a warm greeting, or neutral opening.

"Thank you for your letter of May 20 asking me to volunteer as scoutmaster." In the case of a personal friend, the refusal can open casually: "It was great to hear from you." State your refusal in positive terms: "My commitment to the Safe Neighborhoods Project this year demands all my spare time."

- Be sure to completely identify the request you're refusing by naming the essential information of project, date, and time.
- Direct your letter to the proper person.
- Remember, your objective in refusing a line (or extended line) of business credit request is to keep the customer or client. Offer an alternative solution or counterproposal, whenever possible. It is especially important here to set up the logic of your explanation, and lead the reader through it in an effort to appeal to his or her sense of fair play. It is also important to be firm and positive in tone: "We extend a line of credit to businesses that have operated in this location for over one year. We invite you to reapply to Mr. Albert Green in November with the references listed on the enclosed sheet, and we sincerely hope to do business with Sun Screens at that time. In the meantime, please consider the advantages of setting up all your company checking on First Bank's 'System One Plan' as a preliminary step."
- Refusing inducements and gifts can be done by thanking the reader, and then stating a firm policy of turning down all such offers or items.
- In refusing a bid for a job or project, be as helpful and informative as applicable regulations will allow. The bidder probably expended a considerable amount of time, energy, and funds in an effort to get your business. He or she deserves as much courtesy and support as you can offer. Also remember, the reader may be a future supplier. List areas or items where the bid did not meet specifications or guidelines, and, if possible, list why the winning bidder was awarded the work. Close on an upbeat note.

- Keep blame out of your refusal letters. When terminating business or personal relationships, objective information and taking participant responsibility are the best approaches. Honesty, tact, and kindness are the principles here, and it is wise to avoid detailed explanations. Your decision should be briefly stated, firm, and clear.

SELECT A FORMAT

- In refusing a job offer, respond first with a verbal answer and then follow it with a formal written refusal.
- Personal refusals are often handwritten.
- Business refusals should be typed on the proper letterhead.
- To make form refusals as individual as possible, create a template ("boilerplate") you individualize in the writing process.
- When refusing an invitation, respond in the same form as the invitation was issued. (See "Invitations," page 65.)

SELECT APPROPRIATE WORDS

apply	final
conclusion	invite
considered	opportunity
decision	reapply
decline	refuse
deny	regret
determination	revisit
encourage	unable
evaluated	unfortunately
extend	welcome

CONSTRUCT EFFECTIVE PHRASES

after careful consideration
are not now accepting
cannot participate
determined after study and comparison
doesn't qualify
due to other commitments

I am sorry to be the bearer of bad news
I must tell you we cannot
I recommend you contact
I'm sorry to have to say no
I'm sure you will find support
if you care to resubmit next year
may we invite you to apply again
must conclude that
not able at this time
our application period is closed
our final decision
thank you for applying
there is no way
there's no easy way to say no
unable to help
unfortunately, your application doesn't meet the
  requirements
unquestionably, I must decline
we are so disappointed we cannot
we are unable to invite you
we have evaluated your
we have no other choice but to refuse
we look forward to another opportunity
we must decline your kind invitation
we must deny
we must say no
we regret to report
we will be unable to attend
we wish you great success
will reconsider next year
your idea is a good one
yours is a worthy cause

WRITE STRONG SENTENCES

Start with a strong, positive verb and build your sentences carefully.

I must cancel my conference reservation.

My volunteer calendar is completely full at this time.

I appreciate you asking me to join the Jumpers' Club.

We have selected a bid that more closely meets our specifications for the number of workers to be on site during the contract period.

Please call me next year.

We appreciate all the outstanding work that went into your preparation of the Crichton proposal.

We look forward to receiving your bid on a future project that is closer in scope to your resources.

BUILD EFFECTIVE PARAGRAPHS

Thank you for submitting your proposal for the Wayland Project. We felt your graphics were especially strong.

I enjoyed talking with you on May 10 about the product manager position at Harper. Our selection task was made very difficult by having over 25 extremely qualified applicants.

I am honored at your invitation to speak to the Farmers' Association. I am aware of all the good work the organization is doing.

Thank you for your letter of March 19 describing the problem with the golf clubs. You are correct in assuming that we want to hear about any sales problems.

I have carefully reviewed your letter of June 7 describing the problem with the evening gown. I know that as a 12-year Marks customer, you know we make every effort to satisfy our customers.

We have received your notification that you will be unable to attend day two of the Martinville Conference. Our policy is that we must charge attendees the total conference fee, since our costs for the accommodations remain the same.

EDIT, EDIT, EDIT

Be sure your message is clear, firm, and ends on a good note.

Refuse Customer's Request to Accept Return of Damaged Goods

[Mailed]
(Date)

Dear Mrs. Whitmore:

Start on a positive note. Thank you for your letter of April describing the problem with the red ball gown. As you know, we at Bates try very hard to satisfy our customers.

Show due consideration. Three of us in customer service reviewed the problem after you brought the gown back to the store on April 10. I have also discussed the situation in detail with the manufacturer's representative to try to come to a solution.

Explain. Since the gown was worn and stained, we cannot, of course, sell it as new merchandise. And, as the manufacturer explains in the enclosed letter, the staining problem is a characteristic of the silk fabric, and not a defect in design or construction.

Offer a solution if possible. I am returning your gown to you. Both the manufacturer and I suggest you may want to contact Lace's Dye in Evanston to see if they can dye the garment.

On behalf of Bates, I would like to offer you, as a long-time, valued customer, the enclosed gift certificate for $25, which can be used at any of our stores within the next year.

End on a positive note. We look forward to serving you in the future.

Sincerely,

Judi Wolf

Refuse to Be Club Officer

[Emailed]

Bob,

I'm flattered at the suggestion that I would make an excellent president of the Futures Club, but I have committed all my free time for next year to Jamie's Scouts and Jennie's Little League.

I would certainly consider it next year, and I appreciate your vote of confidence.

Sincerely,

Douglas Viders

Refuse an Invitation

[Handwritten]

Dear Jack and Joan,

Start with thanks, if possible. *How very nice of you to invite us to the reception for Susan on June 10. We have, unfortunately, committed to be adult sponsors at Gary's Young Republicans' party that night. We're very sorry to have to miss such a special occasion.*

Offer an explanation. *Susan is dear to us.*

End on a positive note. *Please do give her our best. We look forward to toasting the new graduate soon.*

Sincerely,

Mary and Jack Burrus

Refuse Employment Candidate

[Mailed]
(Date)

Dear Martin:

It was a pleasure meeting you and discussing how your qualifications might fit the position of sales manager at Basco. You have especially strong leadership skills. However, I believe you'll agree the position requirements aren't the right match for you. All of us here—Jack Mason, June Lockham, Alice Kardon, and I—wish you the best in finding the right situation.

Thank you for your interest and time, and our best wishes for your future success.

Sincerely,

Joe Wagner

Refuse to Volunteer

[Emailed]

Dear Robin:

It's indeed a compliment to be asked to serve on the Program Committee for the Authors' Club, but I have filled my volunteer capacity for this year with several other commitments.

I believe the programs are a very important Authors' Club function, and I shall be happy to consider serving next year, if you need me.

Sincerely,

Eleanor Quinn

Investment Opportunity Refusal

[Emailed]

Saurabh:

Thank you for thinking of me in conjunction with the slot machine investment. Yes, I have heard this is a very hot area, and your plan sounds like a sound one. Potentially a very profitable one.

Unfortunately other commitments have my capital tied up for the next two years. I'm sorry to have to pass, but there it is.

Do contact me again in 20 months, if you have a group you're putting together.

All the best,

Bambi

Refuse Order Due to Past Credit Problems

[Mailed]
(Date)

Dear Mr. Vilas:

Thank you for your Order #3423 of March 10 for Marker Tools.

You may recall that your last purchase in 2005 resulted in our taking collection action for payment through Action Collection.

To establish a new working relationship, you need to send payment for this present order in the amount of $1,582. We will immediately respond by rushing you the tools within 48 hours.

Thank you for considering us again, and we hope to hear from you soon.

Sincerely,

Holly Parker

College Application Refusal

[Mailed]
(Date)

Dear Rubin:

Thank you for applying to Hudson College for your undergraduate studies. The admissions committee has now finished their evaluation of applications for the 2007 fall semester at Hudson, and we regret that your application has been denied.

We'd like to encourage you to consider applying for entrance to Abbott Community College in your city for the fall semester and reapplying to Hudson in the spring. Successful completion as a full-time freshman at Abbott with a 3.4 GPA will give you an excellent chance of qualifying as a sophomore transfer student here.

We wish you every success in your academic endeavors.

Sincerely,

Jennifer Stiffle
Director of Admissions

VII. PROBLEMS, SENSITIVE MATTERS, AND RESOLUTIONS

44
COMPLAINT

Come now, let us reason together.

—ISAIAH 1:18

The letter of complaint has a single objective: to get a problem solved in a positive way. To accomplish this, try to take the place of the recipient so you can make a simple list of what he or she needs to know in order to take corrective action. This letter demands careful organization of the facts, a direct approach, persuasive writing, suggestion of a resolution or statement of further action, and, whenever possible, a statement of goodwill. It's often helpful to think in terms of what will reasonably make you whole again.

Simple complaints may be quickly handled with a telephone call, or by email to the customer service online address. Detailed or complicated ones, or those that could involve legal action, should be handled with an emailed or mailed letter.

DECIDE TO WRITE
You may need to write this letter for one of the following situations:
- A purchase that is wrong, damaged, defective, delivered too late, spoiled, broken, has missing parts, no instructions, or lacks the warranty
- Neighborhood problems
- School problems
- Pet problems
- Social, club, and community problems
- Errors in billing, order, financial statement, minutes, or a collection procedure has been initiated against you
- Employee problems of payment, productivity, attitude, incompetence, or sexual harassment
- Whenever legal problems are suspected
- Illegal activities such as fraud or false advertising
- Misrepresentation
- Legislative problems or disagreements
- Business policies and practice disagreements

THINK ABOUT CONTENT
- A written complaint shouldn't usually be your first course of action. If, for example, the neighbor's dog barked all night, a telephone call is a better response than a two-page letter. As a matter of fact, a telephone call should be the first line of complaint for most problems.
- Gather and review all the facts, so you have them firmly in mind and logically and chronologically in order.

- In social, personal, pet, children, and school complaints, it is usually best to try to resolve these disputes with a calm and tactful, face-to-face conversation with those involved. First review the rules and policies, then state your complaint in terms of infractions, and corrective action or resolution.

- Emphasize the solution or corrective action in objective terms. Stay away from "I" statements like "I want," "I feel," "I need." Use statements like, "To correct this problem . . ."

- Make a written record of all the facts, persons, contact addresses, and telephone numbers involved in your complaint each time something new happens. This will allow you to be accurate, precise, and complete. Include in your information the date, time, and any person spoken to, and the content and outcome of each conversation.

- Keep all original documents, and make copies to send with your letter. Also keep all subsequent correspondence and documents in a file.

- Offer additional documentation, like photographs of broken merchandise, whenever possible.

- Write your letter in a timely manner. Although you may need time to get over the initial anger before writing, it is important to write as soon as you have documented all the facts of the problem. Not only will your letter be stronger, but your chances of getting the corrective action you desire will be better.

- Begin by using a positive statement such as the fact that you chose the product because of its reputation, and write in the full expectation that the reader desires to take corrective action.

- Unless you are stating a number of items that point to a central problem, use the one-complaint-per-letter rule. If, for example, you are complaining about the lack of service of a department store, and you state three examples that took place during your last visit to the store, you should list them very briefly. If you want to complain about three separate policies your senator endorses, write three separate letters.

- Cover the problem completely, even if you discussed it with the reader on the telephone and he or she has some knowledge of the facts. You might start, "As we discussed, I received . . ." Remember, your letter may be referred to someone else within the organization.

- Address your letter to a real person. This may require calling to determine the proper person's name.

- Whenever possible, complain to the person with the authority to take corrective action. Otherwise, you can waste much time and effort, and/or the problem may be exacerbated by dealing with the wrong person.

- Use a "Reference" or "Subject" line, if appropriate, to focus and direct the reader's attention to the problem. State the problem here and/or in the opening sentence of your letter.

- Be direct and state specifically what is wrong.

- Present the facts briefly and clearly, using any reference dates, persons, invoice numbers, inventory numbers, order numbers, prices, and specifications that are applicable. State these in logical or chronological order.

- Use bullets, numbers, and indentation to emphasize your points, and to make it easier for the reader to note and respond to them. This works especially well if you have points to list or chronological events to note.

- Tell the reader why your complaint needs to be resolved.

- State the specific adjustments, corrections, or action you seek. If possible, include a couple of choices for the reader.

- Be polite. The person to whom you are writing is often—if not usually—not the person who created the problem.

- Use a third-party expert if an objective opinion or evaluation is needed, and mention this person in your letter. If the person offered a written opinion, refer to it, and enclose a copy. (Indicate the enclosure on the copy line of your letter.)

- Give the reader a time frame for taking corrective action.

- Close on a positive but firm note. State your confidence that the matter will be taken care of as you suggest.

- Include your complete contact information: name, home and email addresses, and work, home, and/or cell telephone numbers.
- Attach copies of any pertinent documents that support your letter.
- Close with a statement of when you will make your next contact if you doubt the recipient will resolve the matter in a timely manner without urging.

ELIMINATE WRONG MESSAGES

- Do not use harsh, accusatory, sarcastic, abusive, blaming language or terms that could be interpreted as a personal attack.
- Never let your letter wander into side issues or nonissues.
- Don't be vague.
- Do not leave the course of corrective action or the response date up to the reader.
- Do not threaten to sue. It is far better to send a positive letter and indicate a cc: to your attorney with the title of "attorney at law" listed after her or his name. You certainly may state—if applicable and if you are prepared to do so—that if you do not receive a satisfactory reply by a specific date, you will take the matter to small claims court. But be sure you have exhausted every possibility of negotiating first.
- Do not use unreasonable or out-of-line suggestions for corrective action.

CONSIDER SPECIAL SITUATIONS

- Many complaints must take a certain form. First call the organization, and talk to customer service to get any required complaint form or number. Get the correct name and title of the person to send it to, the information to be included, the name of the person to whom you are speaking, etc. A primary example of this is a complaint about a problem with your credit statement.
- In disputes about purchased merchandise that you have charged on your credit card, you must immediately let the credit-card company know there's a problem. Call the 800 telephone number first to make sure you follow their complaint procedure.

- For airline problems, state the flight number, departure and arrival locations, times of departure and arrival, where and when the problem occurred, a description of the problem, the names of airline employees involved, the names and contact information of witnesses, and the course of corrective action you suggest.
- Often wrongs exist on both sides of a complaint. Take responsibility for your part of the problem, apologize if appropriate, and suggest a mutually beneficial solution, whenever possible.
- There are usually several possible solutions to a problem, so be ready to negotiate and compromise.
- Complaint campaigns to political figures and corporations should be made individually, that is, each person should send his or her own letter. Another approach, which may be preferable in some circumstances, is to send one letter or petition with many individual signatures. Check this out before deciding. Also consider other complaint actions such as writing a letter to the editor of your local newspaper, initiating local television and radio station news coverage of the issue, or another type of political action.
- When merchandise arrives damaged by a second-party shipper, you should immediately notify the shipper, and follow their procedure for making a complaint.
- It is often most effective to use a list form and to simply state the facts—what is wrong—in just enough detail to enable the reader to take action. Include pertinent information like dates, and persons involved; and refer to relevant documents by identifying numbers wherever possible.
- If you are angry about a problem, it will be necessary to return to a calm and objective state of mind before you write. Or, you can write your angry letter, read it, then throw it away. Then start over on your real letter of complaint.
- Attach all copies—keep the originals—of any pertinent documents showing the item, situation, date of transaction, place of transaction, cost, sales receipt, invoice, original request, and original inventory certificate. If there are a number, reference them in your letter, and number them.

SELECT A FORMAT

- Your complaint should look official. Type it on business letterhead, personal business letterhead, personal letterhead, or quality bond stationery.
- Complaint or claim forms are often required. Type these or print very neatly.
- If your letter must be handwritten, make it neat and clear.

SELECT THE RIGHT WORD

acceptable	inaccurate
accurate	incident
adjust	judge
apparent	misrepresent
appraisal	mistake
attention	negotiate
aware	oversight
complain	quote
compromise	reasonable
damage	recompense
defect	register
desire	replacement
dispute	resolve
dissatisfied	responsible
error	restore
estimate	satisfy
experience	settle
fault	situation
grievance	true
guarantee	warrant

BUILD EFFECTIVE PHRASES

bring this matter to your attention

does not perform as advertised

I know you will want to correct

I look forward to resuming a

I noticed the error in

I would like to be reimbursed for

I'm sure you will want to correct this

I've enjoyed being a client

not up to your usual customer service standard of

parts were missing from the package

please check your records

please credit me with

please ship me a replacement immediately

product is defective

restore this item to

resulted in work loss

the order was delayed

this is inconsistent with your usual standard of fine service

uncharacteristic error

was inconvenienced

WRITE STRONG SENTENCES

I am writing regarding your invoice #7556, dated May 17, 2006, for the Model 1664 Adapters.

I am depending on you to resolve this problem in one of two ways.

I certainly don't want our working record of five years blemished by such an error.

Please get these parts to me by Friday.

I suggest we simply settle the matter by you issuing Bonders a $500 credit for the broken parts.

Please send a corrected invoice by May 20.

May we please resolve this situation by June 14?

I think you will agree that my request for equipment replacement is a reasonable solution.

I believe this can be easily resolved if you will record a $30 credit in your database, and I'll use it against my next charge.

Your bookkeeper simply charged my account twice.

I'm confident that we can resolve this dispute.

I employed an independent antique appraiser listed on your website to estimate the replacement value of my French leather screen, and a copy of that estimate is attached.

I wish to register my dissatisfaction with your position on this issue.

Your most recent vote in Congress does not reflect the view of your constituency.

My main objective is to ensure that this doesn't happen again.

There are a number of solutions to the barking problem that you may want to consider.

BUILD EFFECTIVE PARAGRAPHS

I am returning for credit the three dozen ceramic yellow bumble bees that I did not order. Please refer to my attached order #3210 that lists three ceramic yellow bumble bees and two dozen little foxes.

My fall sale begins September 20. I must have the corrected order by September 15.

This is the fourth time our shipment of paper bags has been late. As you know, we cannot operate our store without them.

I have not received a return telephone call in response to my email of April 10. (Copy attached.) The assembly line gears supplied by Gears Inc. are not performing to specifications. I need your immediate response to get this problem solved. We are losing 20 percent of our production each day.

EDIT, EDIT, EDIT

A cool, clear communication will win the day.

Returning Product for Refund

[Mailed]
(Date)

Dear Mr. Stark:

I am returning the "Fantastic New Body" kit for a full refund of $49.95, as your advertisement states: "Simply return the unused portion for a full refund if you are not completely satisfied."

After using the products for two weeks, I have experienced no weight loss.

Please send a check for $49.95 to Ellen Worthington, 223 East Drury Lane, Littleton, CO 80223.

Thank you.

Sincerely,

Ellen Worthington

Complaint Offers Two Alternatives

[Faxed and mailed on 8 ½ by 11-inch stationery]
(Date)

SUBJECT: Cool Daze Air Conditioner, Model 1755A, Serial No. 3745, Purchase Order #6654

Identify problem.

Dear Mr. Ricks:

The air conditioner I ordered from Cool Daze on April 1 is not performing according to specifications. (See purchase and delivery documents attached.) After I called your 800 number, your Mr. Wally Cranks came and inspected the unit. He determined the problem is an internal defective seal, and he recommended replacement with a new unit. (See the copy of his report attached.)

Give history and/or facts.

When I called your office on April 20, Mr. William Chatter said you have no units in stock, and don't have any scheduled for production until fall. He said you do have several Model 3755As available at $500 more.

Since the weather is already heating up, I suggest we settle this one of two ways:

Offer solutions.

(1) Cool Daze supply and install the Model 3755A at no additional cost, or

(2) You remove the air conditioner from our roof and immediately refund our money.

Please respond by May 15.

Give response time frame.

Thank you.

Sincerely,

Kim Beerli

Complaint to Moving Company

[Faxed and mailed on 8½ by 11-inch stationery]
(Date)

REFERENCE: Move on August 20, from
110 West Trinchera Peak to
2340 Sundown Mountain Drive,
for Walt and Mary Downs

Dear Mr. Richman:

State the problem.

As I stated on the telephone, there were a number of problems with our move by Westward Ho:

Present the facts.

1. The packing sheets were changed to indicate scratches and dents that were not on the original sheets (see the two sets of sheets enclosed),
2. A drawer that belongs to the antique credenza (see photo) is missing,
3. The Chinese screen was somehow crushed, ruining the surface, and
4. The white brocade sofa received a number of stains that my cleaning consultant, Mr. Cloudy Coils, says will not come out.

Mr. Richman, as I told you, these damages amount to over $12,000. (See the value, repair, cleaning statements, and estimates listed on the attached sheet, and the estimate copies enclosed.) I have also enclosed statements from two antique authorities who saw the items the day Westward Ho packed them, and have since examined the damage.

Ask for action.

Please fax me your damage claim form, and I will immediately complete it and fax it back to you today. I'm sure you will agree that coming to an equitable settlement by October 15 will be an advantage to both of us.

Thank you.

Sincerely,

May Michelle Riley

Complaint About Workmanship in Contract Work

[Faxed and mailed on 8½ by 11-inch stationery]
(Date)

SUBJECT: Installation of Exposed
Aggregate Walkways,
Sun Club Resort, May 15

Dear Mr. Bailey:

When our maintenance man reported a series of cracks in the new exposed aggregate you installed two weeks ago, I asked him to check the thickness. He reported that the sidewalk is 2 inches thick in most places and 3 inches thick in others throughout the 150-yard length.

Since the specifications (see attached, line 15) call for a 6-inch uniform thickness, I must insist this installation be corrected. I suggest either:

1. Maco Concrete completely remove the existing exposed aggregate and reinstall a new walkway according to the specifications and under the supervision of Mr. Ted Walker, our maintenance engineer, or

2. Maco immediately refund the payment of $4,500, plus a removal charge of $2,000.

Please call me by April 15 with your decision, so we may avoid seeking a legal remedy.

Sincerely,

M. B. McDermott

Complaint About Neighborhood Dog

[Mailed]
(Date)

Mr. Backus:

I'm writing after leaving several messages on your telephone answering machine. As I stated, I have a real concern about the safety of our children given the fact that your dog, Bunky, has jumped the fence around your yard several times and displays a vicious nature. My daughter, Karen, who is five years old, is terrified to pass by your yard because of Bunky's fierce barking and efforts to jump over the fence.

Please call me this evening after 6:30 P.M. to arrange a time to discuss this. I'm sure you'll agree this matter needs our immediate cooperative attention. Surely we can come up with a satisfactory solution.

Sincerely,

Annette Korslund

Doctor Overcharging Insurance Company

[Mailed]
(Date)

Dear Rose:

As we discussed, the insurance company was overcharged $1,000 on my August 15 annual checkup billing. I have notified the insurance company, and am copying them with this letter.

State the problem.

Thank you for taking care of this immediately.

Ask for action.

Sincerely,

Carole Sparrow

Incorrect Item Returned for Credit

[Emailed]

Dear Teddy:

Shock and awe—as I stated on the telephone—are what I experienced when I opened the parcel I received today. Not only is the silk dress the wrong color (I ordered sage and received saffron), but also it's not a size 8 but a size 18. The real problem, as I stated, is that I must wear the dress on Saturday.

Please immediately ship the dress I ordered at no charge. I'm returning this one today in its original packaging with the provided label.

Thank you.

Sincerely,

Cecilia Shook

Webmaster Overcharges

[Emailed]

Jim:

I believe, as I stated on the telephone, it was a simple error. I came to you as part of the PubClub, and under your agreement to offer members a special website creation fee package of $1,500. So, when I got your invoice for $3,200, I was shocked.

I know I'll be making routine changes to my website, and want to continue working with you. I'm sending a check for the $1,500 payment, as we agreed. And thank you for a great online image.

Sincerely,

Susan Webber

Complaint of False Charge Card Billings

[Faxed and mailed]
(Date)

REFERENCE: Bank Credit Card #34-34456-4445
Expiration Date 05/12/09

Dear Customer Service Manager:

The charge #23 for $95 that appears on my current statement (see attached) is in error, and I hereby dispute it.

As you will notice, the next item, #24, is a charge for Scissors Salon services in the amount of $78. The clerk overcharged me for a "sparkle" and hair cut, and then rewrote the charge slip, but obviously failed to destroy the errant one. (The charges are for the same date and time.)

Thank you for contacting Scissors Salon to correct this error and for crediting my account.

Thank you.

Sincerely,

Brenda Schaak

Complaint of No Credit for Returned Parts

[Faxed and mailed]
(Date)

REFERENCE: Account #19778,
Jennifer A. Watts, Watco

Dear Mrs. Calvin:

Our monthly statement dated October 30 still shows the item #33 for the three dozen computer parts. These parts were returned on August 10. I'm enclosing another copy of the receipt your Mr. Bill Denson marked and signed when he received the returned parts.

Please send a corrected statement showing that we have been credited with the $89.99 for the computer parts and we will remit a check for the balance owed.

Thank you.

Sincerely,

Sue Atkinson

Also see APOLOGY, page 278; CREDIT: REQUESTING AN ADJUSTMENT IN PAYMENT, page 314; and OPINION EDITORIAL, page 375.

45

DISAGREEMENTS AND DISPUTES

The only agreements I ever had problems with were those I signed with a handshake.

—ANONYMOUS

Disagreements arise in every relationship. Unsnarling and resolving them before they become major disputes are true tests not only of communication skills, but also of the code of ethics and character of the people involved. The steps to satisfactory resolution are often simple, except when emotions and ego intervene. To defuse the emotional component in a conflict and set the stage for resolution, it's important to communicate calmly and clearly that you are determined to work out a fair and equitable solution.

DECIDE TO WRITE

Common areas where disagreements and disputes arise include:

* Written contracts of all kinds (employment, union, client, customer, rentals, home purchase, contractor, subcontractor, literary agent, publishing, etc.)
* Verbal agreements (contracts)
* Orders and sales
* Delivery of services or products
* Schedule of payments
* Employee, employer relations
* Government requirements and policies

* Land use and property lines
* Neighborhood living
* Friendship disagreements and misunderstandings
* Family issues and inheritance

RESEARCH

* Review the terms of the original agreement.
* Collect any additional information that could have an impact on the agreement (e.g., terms of a preceding contract, relevant laws, current practice, settlements, opinions, and/or resolutions; legal documents, such as property boundaries, etc.).
* Review the beliefs and opinions held by the other person or party.

THINK ABOUT CONTENT

* Allow yourself to vent in writing if your emotions are elevated.
  — Sit down, put your pen to a sheet of paper, and without lifting the point, write it all out. Begin with "I'm so upset because . . ." Be sure to include the part about how you feel you've been wronged or injured, and what you're feeling as a result.

—In the solitude of your own office, and out of earshot of others, read aloud what you've written (in full voice and expression, if you like).

—Tear up your letter after reading it.

—Take some deep breaths, and, if you're still feeling less than calm, take a walk or do something fun.

—When you feel calm and able to be objective, try to open yourself to the position of the other person's point of view.

—Communicate, dispassionately, with the other party. State that you are researching and/or considering the matter and will be back in contact on a specific date, if necessary.

- Write your response in a timely manner after your initial emotions have cooled and you are able to be objective.

- Open on a positive note. "Jim, I'm sure we both want to resolve this problem . . ." or "Dick, I know you are very fair and will work to resolve this problem . . ."

- State your points of agreement. "I know we agree that the number of light fixtures originally ordered was . . ." "I'm sure we both want to arrive at the same end result: a fair resolution."

- State your point of view, position, or side of the argument and what you want, complete with relevant supporting facts, documentation, sources, law, and other relevant information. Do it in a calm, factual, and rational manner: "What follows here is my experience . . ."

- Ask the other person for input whenever possible. "This is how I see the matter. Please give me your views . . ."

- Offer a solution—with several alternatives, if possible. This step is likely to find more receptivity if it includes compromise from both sides. "Jane, it seems there are several possible resolutions . . ."

- Allow the reader to save face by stating what you want as an end result in a manner that makes him or her appear generous, powerful, gracious, willing to negotiate, and/or compromise. "With a single word from you, this can be resolved . . ." or "Would you be willing to settle the matter . . ."

- State when you will contact the reader, or request a response by a certain date. "I'll contact you on Wednesday after you've had the opportunity to consider the alternatives" or "Please get back to me by Wednesday with your decision."

- Conclude with a goodwill statement that includes your wish to have a good relationship in the future. "I'm sure that by putting our two reasonable heads together, we can come to a negotiated solution that will allow us to pursue our usual mutually beneficial relationship in the future" or "I'm certain you will give this the kind of consideration that has earned you a reputation for working out fair and equitable solutions."

- Test your letter: (1) give it a little breathing time, then reread it aloud to check the tone. (2) Ask a couple of objective experts in the matter to read your letter. (If there are possible legal consequences, ask an attorney to read it, and give you an opinion.)

ELIMINATE WRONG MESSAGES

- It's important to remember that your foremost objective is to reach a solution. It is not to seek revenge or get even. Eliminate inflammatory words or phrases such as "outrageous," "wrong," "ridiculous," "unacceptable," "insulting," "egregious," "unfair," "no way," and "resounding no."

- Refrain from using personal pronouns in an accusatory manner: "You said that the total fee would be . . ." or "You acted unprofessionally . . ." Instead, use positive or neutral statements of fact whenever possible: "On page two, the fee is stated as . . ."

- Concentrate instead on keeping to objective statements of fact, and solutions. Don't, for example, use "I" or "me" phrases like "I believe this is unfair" or "Others agree with me that I've been treated unjustly."

CONSIDER SPECIAL SITUATIONS

- There are situations where you will not want to compromise or negotiate. In such a case, state your position, then soften it somewhat by appealing to the reader's sense of fairness: "I request a full refund of $550.00. I believe you'll agree that this is a reasonable resolution."

- Because we live in a litigious society, caution must be exercised in writing your letter. Assume that what you write may end up in a court of law, and if you don't want to defend it, don't write it. If there is any possibility that your statements may be actionable, consult legal counsel before sending your letter.

- Red flags that indicate the disagreement is escalating beyond a retractable point include statements of accusation, statements of admission, or threats of legal action. This is the time to seek legal counsel, and/or request arbitration by a third, mutually agreed upon, independent party. Unfortunately, these situations often involve personal matters, such as the division of a family estate; marriage dissolution; business partnership dissolutions; child custody issues; matters of guardianship of a dependent; or when types of legal action are threatened or initiated by another person.

- Letters to the editor of the newspaper disagreeing with a political position, public policy, proposed law, or social issue will be most effective if you quote the other party's published statement and source, then make your objection in rational, well-documented terms.

- Letters to policy makers expressing your views can be effectively handled if you reference and quote the published policy and source, and clearly state your dissenting view or position objectively and with careful documentation.

- Create your own email lists of people who share your views. Use email alerts to inform them of public policy discussions or pending decisions or laws, and request that they join in a letter-writing campaign. This can be effective in giving voice to your shared views and getting public policy changed, or in initiating a group (class) legal action. Creating online discussion groups will be helpful too.

SELECT A FORMAT

- Letters of a financial, personal, or personnel nature should be sent by email only when you are responding through an organization's secure online computer system and there is an established policy to do so. Otherwise, send such communications by registered mail.

- Disagreements and disputes of a personal nature are best handled in a handwritten letter. Whether you use personal and small formatted stationery (5 by 7-inch sheets), full-sized letterhead ($8\frac{1}{2}$ by 11 inches), or a personal notecard will depend upon the nature and length of your communication. (A notecard denotes a more personal and informal communication; a small letterhead an informal one; and a full-sized letterhead one that is a bit more formal in nature.)

- For business or legal disagreements or disputes, type your response on full-sized letterhead ($8\frac{1}{2}$ by 11 inches), and send it by registered mail in a legal-sized envelope.

USE POWERFUL WORDS

appeal	objective
compromise	offer
determine	propose
discover	resolve
discuss	satisfy
negotiate	solution

CONSTRUCT EFFECTIVE PHRASES

a win-win solution

accommodate both parties

agree to a compromise

an equitable solution

avoid further disagreement

come to terms with

I do not disclaim the fact that

do please consider the following

I am willing to settle the matter

I estimate the loss to be

in the interest of resolution

in total and complete repayment (settlement)

move toward resolution

my understanding of the matter

our future mutually beneficial relationship

perhaps you were not aware of the fact that

please consider the following facts

resolve the matter

the agreed settlement will consist of

the disputed points

the points remaining to be resolved

to resolve the matter completely

we agree to resolve the matter completely

work toward a compromise

your reputation for dealing fairly

WRITE STRONG SENTENCES

I'm sure we can reach a compromise.

I am willing to absorb the cost of replacement of part of the order.

I can move in the direction of excusing the extra work time involved to complete the replacement.

I know you to be a very reasonable person.

There is no reason we can't settle this matter between us and remain friends.

I refuse to let this cost us our friendship.

I believe we can both agree to move slightly from our current positions in the interest of settling this matter.

I would be very willing to have this matter arbitrated by a mutually approved independent party.

Please let me know if you will accept these terms and agree that the matter is now settled in full.

I can negotiate on three of the items you have listed.

I am willing to settle the matter if you will repay me in the amount of $5,200 for the cost of having the work redone. (See my receipt for services enclosed.)

There are several ways, which I will list here, we may go to resolve this matter.

I have documented what happened with the attached copies.

It seems we have reached an impasse, so I shall now take the matter up with your superior at Tress, Mr. Ralph Suitor.

I believe we have been able to agree on all but one item of your proposed resolution.

CREATE EFFECTIVE PARAGRAPHS

Let's settle this matter immediately. I'll reduce my claim by $5,500 if you'll increase your offer by the same amount, for a total settlement amount of $10,500 to be awarded to me immediately. This isn't just fair; it's also prudent. With this resolution, neither of us will have to engage an attorney, which would, in the end, be much more costly and far less satisfactory. What do you say?

While we can still be friends, I suggest that we agree to chalk up the incident of the wrecked rental car to "one of life's unfortunate accidents," and agree to split the outstanding bill equally between us. That seems to me the only rational way to settle the dispute, since we will never agree on degrees of culpability and who owes the greater amount.

If we can't agree to put the past behind us and act like adults responsible for the care and upbringing of Alicia, neither of us will "win," and she will most definitely lose. So, for her sake, I've decided not to continue to fight for sole custody. Instead, I've come up with a schedule for shared custody that I hope you'll find as fair as I've tried to make it. Please look at it carefully, and let me know if you suggest any adjustments, and if you will agree to it.

OK, Rachel, as I see it, we can take your approach, and start down the path of legal action, as you suggest, or we can accept the settlement offer, as I prefer, and end the whole matter right here. I've reviewed our situation thoroughly with three leading attorneys who specialize in personal injury cases, and I've attached three transcripts of those discussions. Please review them, and then let's talk about this again. But I must tell you that I think the settlement amount is fair, and I'm unwilling to submit myself to the emotional toll this kind of litigation would require.

Archie, this is crazy. After 10 years as business partners, who remembers who brought the pencil sharpener when we went into business? If you think it was you, take it. I suggest we settle the division of the remaining office equipment by having an appraiser come in and put a value on each item. Then we can take turns picking those items we each want (adding values to come out as near equal as possible). For the stuff left over, we can sell and equally split the proceeds.

Let's not let this disagreement escalate. I suggest we ask Jimmy to cast the deciding vote in selecting the investment vehicles for Dad. Jimmy's the expert. I'm totally against dividing the assets at this point and each of us investing half, as you suggest. The interest this money can earn, if properly invested, can be used to take care of Dad for as long as he needs care. What do you say, Billy?

You are absolutely right: your check for $765 was credited to the wrong account. The error has been corrected. Please view the change in your account balance owed online. We appreciate your help in resolving this dispute quickly. Please accept our apologies for this error and the inconvenience it caused you.

You were right. The books you shipped us were from our warehouse, and the amount of the disputed bill you received has been credited to your account. My apologies for our errors in this matter. Please accept the enclosed coupon for $50 off your next purchase from Blunders Books, Inc.

Failure to Pay Warranty Claim

[Typed on 8½ by 11-inch stationery and sent via registered mail]
(Date)

REFERENCE: B&H Paint Failure, Claim #45562 — Identify dispute.

Dear Sam:

I'm sure we both want to get this dispute settled as quickly as possible, and without further negotiation. We've discussed your response to our initial claim. It isn't acceptable. Here's what we're prepared to do.

First, I'll review the facts as I stated in my call: (1) the pigment on the B&H paint for our home exterior was unstable, so the south-facing exterior wall is discolored and has seriously deteriorated. (2) B&H warranty states (see attached copy, Exhibit 1) that product and cost of application will be covered completely in the case of paint failure. (3) B&H's representative inspected our home exterior and agreed to supply the paint and cover the labor of repainting the south side of the house only, or a total payment of $2,500. (See Exhibit 2.) — State the problem clearly.

Since the other three sides of the house covered by B&H also failed to hold the color (though the fade and deterioration are considerably less), we requested enough paint for complete coverage and a check from B&H for the total labor cost for repainting of $9,900. (See Exhibit 3.)

The B&H representative, Ron Grinch, told us after his inspection that B&H would pay only $2,500 in labor costs, and would supply enough new paint to cover the entire house. (See Exhibit 4.)

In the interest in getting this resolved, we are prepared to settle the matter for $7,500 for labor and enough replacement paint to cover the entire house with two coats, if this can be settled no later than Friday of next week. We have checked with our homeowners' insurance agent, and he stated that ours is "a generous offer." (See Exhibit 5.) — Offer resolution.

Please consult with your committee members, as we agreed. I'll call you Tuesday to learn your final decision. If you agree to this, we want to receive your check for $7,500 and 45 gallons of "Tobacco" B&H's Best Exterior Paint by next Friday, April 15, 2006. — Ask for action and set a time frame.

Sincerely,

Steve and Susie Swindled

Model for Employment Dispute

[Faxed and mailed]
(Date)

Dear Ms. Jitters:

State the dispute clearly. As I stated in my letter disputing the amount of my paycheck for last week, Reddy Boot can confirm that my overtime was authorized and that I am entitled to be paid at the time-and-half rate for the additional 30 hours. The total amount still owed is $1,500 ($45 per hour for 30 hours.)

Ask for action. Please issue my check for that amount today.

Sincerely,

Jack Boxer

Rental Payment Dispute

[Typed on letterhead and sent via registered mail]
(Date)

Dear Jack:

As I stated on the telephone, our agreement on the rental lease for the house at 3222 Winchester, Darby, CO, on July 1, 2006, was that we would purchase paint and supply the labor to paint the house interior, and the amount of $1,500 would be returned to us with our security deposit of $2,500 — a total of $4,000 — at the end of the lease term.

I've enclosed a copy of our agreement, and a copy of the receipt for paint and supplies purchased a year ago. I'm prepared to file a claim in small claims court if we do not receive your check for that amount within the legal period by the end of next week.

Sincerely,

Ginger Scammed

Personal Family Disagreement Letter

[Handwritten on personal stationery]
(Date)

Dear Brother Jim Bob:

Thanks for your note expressing concern about Mom and Dad. Yes, now that Dad has been diagnosed with Alzheimer's and his behavior has dictated that he needs to be in a care facility for his and Mom's safety, there will need to be some immediate changes in their living arrangements.

But, while I agree their living situation must be changed, I firmly disagree that we need to step in and make their decisions for them, take over their finances, and move them to an assisted living community.

While Dad is now unable to be involved in the decision making, Mom is fully capable of making these decisions and has expressed her desire to do so. (I believe her direct words were, "Butt out.") Our job, as I see it, is to offer as much emotional support and hands-on help as will assist her through this very difficult time. (Difficult for all of us, to be sure.)

Mom and I have surveyed all the suitable facilities for Dad in the area where she wants to live. There are precious few, as it turns out. We selected the best one, and Dad will be admitted to Shady Meadows in Grand Plains tomorrow. Mom will pay for his care from their savings.

Mom wants to sell the house and buy a suitable townhome within a few miles of where Dad will be. I will certainly help her through that process. I will also help Mom arrange for a mover, and help with packing and moving.

I've suggested to Mom that she use several services for home maintenance for things I can't cover from this distance. She has promised that she will take a driver's refresher course since she hasn't been driving. (I'll set that up this week.)

As for her finances, Mom probably is more frugal than we are. We'd probably both benefit from her budget advice.

Please give all this your careful consideration. Mom has promised to ask for help when she needs it, and I firmly believe what I've covered here will work well for the foreseeable future.

All the best,

Cheryl

Also see APOLOGY, page 278; COMPLAINT, page 257; and REFUSAL, page 250.

NEGOTIATIONS

Let us never negotiate out of fear, but let us never fear to negotiate.

—JOHN FITZGERALD KENNEDY

While negotiating is often approached with all the transparency of playing a hand of poker, your objective shouldn't be to bluff the other party or parties in order to win the result you want and insure that the other party will lose. Your objective should be to carefully consider all the factors and to arrive, together, at a solution that will leave all parties reasonably satisfied.

Much of this process will be conducted verbally. Often it's wise to wait to commit the items of a negotiation to writing until: (1) the points of negotiation have been clarified, (2) possible solutions have been identified, (3) possible concessions are offered or requested, and/or (4) final terms and details are being considered, debated, and recorded. Usually the final discussion will take the form of a letter containing proposed terms (and counter proposals) spelled out. The final negotiated agreement may be a simple letter stating all the details; a formal agreement; a contract; or a legal document of settlement. (See "Disagreements and Disputes," page 265, and "Settlements," page 275.)

DECIDE TO WRITE

Skills of negotiation are essential any time two or more people are involved. Some very common situations with important consequences include:

- Contract terms of agreement
- Sales, purchases, and payment terms
- Product orders and delivery schedules
- Working arrangements
- Neighborhood living
- Change orders

RESEARCH

- Gather as many related facts about the other negotiator(s) as possible: strengths, weaknesses, financial standing (if important), past similar negotiations and outcomes, etc.
- Research all aspects of similar transactions to discover how you may best approach your own situation.
- Approach the process with openness and a willingness to compromise.

BEGIN THE PROCESS

- Define—only for your own review at this stage— the optimal list of the elements that you want to achieve; and then create your acceptable list of the elements (or take-aways) that you will accept. Use these to create two lists.
- Ask the other negotiator(s) to list the elements she/he wants to achieve. (This may be done verbally or in writing.)
- Propose using a mutually agreed-upon arbitrator (third, independent party) should the negotiations stall or become overly adversarial.
- Listen (or read) the other negotiator(s) list(s) carefully, and ask for clarification when in doubt.
- Indicate you've heard (and/or understand) the negotiator(s) by restating his or her elements listed.
- Make a statement of goodwill and your desire for a win/win resolution.
- State your optimal and/or acceptable list of elements. (This is usually best done by starting the process with only your optimal list, unless you have already ascertained that this will stall or stop the process entirely.)
- Engage the other party in a process of creative brainstorming that may open the door to possible new alternatives or solutions.
- Offer your concessions and request concessions from the other negotiator(s) verbally or in writing.
- Debate areas of nonagreement, maintaining a spirit of give-and-take.
- Close the negotiations with a written listing of the compromised elements upon which you've both agreed.
- Give yourself and the other negotiator(s) time to reflect on the compromised elements, if necessary. (Sometimes a letter of agreement, which is signed by all parties, is in order.)

ELIMINATE WRONG MESSAGES

- Early in the process, avoid words that reflect inflexibility, such as insist, non-negotiable, and unwavering.
- Using a heavy-handed or negative attack usually doesn't work: "You're not willing to compromise."

- Issuing ultimatums like, "This is my last offer," can backfire.
- Avoid, when possible, statements that inflame emotions, like "I'm making all the concessions here" or "You aren't really making a good faith effort."

CONSIDER SPECIAL SITUATIONS

- When emotions become elevated, allow a cooling-off period or time-out of several days or a week, before resuming discussions.
- When negotiations stall or discussions become incendiary, initiate the use of the arbitrator.

SELECT A FORMAT

- When there is an established policy to do so, emails containing financial, personal, or personnel information should be sent only after proper authorization and only on an organization's secure online computer system.
- Send communications via fax only after agreement by the party(ies) involved.
- Business or legal negotiations should be typed on letterhead stationery ($8\frac{1}{2}$ by 11 inches) and sent by registered mail.
- Negotiations of a personal nature may be written on personal and small stationery (for example, 5 by 7 inches) or full-sized letterhead ($8\frac{1}{2}$ by 11 inches).

USE CAREFULLY CHOSEN WORDS

accept	fair
agree	gain
alternative	offer
compromise	satisfy
concession	substitute
consider	suggest
equal	value

CONSTRUCT EFFECTIVE PHRASES

please consider this alternative

a better and more satisfactory solution may be

of equal value to both of us

give the following concessions

offer to negotiate these terms

possible resolutions may include

both end up satisfied

a win-win solution

an equitable arrangement

accommodate both parties

come to agreeable terms

please give this careful consideration

WRITE STRONG SENTENCES

I believe we can reach an equitable compromise.

Thank you for offering your list of concessions.

I feel your points of concession are most generous.

I believe we are both determined to reach a happy resolution.

I want us both to be satisfied with this agreement.

There remains only an item or two to negotiate.

I think we're almost there.

There are several ways I'll list here to suggest how we may come to an amicable agreement.

CREATE EFFECTIVE PARAGRAPHS

If you can see your way clear to offer me the pick of the litter from your bitch, "Sally," I will forego my usual breeding fee and agree to the deal. Is this agreeable to you?

I do hope you can allow our family to pay for Rachael's lunches each week instead of the required quarterly pre-payment requirement. I believe I've explained why we need to have this alternate agreement in place.

I can't take on the volunteer commitment as required in the agreement you sent. I can, however, commit to drive the after-school program bus for the children every Tuesday and Thursday. I've made those alterations on the agreement, and I've signed it. Please let me know if Mr. Brown can use me on this basis.

If you can raise your salary offer by $15,000 per year guaranteed, I will accept the expanded territories of New Mexico, Utah, and Arizona. Under this arrangement, I would receive the same bonus percentage payments on total sales volume offered in your original employment contract. If this is agreeable to Master Quirks, I believe we've reached a win-win agreement.

We are willing to be reasonable on this, Jim, but your offer to settle our insurance claim for $500 for the loss of our credenza, desk, and Chinese screen isn't fair. Here are the value estimates (attached) that I received from the appraiser (her qualifications are also attached): credenza replacement value, $4,500; desk, $750; Chinese screen, $9,500. That's a total of $14,750. We are willing to accept the amount of $14,000 as payment in full if we can get a check for this amount by April 15.

Personal Response to Neighbor

[Typed and hand delivered]
(Date)

Dear Dirk:

Sue and I want to be reasonable and reach an agreement with you, but your demand that we turn off our air conditioner each day at 4:00 p.m. so you and Alice can enjoy sitting on your deck without our air conditioner running just isn't possible. This is the exact time when the heat buildup in our home requires that we run the air conditioner. — State your willingness to negotiate.

After much consideration and discussions with a couple of experts, we'd like to suggest two possibilities: (1) we are willing to install a sound-reducing housing around our air conditioner; and/or (2) we suggest you build a sound barrier on the side of your deck. — Offer possible solutions.

I'd be happy to show you the plan for the housing (see attached bid for $500). We are willing to put $500 into this project to try to reduce the present noise level of the unit.

We look forward to hearing your response. — Close on a positive note.

Regards,

Ted and Sue

Shared Fence

[Typed and hand delivered]
(Date)

Dear Joey and Trix:

We're sure you will agree that the fence between our yards is in need of replacement. We would like to negotiate with you to install a new one.

We have obtained three bids, as I mentioned to you, for the total replacement of the fence around our entire yard and just the section between our two yards will cost $1,200 to replace. (We have samples of the replacement materials, which are exactly like those in the existing fence, and the proposal, if you wish to see either.)

We propose that we pay $700 of the cost since we are requesting the fence, and you pay $500. This payment would be made directly to the contractor, due on April 1, when the materials are delivered and construction begins.

Please let us know if this is agreeable to you by March 2.

Sincerely,

Buck and Eddie

Employment Salary and Benefit Package

[Typed and sent by registered mail and faxed]
(Date)

Dear Mr. Meech:

I'd like to counter your proposed salary and benefit package offer for the sales manager position with the following, which I believe you will agree allows us both to come out in the winner's circle:
- Squeeze & Company pay me $115,000 per year (instead of the proposed $90,000);
- I will forego enrollment in the company's medical insurance coverage plan;
- I receive an added annual bonus of 2% on net sales.

I believe this will allow both Squeeze & Company and me to receive the maximum benefit from our relationship. I'm hoping you and Rob agree, and we can finalize our employment contract and begin a working relationship.

I, and my family, look forward to hearing your response.

Sincerely,

Mike Glad

Assisted Care of Elderly Parent

[Typed on letterhead and mailed]
(Date)

Dear Mr. Soldier:

My mother would like to reserve the two bedroom unit in Restive Acres, if we can arrive at an agreement concerning the following points: (1) each morning between 10:00 and 11:00 a.m., a female personal care assistant will help her with personal hygiene, dressing, medications, and breakfast preparation at no additional charge; (2) Restive Acres will forego the $250 per month unit cleaning fee, as my mother has relatives in the city who will do this for her; and (3) Mother be allowed to have her cat in the unit if she puts down a security deposit of $200.

Additionally, my mother would like to have Restive Acres waive the requirement that she eat one meal each day in the dining room.

We await your response, and hope that we can reach a mutually beneficial agreement.

Regards,

Mason Bent

Also see DISAGREEMENTS AND DISPUTES, page 265; and SETTLEMENTS, page 275.

47

SETTLEMENTS

What has once been settled by a precedent will not be unsettled overnight, for certainty and uniformity are gains not lightly to be sacrificed.

—BENJAMIN NATHAN CARDOZO

A settlement agreement or statement is a tidy way to seal a deal and avoid any further discussion or litigation. It often comes after intense negotiations and defines the final payment or division of assets. It simply says the matter has reached a conclusion. Often the phrase, "in full and final settlement," or "in full and final payment" is part of the verbiage used to make this fact crystal clear. (See also "Negotiations," page 271.)

DECIDE TO WRITE

This agreement is commonly used to resolve disputes resulting from:

- Cohabitation
- Failed business partnerships
- Family inheritance
- Insurance claims
- Outstanding debt
- Prenuptials
- Real estate transactions (The settlement statement, or the closing statement, is the document that gives a complete breakdown of all the costs in a real estate transaction, and indicates whether the seller or buyer pays them.)

RESEARCH

- Review the original agreement.
- Collect all related information that has an impact on the agreement; for example, relevant laws and restrictions, current practice, legal documents, related financial debts and expenditures, infractions by the other party(ies), and so on.
- Consult an attorney and/or local and state officials concerning any other restrictions and/or requirements involved, and to assess your legal rights and obligations.

THINK ABOUT CONTENT

- Any efforts at settlement should come only after you have taken time to reflect on and assess the situation, and you have allowed yourself to grieve and/or vent any feelings of anger and loss. This is best accomplished by writing out your feelings for your own private review and evaluation.
- Whenever emotions are elevated, be sure to allow a cooling-off period before continuing the drafting of your settlement agreement.
- In our litigious society, you must use caution in writing your settlement agreement. It's important to remember that your statement can end up in a

court of law. Consult legal counsel if you are uncertain.

- An equitable settlement requires objectivity and sometimes this is impossible for the parties involved. In this case, a third, impartial party should be consulted to give input and assistance.

ELIMINATE WRONG MESSAGES

- To reach a settlement, it's necessary to renounce revenge. (Remember, if you conclude a very difficult agreement or relationship, you have won!)
- Eliminate inflammatory words that will rekindle conflict.

CONSIDER SPECIAL SITUATIONS

- When you are owed a debt and no longer wish to negotiate, you may be best served by offering to settle the matter for less than the outstanding balance. In this case, initiate the resolution by stating you will forgive interest on the debt and even some of the principal if paid on your schedule or in whole by a stated date. This may allow you to recover something and eliminate further collection costs.
- If you owe a debt you are unable to pay in full, you might propose a settlement. This can have the benefit of stopping further damage to your credit, and it could restore your ability to purchase supplies for your business, for example. It's important in this case to offer the other party something of value, if at all possible.

SELECT A FORMAT

- Use email only when you are communicating on an organization's secure online computer system, all parties have agreed to do so, and there is an established policy that allows it. Otherwise, send your statement by registered mail.
- Personal settlements may be handwritten on personal stationery (e.g., 5 by 7-inch sheets) or on full-sized letterhead ($8^1/_2$ by 11 inches).
- Business or legal settlements are usually typed on full-sized letterhead ($8^1/_2$ by 11 inches) or legal sheets ($8^1/_2$ by 13 inches), and are sent by registered mail.

USE POWERFUL WORDS

agree	equitable
careful	final
complete	negotiated
consideration	resolve
dissolve	settle
divide	

CONSTRUCT EFFECTIVE PHRASES

after in-depth negotiations

the final disposition of

this ends our relationship as

to dissolve the partnership

to equitably divide the assets

to settle the matter in full

we agree not to divulge details of this dispute

we agree to resolve the matter completely and finally

we will not disclose the details of this settlement agreement

with due consideration of

WRITE STRONG SENTENCES

I believe this is a fair and equitable division of the remaining assets.

Each party shall receive an equal amount of the liquidated estate.

All parties shall share equally in the proceeds.

The following list is settlement in full of this dispute.

The final division of remaining assets shall be made on the basis of each party's percentage of ownership in the company.

In full consideration of the initial capital investments of the parties involved, this settlement statement defines the distribution of the remaining assets of Mickey Motor.

The final settlement can only be made after all outstanding expenses have been paid.

I am willing to settle the matter in full for $4,445 if you will have a certified check for that amount in my office by 8:00 A.M. on Friday, March 24, 2006.

BUILD EFFECTIVE PARAGRAPHS

After our many discussions, here's the settlement statement. The three heirs, William, Cary, and James, will divide equally the 900 shares of Capital stock. Each heir will receive 300 shares.

In full and final settlement of the outstanding debt of $10,500 incurred by Squeakers, Charles Baker will repay the amount of $6,500 to Checkers Corp.; and Joan Dithers will repay the amount of $4,000 to Racey Inc.

The following listing is a complete and final settlement statement for the disposition of the remaining equipment at Dolly's Deli.

Personal Cohabitation Dissolution Settlement Statement: With the signatures of both parties, Ruth Ann Bittles, and Bobby Ray Effel, the attached list of the items and designated distribution is hereby agreed to by both. This represents the total claims and assets subject to consideration in this dissolution. [Complete listing of the property items to be awarded to each of these people follows.]

48

APOLOGY

Three things in human life are important: the first is to be kind. The second is to be kind. And the third is to be kind.

—HENRY JAMES

 Writing an apology takes a pen, a contrite heart, and a desire to make a positive change in your behavior. Civilized society is based on the agreement to not harm each other. But sometimes we do harm those around us—by acts of omission or commission. Opening the door to healing those hurts and restoring a relationship requires that we effectively apologize.

A true apology is an act of moral courage. It takes strength of character. You must demonstrate remorse, take responsibility, show empathy for the person harmed, and be willing to remedy a wrong. Apologizing may mean you admit such things as a personal weakness, a failure, a mistake and/or an act of wrongdoing. It may also require that you express your guilt, shame, and remorse in order to create the possibility for true reconciliation.

A written apology can be more effective than a verbal apology because it allows both you (the offender) and the reader (the offended) to reflect upon, absorb, and react after careful consideration. It underscores your sincerity. It can help to diffuse heightened emotions, and it can allow you the opportunity to be completely "heard."

DECIDE TO WRITE

Offenses that require apologies may range from trivial to very serious. They may be personal, social, or of a business or public nature. Some require legal action.

Some common everyday offenses include such things as:

- Not responding to an invitation or request in a timely manner
- Taking for granted the opinions or views of another person
- Treating someone unfairly (consciously or unconsciously)
- Making an error that affects someone else (billing, credit, shipping, accounting, etc.)
- Causing damage to someone's property
- Acting in a boorish or offensive manner
- Disseminating incorrect information that affects another person
- Making a statement that discredits another person
- Making insulting or insensitive comments
- Falsely accusing someone
- Exceeding personal boundaries
- Acting inappropriately or in an abusive manner toward another person: verbally, physically, sexually, etc.
- Lying to someone

THINK ABOUT HOW AND WHEN TO COMMUNICATE

- If you've offended someone, the apology process must start with a real sense of remorse and the desire on your part to make things right.
- Apologize in a timely manner—usually immediately—to avoid the possibility of a small offense growing into a long-lasting grudge. But there are times when waiting for a period of time is necessary to give your apology the weight it needs for the offense involved. Or it may be necessary to wait to first allow the offended person an opportunity to express how the offense affected him or her so you completely understand before writing your apology.
- Be sure your apology measures up to the offense and its consequences.
- For minor offenses, like failing to introduce a friend during a conversation, bumping into someone on the sidewalk, failing to offer the courtesy of allowing an elderly person to precede you in line, or interrupting when someone else is talking, an immediate verbal apology is usually best and adequate.
- For social and business situations, like forgetting (and missing) a dinner party, breaking an item while a guest in someone's home, or making a customer billing error or credit mistake, a handwritten or typed (for business offenses) apology needs to be accompanied by a restorative act. If you missed a dinner party, for example, you may want to deliver a bouquet of flowers with your handwritten apology. If you have broken a vase while a guest, you need to replace it with one of equal value or work out another way to repay the debt.
- In business, when you have failed to issue a credit when one is due, you need to send a typewritten apology and include the credit issue. You may also need or want to call the person immediately to admit and correct the error, and/or offer the customer a token of recompense or goodwill, like a discount on a future purchase.
- For a serious offense, the apology needs to include something to restore the person. For example, if a banking customer's account was shorted years earlier, not only should the amount be restored to the account, but the customer also is due the interest the funds would have earned during that period. Perhaps other restorative steps are needed, too, depending on the circumstances.
- Sometimes apologizing in writing may seem cowardly because it allows you to avoid facing an embarrassing situation in person. If this is the case, it may be necessary to apologize face to face. And, perhaps, follow the verbal apology with a written one.
- It's important to remember that the measure of the apology needs to be in proper proportion to the offense. Not smaller, not bigger.

THINK ABOUT CONTENT

Offending someone robs the person of power or diminishes him or her. Apologizing gives that power back. It's this second exchange that allows the healing process to begin.

- Write out your apology. This allows you to examine why and how you offended someone, and to experience remorse. Writing words that express your regret and desire to make amends is an opportunity for real character growth. Reading your written apology allows the other person to process the offense.
- A genuine apology can also be a solution: it can eliminate the problem, and it can offer the opportunity to restore your relationship with the other person.
- Acknowledge the offense and accept responsibility for it.
  - State the offense and how you violated a moral code. "Lexy, yesterday, Jim gave me credit for doing the Chase brochure you created. I should have corrected him immediately, but I didn't . . ."
  - Accept responsibility without excusing yourself. "That was wrong of me."
  - Acknowledge how you injured the person. (This sometimes must be accompanied by an invitation to the person to express her injury and how it affected her.) Show empathy with the offended person. "Not correcting Jim immediately robbed you of the credit you deserve for such fine work."

- Explain. Give any extenuating but valid circumstances, if they exist, but don't create excuses for yourself. "Here's how it happened. Jim and I were talking in his office while he waited to be connected to Roger Graham in Chicago. Immediately after he credited me with your work, Roger came on the line . . ."

- Communicate your regret. This is key. Be sure to include a statement of your emotions of anxiety, sadness, guilt, and shame. "I'm ashamed of myself for not immediately emailing or phoning Jim to correct his impression. I didn't realize, of course, that he would put a credit in the employee newsletter. I believe that on some level I envied the great job you did, and when it was assumed that I'd done the brochure, I just didn't correct it. Lexy, I've called Jim and told him you deserve all the credit because it was totally your creative concept, copywriting, and execution. I also wrote a correction for the newsletter that will come out next week."

- Make reparations. An offense creates a debt that needs to be repaid. Often such repayment is symbolic, and the apology itself is the reparation— in part or in whole. But sometimes, to even the score, you need to replace what was lost or otherwise make amends. "Lexy, please also accept this bouquet as a token of my heartfelt apology. I've also recommended that you get the Leaf job, as you requested, because your work on the Chase brochure demonstrates that you have the right balance of creative talent and product knowledge needed to do the job."

- For major offenses—infidelity, chronic alcoholism, abuse, theft, etc.—a very strict plan for change in behavior and restitution must be part of the apology. This includes such things as a step-by-step plan by the offender and an organized plan by the offended (injured). Both plans need to include the corrective steps the offender must take before complete reconciliation can take place (if reconciliation ever does take place). This includes demonstrated behavior changes over time that must be achieved before a relationship is restored.

- Offer an olive branch. Reestablishing a relationship after an apology has been made and accepted may begin by the offender initiating an act of friendship. Restart communication with a new or neutral topic, or offer an invitation to an event. Either of these approaches can help eliminate any remaining awkwardness. Sometimes a period of time is needed, too, before the relationship can be resumed.

ELIMINATE WRONG MESSAGES

- Don't make excuses. This detracts from your apology, or eliminates its effectiveness altogether.

- Don't offer a false apology that shifts responsibility to another (or the other) person. Here are some examples:
  - "Sorry." This tells the offended person you want to end the discussion, and/or close the subject immediately without really taking responsibility.
  - "I'm sorry you're upset" or "I'm sorry you feel that way." Instead of taking responsibility, these statements place responsibility squarely back on the offended person. It infers the offended person is obviously too sensitive.
  - "You know I didn't mean it" and/or "You're trying to make me feel guilty." These statements attempt to make the offended person feel responsible.
  - "I regard you as a friend. I would never intentionally hurt you." The offended person is left to conclude it is her fault she feels injured. She's obviously too thin-skinned, she misunderstood, or she attributed a mean or wrong motive where there was none.
  - "I wouldn't have done it if you hadn't . . ." This excuse aims at escaping responsibility and placing blame on the offended person.
  - "I know how you feel," "I see where you're coming from," or "I'm working to correct the situation . . ." When glibly offered, these statements avoid taking responsibility.

- Don't deny, trivialize, or dismiss your behavior if someone tells you he or she was offended. Offer, instead, to hear him or her out, and then offer your apology if you are culpable.

- Don't overapologize, or apologize inappropriately. If you apologize automatically or when you are not responsible, you devalue your apology. You may be trying to please or placate. In business relationships, overapologizing can brand you as incompetent.

CONSIDER SPECIAL SITUATIONS

- The process of apologizing for a personal offense is a dynamic transaction between two people. There's no guarantee of a particular outcome, and sometimes apologizing takes negotiation. It takes a commitment to the process to see it through to resolution.
- When your actions or words affect (or are heard by) more than one person, your apology needs to be made to all those involved. "Tim, I know you overheard my boorish comment criticizing the way Giles handled the Fisher problem. That was wrong of me, and I feel terrible about voicing such a criticism. I apologize both for the comment I made, and also because I neglected to first get all the facts. In the future, I promise to be far less critical and much more circumspect."
- In business situations, an apology that includes a complete written explanation is often needed to provide an accurate record of what happened.
- Sometimes, in situations that involve customer relations, it's important to apologize when you don't bear nearly as much responsibility for an error as the customer. For example, if an irate customer complains that she received five polka-dot dresses, instead of one, and you determine that the error occurred because the customer placed her order five times, you may need to write: "I'm sorry that an error occurred in your order. You are right; I should have called you to check the quantity of dresses you intended to purchase." In such a case, you may want to follow your apology with an explanation of proper ordering procedure, and close with a goodwill statement like "We look forward to continuing to

serve you in supplying the latest-trend solutions to all your wardrobe needs."

- For customer apologies, effective use of discount coupons, gifts with purchase, entrance to special sales, valued-customer premiums, or other things may be included with your apology. "Along with our apology, please do accept the enclosed coupon for 20 percent off your next purchase."
- When your child offends, injures, or causes damage to someone's property, apologies need to come both from you, as the responsible parent, and from your child (in an age-appropriate and situation-appropriate fashion). "Mr. Winters, I am so sorry that Icky rode her bike through your flowerbed. She's not yet quite in control of her training wheels, and I was several steps behind her when I realized she was unable to stay on the sidewalk. I've tried to telephone you, but I have been unable to reach you. May we come over Friday at 3:30 P.M. with the replacement petunias, and so that Icky can apologize in person?"
- When a major offense includes apologizing for a legally actionable offense, e.g., driving while drinking, causing an accident, theft, remarks that may be interrupted as sexual harassment, etc., you should first consult an attorney who specializes in the area of offense before writing your apology. It's important in such cases to carefully word your apology and include statements that indicate you are not only sorry for such behavior, but you will take corrective steps so that the behavior will not be repeated.

ASK FOR AN APOLOGY

- If you've been offended, and you want to heal and restore a relationship with the offender, you may need to ask for an apology.
  — First, give yourself some time to reflect or cool off if you're angry.
  — Write how you feel to the other person. (Don't accuse.)
  — Ask for an explanation or an apology: "I value our friendship, and I would like to resolve this . . ."; "Would you think about this, and

discuss it with me?"; "I believe you owe me an apology" or "I'd like to discuss the matter and learn how this happened in case I have misinterpreted something . . ."

— Don't avoid asking an offender for an apology. Allowing someone to continue to offend you tells the person you are weak. Instead, tactfully state how you feel: "I felt insulted when you said . . ." or "Your statement troubled me. What did you mean when you said . . ."

— If the offender doesn't apologize and won't discuss the offense and try to work it out, you may decide to discontinue the relationship. Remember, the most common reasons people don't apologize are: (1) pride (fear of shame), (2) egocentricity, (3) fear of the offended person's retaliation, (4) fear of being rejected, and/or (5) fear there will be requirements to make amends.

— Act honorably and respectfully, and be compassionate and fair.

SELECT A FORMAT

- Business apologies are best typed on business letterhead when the letter is going to a customer, employee, client, or business colleague or associate.
- For personal apologies, use a personal notecard or stationery, and handwrite your apology. Apology greeting cards are available, too, and may be appropriate for some situations, but don't fail to write your apology in your own words inside the card.

CHOOSE THE RIGHT WORD

accept	fault
acknowledge	mistake
admit	offended
apologize	rectify
callous	repair
committed	repay
conclude	responsible
confess	restore
determine	tactless
failed	thoughtless

BUILD EFFECTIVE PHRASES

am guilty of
bear the shame of it
can offer no explanation
can you find it in your heart
can't believe my own actions
cannot offer a viable explanation
correct the situation
distressed by my behavior
given the same situation again
I admit
I am responsible
I am so contrite
I can offer no excuse
I regret to inform you that
I reproach myself for
I take responsibility
I wish to apologize
I've offended you by
if do-overs were allowed
if it's any consolation
make amends
my intent was
never again will I
offer you this recompense
owe you an apology for
please allow me to make this right
promise to act very differently
repair the damage
sincerely regret
there is no logical reason for such behavior
will always live with the regret of
will compensate you for
will correct the matter by
wish to completely replace

WRITE STRONG SENTENCES

I apologize for my bad behavior.

I know I offended you, and I am so very sorry.

Please accept my apology.

There is no excuse for such boorishness.

Yes, if I had been in your shoes I would feel offended; I'm so sorry.

I'm so sorry I neglected to see the matter from your point of view.

I would like very much to hear how my insensitivity made you feel, if you care to tell me.

I know I hurt you, and I am thoroughly ashamed of myself.

I sincerely apologize.

I so regret my actions.

I can't explain, with any reasonable explanation, why I didn't respond better in the situation.

I'm so sorry my actions caused you such pain.

The error was completely my fault, and I apologize.

May I please have the opportunity to make things right?

If only I had acted honorably, things would have turned out much differently.

I know a simple "I'm sorry" may seem too easy, too weak.

Please don't give up on me.

I do promise to be more sensitive to your feelings in the future.

I can make this right, and I will.

I acted completely inappropriately.

The error was completely mine.

I certainly don't blame you for being angry with me for such behavior.

I do pledge to right this wrong.

I won't ever let you down by not allowing you to offer your opinion again.

I do hope you can forgive me for being so dense.

Yes, you are correct, the amount of the bill should have been $534.

It was wrong of me to take the credit.

Your complaint won't go unnoticed.

I'm sorry you were treated in such a rude manner, and I plan to correct the situation.

Yes, my son was completely out of line, and I apologize.

I will certainly correct our error, and restore the funds owed you.

We do apologize, and ask you to give us another chance to serve you better in the future.

Here's my plan for correcting the error.

I'm intent upon righting this injustice done to you.

With a contrite heart, I seek your forgiveness.

I acted completely out of jealousy; I apologize.

I owe you my sincere apology.

BUILD EFFECTIVE PARAGRAPHS

Most apologies are only a few sentences. Sometimes saying more is less effective. Few words can have more impact. The following paragraphs could be most or all of the apology:

Yes, Alycia, I did make that boorish comment. It was completely insensitive of me, I admit. I can only imagine how it hurt you, and I feel terrible about it. Please accept my sincere apology and my promise to be more sensitive in the future. (I've also apologized to Teddy, who I'm sure overheard it.)

Your complaint didn't go unnoticed. After careful research, I agree that we didn't meet our guarantee to replace any item damaged in shipment. I sincerely apologize for this failure, and want to assure you that the new tub will be delivered tomorrow morning between 9:00 A.M. and 11:00 A.M.

Please accept our sincere apology for this blatant error. This does not reflect our committed standard for delivery of services, and we will work with you to correct the situation to your satisfaction.

Roger, this is very difficult for me, as I'm sure you realize, but I wish to apologize from the bottom of my heart for not showing up for the ski trip at the designated time and place. I simply rolled over, hit the snooze alarm, and then didn't awaken until 9:30 A.M., long after everyone had returned home. I know I ruined the trip for all four of you, and I feel terrible about this. I've certainly learned my lesson: redemption doesn't hit the snooze button. (I'm sending a note to each of the other guys too.) I know I can't entirely make this right, but please let me try to redeem myself by both driving and buying the lift tickets for all of you next Saturday.

Yes, you are due the contractor discount of 33 percent off the retail price. I apologize for this billing error. I forgot to inform accounting that you get that rate. Please accept my apology with this refund check of $987.

Trudy, my comments at yesterday's luncheon were completely petty, and I'm truly sorry. (Thank you for telling me exactly how you felt.) Please accept my apology.

I know there's only one chance to make a great first impression, and I blew it. Ben, I'm so sorry. I feel like a complete louse. I know you were looking forward to introducing me to Julia, and I still have no clue as to why I acted so badly. I apologize, and ask for your forgiveness. You have my promise, too, that such behavior won't ever be repeated by your big (and yesterday feckless) brother. (Please pass the enclosed apology note along to Julia.)

First of all, I must take responsibility for the error. I sent you the order before carefully reviewing my spec sheet and making sure I'd included all the parts we'll need. (I'd be happy to tell anyone else in your organization, if that will help, or please feel free to pass this letter on to others who were inconvenienced.) I apologize, and request that you order the drain assembly, Part #453A.

EDIT, EDIT, EDIT

- If in doubt, write your apology out in a rough draft first.
- Reread your apology and make any changes.
- Let it rest for a period of time.
- Reread it aloud to make a final check for tone before you send it.
- Give it verbally, then send it by mail unless there is a compelling reason that it must be emailed.

Newspaper Error on Op-Ed Page

[Handwritten]
(Date)

Dear Miss Elder:

My sincere apology for the omission of your name after your insightful op-ed piece that appeared in Sunday's Sun. *As editor, I certainly failed in my job of catching the error before press time. The error was a simple one of fitting copy to the available space and inadvertently dropping off your name.*

We will run our apology for this error next Sunday, and credit you for the evocative piece.

We invite you to again submit your opinions on the school issue, or any other issue. We look forward to receiving them, and will make every effort to make sure they appear without any such error.

Sincerely,

Woody Beaner

Error in Shipment

[Typed, faxed, and mailed]
(Date)

Dear Mr. Crispy:

Thank you for calling to inform us that you did not receive the overnight shipment of our Model 433A sterilizer. You are correct: it should have arrived at your place of business, 445 Walker, Suite 334, Orlando, FL 32808, at 8:30 A.M. this morning.

I have researched the matter thoroughly and can only conclude that the sterilizer was stolen around midnight from our loading dock. We have reported the situation to the police, and an investigation has begun.

I want to thank you for contacting me immediately. Your call gives us a head start in locating the missing machine.

I do apologize that your machine hasn't arrived. We are shipping you a replacement this afternoon, as I stated on the telephone, and it will arrive at your office tomorrow morning. It will not have the customized features that you ordered, but we will have an installer add those on site within two days.

We look forward to continuing the great relationship we have enjoyed with your company for five years now. And I personally look forward to serving you in the future.

Sincerely,

Russ Wild

Offensive Remarks

[Handwritten and mailed]
(Date)

Dearest Cricket,

There's no fool like an old fool, unless it's an old fool who shoots off his mouth at his niece's bridge luncheon. I realize now (too late) that you were mortified, and I'm so sorry.

I apologize for sharing my (apparently unpopular) political views (in full voice) with your genteel ladies' bridge group. Reflecting now on the horrified faces I saw after I stated I'm in favor of returning to the law of the sword, makes me realize that I was out of line and out of touch with where I was. (It doesn't raise an eyebrow in my neighborhood pub.)

Please forgive me for such an outburst. If ever again you need a bridge substitute, and your Aunt Ruth isn't available, I hope you'll trust me enough to ask me. I promise to keep all such heretical views to myself. (I've enclosed copies of my apology for each of the ladies.)

Please accept this floral bouquet as a symbol of my contriteness. (And, if you can find it in your heart, would you please tell your Aunt Ruth that it's OK to resume speaking to me?)

Your chastised Uncle Browsard

Betraying a Trust

[Handwritten and mailed]
(Date)

Dearest Rita:

It is with a truly contrite heart that I sit down to write you this note of apology. Yes, it is true: I did betray a trust by repeating very personal information you told me in strictest confidence. As I stated last night, I know you must feel betrayed, and I'd like for you to tell me whatever you'd care to about how you feel. — Accept responsibility.

I have no plausible explanation for my behavior, because there is none. I was talking with Squibb in confidence and just blurted it out, completely without thought. — Explain, if possible.

I know it may take a period of time for you to absorb this betrayal and to be willing to talk to me about it; but I do want you to know how very, very sorry I am. I am also repenting of my transgression to Squibb, and am repeating my request that she not share this information with anyone else. — Apologize.

I do hope you can find it in your heart to forgive me. I do want to restore our relationship and will happily do anything you may request to make amends for breaking your confidence. — Ask for forgiveness, if necessary.

I'd like to take you to lunch and discuss any aspect of this you may feel you'd like to discuss—or just let you unload on me. Please do give me a call whenever you are ready. — Offer recompense, if appropriate.

Remorsefully,

Katie

Family Rift Between Sisters

[Handwritten and mailed]
(Date)

My Dearest Sister:

I'm writing this in the hope that, even if you aren't speaking to me, you'll read this note and reflect on my heartfelt apology.

I'm totally ashamed of myself, Bebe, for not complying with your wishes that all the attendants wear full-length dresses to your and Mahesh's wedding rehearsal dinner. It was a selfish and reactionary decision on my part, one rooted in some leftover envy from early childhood, I'm sure psychologists would say. I know I wounded you, and I am so sorry. (I didn't realize there was going to be a photo shoot of the wedding party; and it wasn't until I saw the photographs that I realized the wisdom of your request: I'm the only person in a cocktail-length dress.) I'm totally ashamed of myself.

I know there is no way I can make amends for being so obstinate after you made your wishes clear; but I hope that you'll find it in your heart to forgive me.

I would love to host a smallish reception here in Denver for you and Mahesh after you return from your East Coast assignment. I'd invite those on the enclosed guest list (and/or any others you two would like). I'm thinking of a candlelight dinner for 25 to 30 people at our country club or, if you prefer, in our home. But I'm happy (this time) to comply with any other plan you'd prefer.

Please reflect on this, and let me know. You are most precious to me, Bebe, and I want more than anything for our sisterhood to be restored to its loving best.

Sonia

Rude Behavior

[Handwritten and mailed]
(Date)

My Dear Cherie:

I just want to repeat what I said on the telephone. Please do forgive me for my rudeness this morning in rushing in and rushing out without a civil greeting, or taking the time to meet your interior decorator. I know you wanted me to see the choices she was presenting and give you my advice. Selfishly, I was completely preoccupied with the schedule of getting to three more places before the clock struck twelve! I feel very badly about my rude behavior. Again, please forgive me. — Take responsibility. Empathize with the offended.

Will you please come to a leisurely tea on Thursday, and show me all the possibilities for changes you'll be making in your home? I promise to pay full attention and to offer any advice you'd like. — Make things right.

Sincerely,

Max

Confessing a White Lie

[Handwritten and mailed]
(Date)

Dear Pet:

My sin, to be sure, has found me out. Well, actually, it's the weight of guilt for telling you a "white lie" that had me pacing the floor at three this morning.

I share your passion for the truth, yet I've lied to you (of all people) about the silliest and most mundane thing. I'm very ashamed of myself. I didn't attend the Roscoe party simply because I didn't want to. I wasn't in San Francisco for the weekend.

I'm at a loss to say exactly why I lied. I know we'd talked about seeing each other there. I hope my actions didn't cause you any discomfort, but I just didn't feel like going out. I wasn't in a party mood and was just feeling generally deflated.

Please do forgive me. I do promise in the future to keep our shared standard of truth.

Yours,

Griggs

Failure to RSVP

[Handwritten and mailed]
(Date)

Ginny:

As I said on the telephone, I'm so sorry I didn't RSVP on time to the invitation to the Grand Pooh Bah Ball.

I do know better. I've actually done your job and know what a hassle it is to have to call people to find out if invitees will be coming so the number of reservations can be made to the caterer on time. I'm so sorry you had to call me to check. It was inexcusably rude of me.

Thank you for letting me do the rest of the follow-up calls as a token of my contriteness. As we agreed, I'll email a list of RSVP responses to you by Wednesday.

All the best,

Rachel

Job Performance Failure

[Emailed on a secure server]

David:

I know I committed to have the Bennett progress report complete and to you by Friday at 2:00 P.M. I realize, too, that this impacted your ability to make your report to Sattersfield. I then compounded the failure by not letting you know Friday morning that I'd be unable to complete the report. I'm sure this put you in an awkward position, and I'm truly sorry. (Please forward this to Sattersfield, if you like.)

I should have notified you as early Friday as possible that I couldn't get all the numbers together until today. The storms in Raleigh made things impossible for the field guys to get their counts complete. I have, in fact, just gotten the final figures, and I'll have my report to you by the end of today.

In the future, I will let you know immediately if there is a problem with keeping my commitment. If there is any other way I can right this wrong, please let me know.

Sincerely,

George

Pet Apology

[Handwritten and mailed]
(Date)

Dear Nigel:

As I said on the telephone, we are so sorry that Nipper bit your cat, Roughy, this afternoon. I can only imagine how distressed you were.

We have never had such an incident, and Bobbi Anne has walked Nipper on his leash every day for a year. We felt confident that she was able to control him, but she has never faced the situation of a cat approaching him.

We will, of course, pay the veterinarian bill if you decide to take Roughy for a checkup. Nipper is current on all his shots, as I said, and Ben Wright at Animals R Us on Nappa St. is the vet we use (312-555-0123). Nipper sustained a serious cornea scratch and several bites we are treating.

In the future, Bobbi Anne will not be allowed to walk Nipper on your side of the street. Hopefully, that will avoid any further potential for conflicts.

Sincerely,

Mavis Moore

Also see COMPLAINT, page 257; DISAGREEMENTS AND DISPUTES, page 265; FORGIVENESS, page 287; NEGOTIATIONS, page 271; RESPONSE, page 234; and SETTLEMENTS, page 275.

FORGIVENESS

Only the brave know how to forgive. . . .
A coward never forgave; it is not in his nature.

—LAURENCE STERNE

Although we often think of forgiveness in religious terms, it is true that we need to forgive one another when we injure someone else or someone injures us. Forgiveness is usually linked to the apology process (see "Apology," page 278) as the last step before reconciliation.

When you've been hurt by another person, the natural responses are denial, anger, and/or even the desire for revenge. The decision to dispense with these responses (or pass through them without getting stuck there), and instead to forgive your offender, requires a change of heart and mind. That usually doesn't happen immediately.

Choosing forgiveness is a dynamic way of canceling a debt owed to you (created by an offense). While you offer the gift of forgiveness to your offender, you are the one who realizes the benefits of increased health: the reduction of anger, stress, and even physical problems like headaches, backaches, colds, and other maladies.

Writing out your message of forgiveness—either asking for or offering forgivness—will benefit both you and the reader by allowing you both to process the offense, have a change of heart, change undesirable behavior, and/or begin to work toward reconciliation.

DECIDE TO WRITE

The Offender

- When you've injured someone, you may want to apologize and ask for forgiveness immediately. "Buzz, I did say Dad prefers to spend his time at Jimmie's. I didn't think how that comment might hurt you, and, to be clear, Dad never said that. Now, of course, I realize how it did hurt you. Thank you for speaking up. Please forgive me for such a thoughtless and callous remark. I promise to never do it again."

- When someone doesn't respond to your calls, letters, or emails, or responds with anger or acts upset, you may want to ask if there is a problem. Or, ask if you have offended the person in some way in order that you might consider the matter, apologize, and ask for forgiveness, if that's appropriate.

- If another person says you have offended him or her, ask for an explanation so that you may properly consider the matter, apologize, and ask for forgiveness, if appropriate.

The Offended

* When you are harboring angry thoughts toward someone, you may want to examine your feelings to learn exactly why you feel as you do. Isolate the reason for your anger. Be able to state exactly what it is that distresses you.

* When you value your relationship with the offender more than you value your feelings of hurt and you want the relationship to prosper, ask the offender to discuss the problem with you so you may consider all the facts. If it's appropriate, ask for an apology so that you may forgive.

* Start with a statement about how you're feeling: "Jane, I felt hurt when you said my report didn't measure up to the established standard. I'd like to privately discuss with you why you felt my report was substandard." "Jennifer, I'm feeling very disappointed, or did I misunderstand you? I thought you said I'd have my check for the Jazz Session performance last week."

THINK ABOUT CONTENT

The Offender

* Consider your actions. Write them down to more thoroughly understand them.

* Write out your apology in order to consider it. (You may, or may not, decide to send your written apology.) Make your apology (see "Apology," page 278).

* Ask the offended person(s) for forgiveness.

The Offended

* Calm down.

* Examine your anger and its effect on you. Writing it out can be very helpful (though you'll probably not let anyone else read it).

* Decide not to pursue revenge but to take the path of forgiveness.

* Take stock and ask yourself: Can I talk about the hurt with the offender without attacking? Will the other person be objective and not defensive?

* Empathize with the offender, and reframe your thinking about him or her. Allow for his or her weaknesses. Ask yourself "What was going on in his or her life at the time?" and "Was he or she under stress?"

* Accept what happened without tossing it back at the person who offended you or displacing it onto someone else.

* Move forward. You may decide to try to work with the offender (if he or she is willing) toward resolution and reconciliation. Or you may decide to limit or discontinue your relationship. Either way, forgive the offender in your heart.

* Realize your own full release in the act of forgiving.

ELIMINATE WRONG MESSAGES

* Don't expect to forget the offense, and don't ask for the other person to forget. You will undoubtedly always remember the offense. Forgetting isn't a part of the forgiving process, nor is it a goal.

* Don't immediately seek reconciliation when a serious offense is involved (abuse, betrayal, etc.). Reconciling is not a good idea until the offender has undergone extensive therapy and has established a long record of reformed behavior.

* Don't excuse or condone the offender's bad behavior. The offender is still responsible for his or her misdeed; you (the offended) have just canceled his or her debt to you.

* Making amends doesn't mean you are weak. On the contrary, it's a sign of strength and moral courage.

* Don't expect an instant resolution. Keep your commitment to resolve the issue, and know that it may take time. Exercise patience.

CONSIDER SPECIAL SITUATIONS

- Anger, a natural response to another's offense, is initially energizing. But it can grow into a debilitating grudge that holds you captive. Use forgiveness to eliminate the grudge and free yourself from its control.
- The process of forgiving is a dynamic and complex one. It often takes time to work through the stages of anger, loss, and grief. When very serious abuses, death, and/or legally criminal acts are involved, the steps of forgiveness can and must happen independently of the offender paying any legal debt to society.
- Each person must come to forgiveness. True forgiveness is possible only when you are ready to forgive.
- Sometimes two people offend each other, or one overreacts to an offense with a greater (revengeful) offense. It's especially helpful in these situations, after both people can approach it calmly, to discuss the offense and each person's roles. Each person needs to accept responsibility for his or her own part. Writing out your apology, even if you don't give it to the other person, can be very helpful in working through to forgiveness.
- After the offender has apologized to you, even though you know he or she is sorry, your pride and stubbornness may keep you from offering forgiveness. It's important to recognize this and make a commitment to forgive for your own sake. You don't necessarily have to even tell the offender.

SELECT A FORMAT

- There are some greeting cards created for things like a missed birthday, a personal injury, etc. These may be used if you also write your own personal message asking for forgiveness and taking responsibility for your actions or inactions.
- Use a notecard and matching envelope for personal short notes of forgiveness.
- Use personal stationery for longer letters of forgiveness.
- Business matters of forgiveness may require the use of business letterhead, or may need to be sent by secure corporate email.

USE STRONG WORDS

admit	express
anger	forgive
beg	pardon
believe	reconcile
change	regret
commit(ted)	repent
courage	responsible
decide	trust

CONSTRUCT EFFECTIVE PHRASES

acted very badly
blame no one but myself
committed an offense
conduct was wrong
genuinely sorry for
I alone am to blame
need to come clean
no excuse for
responsible for
should never have said
will not repeat
wish to confess

BUILD STRONG SENTENCES

The Offender

I need to ask you for your forgiveness.

I accept the responsibility for offending you.

I promise I will never repeat my offense.

There is no excuse for my rude behavior.

I acted badly, and I'm sorry; please forgive me.

I can only tell you how sorry I am, and ask for your forgiveness.

Please forgive me.

You have every right to be angry with me for my offensive remark, but I do hope you will consider my apology, and forgive me.

Yes, my response was wrong; I do apologize for offending you, and I ask for your forgiveness.

The Offended

Yes, I do forgive you.

Like you, I don't want this to come between us. Let's discuss this matter so that we may both come to an understanding and work toward forgiveness.

I believe you owe me an apology for your statement at the meeting today. Your apology will help me greatly in coming to the point of forgiving you.

I need to tell you that your remark was very offensive to me. But after our discussion, I want to say I do forgive you and wish to move forward.

You totally misrepresented the facts, and I need to discuss this with you before I can take the step of forgiveness.

Please review your actions, which I found very offensive. I must ask you for an apology, so that I may forgive you.

I've tried to understand why you chose to lie about the matter, and I need to discuss this with you in order to take the next step.

I've chosen to forgive you, but at the same time I've elected not to continue our relationship.

I did carry a grudge over your betrayal, but I have chosen to forgive you and, in that act, to release myself from the anger that held me prisoner for so long.

BUILD EFFECTIVE PARAGRAPHS

The Offender

Thank you for reinforcing the fact that my bad behavior doesn't mean I'm a bad person. And thank you for the gift of forgiveness. I do promise to be more considerate in the future.

Please forgive me for my lack of understanding during Dad's illness. You are the one who carried the primary burden for his care. I could have been, and should have been, much more help. I was not. I finally realize how much of a burden I left on your shoulders, and I'm truly ashamed of myself. It's too late to help more with Dad, but I will be a much more participating, and caring, sister in the future. I hope that over time, you will forgive me.

Please do forgive me. In the heat of the moment I called you some very unkind—and all untrue—names. I feel like a complete heel. And I repent. In the future, when faced with a point upon which we disagree, I do promise to make my statements in terms of the idea I object to and refrain from letting it inappropriately become a personal attack.

Jamie, please consider my humble appeal for us to sit down together so you can tell me exactly how my behavior hurt you. I am so desperately sorry, but I believe if I completely understand how it affected you, I will be more certain never to repeat it. Please do forgive me.

The Offended

I can't offer forgiveness at this moment. I'm still processing the offense. But I'll call you in a couple of days to arrange a time to sit down and discuss it.

Yes, of course, I forgive you. I do want us to be "safe friends," knowing we can go to each other with anything and feel certain we'll each be heard.

I'm not finding forgiveness is coming that easily this time. I know we've been over this ground before, and I can only say I need a bit more time to process the injury. I'll get back to you as soon as I can.

We've come to the age when we must forgive each other speedily. We don't have time or energy to harbor hurt or ill feelings toward each other. I know the stress you've been under, and I appreciate the fact that at times such pressure results in unkind words. I love you, and I do forgive you.

EDIT, EDIT, EDIT

The great thing about writing out your forgiveness message is that this helps you to process the offense and work toward forgiveness. Be sure you give your message breathing time, and then reread and edit it before sending. Or you may choose to write out your message and reread it just for your own benefit, and not send it. Either way, writing will help you get to the healing power of forgiveness.

Forgiveness Granted for Breaking a Lamp at a Party

[Handwritten and mailed]
(Date)

Dear Mark,

Yes, I do believe the guests enjoyed the party. (A highlight for many who've called or written was seeing you in that lampshade.)

I do accept your apology. You are forgiven for dropping the lamp while trying to reattach the shade. The check for $257.50 does cover the repair.

Alice

Forgiveness Granted for Thoughtless Remarks

[Handwritten and mailed]
(Date)

Mort,

Can I forgive you? Are you kidding? How many times have I had to beg you for forgiveness? Many more than either of us wants to remember. You are my dear brother, and I shall always have forgiveness for you.

Al

Forgiveness Request for Breaking a Promise

[Handwritten and mailed]
(Date)

Dearest Buckie:

I betrayed a sacred promise I'd made to you, and I am so sorry.

I've told you why, and I am thoroughly ashamed. I can only say I'm devastated at the thought that I so wounded you. And I can only plead that if you'll forgive me, I will never do such a thing again.

Can you ever forgive me? Please do consider it, though I don't deserve it.

Your Cousin,

Ruth

Forgiveness Request for Online Email Personal Attack

[Handwritten note after face-to-face apology]
(Date)

Dear Raz,

As I said today, I had to apologize face to face after I reviewed my post (to the group) and realized I'd allowed the anonymity and facelessness of email to release me from the bonds of normal civility. My remarks were undeservedly harsh. There is no excuse for my personal attack on you, calling you a "twit" for your expressed views. It was your idea and not you that I should have addressed. I'm truly sorry for this ad hominem.

I'm sure you've read my online apology; and have considered my in-person apology. I don't view you as a twit, and I certainly should not have made that statement.

In the future, I promise to direct my comments only toward the ideas expressed. Please do forgive me.

Remorsefully,

Chaz

Forgiveness Request for Challenging an Employee

[Typed on business letterhead]
(Date)

Dear Raylene:

I improperly challenged your numbers on your report at the department meeting this morning. I shouldn't have done that, and what's more, your numbers are correct. I was wrong. (I'm copying all staff members at the meeting.) Please forgive me.

In the future, I'll do the proper research first, and contact you privately if I have a question.

Sincerely,

Frankie

Forgiveness Request for Losing Temper

[Handwritten after verbal apology]
(Date)

Dear Bonzi:

Again, I must ask for your forgiveness for flying off the handle when you brought up your stance about drinking. We don't share the same views, obviously, but a gentleman has a long fuse and a generous tolerance of other views. I displayed a lack of both, and I'm deeply sorry.

Please accept this bouquet as a symbol of my remorse, and consider forgiving me my red-faced rant. I promise not to repeat such behavior.

With true remorse,

Ivan

Forgiveness Request for Bad Manners

[Handwritten]
(Date)

Dear Sis:

Yes, my lack of gentility was on complete and boorish display at your dinner party. I didn't even realize how uncouth my question about money was until I saw the slack jaws and the shocked expressions, and heard the gasps followed by resounding silence around the table.

I'll gladly submit to your etiquette class 101A if you'll forgive me. (And, if you'll ever invite me again, I'll agree to wear a placard that reads: "This is the feckless lout of a brother—a black and cloddish sheep—of the hostess. Please disregard any inappropriate bleating.") I'll also submit to any other recompense you feel is appropriate.

My dear sister, can you find it in your heart to forgive me?

Contritely,

Lenny

Forgiveness Request for Failing to Keep an Agreement

[Handwritten on personal stationery]
(Date)

Dear Antoine,

There's no excuse—none—for discussing our book idea with Jennifer Beales after we'd agreed to keep any word of it completely to ourselves, yet I did exactly that. And, of course, the stupid irony is that I did so only after carefully making her commit not to discuss or reveal the idea to anyone else. (Of course, she kept that promise for exactly what—three minutes, five minutes? I don't introduce this fact to detract from my culpability and guilt for breaking our agreement. I only do it to point out the absurdity of my flawed rationale as well as my wrong-headed and wrong-hearted-ness.)

As I explained to you in my confession and apology, I followed up with Jennifer (after the fact) by having her sign a nondisclosure agreement, primarily to reinforce the terms of her commitment. In fairness to her, she didn't discuss it (she says) with anyone else, but only called you to discuss it because I wasn't available.

I do understand your anger. I empathize completely. I would have reacted exactly as you did, had the situation been reversed.

The only feeble explanation I can offer is that I found myself in the position of having the opportunity to try our idea out on a senior editor at Catherine Publishing and couldn't at that moment get in touch with you to get your consent. (You'll remember I did leave a message to that effect on your cell phone.) I shouldn't have gone ahead without your agreement. But I rationalized that you would certainly want me to take the opportunity presented. (In retrospect, I could have asked Jennifer if we could contact her together on a conference call to discuss the idea. At that moment, this idea didn't occur to me.)

Please forgive me. I do take my commitments seriously, and will never break our agreement again.

Sincerely,

Dutch

Forgiveness Request for Repeating a Rumor

[Handwritten]
(Date)

Dear Hoda:

Yes, I am guilty of passing on the rumor that you were seen interviewing for a job at Mathers. I do know better. It was both unethical of me—by my own standards too—and demonstrates vividly to me just how damaging idle chatter can be. — Admit your behavior.

I've searched my heart, and I don't believe I bear you any ill will. But I did harm you, and I am so sorry. — Express remorse.

I have gone to those six people, including your boss, James Wright, and confessed my role in spreading a completely false rumor.

I know, when I reflect upon it as I have, how angry you must be. And I also know such an injury isn't easy to forgive. Yet I do ask you to consider forgiving me after your initial anger has cooled, and you are able to do so. — Acknowledge how you injured someone. Ask for forgiveness.

And please allow me to make any other amends that are appropriate. May I start by taking you to lunch so you can administer 20 lashes with a wet Vietnamese noodle? — Offer recompense.

Sincerely,

Joni

Forgiveness Request for Long-Term Abuse

[Handwritten]
(Date)

My Dearest Daughter,

If I were to list—and over the next six months of intense therapy I shall—all the ways I've sinned against you and injured you with my abuse of alcohol, I would—and will—undoubtedly fill the pages of your diary many times over.

Why did I do all those horrible things? I'm determined to learn the answers myself in order to change and reclaim my life completely. I'm only desperately sorry that I subjected you to so much suffering. Please be clear: none of what I have done is in any way your fault or your responsibility.

I know it would be improper of me to ask you to reconcile with me immediately. Improper and completely wrong. I must—and I will—demonstrate over time that I have repented of my past and that I have changed, not instantly and miraculously, but by being sober from now on.

Please do forgive me so that you may move on to the healing and happiness you deserve. And I would like to ask you if you are willing to start a correspondence dialogue wherein I can repent of each injury I've caused you over the past 20 years. Consider it, and let me know.

I do look forward to reconciling with you when I've earned the right to do so.

With all my love,

Dad

Also see APOLOGY, page 278.

VIII. ORDERS, CREDIT, AND COLLECTIONS

ORDERS

Reason is the mistress and queen of all things.

—CICERO

Orders, whether they are placed electronically, over the telephone, on a printed order form, or face to face with a salesperson, require specific and clear information. There may still be occasions when it's necessary to submit an order letter for items you wish to purchase. The keys to successful orders: be concise, include complete information about what you want and how you will pay for it, list any order conditions, and provide a contact name and shipping information.

After an order is placed, any number of problems may require you to compose a letter. Using concise, clear, and complete information is always the best approach for resolving problems and keeping customers informed about the status of their orders.

DECIDE TO WRITE

Use this communication to:
- Order
- Confirm an order received
- Explain procedures, change in products, unavailability, issues of payment
- Request additional information
- Make adjustments
- Cancel or change an order
- Inquire about the status of an order
- Clarify payment questions/problems
- Accept or refuse changes
- Refuse or return an order

THINK ABOUT CONTENT
- Cut to the chase in ordering: "Please send me," or "This is an order for" is the best way to start.
- Arrange items with identifying information—number, catalog identification code or number, name, description, unit price, color, dimensions, special information (engraving or monogramming), and total price.
- Set the order out by indenting if you're not using an online form:

  3 copies

  Melvin Batcher, *Clear Thinking*, 2nd edition, 2005 @ $29.95 each

  Total: $89.85

- State any conditions of your order clearly. If you must have the order by a certain date, for example, or if you will accept no substitutions, these conditions must be part of your order.

- Cover tax, shipping information, timeframe, any special instructions, and method of payment.
- Make sure your contact information is complete: full name, mailing address, shipping address, telephone number(s), email address, and fax number.
- Conclude with a friendly comment, if possible.

ELIMINATE WRONG MESSAGES

- Don't confuse the order with unnecessary information.
- Be singular in purpose; don't include other business.
- Don't bury the order in a paragraph.
- Don't order special items without first talking with someone at the organization and confirming it can be done.

CONSIDER SPECIAL SITUATIONS

- If you will accept substitutions, state these clearly.
- Emphasize any deal-breaking information. For example, if your order is only good if the product can be delivered by the 15th, say so: "Order good only if products can arrive by January 15."
- If your order has been lost, emphasize you are submitting a duplicate order in the event the first is found.
- When writing about an order that was placed, always completely identify it by order date and your purchase order number, and/or tracking number and confirmation number, if possible. Also transmit a copy of the order, if you have one.
- If you want to cancel your order, first state clearly that you are canceling your order. Make your contact by telephone, and be sure to get the name of the person who records your cancellation. Repeat all identifying information. If you paid by check, ask for a refund; if you charged the item, ask to have your credit card or account credited. Follow up with an email or letter of cancellation.

- If you must change your order, start by stating you are issuing an order change. Include the original order information. This should be telephoned in and followed by faxing or emailing the change.
- Get confirmation. Telephone orders, especially complex ones over a certain dollar amount, should be confirmed by the supplying organization. If orders will be delayed or must be back-ordered, the supplier should call the customer, and should send a letter that states this fact. A back-order letter should include an apology for the inconvenience, and end with a brief statement of goodwill. More and more these are sent by email, or are faxed.

SELECT A FORMAT

- Official, printed order forms are best. But if a letter is used, be sure to include customer name (with title), business name, shipping and billing addresses, zip codes, purchase order number (if you have one), customer number (if you have one), contact telephone numbers, and fax numbers. Order information should include a catalog number (if available), description of the items ordered, catalog page number (if available), size, color, type (design, motif, etc.), quantity, unit price, and total price. Where applicable, sales, shipping and handling, place and method of delivery, payment information—charge, COD, credit card payment, or payment by check—should all be noted. Include and emphasize any conditions or restrictions, such as delivery deadline, and the acceptability of substitutions.
- Type letters concerning orders on organization letterhead or personal stationery. A legible handwritten letter is also acceptable.

Customer Ordering Supplies

[Emailed]

Jasmine Flowers, Sales Manager

Dear Ms. Flowers:

I am ordering the following from your June 15 price list:

20 boxes	Neenah Parchment bond paper, Dove Gray, 25% rag, 8½ by 11 inches, 20-pound, @ $15.50	$310.00
14 boxes	Neenah Parchment bond envelopes, Dove Gray, 25% rag, 20-pound, size 10, @ $35.00	$490.00
5 dozen	Printer cartridges, #20A, black @ $22.50/box	$112.50
5 each	Stanza computer stands, #1233, Model K in black @ $298.99	$1,494.95
	TOTAL	$2,407.45

Please ship by prepaid parcel post to 540 East Bayaud, Suite 7, Lincoln, Nebraska 68514, and charge the amount on the usual 2/20, net60 terms to The Barker Account #34456.

I'm nearly out of these supplies and would appreciate your getting these out ASAP. Thanks, and call me if there's any problem.

Sincerely,

Joan Thrush

Customer Order Confirmation

[Emailed]

MaryLou Manners, Sales Manager

Dear MaryLou:

This confirms my telephone order, our purchase order #44556, for 435 five-gallon Happy Juniper Shrubs, @ $20.00 each . . . $8,700.00

As agreed, you will guarantee that any shrubs that die or fail to thrive within the first year will be replaced free of charge.

As also agreed, this order is conditional upon these shrubs being delivered by March 15 to 8220 East Dartmouth Avenue, #55.

No substitutes will be accepted.

Thank you for your help on this.

Sincerely,

Henry Wilkins

Customer Received Broken Merchandise

[Emailed]
(Date)

Richard Munch, Customer Service

Dear Mr. Munch:

I just opened the two custom speakers, Model ZZXs, that Stereo Parts made and shipped to me July 2. Two of the membranes over the speaker openings are punctured. As you directed over the telephone, today I am returning the damaged speakers to you for repair or replacement.

I will expect the speakers returned to me by July 15, as agreed. Thank you for your attention to this problem.

Sincerely,

Jack Reynolds

Supplier Notifying of Product Arrival

[Emailed]

Dear Mr. Kowaleski:

It's a beauty! The BMW 735i you purchased through our Munich European Delivery Program has arrived, it has been prepped and serviced, and is ready for pickup. Please call me at 310-555-0123 so I can arrange a time for you to complete the paperwork. My hours are 9 A.M. to 6 P.M. Monday through Saturday.

It will take about 20 minutes to complete the transaction and make any adjustments you may request. You will need to bring the folder of paperwork you received in Munich at the time of purchase and your photo ID (driver's license).

I look forward to hearing from you. You'll be the envy of Englewood.

Sincerely,

George Crawford
Customer Service Manager

Supplier Concerning Back-Ordered Equipment Being Shipped

[Typed, faxed, and mailed]
(Date)

Dear Dr. Hanson:

Give complete identifying information.

We have received the autoclave you ordered (your purchase order #9984) on January 10, which was on back order. I am shipping it to you by Air Service (shipment #44-C-1390), and it will arrive in your office on the 13th.

Thank you for being so patient, and as I said on the telephone, our service representative will call you to arrange a time to come by and check the unit thoroughly.

Conclude with a friendly comment.

We look forward to serving you in the future.

Sincerely,

Ronald D. Servos

Customer Ordering Services

[Typed, faxed, and mailed]
(Date)

Martin Schine, President

Dear Martin:

I would like to order these items from your December 15 proposal:

1) Prepare the site, including, but not limited to:
   a. remove and dispose of existing junipers
   b. grind out pear tree stumps
   c. remove lowest branches on existing Austrian pines
   d. remove and dispose of existing rock mulches $935
2) Furnish and install 5 yards compost . . . 440
3) Furnish and install 110' steel edging . . . 145
4) Rebuild rock wall at west of garage . . . 430
5) Remove and dispose of existing exposed aggregate 460
6) Remove and dispose of existing cobblestone 460
7) Furnish and install flagstone step stones 290

   TOTAL $3,160

I agree to the terms of payment in your proposal: 50 percent upon starting, and the balance on satisfactory completion. Your "General Conditions" for performance will also be part of our contractual agreement. I do wish to take advantage of your winter discount of 10 percent, or $316, that you offered for beginning the work immediately.

Our agreed completion date is February 15, after which there will be a penalty of $25 per day taken off the price.

I look forward to having your company complete this project. Please call me if you have any remaining questions.

Sincerely,

Gladys Poundstone

Author on Books Back-Ordered by Bookstores

[Emailed]

Julie:

When I appeared at the Big Dog Bookstore in Chicago for the book signing on May 16, I was told by Janet Jones, who purchases books, that the books had been on back order for months, and she has been unable to get copies from Ingram, the distributor.

I had checked six different times between March 1 and May 10, and was assured that books were shipped directly from the St. James warehouse on April 1, and would arrive on May 15.

I need to know how this all went so terribly wrong. Please check and call me by tomorrow at noon, so we can get this resolved before my next book signing, May 29.

Regards,

Melville Bounder

Supplier Filling Partial Order

[Emailed]

Dear Ms. Trout:

Thank you for your order (PO #3455), which we just received. We can fill all your order within the next 48 hours, except for 32 of the 65 pairs of Deep Freeze mittens, which we will back-order and ship to you in two weeks.

You will receive your first shipment of the items on the attached invoice within five days; the remainder within three weeks. Thank you again. We look forward to serving you in the future.

Sincerely,

Nighthorse Walker

Order Quantities for Building Project Reversed

[Emailed]

Jerry:

The shipment of "Durango" tumbled travertine tiles arrived today, and we are delighted with the appearance. The condition seems fine. But, as I stated on the telephone, the quantities in the order have been reversed: there are 500 sq. ft. of 18" tiles and 1,500 sq. ft. of 4" tiles, which is the reverse of what we ordered.

As we agreed, Caps Inc. will deliver the missing 1,000 sq. ft. of 18" tiles to, and pick up the 1,000 sq. ft. of 4" tile from, the construction site, without charge, no later than Monday, April 5. And we will incur no other charges for this error.

Thank you for expediting this.

Best,

Charlie Fiddle

Also see COLLECTION, page 321; COMPLAINT, page 257; CONFIRMATION AND ACKNOWLEDGMENT, page 240; CREDIT: OFFERING AN ADJUSTMENT, page 314.

51

CREDIT INQUIRY AND PROVIDING CREDIT INFORMATION

*If you want the time to pass quickly, just give
your note for ninety days.*

—R. B. THOMAS, *FARMER'S ALMANACK*

Credit information—your own and others—
must be handled in a straightforward, diplomatic, and confidential manner. While
computer records are fast and efficient, they also
present unprecedented new challenges to credit security and confidentiality. Both your ability and that of
those with whom you do business may be impaired if
credit information is mishandled. Exercise every pre-
caution to safeguard credit information.

DECIDE TO WRITE
Use the credit inquiry to:
* Routinely check your credit rating and records
* Learn why credit has been denied
* Obtain credit information on a business or person
* Clear up a credit blemish
* Correct credit-report misinformation or mistakes

THINK ABOUT CONTENT
When requesting credit information:
* Call first to learn why credit was denied and to
  determine the agency that issued the credit report.
* Contact the credit bureau (see below), and obtain
  a copy of your credit report.
* Be direct and to the point.

* Give all the necessary identifying information:
  name, address, telephone number, purchase dates,
  item, purchase amount, account number, place of
  purchase, etc.
* For another person's or organization's credit
  information, reference the request of the party
  involved, give any identifying background information, state that all remarks will be kept confidential, and conclude with a statement of
  goodwill and an expression of appreciation.
* For a copy of your personal credit report, write
  to the bureau that issued it. There are three
  major bureaus:

  Experian
  PO Box 2002
  Allen, TX 75013-0036
  (818) 785-3905 or (818) 785-4025
  http://www.experian.com

  TransUnion Corp.
  Consumer Relations
  PO Box 2000
  2 Baldwin Place
  Chester, PA 19022
  (800) 916-8800
  http://www.transunioncorp.com

Equifax Credit Information Services
Consumer Assistance
1600 Peachtree St. NW
PO Box 105069
Atlanta, GA 30374-0241
(800) 685-1111
http://www.equifax.com

The FACT ACT revised the Fair Credit Reporting Act, and you may now obtain one free credit report each year from these three credit bureaus. Make your request through a central source: www.AnnualCreditReport.com (for more information visit www.ftc.gov). Costs for additional reports are $5.95 for one or $25 for all three. Be sure to use the official, secure websites.

You are also entitled to a free credit report copy within 60 days after you have been refused credit. Call the toll-free number if you have questions, then write and mail a copy of your refusal letter with your request. Make it a practice to obtain a copy of your credit report at least once a year, preferably more often—problems or not—to check that your credit record is accurate. Enclose a self-addressed, stamped envelope if you're inquiring by mail.

SELECT STRONG WORDS

application	paid
approve	payment (repayment)
balance	record
character	references
collateral	repayment
credit	satisfactory
debt	savings
deny	substantiate
extend	verify
funds	vouch
lend	welcome
loan	

BUILD EFFECTIVE PHRASES

after careful consideration
all payments on time
application has been received
apply for credit in the amount of
can establish a credit line of
cash basis only
current outstanding balance
delinquent payment record
due to your current credit status
excellent repayment history
lists past-due amounts
my credit record shows delinquencies due to
no delinquent payments
our current credit policy requires
please reapply after
pleased to approve your application
present economic conditions
record of repayment
repayment record indicates
request a credit report
restricted line of credit
substantiate the repayment record
to verify employment
will be happy to consider a credit line in the amount
wish to open the account with
your credit background
your credit policy

BUILD STRONG SENTENCES

I wish to apply for a line of credit in the amount of $200,000.

Please accept my application for a short-term loan in the amount of $125,000.

Mr. Saurabh Beta has listed you as a credit reference.

We are inquiring about the repayment record of Susie Ort's loan to First Federal.

I request to meet with a small business loan officer to establish a business account and line of credit.

Ignacious Dorifo has an excellent credit history with this company, and we would recommend him as a credit customer.

The repayment record of Mark Putz shows five payments over 30 days late.

We would appreciate any credit information you may give us on your customer Matthew Mathers.

SELECT A FORMAT

- For all Internet inquiries and responses, be sure to strictly comply with federal, state, and organizational security requirements in all your communications.
- For mailed inquiries, type your request on personal stationery or letterhead. A neatly handwritten personal letter with return address may also be used for your personal credit report.
- Develop standard (boilerplate) statements consistent with approved credit inquiries and responses. This will allow you to quickly request information, or check off and return a response to credit inquiries.

EDIT, EDIT, EDIT

Your challenge here is to include all the necessary information in a very clear, straightforward, and legally acceptable manner.

Standard Credit Inquiry Form

[Mailed]
(Date)

Reference: Credit Report for _____

Dear _____:

In order to complete a credit application for the above individual/organization, we request the following credit information:

_____ Record of loan repayment history
_____ Standard Credit Response Form

Sincerely,

Joseph Wright

Request for Credit Report on Another Person

[Mailed]
(Date)

Delbert Donavan
Manager, Credit Department

Dear Mr. Donavan:

Regina Merriweather, account #4456, listed your store as a credit reference on her application for a More Credit account. Would you please supply your creditor information on Ms. Merriweather regarding
- length of credit relationship
- monthly and annual billed amounts
- payment record

We will keep the information confidential.

I have enclosed an envelope for your response. I appreciate your prompt attention to this request, and your response.

Thank you.

Sincerely,

Harold M. Miser
Credit Manager

Requesting Credit References from a Company

[Faxed]
(Date)

Mr. Malcolm Meeker
President

Dear Mr. Meeker:

Thank you for your purchase order for our Model SXZ computer system. Before we can finalize the sale, we will need some additional information. Please fax or overnight mail the following information to my attention:

- last quarter's profit-and-loss statement
- copy of certificate of incorporation
- a listing of corporate officers
- the completed attached Form A-345 listing credit references and banking affiliations.

All information will, of course, remain confidential.

When your information arrives, we will review your entire application file, and make a determination on your line of credit.

We look forward to processing your application. Thank you for your interest in Dice Systems.

Sincerely,

Jack Hammer

Company Credit Inquiry

[Faxed]
(Date)

Allen Alexrod
Credit

Dear Allen:

As I explained on the telephone, High Country Duds has just placed a large order, requesting delivery the first of the month. Their purchasing director, Bob Adler, gave your company as a credit reference. *Make your request.*

I realize this company is new, but I'd appreciate any information you have as well as your recommendation regarding an extension of credit. Your comments will be kept strictly confidential. *Give needed information.*

Thanks. I appreciate your help, cooperation, and willingness to fax your response. *Express thanks.*

Cordially,

Nathan Spratt
Sales Manger

Requesting Company Credit Reference

[Mailed]
(Date)

Mr. Milfred Brookfield
Credit Manager

Dear Mr. Brookfield:

Silvers, Inc., located at 500 Silversmith Way in Springfield, has applied for an account with us and has listed your company as a reference.

Their initial order is for $64,500. Can you supply us with information concerning this company's account with you, especially the credit terms, lending limits, and payment history?

We will keep all information you provide in the strictest confidence. Please use the enclosed envelope and it will get directly to me.

Thank you for your help.

Sincerely,

Evelyn Smith
New Accounts

Request for a Copy of Your Credit Report

[Faxed and mailed]
(Date)

Mr. B. Kind, Credit Manager

Dear Mr. Kind:

On September 21, I applied to open a bank account at 1st Bank, 540 West Applegate in Dallas. I was told that there are three negative items on my credit report, and Mr. Jim Bob Aires in the customer service department refused to open the account. (Letter of refusal attached.) *Be direct and to the point.*

I have lived at my present address at 540 Locust in Dallas for five years. Prior to that I resided at 434 East Windsom Drive in Dallas for nine years. I have worked for Lone Star Graphics, 200 Long Horn Trail in Dallas since 2002. *Include all necessary information.*

Please send me a copy of my credit report. If you have any questions, I may be reached at 214-555-0123. *Ask for what you want.*

Sincerely,

Suzanne Richardson

Renewing Credit Relationship with Former Customer

[Faxed]
(Date)

Ms. Mable Bugg, President

Dear Ms. Bugg:

I'm preparing my confidential credit file on your company for extension of a line of credit with us before our visit to your plant next week. I noticed that your financial statements and references date back two years. Our policy for increasing credit lines requires that all such information be current.

Please supply me with updated information for the attached:
- last quarter's profit-and-loss statement
- five current credit references
- current banking affiliation

All this information will be kept completely confidential.

Please fax your response or overnight mail it to my attention by Wednesday so we can keep our appointment for next week.

We look forward to again working actively with Grasshopper, as we did in the past. Thank you, and please call me if you have any questions.

Sincerely,

Mable Karing

Positive Credit Reference

[Mailed]
(Date)

David Jensen
Credit Manager

Dear David:

In response to Bob Adams's request of July 8 to supply you with credit information on BYK, 870 Adair St., Detroit: we have enjoyed a mutually beneficial relationship with BYK for seven years.

All the company's payments have been received on time, and we have extended our credit line with the company from an initial $5,000 monthly limit to a present $25,000 per month line. Annual purchases by BYK have increased from approximately $4,500 to $225,000.

If you require any additional information, please call me.

Sincerely,

Jim Backus
Credit Manager

Request for Company Credit Reference

[Mailed]
(Date)

Dear Mr. Breck:

John Reifer has listed you as the contact person at Manufacturer's Bank for Roller Derby Inc. (See the copy of John's permission-to-contact form enclosed.) In order to establish a line of credit for Roller Derby, we need an indication of their credit performance as well as any comments you can make about their operation and management.

The information you submit will be held in the strictest confidence, and it will be used for credit purposes only. We, of course, welcome the opportunity to reciprocate at any time.

Account opened on: _____

Highest credit in last 12 months: _____

Present balance: _____ as of: _____

Amount past due: _____ as of: _____

Number of late payments in last 12 months:

_____

Comments: _____

_____

_____

_____

Please return in the enclosed envelope. Your prompt response will be appreciated.

Sincerely,

Bill Babcock

Positive Reference

[Mailed]
(Date)

Jeremy Handler
Credit Manager

Dear Mr. Handler:

Our business relationship with Whitcomb Packaging has been excellent over the seven years they have been purchasing our products. They have always paid invoices within thirty days whether they were $2,500 or $17,500 (as our records indicate they were).

We value Whitcomb's business, and have, in fact, just raised their credit limit to $25,000 per month.

I hope this is helpful. Please contact me if you need additional information.

Sincerely,

Raymond Q. Featherlight

Negative Business Credit Reference

[Mailed]
(Date)

Dear Ms. Nair:

We have carried a line of credit for Itchy's Dog Salon for 12 months, which has had a monthly balance of from $3,000 to $5,000. During the 12-month period, there have been seven late payments over 10 days, one for as long as 90 days. While this is a start-up operation and the last four months have shown an improvement in payments, we could not recommend Itchy's at this time.

If you desire any further information, please give me a call.

Sincerely,

Sloan Critter

Negative and Positive Credit Response

[Mailed]
(Date)

Mr. Simpson Alexander
Credit Manager

Dear Mr. Alexander:

Here is the reference requested by Bryant Daniels, your credit applicant, of Flatlanders, 777 West Aberdine, Fort Worth:
- customer from June, 1997.
- high credit balance: $4,520.
- payments were slow from June to December of last year.
- comments: The company underwent a loss of customers and cash flow during that period, but has resumed prompt payment.

We are currently doing business with Flatlanders in a satisfactory manner.

Sincerely,

Joyce Evers
Credit Manager

Also see COLLECTION, page 321; CREDIT: OFFERING AN ADJUSTMENT, page 318; CREDIT APPROVAL, page 306; and CREDIT DENIAL, page 309.

52

CREDIT APPROVAL

. . . for a good character
is what is remembered.

—THE TEACHING FOR MERIKARE

When the decision to extend credit is made—after all the credit information has been collected, checked, analyzed, and the applicant has been approved—you are sending a good news message to announce the fact to the individual or organization. Write it with a welcoming and enthusiastic tone.

THINK ABOUT CONTENT
- State the good news immediately, and cordially welcome the credit customer.
- Define any limitations, and follow that with a brief statement about expanding credit limits.
- Close with a goodwill statement about the future of the relationship.

ELIMINATE WRONG MESSAGES
- Do not include doomsday or negative statements about possible delinquency, late payments, or credit exceptions. If this information has not been conveyed, enclose an explanation and reference it in the letter. Or, to personalize the relationship, invite the reader in for a face-to-face meeting.

- Do not omit a complete statement about immediate credit limits and terms. This could get the relationship off to a bad start.

SELECT A FORMAT
- Use a business letterhead, typewritten.
- Secure Internet communications may be used if organization policy permits.

SELECT STRONG WORDS

accept	funds
approve	receipt
balance	receive
extend	welcome

USE EFFECTIVE PHRASES
accept your application
appreciate your business
approve a line of credit
as a valued customer
become a valued customer
begin a relationship

establish a relationship with you

excellent credit references

extend premier services

find us easy to work with

good payment history

happy to establish

introduce you to our bank officer

join your business team

make available to you

new small business customer

open a line of credit

opening an account in the amount

outstanding credit record

realize business reward in working with us

wish to welcome you

WRITE STRONG SENTENCES

We believe you will become one of our valued customers.

We are pleased to open a Dollars account for you with a beginning line of credit in the amount of $50,000.

We would like to welcome you to our preferred customer group.

Here is a list of the services you will enjoy as a preferred bank customer.

We look forward to working with you for all your widget needs.

Your application has been approved.

You will be happy to learn that your application has been approved for an opening line of credit in the amount of $100,000.

Please check our online services to learn the many ways we are prepared to help you with your business financial needs.

Ordering from Snoopy's was just made a whole lot easier with the approval of your request for a line of credit.

Your small business loan has been approved.

We welcome the opportunity to do business with you as a credit customer.

BUILD EFFECTIVE PARAGRAPHS

We are pleased to report that your loan has been approved for the requested amount of $225,000. Please call my office to arrange an appointment time to complete the necessary loan documents and to receive the check.

After careful evaluation, we are prepared to open a line of credit for Scampy's in the amount of $50,000 for a period of one year. At the end of that period of time, we will reevaluate the line of credit. If your record of repayments has been satisfactory, we will increase the line to your requested $150,000.

Jim, I'll be happy to loan you and Ellise the $20,000 toward the down payment on your house. As we agreed, you will repay the loan in $5,000 increments on the following dates: June 1, September 1, December 1, and March 1. (If you don't meet this payment schedule, Sarah and I take immediate possession of the basset hound, Ralph.) Please countersign on the line below, and this will become our loan agreement. (I was kidding about the dog; it's the kids we want.)

EDIT, EDIT, EDIT

Because of the legal implications, be sure your letter and agreement terms are reviewed by an attorney. If in doubt, give your letter shelf time, and then reread it aloud a bit later to make sure you've said exactly what you intended.

Individual Approval for Department Store Credit

[Mailed]
(Date)

Sarah Wasserstein

Dear Ms. Wasserstein:

It is with pleasure that I welcome you as a preferred credit customer at Oren's Department Store. As a new credit customer, you will have an immediate credit limit of $500.

We believe you will enjoy the convenience and value of our products and services, as well as the special benefits of being a preferred credit customer who is entitled to special sales and discounts.

Please validate your new enclosed Oren's charge card by signing the back. It is good in any of our stores or for any of our services. Enclosed is a copy of our credit terms specifying how you will be billed each month.

Again, we welcome you as one of Oren's preferred charge-card customers.

Sincerely,

Marilyn H. Houser
Customer Service

Offering Limited Credit

[Mailed]
(Date)

Lucille M. Foster
President

Dear Ms. Foster:

We appreciate your credit application. We have now received and reviewed all the responses from the creditors you listed. We would like to offer The Silver Slipper an immediate line of credit for $25,000 based upon our present credit policy.

We will certainly be happy to review and raise this limit to the amount you requested after one year.

We look forward to being of service, and I shall await your first order.

Cordially,

Samuel R. Wright

Organization Credit Approval

[Mailed]
(Date)

Mr. Harold Appleton
President

Dear Mr. Appleton:

After reviewing replies to all the references listed on your application, we are happy to extend to Harold's Way a $75,000 line of credit on a thirty-day billing cycle (2 percent, 10 days). You may order online at Squids.com any quantities you need throughout the month (no minimum order). Just identify the account with your company name and password. We will provide you with free, same-day delivery.

We know you'll find an account with Squid's both convenient and economical, and we look forward to serving you.

Sincerely,

Horacio Blackburn
Account Services

Also see CREDIT DENIAL, page 309, and CREDIT INQUIRY AND PROVIDING CREDIT INFORMATION, page 300.

53

CREDIT DENIAL

Take nothing on looks; take everything on evidence. There's no better rule.

—CHARLES DICKENS

Writing a letter denying credit is a very difficult and delicate task, because this sensitive area is closely tied to character, integrity, and social acceptance. Deliver the bad news in an objective matter-of-fact manner, while trying not to injure the applicant further. Both an indirect approach (see "Refusal," page 250) and an extremely tactful tone are necessary.

Your final strategy will depend to a certain degree on why you are denying credit. If the economy or the segment of the economy that affects the applicant's ability to repay are weak, the job is not as difficult as a refusal based on an unexplained nonpayment of debts. If at all possible, end with a goodwill statement.

DECIDE TO WRITE
Use this response to inform an individual or organization that credit cannot be extended.

THINK ABOUT CONTENT
- There may be local, industry, state, or federal regulations and standards that apply to your statements. Follow them closely.
- Respond to the exact information requested.

- Begin by being direct:
  — Identify the request you are responding to.
  — If the response is one simple answer, give it.
  — If the response consists of more than one answer, start with the major answer. Be tactful, but truthful. Give the points of information with appropriate emphasis.
  — Arrange your answer logically.
  — Make clear, concise statements, visually setting them off, if possible.
- Offer the applicant an alternative plan or hope for a future credit relationship, if either is feasible. People or businesses with weak credit often become good credit risks at a later date.
- End, if possible, with a statement of goodwill.

ELIMINATE WRONG MESSAGES
- Do not supply unsolicited information.
- Do not offer an opinion.
- Don't cite exact "bad" credit references. It is far better to ask the applicant to set up an appointment to discuss these, if he or she desires.
- Don't offer facts you can't back up.
- Do not give confidential information or unnecessary details.
- Don't make promises about the future.

SELECT A FORMAT

Use standard forms where appropriate, or type your response on company letterhead.

USE STRONG WORDS

analyze	future
build	policy
consider	reconsider
credit	record
creditworthy	reevaluate
demonstrate	review
deny	risk
establish	successful
evaluate	

CONSTRUCT USEFUL PHRASES

a review of your debt load

after careful review

after demonstrating a successful repayment

considering your present leverage

financial review committee concludes

in order to build a credit record

loan committee decision

our analysis indicates

past performance indicates

please review the enclosed schedule

to extend further credit

upon further review

we are not authorized

BUILD EFFECTIVE SENTENCES

Our loan committee has carefully reviewed your application for a small business loan.

We have analyzed the profit-and-loss statement you submitted.

Unfortunately our current bank policy requires that a small business loan applicant demonstrate a two-year successful credit relationship with suppliers in order to establish a line of credit in the amount of $250,000.

While we are unable to offer you a line of credit at this time, we do encourage you to reapply in 14 months, and submit a record of the missing financial statements at that time.

We must deny your credit application at this time.

In order to offer you the line of credit you desire, we will need to see a track record of five years of successful operation.

In order to have your application for a line of credit approved, you will need to have the signature of a personal guarantor.

Please reapply once you have completed the items checked on the enclosed form.

We look forward to serving you as your loan institution in the future.

We have every confidence that you will be able to complete the requirements.

EDIT, EDIT, EDIT

Limit the information you give, keeping it as objective as possible. Always be sure you have complied with local and state credit-reporting regulations.

Line of Credit Denied

[Mailed]
(Date)

Dear Ms. Deloy:

Reference: Loan Application #20344

Your loan application for a second mortgage is denied because the home appraisal completed (see attached) indicates a market value below the present loan balance. We understand you are interested in selling the home, and would encourage you to call James Bonder at 202-555-0123 to discuss how you might make improvements that would create a higher market price.

We are all hoping that house market conditions will turn around soon, and Jim will also be able to share with you the most recent forecasts.

Sincerely,

Tu Ryse

Denial of Loan Application

[Mailed]
(Date)

Dear Sharon Shine:

Thank you for considering Foremost Bank as your banking resource for your new women's apparel store. After a careful review of your submitted financial package for a small business loan, the loan committee has declined your application, citing the need for a stronger equity to debt ratio.

We would like to see you qualify for the small business loan and develop a successful retail venture. Therefore, we would like to offer to enroll you in a series of small business seminars that could help build a stronger financial loan package. If this interests you, please call me. I've also enclosed a copy of the loan committee's report that outlines the areas where you may wish to focus attention.

Sincerely,

Joan Saltz

Personal Retail Credit Refusal—Residency Requirement

[Mailed]
(Date)

Ms. Gwen Longfellow

Dear Ms. Longfellow:

Thank you for your interest in a Homestead House credit account. We are pleased you find the quality and variety of home furnishings fit your lifestyle.

Our policy on new accounts requires applicants have a minimum of one year living in the area, so we are not able to open an account for you at this time. As a newcomer, however, we would like to welcome you to the community with the enclosed certificate. It gives you a five percent discount on your next purchase in one of our seven area stores.

We certainly hope you will continue to shop at Homestead House, and we would welcome the opportunity to reconsider you as a credit customer next summer. Please submit an application at that time.

Sincerely,

Rhonda Weaver
Customer Service

Loss of Credit Privileges

[Mailed]
(Date)

Dear Ms. Annoy:

Due to the disuse of your Bonwitt Credit Card (last purchase December, 1999), we are rescinding your credit privileges effective immediately. This means, of course, that you will no longer enjoy the benefits of a Bonwitt customer: flight insurance in the amount of $500,000 for airline tickets charged on the account; insurance against theft of any item purchased on the card; and discounts on 350 major hotels, motels, car rentals, and restaurants.

Should you wish to renew your account with Bonwitt, please complete an application during your next visit to any of our fine department stores across the country.

Sincerely yours,

Darius Drommett

Commercial Credit Refusal—Lack of References

[Mailed]
(Date)

Dick Chancey
President

Dear Mr. Chancey:

Thank you for your order and application for credit. Woods Supplies has long been a friend of new businesses.

We do, however, require five credit references of over two years duration in order to open a charge account for over $50,000. If you have established the additional two references, please submit them to me.

If not, Woods Supplies will be pleased to reconsider a credit arrangement with New Waves after you have been a cash customer with us for one year. Cash orders at Woods Supplies have one great advantage: we offer a five percent discount. Please indicate on the enclosed order form if you would like to place a cash order, or resubmit your application to my attention with the additional credit references or after we have worked together on a cash basis for one year. We look forward to working with you and wish you great success in your new endeavor.

Yours truly,

Roger Crocker
Credit Manager

Commercial Refusal—Additional Information Needed

[Mailed]
(Date)

Kevin Doerr
President

Dear Mr. Doerr:

Thank you for your interest in RayGlows and your application for a line of credit. We have now reviewed it thoroughly.

Our policy requires three more references than you have supplied. If you have these references and current financial statements, please return them to me. We will be pleased to reprocess your application.

In the meantime, we welcome your business on a cash basis and offer you a standard five percent discount on all product lines.

Sincerely,

Lane West,
Credit Manager

Personal Refusal—Slow Pay

[Mailed]
(Date)

Jerald Pearlmutter

Dear Mr. Pearlmutter:

Thank you for applying for a Bullock's credit card. A careful review of your credit references precludes us from offering you credit at this time.

We would like to encourage you to resubmit your application when your credit record indicates timely payments on your present debts over an eight-month period.

We look forward to the possibility of serving you now with cash sales, and in the future by offering you a credit card.

Sincerely,

Jack Bolden
Credit Manager

Personal Refusal—Lack of Work Reference

[Mailed]
(Date)

Mr. Raymond Wayward

Dear Mr. Wayward:

Thank you for your interest in Bowland's and your application for a personal credit card.

Our policy on issuing credit cards requires that applicants have been employed full-time for a minimum of one year at their present place of employment. Your six months of part-time work at Shelby's prevents us from issuing you a credit card at this time, but we will be happy to reconsider your application if you will resubmit it when you meet this requirement.

Thank you again for your interest in Bowland's. Enclosed is a certificate that entitles you to 15 percent off when you make your next purchase.

Yours truly,

Charlene Childs
Credit Manager

Corporate Refusal—Bad Credit Risk

[Mailed]
(Date)

Marshall Feedler
Controller

Dear Mr. Feedler:

We appreciate your interest in establishing an account and line of credit with Whimple and Sons.

We have now completed our review of your application, and have made the credit checks you authorized. We have determined that we can offer Wild Things only a cash arrangement at this time. But, as you realize, cash purchases save money by giving you an additional two-percent discount.

We hope you continue as a Whimple and Sons customer, and we look forward to serving you.

Yours truly,

Marvel White
Credit Manager

Corporate Refusal—Offering Alternate Payment Methods

[Mailed]
(Date)

Doris Misewire
President

Dear Ms. Misewire:

Thank you for your interest in using Formed Container's new line of pop-up packaging for your products. It does make an extremely handsome and marketable combination.

We share your enthusiasm about this venture, and after extensively investigating the credit references you provided in your application, we offer your two initial alternatives for beginning a credit relationship:
- you may pay for the containers in advance of shipping, or
- we will ship containers to you COD.

With either arrangement, we will offer you a four percent cash discount. After six months, we will reconsider establishing the requested line of credit.

We hope to have the opportunity of working with you to fulfill your packaging needs.

Sincerely,

Stanley Shakely
Credit Manager

Corporate Credit Cancellation

[Mailed]
(Date)

Mr. Sheldon Ryder
Credit Manager

Dear Mr. Ryder:

Our records show that during the past 12 months your account balance has remained above our agreed credit terms. As of today, your balance is $2,100.54, and the 60-day, past-due portion of that amount is $1,143.56.

In keeping with our credit policy, we must convert our arrangement to a cash basis. Please make an appointment with Mr. Alex Stitwell this week to review your account and work out a more suitable payment schedule.

If our records are in error, please bring your documentation to your meeting with Mr. Stitwell. We look forward to getting this satisfactorily resolved.

Yours truly,

Norman Nicely
Credit Manager

Corporate Credit Termination

[Mailed]
(Date)

Sidney Boyer
President

Dear Mr. Boyer:

A review of your account indicates that you have an outstanding balance of $5,678.20, and that no payment has been made on your account in 60 days. We must therefore cancel your line of credit, effective immediately.

Please submit your check for the overdue amount, or contact me to discuss alternate arrangements. We hope you will bring your account current so we can reinstate your line of credit.

Yours truly,

Archie Bufford
Credit Manager

Also see CREDIT APPROVAL, page 306; CREDIT INQUIRY AND PROVIDING CREDIT INFORMATION, page 300; and RESPONSE, page 234.

CREDIT: REQUESTING AN ADJUSTMENT IN PAYMENTS

It never hurts to ask.

—ANONYMOUS

When you cannot meet a payment schedule, or a repayment commitment cannot be met as agreed, it is vitally important that you take the initiative, immediately, and contact the creditor or loan institution. Usually face-to-face or telephone contact is the best first course of action. At that time, or immediately afterward, make a written request for—even suggest and outline—an alternative plan for payment. Remember that the creditor holds the power to damage your credit record. Be as tactful as possible. Be realistic about the plan you propose. Think carefully before you suggest an altered payment plan. Enclose some payment with your letter. And by all means, honor your altered schedule of payment.

DECIDE TO WRITE

Use this communication:

- As soon as you know you will be unable to keep the original agreement
- To renegotiate your payment agreement
- To request and/or notify the lender about late payment

THINK ABOUT CONTENT

- Examine every aspect of your agreement and find out everything you can about the practices of the creditor before deciding on your altered repayment proposal.
- Refer to any appropriate account or customer numbers.
- Use the indirect (bad news) approach: make a positive statement that sets up the problem.
- State the problem, and, as succinctly as possible, give the explanation for the necessity to alter the payment schedule.
- Give the proposed altered plan details.
- Assure the reader you will pay the bill in total.
- Remind the reader of your past positive performance, if possible.
- State the fact that you have enclosed a check, and list the amount of the partial payment enclosed. (Always enclose a partial payment.)
- End with a goodwill statement about a continued positive relationship, and ask for the lender's cooperation.

ELIMINATE WRONG MESSAGES

* Do not start with a negative statement.
* Do not fail to include an altered plan for payment.
* Do not fail to enclose a check as a statement of good intentions.

START WITH A STRONG WORD

adjust	necessary
agreement	patience
alter	regret
amend	renewed
arrangement	repay
consideration	restructure
cooperation	satisfactory

USE EFFECTIVE PHRASES

adjust the present payment schedule

after careful analysis

alter our present agreement

appreciate your cooperation

circumstances dictate a change in payments

considering these new developments

have performed satisfactorily in the past

hope this is agreeable

keep my credit record unblemished

lower the payment amount

meet both of our objectives

propose this new schedule of payments

regret that I'm unable

request your cooperation

restructure the payment plan

resume regular payment schedule

trust you can work with me

unable to meet

will be able to pay

will keep the new plan

BUILD STRONG SENTENCES

I request that my present payment schedule be altered.

I need to request an extension on the payment schedule.

I would like to suggest restructuring the repayment plan to the modified schedule below.

Since making our original loan agreement, we have experienced several financial changes that require us to request a repayment adjustment.

We will be unable to meet our agreed payment schedule.

Our June and July payments will be late.

I will make up the missed payments in the month of December when I will pay off the loan in full.

Please allow us to complete our loan agreement without incurring late fees or a negative credit report.

We look forward to continuing our banking relationship in the future without further interruptions in the payment schedule.

I believe you will find us worthy credit partners in the future.

Thank you for your consideration of our request.

SELECT A FORMAT

* Use a business letterhead; or, for a personal loan, use a standard $8\frac{1}{2}$ by 11-inch sheet with return address.
* For communicating by email, use a secure website for all financial matters.
* Type for business; type or use neat handwriting for a personal letter.

EDIT, EDIT, EDIT

Let your letter sit for a period of time. Then reread it to be sure it is correct in tone as well as clear and concise in content.

Request for Repayment Extension

[Faxed and mailed after telephone discussion]
(Date)

Ms. Sudi Bastra, Vice President

Dear Sudi:

As you know, I suffered a back injury in an auto accident on July 1, and have been unable to work for two months due to acute back pain. This has resulted in my loss of the Thompson account and several smaller accounts with project due dates in July, August, and early September.

I'm now greatly improved and shall resume a full-time work schedule next week. But, as a self-employed writer, the loss of income over ten weeks has left me temporarily financially stretched.

I have just signed a new agreement with Phillips in the amount of $150,000 for the completion of two books, and an agreement with Leopard for $75,000 for copywriting on their Williams and Courtesy accounts, so the future looks bright once again.

I request that you extend my repayment schedule for September, October, November, and December (a total of $6,000), and allow me to pay these payments in one total payment on January 1 to coincide with installments I will receive on the Phillips and Leopard contracts. (I have enclosed the payment for August in the amount of $1,500.) I will, of course, expect to pay interest on the payments for the additional time at the current preferred loan rate. I also request that no negative note be made to my credit rating.

Thank you for your consideration of my situation. I look forward to our continuing banking relationship, and to being a valuable bank customer long into the future.

Sincerely,

Bebe Rice

Request to Restructure Payments

[Mailed after face-to-face discussion]
(Date)

Mr. Fred Aster
Accounts Receivable Manager

RE: Account TR-4578

Dear Mr. Aster:

Following our discussion, I am enclosing a check for $450 to be applied toward our account number TR-4578. This is, of course, less than the scheduled payment of $1,800 designated in our payment booklet. As I stated, we have had a temporary but marked downturn in business because our farmer-customers have experienced severe flooding, as I'm sure you've heard on the news.

We will need to adjust our payments to $450 a month for the next 12 months, since farmers will not be purchasing seed or planting this season. We plan to be able to pay our account in full in April of next year; plus, of course, the incurred interest on the loan extension.

We have enjoyed a long and satisfactory relationship with your company; and we look forward to resuming a mutually profitable one next season.

We will greatly appreciate your cooperation and patience in this difficult time.

Sincerely,

Jacob Stern

Request for 30-Day Extension—Slow Receivables

[Mailed after telephone discussion]
(Date)

Alexander Fishbein
Collections

Dear Alex:

I'm enclosing a check for $200 instead of the $1,300 balance due because, as I detailed in our conversation yesterday, we have unfortunately had a delay on several large units. Those have now been shipped, but the accounts receivable pipeline hasn't been replenished.

I am sorry about this reduced payment and certainly do not want to blemish our 10-year, excellent credit record. We'll be back on track and pay this in full in 30 days, bringing our account current.

We ask for your patience with this delay. Thank you.

Best,

George Buckingham

Payment Withheld Because of Creditor Error

[Faxed and mailed after telephone discussion]
(Date)

Suzie Stith
President

Dear Suzie:

I'd like to pay the outstanding balance on our account RR-440, but I haven't received a response to my letter of March 10 requesting that you check the balance and correct the error in your bill dated February 15. (See copies attached.)

I will gladly pay the corrected balance of $765.20 in full when I receive a corrected statement. Thank you.

Sincerely,

Jennie Garrison

Request for Return for Credit

[Faxed after telephone discussion]
(Date)

Esmeralda Squat
Customer Service

Dear Esmeralda:

As discussed on the telephone, I wish to return 50 boxes of the 18 by 18-inch "Durango" travertine stone tiles (priced at $8.76 per sq. ft.) for full credit in the amount of $1,292, including tax. I understand that this was a special order, but it is a frequently ordered product and the local supplier, Quido, has stated that they will accept the return of the tile for full credit without a restocking charge.

If you prefer, I would be happy to have a store credit in the amount of $1,292 rather than a refund.

Thank you for your cooperation in this matter. I shall return the tile on Wednesday if you give me a call today with approval.

Sincerely,

Rachel Chance

Request Concerning Late Payment

[Mailed after telephone discussion]
(Date)

Sherri Grove
Accounts Payable

Dear Sherri:

As I explained on the telephone, I inadvertently left my mortgage payment for October in the amount of $1,564 in my purse for more than three weeks. (Yes, I must clean out my purse more frequently. In my defense, I changed purses, and just pulled this one out of the closet to use again.)

I would like to avoid having this appear as a late payment on my record, if possible, and request your consideration. I'll also promise not to let it happen again. Please do initiate the automatic withdrawal of the mortgage payment from my account to start with my next payment.

Thank you for your help with this.

Sincerely,

Jade Jewell

Applying Credit to Accounts Payable

[Mailed after telephone discussion]
(Date)

Jesse Choice
Accounts Receivable

Dear Jesse:

As we discussed, I've shipped the valves that are missing seals back to you. You will have them this morning. The total charge for these (your invoice #12221) is $5,455.23.

I've reduced our outstanding invoice #122554 for July of $15,897 by the refund credit amount of $5,455.23 we paid for the valves; and I've enclosed a check for the balance of $3,866.23.

Sincerely,

Pablo Martinez

See also ORDERS, page 295, and CREDIT: OFFERING AN ADJUSTMENT, page 318.

55

CREDIT: OFFERING AN ADJUSTMENT

It takes two to speak the truth—
one to speak, and another to hear.

—THOREAU

When you are offering a product or service and something goes wrong, it's your responsibility to take the necessary corrective steps to maintain the goodwill of your customer.

Quick action increases your chances of maintaining a positive relationship and the esteem of the other party. In the ideal situation, of course, your follow-up is so impeccable that you are aware of a problem before the customer has registered a complaint. This often is not the case, of course. But do act immediately. This is when your efforts will be most effective.

Communicate directly, accept proper responsibility, resolve the problem fairly, and work toward complete customer satisfaction, if possible. The critical factors in the adjustment letter are the tone of the letter and the emphasis. Be both respectful and positive, regardless of the factors involved, and emphasize customer satisfaction.

DECIDE TO WRITE

Timing is vital. Write this communication immediately when:

- An error has been made in the delivery of your services or products
- A customer registers a complaint

- A damaged product has been received
- An exchange is requested
- A refund is requested
- There has been a change in payment terms or amounts
- There has been a billing error

THINK ABOUT CONTENT

- Open with good news the customer or other party will want to hear. Focus on a positive solution. In a simple situation, this may be the granting of an adjustment. In other situations, it may be acknowledging the customer was right.
- Quickly identify the complaint you are responding to. Do not go into a lengthy explanation of the negative aspects of the complaint or problem.
- Briefly, and in positive terms, explain what caused the problem if this is essential to restoring the reader's confidence in you and your organization.
- Explain exactly how you will correct the situation. Make your statement sound eager, not begrudging.
- Give any steps you will take to prevent the problem from recurring, if this is appropriate.
- Thank the customer for bringing the situation to your attention, if this is appropriate.

- Close with a friendly, positive statement that will help to reestablish rapport, but don't apologize again.

ELIMINATE WRONG MESSAGES

- If the customer or other party was at fault, do not state this outright. Rather, let it be known by implication or understatement.
- Do not overapologize or overemphasize the problem.
- Do not make statements that could be construed as you accepting liability beyond the scope of your responsibility or admitting that you acted in a negligent manner.
- Do not place blame. Keep your statements, whenever possible, objective, brief, and simple.

CONSIDER SPECIAL SITUATIONS

- In all situations where there are serious issues of neglect or liability, consult your attorney on how your letter should be worded.
- If the problem has resulted in a loss of income or other consequences for the customer, try to arrive at a solution that will rectify the situation. Perhaps something such as a future discount that allows the customer to recoup lost revenue could be proposed.

SELECT A FORMAT

Use a standard letterhead, typewritten.

EDIT, EDIT, EDIT

Make your letter factual, brief, and concise.

Delayed Shipment Due to Strike

[Emailed with attachment]
(Date)

Nigel Redenbacker
President

Dear Mr. Redenbacker:

Thank you for your call today. I had just dictated a letter to you to keep you up-to-date on your shipment (order #4456) of April 14. The dockworkers' strike in New York persists; however, we have heard that a settlement is expected this week.

In the meantime, I'm enclosing pictures I took this morning of some great rugs we have in house that I can ship to you immediately if you need them to fill out your inventory for your upcoming sale. I am willing to offer you a five percent discount on the prices listed.

The minute the strike is settled I will be in contact, and if you decide to order any of the rugs pictured, please give Gertrude a call at (617) 555-0123.

Sincerely,

Hasan Raheeb
President

Data Entry Error

[Mailed]
(Date)

Mr. Edward Fishwhacker
President

Dear Mr. Fishwhacker:

Thanks for your call this morning concerning the error in your bill dated April 12 for $2,456. In investigating, as I stated in my return telephone call, I found that due to a data entry error, your check #8998 was credited to the wrong account. *Offer information.*

Please accept our apology. The correction has now been made showing your account paid in full. (Copy enclosed.) *Prevent further problems.*

Would you please review your company listing below to ensure that we have complete and correct information?

Customer:	Whaler's Cove
Address:	Worthy, MA 01075
Telephone:	(617) 555-0123
Account #:	55420-98

I'm enclosing a 15 percent discount certificate for your use on any products you purchase before September 1. We look forward to serving you in the future. *Close on a positive note.*

Sincerely,

Stan Swinebuckle
Customer Service

Replacement of Damaged Goods—Problem Unknown

[Mailed after telephone discussion]
(Date)

Mr. Arthur Knight

Dear Mr. Knight:

Apologize. I am enclosing a check for $553.12, the amount you paid for the custom-made Wright suit. We are very sorry this unfortunate accident occurred.

Give any explanation. My investigation did not turn up the exact source of the stains on the suit. Our laboratory determined that the stains were made by an acid of the kind used in automobile batteries. Evidently something was spilled on the package during shipment. In 18 years, we have never had such an occurance.

Make a positive gesture.

End on a positive note. I am also enclosing a certificate for a 15 percent discount should you want to order another suit. We would be happy for the opportunity to serve you.

Sincerely,

Frank Fong
President

Supplier Sent Wrong Product

[Mailed]
(Date)

Ms. Vivian Waverly

Dear Ms. Waverly:

I was sorry to learn that an error was made, and that you were sent the wrong fabric color on the sofa you ordered from us May 15. Our source at the factory has located your sofa, and it is being shipped to you tomorrow. It will arrive on Thursday, and someone will telephone you on Wednesday to arrange an exact delivery time. The delivery people will pick up the burgundy sofa at that time.

You have selected the finest sofa of the season, and I'm sure it will offer you great enjoyment. I am enclosing a brochure on a pair of chairs the manufacturer is showing with your sofa. If you wish to order these, we would be happy to offer you a 10 percent discount. Just show the salesperson this letter.

Sincerely,

Janice Placid
Customer Service

Negative Response to Request to Return Merchandise

[Mailed after telephone discussion]
(Date)

Mr. Charles Reeves

Dear Mr. Reeves:

State your response as simply as possible. Thank you for your letter of March 19. I was sorry to hear that sales of the custom-made hutches did not go as you expected. The question of returning the 32 remaining miniature hutches you have in stock is a difficult one. Since you ordered these 16 months ago and we had them made to your specifications and delivered them to your stores 11 months ago, any return policies have long expired.

Offer additional help, if possible. I have checked with the manufacturer and with other retailers, and have been unable to locate other stores interested in purchasing them. Bill Hornblower at Country Way in Boston (617) 555-0123) and Henry Hopewell at Repasts in Rhapsody (213) 555-0124) both offered to discuss with you some ideas for selling them.

Additionally, we have received infrequent calls from interior decorators in your area for similar pieces: Ted Booker at Draper Designs (555-0125) and Hillary Groves at Design Works, Inc. (555-0126).

End on a positive note. I hope this is helpful, and I look forward to serving you in the future.

Sincerely,

Sherman Taylor
Customer Accounts

COLLECTION

Time is money.

—BULWER-LYTTON

Unpaid debts are growing losses to the seller. The goal here is to collect money owed as soon as possible, while at the same time retaining customer or borrower goodwill.

Don't bypass the friendly reminder telephone call. This is often the first and best approach in collecting. (But do check, first, all call restrictions.) In writing the first collection letter, use an indirect approach (see "Refusal," page 250) and write the letter in a persuasive tone. Collection letters to individuals should take an empathetic "you" attitude, and business-to-business letters should also ring with sensitivity to the reader.

Most organizations develop a series of four stages of progressively stronger collection letters. They must be well timed to be effective, and although the computer makes this process very easy, you must carefully monitor it. (Any emails with financial subject matter must be made on secure servers.)

The first-stage letter is usually a *reminder,* the next an *inquiry,* followed by an *appeal,* and finally a *demand.* The wording and timing depend on whether the customer is a person or a business, the balance owed, your type of business, and a number of other financial and industry factors. All stages should be completed in a courteous manner.

There are local, industry, state, and federal standards and regulations concerning collection practices. These must be carefully followed.

THINK ABOUT CONTENT

- Let the reader know in the first sentence that this is a collection letter.
- You can then ask him or her to act.
- Put the responsibility to communicate or explain on the reader. You may even ask the reader for an explanation on the back or bottom of the letter or statement.
- In each letter, state the total amounts owed, the original due date, suggest an alternate plan, and invite the reader to call and discuss it.
- Make it easy for the reader to respond. Enclose an envelope and provide a telephone contact name and number.
- Be flexible and as generous as possible in trying to work out terms for repayment, especially if the debtor expresses that difficult circumstances have caused nonpayment. This, of course, can be easily checked out.
- Use a polite tone in the first series of letters and gradually make it stronger.

Early or Reminder Letter

- Begin by identifying with the reader, then remind the reader of the past-due bill.
- Include a statement that shows confidence the reader will pay.
- End with a goodwill comment, or a statement about your future relationship.

Inquiry or Stronger Reminder Letter

- Following the steps for the early reminder (above), start with a neutral inquiry in an effort to start a dialogue, but make a stronger statement about the necessity of paying the overdue bill.
- Assume circumstances are preventing invoice payment, and ask directly for payment.
- Inquire about problems, and suggest alternatives like partial or installment payment plans if you can offer this.
- Offer a toll-free telephone number, a fax number, and/or a Web address where payment may be made with a credit card.
- Mention the importance of good credit, and remind the creditor that he or she has received considerate treatment from you.
- Make it easy for the customer to respond by including a toll-free telephone number; an email address; and/or a stamped, addressed envelope.

Middle or Appeal Letter

There may be a number of graduated letters in this stage, starting with ones with lots of goodwill statements to ones with fewer goodwill statements. In all these letters, you should do the following:

- Begin with an attention-getting statement that sets up your appeal.
- State your appeal using the second-person ("you") viewpoint and persuasive language.
- Ask for payment.
- Optionally, repeat the appeal.

Develop a persuasive strategy that will appeal to your particular reader:

- The *pride* approach appeals to the reader's self-respect and desire for social acceptance.
- The *ethics* approach appeals to the reader's moral standards of honor, character, integrity, and "doing what's right."
- The *self-interest* appeal stresses the importance to the reader of keeping his or her credit rating and buying power.
- The *fear* approach is the flip side of self-interest: the consequences of not paying, such as legal action, and not being able to buy on credit, etc.

Final or Demand Letters

- You must first consider any federal, state, and local laws governing collection procedures, business practices in your industry, and the image you wish to convey about your organization. Your objective is to get the debtor to take action and pay the delinquent account. It is not to harangue or demean.
- In most cases, you have three courses of action if payment is not made:
  1. Report the delinquent account to a credit interchange group such as a credit bureau.
  2. Turn it over to a collection agency.
  3. Take the debtor to court.

Decide which alternative(s) you will take, then write your letter accordingly.

- Begin by stating which course of action you are taking and why.
- Explain the effects of this action matter of factly.
- Offer the reader one last chance to pay by setting a deadline and urging that it be met.
- Optionally, end with a statement that the reader can stop the action, or the reader will cause the action by his/her inaction.

ELIMINATE WRONG MESSAGES

- Never write an angry letter.
- Don't apologize.
- Do not use stilted language.
- Never repeat an appeal made in a previous letter.
- Never imply that your customer is not an honest person.
- Do not lapse into abuse or threats.

- Do not use inflammatory or demeaning words or phrases such as "demand," "failure," "repeated failure to respond," "failure to pay."
- Don't use sanctimonious, coercive, or false reverse psychological terms or phrases in an effort to manipulate.
- Do not include any statements that could be considered libelous.
- Do not violate an individual's right to privacy. Do not send statements or make collection telephone calls to his or her place of employment, for example.

CONSIDER SPECIAL SITUATIONS

Handle collection of personal loans to friends or relatives with pleasantness but with firmness. "Dear Jill: Did you forget? My records indicate we agreed you would repay the loan ($5,000) on January 15 . . ." Or use humor if it's appropriate: "I've reached that scary stage of not being able to remember if I remembered! Didn't we agree the loan of $5,000 would be repaid on June 1?"

USE CAREFULLY SELECTED WORDS

agree	eliminate
alter	outstanding
alternate	overdue
amount	partial
arrive	reimburse
balance	remember
check	reminder
contact	repayment
cooperate	resolve

BUILD EFFECTIVE PHRASES

according to our agreement
did you forget
do not wish to discontinue deliveries
don't want to disrupt
due the first of the month
experiencing financial difficulties
find a delinquency
friendly reminder

invite your call to discuss
let us know your plan to repay
let's discuss alternatives
payment now due
please contact us immediately
preferred customer
request partial payment
review our records
show your account overdue
use our convenient website

CREATE STRONG SENTENCES

Please call me to discuss your payment schedule.

Please go to our convenient website and make your payment to immediately resolve this matter.

Perhaps a simple accounting error has been made.

We wish to discuss with you how you may bring your account up to date.

This is a reminder that your June 1 payment has not been received.

Alice, please give me a call to discuss the matter.

I know there is a simple explanation as to why the payment has not been received.

Have you somehow overlooked paying the August invoice?

By sending a check today, you will preserve your excellent credit standing.

We are concerned that we have not heard from you.

Partial payment arrangements can be made if you will call me today.

Please use the enclosed envelope to send in your November check, or call me toll-free at 888-555-0123.

We will work with you in every way possible to bring your account up to date.

Your account in the amount of $5,650 is now 120 days overdue.

Because you have not responded to our reminders and notices, we must turn your account over to Credit Mongers Inc. for collection of the outstanding balance of $6,322.

You can easily avoid the nonpayment status by calling me today at 800-555-0123.

Don't endanger your fine credit standing by ignoring this notice.

You can easily resolve this problem by sending in your payment or calling today.

SELECT A FORMAT

Use a business letterhead, typewritten.

EDIT, EDIT, EDIT

In addition to verifying the facts in your letter, be sure to eliminate any grammar and spelling errors. But most important, check the tone of your letter to ensure that it promotes cooperation and ends with a goodwill statement.

Initial Corporate Reminder Letter

[Mailed]
(Date)

Antiqua Brookner
Accounts Payable

Dear Ms. Brookner:

Just a reminder that your account balance of $1,545.24 at Highlands' Ranch is now overdue. Please mail your payment today, or if your check has crossed this letter in the mail, please accept our thanks.

Yours truly,

Charles DeVoe
Accounting

Personal Reminder Letter

[Mailed]
(Date)

Jeena Bucarra

Dear Jeena:

This is to remind you that we've not received your payment for April's club fees of $185. Please mail your payment today to avoid overdue charges in the amount of $20, which will be added to your account balance on the 15th. Or, simply go our website, www.fitforaction.com, and make your payment with a credit card.

Jeena, you may wish to initiate our automatic withdrawal payment plan for future use and eliminate the monthly check-writing exercise altogether. To do this, give me a call at 213-555-0123, or return the enclosed form.

I've also enclosed our monthly specials for June. I hope you will again be joining us for the weekly tennis drills program.

Sincerely,

Rafael Truss

Intensified Business-to-Business Reminder Letter

[Mailed after telephone call]
(Date)

Melissa Beale
Accounts Payable

Dear Ms. Beale:

This is a follow-up to our telephone conversation regarding your order #5443 of April 30 for seven chandeliers, totaling $7,540.76. We invoiced you on May 7, the day the chandeliers were shipped. They were received by you on May 15. (See copies attached.)

We agreed that you would send a check for the chandeliers upon receipt, but that was 60 days ago.

Please remit payment immediately so we can get this resolved and ship your present order sitting in our warehouse.

Sincerely,

Jeannie Dickson
Account Services

Appeal for Further Business Communication

[Mailed]
(Date)

Derek Dietz
Controller

Dear Derek:

Concerning your nonpayment of our invoice #8990 for consulting services in the amount of $1,425, presented on April 17: I'm again asking you to call me or Eleanor Jeffries at 529-555-0123 to discuss any details you still have unresolved.

Perhaps if we talk, we can arrange an alternate payment schedule. Please call by Friday so we can get this settled.

Sincerely,

Sharron Decker
Accountant

Appeal for Action to Customer with Financial Problems

[Faxed]
(Date)

Mr. Kirk Foster
President

Dear Kirk:

We understand the trials and tribulations of a rotten season for retailers, but we still need to hear from you on the overdue payment of invoice #4559 for $4,650. (Copy enclosed.)

We'll work with you to reschedule payments so when things pick up in the next couple of months you won't be without a supplier.

Call me today. I'm going to be in Steamboat on Tuesday, and I can stop by to resolve this.

Sincerely,

Joan Dickson
President

Appeal for Payment

[Mailed]
(Date)

Vadi Kroft
Accounts Payment

Dear Vadi:

I'm concerned that I haven't heard from you concerning the outstanding invoice #32222 in the amount of $4,520 even though I've sent three reminders over a 90-day period. We've had a mutually rewarding credit relationship over the past five years, and this is quite out of character. I'm wondering what extraordinary circumstances have caused this delay of payment.

Please do send in your check today, or call me at 729-555-0123 to arrange a payment plan. I'm certain that if we put our heads together, we can satisfactorily resolve this.

I've enclosed an envelope for return of payment. Or, you may always pay by credit card through our website, www.cycle.com. I look forward to talking with you, and getting the issue of your line of credit resolved.

Sincerely,

Yuri Stern

Demand Business Letter

[Emailed on a secure server]
(Date)

Asa Blizzaard
Sun Thongs

Dear Asa:

Your outstanding balance of $3,200 is now 120 days overdue (pull up your account and take a look), and we can no longer extend additional time for bringing the account current.

Since we haven't heard from you, we will have to turn your account over to our attorney for collection if we don't receive payment in full by Friday. This may, of course, adversely affect your credit.

Please do take care of this by issuing your check for balance, and sending it today, or by going to the website, www.reflections.com, and paying by credit card. You may also call me at 800-555-0123 to discuss the matter.

Sincerely,

Jorge Ruff

IX. SALES

57

DIRECT MAIL

He profits most who serves best.

—ARTHUR R. SHELDON

While it's true that nearly every letter you write has some sales message, the direct-mail sales letter is designed and written with the sole purpose of persuading the reader.

The term *direct mail* means that the letter is sent out directly to the target market instead of being sent in response to an inquiry. It may promote a product, service, concept, or even a person.

In order to sell, the effective letter must (1) get the reader's attention, (2) appeal to the reader's interest by relating to his needs or desires, connecting the point of your message to a reader benefit, (3) explain the product or service, again in terms of reader benefits, and (4) motivate the reader to take the directed action.

First you must identify the selling points of your product or service. With these in mind, you must select the right recipients or target audience. This can be scientifically done by using a variety of marketing techniques and data to select the names of people most likely to be interested in what you're selling. There are a great number of firms that do this. Or, with some work, you can develop your own mailing lists.

Many products or services have more than one target audience. But each audience will undoubtedly need its own specially tailored sales letter. If you are selling a new product, your first mailing list is almost always your present customers and the next list is your current prospects. You have already established a positive relationship with the first and are well on your way with the second.

To tailor your letter to these readers, learn as much about them as possible. If your mailing list hasn't designated it, learn the sex, age, marital status, vocation, income level, geographical location, interests, hobbies, etc., that will help define your readers in terms of people most likely to buy your products or services.

Write your letter to fit this individual target audience, emphasizing how your product or service can benefit the reader. When possible, phrase these benefits in the second-person viewpoint. Remember to test your letter for any overstatement, and check it against any possible liability statements.

Aim the closing at bringing the reader to the point of the desired action. In the case of big ticket or complex-concept sales, this will probably mean leaving the door open to make, or setting up, the next contact. So instead of ending with "Give me a call for more information," you will write, "I will call you on Friday morning about nine o'clock to give you the details."

In our electronic age of computer mail-merge, it is easy to "personalize" you letter's inside address and salutation. With the present wide use of email, the direct-mail piece can be instantly and cost effectively electronically delivered to your target market. (The key to email marketing is a tantalizing subject line that gets readers to open your email and appealing content to keep the recipient reading.)

DECIDE TO WRITE

Use this letter to:

* Introduce a new product, service, or candidate
* Introduce other products after a sale
* Sell to known prospects
* Invite customers to a grand opening
* Announce a special sale or promotion
* Announce a business closing

THINK ABOUT CONTENT

Collect direct-mail sales letters. Test your own reaction to the messages. Examine what the writer did well and what he or she did poorly. Look especially at letters concerning the type of product or service you have to offer.

Direct mail has become so commonplace that only the very best will be read. Be sure to make yours as brief and complete as possible to give it the best chance. This includes having something unique to say, keeping paragraphs short, using white space to make the letter appear easy to read, and using visuals to attract attention.

Consider writing a series of letters. This will affect the letter content and approach.

Look at the length of the messages. It's best to keep your letter shorter than a single page, or screen length for email, if possible. There are certainly exceptions, but not many. If your letter is over one page, ask yourself if the sales process should have been broken into more steps. Maybe the letter should have the goal of setting up a face-to-face meeting, participation in a seminar, or a personal sales call, rather than a "sales-in-one."

Get Your Reader's Attention

When you are ready to write, lead with a statement to get the reader's positive attention and set up your strategy. Use what you've decided is your strongest psychological sales point that's keyed into a benefit to your reader. Build your message around it. Open with your strongest psychological point and use your best creative efforts. Think your lead all the way through to the follow-up sales letter and the final sale. An announcement letter telling the reader about a new home loan interest rate of 3.5 percent in a 5 percent market, especially if the letter was mailed to a special list of targeted new-home shoppers, would get the reader's attention, preparing the reader for your loan message, your follow-up telephone call, and your sales presentation and closing statement.

A statement or question opening that introduces a need the reader has that the product will satisfy works well. This one is based upon a rational appeal:

> "A Capital Loan can save you $125,000 in house payments."

> "You can qualify for a 3.5 percent home loan."

Or try a question:

> "Will you pay too much for your new home loan?"

> "Would you like to save $420 each month on house payments?"

> "How can you pay $225,000 less for your new home?"

> "How can you get $175,000 more house and pay $95 less each month?"

Or your opening may be based on an emotional appeal, like this letter for aid to children:

> "Pablo is seven years old today. As he sits inside the darkening hut that is his home, an old pot sits on the dirt floor beside him to catch rain dripping from the tin roof. He's very hungry. But he knows there will be no dinner tonight."

Select an approach appropriate to your product or service and your audience. Often there will be both rational and emotional elements in the same opening. The use of gimmicks in conjunction with the opening can work well if the gimmick supports the theme.

Select the Right Viewpoint

Use the second-person ("you") viewpoint whenever possible to make the reader a participant in your appeal. This works well in the home loan example. The second example ("Pablo") relies on the narrative, or "story," technique to draw the reader in. The second-person viewpoint or the reader-benefit approach helps focus the message and keep it direct and to the point.

Develop Your Strategy

After the "grabber" first sentence, you must make the transition to telling your reader how your product or service will fulfill his or her need or desire. This must logically follow, of course, from your opening statement. In the example of the home loan, you would follow this rational opening with, perhaps, a true example that your targeted reader can relate to: "Lynne and David Ross pay $1,457 each month on their home loan . . ."

Choose Your Voice

Make your writing conversational, fast paced, and assertive. You must gain and hold the reader's interest very quickly. To perfect your style, you must write and rewrite.

Select Your Words Carefully

Shades and nuances of words are very important. Strive for words that enliven your sentences. Check the difference in the effect of these words:

Instead of	Try one of these
Hot	sweltering, steaming, fiery, sizzling
Cold	freezing, frigid, frosty, cooling
Delicious	sumptuous, delectable, feast, ambrosia

Very important here, too, is selecting positive words of persuasion. Negative words or statements are seldom the best choice:

Negative Wording	Positive Wording
Reduce downtime by 10 percent.	Increase your production by 10 percent.
Less than 2 percent of our clients do not get a new career.	We place over 98 percent of our clients in new careers.
Easy Press eliminates wrinkles.	You get a wrinkle-free shirt all day long.

Enliven Your Text

Use visual techniques to add interest. Consider using bold-faced type of various sizes, italics, color, and graphics.

Give the Reader the Necessary Information

You must accomplish two things: (1) answer the reader's questions and overcome his or her objections, and (2) supply enough convincing information and facts to motivate the reader to take the next step. This requires a careful balancing act. You must include enough information without bogging the reader down. The fine details of most sales presentations require that you enclose supplementary collateral pieces. But again, this is a balancing act. Too many pieces and the reader will toss the letter and the supplements into the wastebasket.

So keep supplemental materials to a minimum, and coordinate them with the letter by referencing them: "Price details are covered on page two of the enclosed brochure." Another good example of this might be a cruise with a whole variety of price possibilities. Your letter could include a statement like: ". . . from $234," or "Prices begin at $234."

There are many visual possibilities when you deliver your direct mail piece via email. But remember that many of the same rules apply: keep it simple. Use visuals whenever they promote, but do not detract from, the message.

The Action Step

There are several ways you can bring the reader to the point of taking action. Select the one consistent with your product, and audience, but be sure to make your close clear and specific, preferably with only one course of action to take. Here are the best ways to initiate the next step:

- Call for action. If you offer an incentive to act now, this step makes sense:

  ". . . to get your free sample, mail in the enclosed card."

  "Just hit 'reply' to sign up for our free newsletter."

  "Order your GlowBright bulbs now, in time for Christmas."

  "Order now, online, and receive a 20 percent off coupon to be used on your next restaurant visit."

  "Order your original print now, before they are gone."

- Complete the circle. Take the reader back to your opening. This is sometimes referred to as the pay-off on your teaser lead:

  "Start saving $295 each month on your home mortgage payments now . . ."

- In the case of the narrative story, end with the possible happy ending:

  "With your help, Pablo can eat three meals a day, go to school . . ."

- Add "postscript punch." Sometimes overused, but often effective, is the added postscript (PS) that makes one last pitch for the reader to act. This should be short, punchy, and call for a precise action. It is usually done in script, or what at least looks like a handwritten note:

  "Call now. Offer expires . . ."

  "Order Christmas gift subscriptions now for only $9.95."

  "To take advantage of this offer, place your call now."

Take the Final Steps

- Double-check your letter to be sure you have included all the information the reader needs in order to act, and make sure it is easy for him or her to respond.
- Hand-address the envelopes, if practical, and affix with stamps (make them commemorative). This is more appealing to readers than envelopes with address labels and metered postage marks.

ELIMINATE WRONG MESSAGES

- Avoid "hard sell" pushy techniques. Most readers find these a turnoff.
- Eliminate negative pitches unless they are the strongest.
- Do not give too much information or a fragmented message in your letter. Keep the information simple and straightforward. Use a brochure to provide details, and tie the brochure and the letter together.
- Don't be too familiar. Many readers who are strangers don't want to be instant "friends."

CONSIDER ALL YOUR MAIL-OUTS

- It is important to think of the direct-mail sales letter as part of all the letters you send to customers and clients. It is also important to think of the sales aspects of other letters you send.
- Create a complete family of letters. This is part of building an identity for your organization.
- Don't miss an opportunity to get the word out about your product or service. Think of everyone you do business with in terms of whether they can be customers.
- Think about creating specials for "valued customers" to build loyalty. This is usually easily done by offering special discounts or pre-sale access to merchandise.

SELECT A FORMAT

- Use a format consistent with the product and audience. Two-color embossed letterhead isn't the best choice for catalog sales, but it usually is for announcing new banking services, investments, and life insurance.
- Computer-generated letters make personalizing a simple task.
- Email offers are a great way to give a special class of customers a special deal, and coupons can be easily printed out for use in redemption.

EDIT, EDIT, EDIT

Double- and triple-check the facts in your direct-mail piece. Then check for typos and have at least several reviewers (preferably people like your target reader) review your piece before sending it. Make sure, too, the tone is right.

Special Customer Offer

[Emailed and mailed]
(Date)

Dear Janice:

This is your special preferred customer invitation to Cricket's "Pre-Season Preferred Customer Sale." This year our Spring Trunk Show and Sale includes the hottest new fashions that will flatter your figure.

As usual, it's one day only, January 15, from 2:00 P.M. to 8:00 P.M., and our doors will be closed to all other customers.

Print out the coupon below, and come on in for our best preview ever. We've even upped the preferred customer discount to 25 percent off your total purchases.

High tea will be served, and your favorite models from the Junior League will be modeling the latest hot designs. A 10 percent contribution of all sales for the afternoon will be donated to the Junior League Little Miss Scholarship Fund.

See you on the 15th!

Best regards,

Betty Gossamar

Bike Promotion

[Emailed]

SUBJECT: Your Invitation to Ride the Rockies!

There are only 90 days until you'll be meeting at the Park Meadows Roundup! Are you ready? How about your bike?

Print out this coupon, and bring in your bike for our special customer tune-up for only $39.95. That includes a total Mountain High reworking of brakes, tires, lights, chains, all moving parts, and frame integrity.

The offer's good from April 15 through May 15. Give us a call now at 303-555-0123 to subscribe to our free online "Readiness Teleseminar" and to make an appointment to get your bike in. Or, click here to set up your appointment now.

Limited-Time Offer

[Mailed on postcard]

Act now, and receive six additional months of *Modern Women* magazine at the same great introduction price of $1.00 an issue.

Just complete and return this postcard, and we'll rush you your first issue of the magazine described as "What every woman wants to know about her world."

PR Company

[Mailed]
(Date)

Dear Archie:

Over the past five years, Scream Communications has served as King Sausage's public relations agency, netting your company a market share increased by 150 percent each consecutive year. That's a record your competition has openly coveted!

Now that representation for your corporation is coming up for review and bid, we would like the opportunity to again make a presentation to your marketing committee on how we feel we can improve—*even more*—on our past outstanding record.

We have some new and exciting ideas for King Sausage, including plans that will appeal to three new market areas. I will call your office next week to set up a presentation meeting with your selection committee. We look forward to sharing our dynamic ideas with you.

Sincerely,

Manning Traceconsc

Charter Membership Offer

[Mailed on oversized postcard]

Dear Charles:

You are nominated for membership as an honored "Charter Member" of the Regional Air and Space Museum to be opened at the spectacular George Q. Queezy Center. Congratulations! This magnificent center will be constructed entirely with private funds, and, as a noted pilot, you qualify for recognition as a "Charter Member."

We cannot accomplish this without your support. Will you join my wife, Gertie, and me in choosing to make a contribution and bequest in commemoration of the Century of Flight?

If you want to create your legacy for the Regional Air and Space Museum, please complete the back of this card, and we will send you a contribution and bequest agreement form. Or, you may call or email for more information from the Office of Development's Gift Planning Department either at 800-555-0123 or at legacy@flight.com

Thank you for considering the Regional Air and Space Museum in your estate planning. With your help, we will be able to construct and operate this as one of the leading regional museums worldwide.

Best regards,

General Dizzy Daft

Seminar Promotion

[Emailed]

SUBJECT: Do You Want to Make Your Book a Best Seller in Just 21 Days?

On Tuesday, January 15 you can learn how to hit the Best-seller List and sell up to $200,000 in books, even if you're a first-time author, and a marketing and sales novice.

Dagwood Dugan and Greer Slough have perfected a simple, four-step formula that you can use to achieve book-sale success. Rob Chock used it to hit four regional best seller lists and sell $500,000 in books. The cost to implement the formula is less than a good meal out. And it works for all authors—fiction or nonfiction—and all subjects.

Here's your pass to success: tune in for the 45-minute FREE telephone seminar on Tuesday, January 15 at 6:00 P.M. EST.

To register, go to www.bookbust.com, or call toll-free 800-555-0123.

Cruise Promotion

[Mailed]

Dear Mr. and Mrs. Gripe:

To help with your life-changing travel discoveries for this coming year, we are enclosing your copy of Tiny Ship Travel Catalog, which features the very first announcement of our most popular vacation trips. (Check out what other discriminating travelers like yourselves have to say.)

You may become a Gold Star Traveler if you sign up before December 1. You'll received a 10 percent reduction on your total trip fee.

We look forward to traveling the world with you again this year.

With warm regards,

Harriet Molher

Also see ANNOUNCEMENT, page 21; CONGRATULATIONS, page 30; INVITATIONS, page 65; PRESS RELEASE, page 350; THANK-YOU, page 76; and WELCOME, page 59.

58

SALES FOLLOW-UP

If at first you don't succeed, try and try again.

—ANONYMOUS

A follow-up sales letter is any letter that follows an initial contact and has a sales motivation. A number of studies have shown that sending a follow-up sales letter to a prospective customer can get as good or better results than the initial sales letter (see "Direct Mail," page 327).

In fact, the first sales letter or sales contact seldom produces enough results from readers to eliminate them from your follow-up sales list. You may want to plan a series of sales letters, often four to six, as part of your total sales campaign.

Follow-up sales letters should contain some of the same vital information as the initial sales letter to build on the message already begun. Making this reference helps to build your sales effort.

A progressive number of follow-up sales letters—a sales-letter ladder—is actually required by some audiences. Probably some of the best examples are those involving ideas readers are initially opposed to, such as buying an insurance plan for an extended-care facility or buying a new product that uses brand new technology.

Many follow-up sales letters also wear other labels: *thank you, congratulations, response, invitation,* and *request.*

DECIDE TO WRITE

Use this letter:
- After an initial direct-sales letter has introduced a concept
- In response to an inquiry
- After a sales call
- As part of a planned, multicontact sales campaign
- After receiving a sales referral
- With new customers

THINK ABOUT CONTENT
- Reference how the reader has come to your attention. If he or she is a referral, name the person. If you are following up after a sales call or a telemarketing call, thank the reader for his or her time; if you met the reader at a meeting, say so. This information establishes a relationship and may increase the reader's receptivity to your message.
- Describe the product or service you are offering. Refer to the first letter, if appropriate.
- Stress the customer benefits.
- Back up your lead with facts and information. Make statements that will overcome the reader's objections, and answer needs and desires.

- Give new or additional information that may arouse the reader's interest.
- Make a strong close by tying a special offer or incentive to your lead.
- End by leaving an opening for your next contact.
- Follow up by thanking those who give you leads. Write a thank-you letter and report your progress, if appropriate. As a point of courtesy, always let your referral source know if you make the sale.

ELIMINATE WRONG MESSAGES

- Don't send the exact letter you used for the first mailing if it got little or no results. Try to determine why there was little response and make some changes.
- Don't close the door to future contact. Close with a statement that you will make the next contact and/or that invites the reader to contact you.

SELECT A FORMAT

Match or coordinate the look of this letter with any others you have sent the reader. You want to build recognition of your organization's name and products or services.

EDIT, EDIT, EDIT

Transforming your letter into an arresting, clear, and concise form is your challenge. Reread your letter to make sure it (1) gets the reader's attention, (2) creates interest, (3) convinces the reader your product or service meets his need or desire, and (4) asks him to take the next action you suggest.

Follow-Up after Direct-Mail Letter

[Mailed]
(Date)

Richard Munson
Photographer

Dear Mr. Munson:

I'm glad you and four of your staff are considering attending our Fifth Annual Shoot 'em Up Seminar October 20–22. We will cover advanced photo techniques and high-tech photographing in several hours of instruction on each of the three days. I have marked these sessions on the enclosed brochure.

International expert Flash Weasel will teach three of these sessions, and Edsel Redeye will teach the other three.

I've enclosed six applications for your staff to use. If you return the completed applications with tuition payments before Friday, your staff will be assured of getting places, and you will save $25 on each tuition fee. I will call you Wednesday to see if you have any additional questions.

Sincerely,

Miriam Foil
Program Coordinator

Follow-Up to Set Sales Presentation Appointment

[Mailed]
(Date)

Sybil Snidvider
Marketing Director

Dear Sybil:

It was a pleasure talking to you today. Yes, Marketing Communications is a full-service marketing, advertising, and public relations agency. We specialize in technical accounts and have been able to get great results for our clients using a personalized program emphasizing public relations. Our capabilities statement and a list of some of our clients are enclosed.

I will be in Orlando on the 21st, and would like to talk with you about the possibility of LiveWire using us on a per-project basis. As I mentioned, you may call Roy Bender of B/PAA and discuss with him how we have helped that organization gain a 74 percent market share—an increase of over 50 percent.

Your new energy products sound very exciting, and I'm already percolating some great, low-cost promotion ideas. Would you be able to give me 30 minutes from 1:30 to 2:00 P.M. on the 21st? I'll call your office on Friday to see if I may schedule that time.

Sincerely,

Eric Muskgrove
Account Manager

Follow-Up on Request for Samples

[Mailed]
(Date)

Dear Mavis:

Here are the Prestige silk shantung samples you requested in both the silver fox and the pewter blue. We also produce a wonderful embossed and corded shantung in coordinating colors, and I've included samples of those too. Any combination of these fabrics will provide the elegance you are seeking.

Our shipping schedule is enclosed for your reference. Quantities for the draperies, pillows, bedcover, and chaise are available.

If you place your order this week, we can offer you a 7 percent discount on these fabrics. Please call me if you have any additional questions.

Sincerely,

Rachel Trapp

Follow-Up to Request for Search

[Emailed]

Dear Ruby:

I'm amazed. I've actually located two lemon-yellow Model 77s in vintage condition and have attached photo files so you may take a look yourself.

My advice: if you love one or both, please authorize me to make an offer. On the File A bike, I suggest offering $11,500, and I'd try for this one first; and on the File B bike, I think the seller will let it go for $13,000, though as you'll see, it's slightly less desirable.

All the relevant stats are in the photo files.

Best,

Mike

Follow-Up to Request for Information

[Emailed]

Dear Ryan:

Yes, you can get the Roadster Rabbit Model X2 in carmine red in time for Christmas—if you order this week.

There's more good news: we are offering you a Model X2A, an upgrade that includes two new features this year, for the same dealer-plus price.

If this is the automobile you've had your heart set on, now's the best time ever to make the decision to purchase.

I've put a hold on this particular car for 48 hours. Give me a call today, and I'll run through the pricing and payment structure with you.

All the best,

Rudy Rotor

Follow-Up to Sales Call

[Mailed]
(Date)

Alexander and Elle Callan

Dear Mr. and Mrs. Callan:

It was a pleasure meeting you last evening. Thank you for the opportunity to introduce our insurance plan. I believe Plan D in the brochure is ideal for your first goal of sending Derek to college. The other elements of the plan will meet your family protection, retirement income, and other education needs.

I will be conducting a luncheon workshop on Thursday for about 20 people. I'd like to invite you to attend because I will be covering the plan elements in depth. Or, I would be happy to meet with you again on Thursday evening to answer any additional questions. I will call you on Tuesday evening to discuss which you would prefer.

Sincerely,

Charlie Sellwell
Insurance Manager

Follow-Up Sales Letter

[Mailed]
(Date)

Jonathan G. and Louise Kettering

Dear Mr. and Mrs. Kettering:

Welcome to Tucson. Thank you for requesting our brochure from the Welcome Wagon. I've enclosed it along with several photos you requested in our telephone conversation. These are five of the homes we have landscaped in your area.

We have been giving homeowners the best of the desert Southwest for over 25 years. Please feel free to check with a few of those customers from the enclosed list.

We do have a small welcome gift for you, which I will bring by after I call you next week to set up a time to give you a landscaping estimate.

Sincerely,

James Morningflower

Follow-Up to Returned Postcard

[Emailed]

Hi, Brad,

Yes, you are registered for the FREE teleseminar on Wednesday, June 15 at 6:30 P.M. EDT. You'll want to be prepared to take notes, as the information Randy and Ralph will share is truly phenomenal.

Ginger Rogers

Sales Follow-Up/Thank-You to New Customer

[Mailed]
(Date)

Darrel Covey

Dear Mr. Covey:

Thank you for your order for the Bridgestone Model AS-34.

I was happy to hear about your increase in production with this fine machine. As I mentioned to you on the telephone, I believe you will be interested in the two Bridgestone grinders, Models RE-34 and RE-50. These will replace your present machines, and offer the efficiency and increased production you desire. I've enclosed the spec sheets for both.

I will be demonstrating these grinders during our open house on the 15th, and you could see all the benefits to your present operation with this hands-on opportunity. I will also have a complete sequence of machinery set up to demonstrate an operation similar to yours. You're welcome to bring some of your own parts and try these new machines.

I'll call you later this week to see if I can sign you up for this session (it's free), or exactly how I can help you with your next step.

Sincerely,

Frank Sharpe
Customer Sales

Follow-Up to Inquiry

[Emailed]

Dear Sudi:

Thank you for your inquiry concerning Freddie's Hand-Printed Wallpaper. The design you're inquiring about may be seen by going to our website FreddiePrints.com, and searching by design name.

Orders may be placed through the website. We look forward to supplying you with the world's best hand-printed wallpapers.

Best regards,

Ara Glibb

Also see DIRECT MAIL, page 327; REQUESTS AND INQUIRIES, page 224; RESPONSE, page 234; THANK-YOU, page 76; and WELCOME, page 59.

X. PUBLIC RELATIONS, PUBLICATIONS, AND PUBLICITY

59

PITCH

Writers are like baseball pitchers.
Both have their moments.
The intervals are the tough things.

—ROBERT FROST

 When you wish to promote an idea to be covered by the media, you'll "pitch" the editor, TV reporter, movie producer, or other appropriate person. This is done either verbally or in written form, and it's best to find out the form preferred by the individual or individuals you wish to convince. You will want to carefully develop and hone your pitch, a sales tool cut to its most concise and persuasive best.

Most editors at magazines and newspapers will insist you send a letter—transmitted by email, fax, or mail—explaining your idea or the subject you are requesting they cover. But sometimes you will get the opportunity to make a pitch over the telephone.

A good pitch message must not only suggest a newsworthy idea, or an idea with human interest, it should also offer the editor a bit of background information, and sometimes the opportunity to set up an interview (if you are suggesting the editor cover the story rather than you writing a piece). When appropriate, also include a product sample (like a book, if you have a new book out). Include all the ingredients that will make it convincing and easy for your reader to make a decision to cover your story. (The pitch is usually a short version of the query letter, but the terms are often used interchangeably.)

THINK ABOUT CONTENT

- Be sure you understand the subject or product thoroughly so you can explain newsworthy aspects well.
- Know the target media and appeal to their particular interests.
- Make sure you target the right editor.
- Call the person—editor, reporter, or interviewer—and, if appropriate, make a verbal pitch, stating you will follow up with a letter.
- Determine how the person prefers you submit your pitch: telephone, mail, email, or fax. It may be necessary to offer an "exclusive" on the story. If there are competitive newspapers, for example, try to get one to do a feature by using this approach.
- Check the spelling of the person's name, title, and address.
- Personalize your letter to your reader, offering a "slant" for his or her readership.
- Use an intriguing first sentence to hook the reader immediately. This "hook" can be a news angle or something the reader needs or wants.
- Use a professional but friendly tone.
- Keep the pitch short—no more than a single page or one computer screen in length—pithy, and full of information.

- Conclude with a statement taking the initiative to make the next contact; for example, "I'll call you on Thursday to see if this will work for you."
- Follow up exactly as you promised to increase your credibility.

ELIMINATE WRONG MESSAGES

- Do not use a first name in the salutation unless the reader is a personal friend, or you know it will be OK.
- Gimmicks are high risk. Don't use them unless you've tested them on a substantial market sample and know they fit the reader well.
- Avoid overused adjectives like "unique," "fantastic," "greatest," "incredible," and "best."

CONSIDER SPECIAL SITUATIONS

- If you are pitching a product, single out the most newsworthy and interesting aspect of the product and make that the first sentence.
- If you are pitching the results of a survey or a personality for an interview, use a provocative opening, either a statement or a question:
  — "Did you know that over 97 percent of husbands are unfaithful?"
  — "How frequent are accidents at work?"
  — "Today nine accidents will happen within 25 feet of your desk."
  — "The job market for sports editors is drying up."
  — "Did you know that 93 percent of working mothers will only get six hours sleep tonight?"
- Back up your first sentence with facts, an explanation, and/or an expansion on the lead.
- Put the meat in the middle of your pitch, but keep it short and snappy.
- Use bullets and indentations to make important points.

- Keep your purpose in mind: to get the reader to agree to do an interview, take a tour, assign a feature for you to write, or some other request.
- Be sure you close asking for what you want:
  — "Will this work for you?"
  — "I'll call you Wednesday to answer any additional questions."
  — "May I write this in 1,500 words?"

SELECT A FORMAT

- Use 8½ by 11-inch letterhead.
- Use a clean and open email format.
- Use verbal pitches when requested.

SAMPLE-PITCH FIRST SENTENCES

- Robert Wright had no idea that the chimp, Axel, he'd raised from a two-month-old orphan would try to kill him.
- Why does the US lead Third-World countries in infant deaths?
- Jason Quit had no idea as he ate his Cheerios Tuesday at 7:45 A.M. that he would face death not once, but twice, before dinner time.
- The candy craze now accounts for a quadrupling of your family's dentist bills.
- You can save $10,000 per year on your son or daughter's college tuition.
- Would you buy this car if it promised to save you $15,000 this year on gasoline?

SELECT STRONG WORDS

act	now
assign	only
exclusive	please
feature	readers
first	research
learn	results
new	survey

BUILD EFFECTIVE PHRASES

findings revealed

first time

new facts

new research indicates

new survey

recent research

research results

secrets revealed

survey results

budding trend

CREATE STRONG SENTENCES

New research indicates medical treatment for AIDS is near a cure.

Mom learns how to raise thankful kids.

Secret hooker life of Mom is revealed.

Is this the cure for breast cancer?

More than 100 pounds lost in just 20 weeks with this diet.

Lifting cans of soup results in strong bones.

Will the new transit system eliminate the brown cloud?

Tuesday is a free day at the zoo for kids.

Do you have the kind of blood that will save a child's life?

Here's a new way to give the gift of life on your lunch hour.

Do you know how to apologize?

Forgiveness isn't about forgetting.

Pitch Letter

[Emailed]
(Date)

April Meehan, Senior Editor

Dear April:

I suggest a feature story on Blanchard Banks of Detroit, who, at the age of sixty-four, has just read his first book ever to his granddaughter, Jasmine, age four. "It's a miracle," the silver-haired man explains.

Blanchard began life as a farmworker in Mississippi and migrated to Detroit as a young man in 1940. Working in a factory, he managed to get by without reading, by meticulously following instructions and occasionally asking someone to "clarify" written communications.

When Marks Industries, where Blanchard works, joined the fight for literacy, Blanchard signed up for the after-work tutoring program offered at his local library. In June he will graduate in a special program to be attended by several members of the U.S. Congress.

In the Marks Industries program alone, fifty people have already been able to experience the joy of learning to read. It wasn't easy for Blanchard and the others to admit their reading deficiencies; it wasn't easy to overcome the obstacles of getting enough volunteer instructors and a suitable meeting place; but the Marks program is making a big difference. In fact there are now plans to expand it into a fifteen-state partnership with local community organizations.

I believe your readers would be inspired by Blanchard's story. There are great photo opportunities here. I'll give you a call in a few days to discuss your interest.

Sincerely,

Samantha Gerkins

60

FUND-RAISING

Cast your bread upon the water, and it may come back to you with peanut butter and jelly.

—ANONYMOUS

The fund-raising letter is a sales letter with a heart tug. But it must be tempered with the kind of persuasive and cogent writing that brings results without broadcasting that it is selling the reader something.

Many charities compete for the same dollars, and unsolicited direct mail has gone beyond the saturation point. Frustrated, people often toss requests for donations after only a cursory glance, or less. To be successful, a fund-raising letter must be part of a larger campaign that has established the organization as one with worthy goals and a demonstrated accountability for donations. It helps a great deal if the charity is immediately recognized as a good cause.

For economy, the letter's recipients should be people who have demonstrated interest in the charity's work or who have track records of giving to similar charities. Then the letter must deliver a simple, concise, and convincing message.

All these factors make the fund-raising letter very difficult to master.

DECIDE TO WRITE

You'll use this special communication to:
- Elicit monetary or other contributions
- Request volunteers
- Invite contributors to a fund-raising event (also see "Invitations," page 65)

THINK ABOUT CONTENT
- Grab the attention of the reader in the opening sentence.
- Identify the charity and its purpose.
- Convince the reader of the need to contribute.
- Define exactly how the reader's contribution will be used.
- Explain the benefits of the reader's contribution to charity recipients.
- Explain the benefits the reader will receive by contributing.
- Make the act of contributing as easy as possible.
- Use language and a tone that indicate that you expect the reader to help.

- Tune your message to your reader as closely as possible.
- Use positive, clear, and concise language that focuses on benefits to the reader. Rather than writing "Jose Perez won't eat tonight unless you give," it is far better to say "Helping children like Jose Perez feels good" or "You can make sure Jose Perez eats tonight . . ."
- Define specifically your contribution request.

    There are several ways you can help:
    — Return a check for $15 or more.
    — Check the box that says, "I volunteer to be a telephone operator one hour a week."
    — Call 555-0123 and tell the operator you have an item to be picked up Tuesday for the auction.

- Remember, your message should entice the reader to act immediately: "Return your contribution in this envelope now to help." Statistics indicate there's a dramatic drop in response if action is delayed by the reader.
- Construct your letter using informal language, including contractions, some short sentences (but don't make it choppy or staccato), questions, and perhaps even acceptable slang to achieve a conversational tone. Contractions are useful: *isn't, don't, can't, won't, isn't,* and *we're.* But don't overdo it. Some short, useful sentences include these:
    — "We're almost there!"
    — "Just $50,000 more and we'll start building."
    — "Can you believe it?"
    — "You've been wonderful!"
    — "And now for the final lap!"
    — "We need your help."
- Include a mission statement. Briefly and exactly tell the reader what you want to accomplish: "In just three months, we have raised $500,000 of the $5 million needed to build the new Lily Women's Center."
- Expect the reader to fulfill his or her commitment. If this is a letter in a series that follows a pledge on the part of the reader, you might say, "Your pledge is important to finishing the job."

- Remind the reader of his or her pledge, but don't let your letter slip into a harping, pressuring, or threatening tone.
- Use a postscript to attract additional attention. By placing a punchy, handwritten (script) point outside the body of the letter (perhaps even in colored ink), you may create a strong emphasis.

ELIMINATE WRONG MESSAGES

- Don't let your letter take on negative, moralizing, or guilt-inducing tones. Givers want to feel their motivation is prompted by their own best intentions.
- Be sure your letter doesn't have a slick or patronizing tone. Test it on a number of readers to be sure it rings genuine and sincere.
- Don't include more than two inserts. Too many inserts dilute and clutter your message, prompting the reader to classify your letter as junk mail.
- Avoid creating undue pressure, but make it easy for the reader to respond.
- Don't use gimmicks that will detract from or cheapen your message.
- Don't pressure contributors to give you the names of friends and associates.

CONSIDER SPECIAL SITUATIONS

- Target your letter to a specific audience. If a form letter is sent, be sure it is tailored to a carefully selected audience to increase your response. Then change it and tailor it to another audience.
- Computers make it possible to personalize form letters to recipients. Use this approach, if possible.
- Email fund-raising can easily be viewed as spam, and therefore isn't usually effective as a first communication plan. However, it can work nicely as a follow-up plan, after responders have indicated they want to be contacted by email. You may want to create a newsletter or progress email memo or blog approach to keep contributors involved.

- Successful direct-mail solicitation receives a 2.5 percent positive response. A 5 percent response is excellent. This illustrates how important it is to be very selective about the people to whom you send a fund-raising letter. And it also makes a vital statement about the necessity to write an effective letter.

- It's important to have contributors feeling good about giving, even if it involves a dozen mailings.

- Enfranchise contributors, bringing them into the action. Make sure they feel a part of the fund-raising: "We've almost met our goal."

- Fund-raising requires a multifaceted approach to be successful. Appealing for contributions through direct mail is only a small part of it. Many other parts of your campaign, like effective public relations efforts, will be needed to help make your fund-raising letters successful. (See "Announcement," page 21; "Opinion Editorial," page 375; and "Press Release," page 350.)

- Fund-raising often involves functions like luncheons, gala events, dinners, dances, and the like. Use the appropriate invitations for contributors. (See "Invitations," page 65.)

SELECT A FORMAT

- Invite readership with an appealing letter layout. Your letter appears shorter and more inviting, for example, if you select a typeface that is easy to read and has space between the lines of type. Indenting also creates an impression of being attractive, open, and easy to read.

- Individualize your letter, if possible, by using the reader's name in the inside address and salutation. This is true, too, of memos and other updates you send by email. Personalize them whenever it's practical.

- Have the letter signed by the highest and/or most recognized official of the charity organization. Respected celebrity endorsements can also be helpful.

- Consider using a postscript to attract additional attention and get action.

- Design and create a website where contributors can always go to respond with a contribution. This, too, will give you a venue to keep fresh information flowing to contributors, and to help build interest and participation. One example might be to show the donations building toward the goal. Another might be an update on research for a cure. Another might be a blog that keeps fresh information flowing, and reader interest high.

SELECT POWER WORDS

assist	partner
benefit	plan
build	power
change	prosper
charity	receive
construct	reconstruct
contribute	relief
cooperate	rescue
donate	reward
drive	share
encourage	sponsor
endow	survive
generous	thanks
grant	tribute
gratitude	urgent
heartfelt	volunteer
participate	

WRITE EFFECTIVE PHRASES

almost complete

continue to work

count on you

direct help

donate what you can

give a helping hand

help is needed

here's how you

join with us

make a difference

meeting the need

near our goal

only need three more contributions of

open your heart

plan to contribute

respond today

send your donation

three-fourths complete

volunteer to make

will you commit

you can help

your contribution

your generosity

WRITE STRONG SENTENCES

Start with an action verb and then construct lean sentences with a strong message:

Let's all work together to eliminate this devastating disease.

Only $500,000 remains to be contributed before we can begin work.

Your contribution can help send 50 underprivileged children to Cower's Camp for a week.

Please use the enclosed, stamped envelope to return your check, and thank you for your help.

Share your love with others.

Contributors of $5,000 or more will become listed in next year's program under Patrons of the Library.

Friends of the Library enjoy several special privileges.

Why not send your contribution today?

Books are a wonderful thing to contribute!

BUILD EFFECTIVE PARAGRAPHS

Let's eradicate this debilitating disease. Researchers believe one more year at a cost of $1,500,000 will produce the needed vaccine. We're that close to a solution. Won't you help with a contribution of $25 or more?

You can help now in two ways: (1) write Senator Allen Dirkson and congressional representative Alice Schroeder, and state your objection to the legislation, and (2) return your check for $25 today.

Operating Angel's Kitchen takes $3,500 and 400 volunteer-hours each week. You can help by signing up to serve for one or more of the time slots indicated below, and by returning your contribution of $25, $50, or $75.

United Foundation will be canvassing neighborhoods again this year for contributions. Will you help?

The Sisters Against Crime meeting to organize for this year's campaign will be Tuesday, September 10, at 7:30 P.M., in the Logan School Auditorium. Please call Sarah Crimpton, 555-0123, and tell her you'll be on hand to help.

It's spring again and time to get our after-school program organized. Without your volunteer efforts, the children of Burton Township will not have this enriching experience.

Your contribution to the Dempster Project has made it possible to make the recreation program a reality. Thank you.

EDIT, EDIT, EDIT

Fine-tuning this communication will increase your response. If possible, have several other people read your communication and check for tone and typos. Always run your spell-check, and read the communication aloud to hear any words that don't ring true to your message.

Community Fund-Raiser

[Mailed]
(Date)

Dear Alice:

This Holiday Season we will again sponsor the Noel House Tour to benefit the Opera Society. Since last year's tour raised $650,000, which went directly and completely to the opera, we felt it was extremely profitable. Our contribution paid for the renovation work that's been done to the Opera House. A complete breakdown of how the money was spent is itemized on the enclosed sheet.

This year our goal is $675,000 for enlarging the stage area and providing two new sets. We believe we can meet this goal with all our members' help. Contributions from florists, designers, and interior decorators are already rolling in.

The Tour Committee is requesting that eight members of the Park Hill neighborhood volunteer their homes for the tour, 50 members volunteer to function as tour guides and receptionists, and 225 members volunteer to serve on the preparation subcommittees.

We know you'll want to help. Please return the volunteer card indicating your choices, or go to the website, COC.com and sign up.

Sincerely,

Roger Wagner

Alumni-Related Fund-Raiser

[Mailed]
(Date)

Dear Manny Lester:

The Hi Phis are again sponsoring the "Gifts for Children" program this Holiday Season. Last year your generous gift helped provide a party and an individual gift for all 90 children hospitalized on Ward B at Children's Hospital.

Can we count on you this season?

Please indicate your contribution, and return the enclosed card now so the preparations can begin. Thank you.

Sincerely,

Sally Strutter
Chair

Request for Volunteers and Money

[Mailed]
(Date)

Dear Sally:

High Achievers has turned the lives of 79 children around in just two years. The first year we sponsored the program, school officials reported that the 79 children who attended were at high risk of dropping out of school. The second year the number was only 20 of those children. This year all 79 are performing far above average, and are committed to completing their high school studies.

You can thank yourself and all the volunteers from Chambers Corporation who dedicated after-school hours to be tutors at Elbert Middle School.

This year we're taking on an even bigger challenge. In order to purchase needed supplies and operate a store where students can purchase things with their "achievement dollars," we are asking for money contributions. Chamber Corporation's president, Robert Elliot, has pledged a matching $35,000 for the program if we raise that amount and enlist volunteers for 4,000 tutoring hours.

It's a great way to be involved in our community—and to make a difference in a child's life. Please put your commitment on the enclosed card and return it today.

Yours truly,

Angel Martin

P.S. Production has already pledged $2,000 and 600 tutoring hours. Can your department top that?

Call for Time and Commitment Pledge

[Mailed]
(Date)

Dear Jim:

Little League time is here! And we need to get organized!

We already have enough kids to field 14 teams. That means, of course, we will need another $3,500 for equipment and supplies, and a total of 60 coaching volunteers. At this moment, we have $1,250 and 10 head-coach volunteers.

The team families committee feels it can raise over $3,500 at the bake sale next weekend, so that leaves the coaching volunteers.

This promises to be Little League's best year ever. But we'll need your help. Please call Joe Baker at 415-555-0123 by March 15 to sign up.

Yours truly,

Sparky Henderson

P.S. The Jaguars are determined to take it all this year, Jim!

Special Invitation to Fund-Raising Event

[Mailed]
(Date)

Dear Andrea:

The North Bay Arthritis Foundation counts on you. In fact, if it weren't for you and our other 500 members, the Foundation would have been unable to fund the Remus Research Project last year. Your help meant that we got closer to finding a cure for this debilitating disease.

Our goal for this year is to again fund the Remus Research Project. (See the encouraging progress report enclosed, and check the "Progress" column on the website, RemusResearch.com.) We will all need to work together like last year—even harder—to achieve our goal of $500,000.

This year's art show, Contemporary Artists of America, will include 200 pieces of art by contemporary artists. It's the second largest show of its type in the country. A blind-drawing, fixed-price sale will be conducted at the opening gala at the Historical Society Hall on September 15. Works not sold that night will be available on a first-come basis starting the following day.

Tickets for the gala will be $125. The fee will include a cocktail party, a souvenir medallion designed by Hugo Halsey of Santa Fe, admission to a private preview of the exhibit, and an art seminar at the downtown Chilcott on September 12.

Please call 708-555-0123 to order your group tickets today and sign up online to contribute in a number of other ways.

Sincerely,

Horatio Gailbladder

P.S. This year we will have 75 of the artists attending the gala.

Plea for Food Contributions

[Mailed]
(Date)

Dear Alice:

Channel 4 is starting its Fifth Annual Holiday Basket Drive on Thursday, October 17. Trucks will be parked at convenient locations listed on the back of this letter.

Your help last year meant that 1,900 families throughout the metro area got holiday baskets. This year you and other captains requested we make our appeal to clubs, schools, and businesses as well as to the general public. And that's why you're getting this letter.

Won't you organize the efforts of your club to make sure the drive receives enough canned foods for 2,500 families? That's our goal.

Please list your club name and number of members on the enclosed card, selecting the type of participation you'd like to volunteer for.

Let's make this the city's brightest holiday season.

Sincerely,

Levitt Lighthorse

Fund-Raiser for Church Program

[Mailed]
(Date)

Dear Sarah and Ted Ellis:

Isn't it exciting that our church has taken the step of faith to increase our outreach by 50 percent for the coming year? On Thursday, October 10, at 7:30 p.m. we will discuss how we can exercise our faith.

Please plan to be there. Both the outreach and the increased youth activities will mean a commitment of $50,000. Split among us, each member will need to pledge to help meet this goal by helping in the planned fund-raisers, or making a donation commitment.

Please consider the choices on the enclosed pledge card, fill it out, and bring it to the meeting.

Yes, this is an exciting time to be a member of our church and have the opportunity to exercise and increase our faith.

Sincerely,

Dollie Parish

MEDIA KIT

What the mind doesn't catch,
the mind grieves after.

—JACQUES BARZUM

The media kit or press kit is a collection of written pieces in a folder used together to give editors, reporters, interviewers, and other media people background information on a subject. Usually the kits are made available to media people at large-scale, newsworthy events, and may include:

- New releases describing something that will be announced at the event
- Biographies of speakers
- Backgrounder or organization brochure
- Copy of speech delivered at the event
- Q&A
- Photo

At large trade shows, regional or national book fairs, political meetings or sports events, there will usually be a central press room where all participants may make such information available to media people.

Keep the pieces to a few, comprehensive ones to maximize impact. Don't clutter the media kit with nonessential pieces.

See the chapter for each of the elements that may be included in the press or media kit: "Backgrounder," page 360; "Bibliography," page 366; "Biography," page 358; "Brochure," page 380; "Press Release," page 350; "Questions and Answers," page 355; "Fact Sheet," page 362; and "Timeline," page 364.

Media Kit Sample

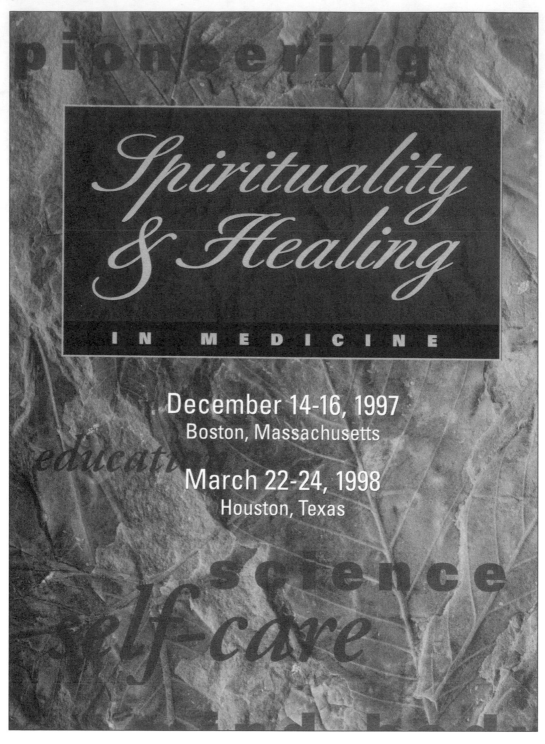

John Templeton Foundation—The Mind/Body Medical Institute at Beth Israel Deaconess Medical Center—Harvard Medical School "Spirituality & Healing in Medicine II." Public Relations Society of America 1997 Silver Anvil Award–winning entry in the category of special events and observances.

Backgrounder Included in Media Kit

- At the time of discharge, hip-fracture patients who are religious walk longer distances and have less depression than non-religious patients do (Pressman et al 1990).

- Rel
  fast
  199

- If p
  198

- He
  reli

- Ho
  affi
  san
  reli

- Bla
  con

- Pat
  pai

- He
  sta

Religio
beliefs.
180:67

"Syste
epidem
792-79

"Throu
spirit i
practic
the po
Healin

Clinical Study Data
Spirituality, Religion and Healing in Medicine and Health Care

Our growing understanding of the biological basis for disease and healing, combined with modern medications and procedures, have produced dramatic improvements in mortality and morbidity in the United States. Yet, our current state of knowledge does not fully account for the individual experience of many patients that mind-body interactions, and specifically, spirituality and religion have resulted in better health outcomes. Survey data suggest that most Americans and their physicians see this connection as viable (Time/CNN poll, Time Magazine, 1995; Templeton Foundation Family Physician survey, 1996. Both surveys by Yankelovich Partners).

The value of research on the impact of spirituality and healing can be seen as two-fold. First is the potential for more targeted and effective use of such interventions, with improved health and potential cost savings as the result. Second, many patients are intuitively aware of the power of spirituality and religion and desire validation of their natural inclination. For example:

- 40% of hospitalized patients say their religious faith is the most important factor that enables them to cope (Koenig, 1997). This has also been documented for patients with gynecologic cancer (Roberts et al 1997), other types of malignancies (Kaczorowski 1989), endstage renal disease (O'Brien 1982), open-heart surgery (Oxman et al 1995), cardiac transplantation (Harris et al 1995), Alzheimer's disease (Whitlatch et al 1992) and health problems related to aging (Conway 1985).

- A prospective, matched-control study of persons living in religious kibbutzim versus secular kibbutzim in Israel, demonstrated pervasive morbidity and mortality advantages to those who led religious lives, even in comparison with those in a tightly-knit community without religious focus (Kark et al 1996).

While the scientific literature on spirituality, religion and healing is growing and is highlighted below through both epidemiologic studies and clinical trials, ongoing work should produce more results over the next few years.

Studies that Demonstrate Clinical Effectiveness

- Patients are three times more likely to survive open-heart surgery if they depend on their religious faith (Oxman et al 1995).

- Over a 28-year study period, the risk of dying was almost 25% less (35% in women) for frequent religious service attendees, after controlling for health practices, social ties, and well being (Strawbridge et al 1997).

- Similarly, those who attend religious services, at least once per week, have been shown to have stronger immune system functioning (Koenig et al 1997a) and maintain their physical activity significantly longer (Idler & Kasl 1997), compared with less frequent attendees.

62

PRESS RELEASE

A word to the wise is not sufficient if it doesn't make any sense.

—JAMES THURBER

The press release is a vital tool—the workhorse of any personal promotion, or organization's public relations program. Used properly, it can raise your visibility in the public eye, help create a positive image, and assist you in marketing your own or your organization's services or products.

A press release should describe an event or new facts of importance: a personnel appointment or promotion, the release of a new product or service, a new business opening, major expansion, reorganization, an achievement, or a change in management or philosophy.

Write releases in journalistic style, answering *who, what, when, where, why,* and *how.* Present the information in order from the most important to least important, from the central idea to specific facts. Imagine that an editor will take a pair of scissors and clip from the bottom of your release. To keep the essential facts in place, include all critical information in the first paragraph——the first sentence, if possible. The press release should be objective, clear, and easy to read, and it should not include extra words or superlatives. Photos, if used, should be carefully identified on the back or with a paper glued to the bottom. Attach the photo to the release with a paper clip, taking care to use a clip that will not mark the photo. When sending the press release by email, the photo may be sent as an attached file.

No cover letter is necessary when mailing the press release, and the format described in this chapter should be strictly adhered to. When your press release is emailed, you may want to preface it by a very short personal message to help distinguish it from spam.

THINK ABOUT CONTENT
- Determine what about your subject is *newsworthy*—new information. Ask yourself:
  — Who will care?
  — Will the release answer the questions it will undoubtedly raise?
  — Will it advance my objectives?
  — Have I gathered all the facts and double-checked them for accuracy?
- Determine if the release is hard news (personnel appointments, new products, company openings, new services, events, research or survey results), or soft or feature news (human-interest items, business trends, ongoing research or projects).

- Create an outline to ensure a logical and clear flow of information. Answer the five w's: *what, who, where, when,* and *why,* and then answer *how.*
- Use the journalistic style of the inverted pyramid: the most vital information should come first. The rest of the information should follow in order of its importance. Include all critical information in the first paragraph; the first sentence if possible.
- The lead is all-important. It should read like the lead of a news story.
- The personnel appointment should focus first on the responsibilities of the appointee. Then it should give the appointee's background.
  1. State the appointee's title and credit the announcement to the proper organization official.
  2. Give the name of the person to whom the appointee will report and the start date.
  3. State the appointee's responsibilities. (In the second paragraph, you may want to use a quote by the organization official.)
  4. Describe the appointee's professional experience and educational background. Social and personal information like marital status, professional affiliation, charity, and/or social affiliations is sometimes included.
  5. State if the position is new. You may also want to give the name of the person being replaced if the circumstances are positive.
- Rewrite and edit for clarity, trying to keep your release to one or two pages. Make sure your copy is clear and concise.
- Define any technical terms.
- Quotations add interest and lend personal authority. Use some if possible, but only those that provide relevant information. If you use a quotation—and be sure to quote the correct official/authority here—check it with that person for approval. If you obtained a direct quote in an interview, you should still get the person's approval to quote before using.
- Samples, photos, and review copies (books, CDs, DVDs, etc.) add interest to your release, so include them when it's practical. If not, make an event, press conference, or interview available to the editor.

CONSIDER SPECIAL SITUATIONS

- Send the release to a specific person if possible. If you cannot, address the news release to a particular editor, for example, business editor, social editor, sports editor. It is worth calling major media such as daily newspapers or television stations to learn the correct person's name, title, department, and specific address (4th floor, Department 4-A). It's often worth a telephone call to that editor stating you are sending a press release.
- The official statement, for use in crisis situations or when controversial situations arise, should be developed and distributed to the press and internal organization representatives to help control rumors and eliminate misinformation. Timeliness and the frequency of these reports are key to keeping the media informed, eliminating the start or growth of false reports, and preventing public anxiety caused by misinformation. Obviously, these are most often sent by email to provide the fastest means to keep the media informed.
- It is extremely helpful to have a crisis public relations team ready to act in emergencies like a flood, fire, earthquake, or other disaster. This team should draw up and have in place a crisis plan. Preparations for disasters should allow you to create and send releases from another location on official letterhead if faxing or mail is also necessary.
- Use electronic distribution of releases and updates—fax or email— when the editor or reporter makes subsequent communication requests.
- Check and note publicity policies of the particular media. Some organizations do not welcome unsolicited emails, faxes, or other electronically transmitted information.
- Consider these additional factors in crisis situations:
  — Estimate the audience scope and send releases to local, state, regional, national, and international media as appropriate.
  — Write in a brief, concise style, using bullets so the facts can be easily pulled out.

— Type in the time after the date on page one, and put the date and time on every page. (Exceptions to this rule are press releases that aren't time-sensitive such as new-book press releases.)

— Add "Issued by: [person's name]" or "Contact: [person's name]" with a telephone number.

— Include contact name and telephone number(s) on a 24-hour basis.

— Issue updates as frequently as new information is available.

— Get legal approval, if possible, before releasing.

— Keep a release log covering when, and to whom, releases were made.

— Use recorded telephone messages, and update them, if possible, for incoming calls.

— Set up a schedule of briefings.

— Make videotapes and/or live reports from the disaster scene available on a website, if possible.

— Use audiotaped official statements for radio, if possible.

— Have press kits with background information about the organization available, if possible. Have all this information available on a website, if possible.

USE THE CORRECT FORMAT

- All releases must be consistent, be sent on official letterhead, and look professional. For those emailed, use standard format.

- For mailed or faxed press releases, leave the top third of the first page blank for the editor to write his or her headline.

- All press releases must have six key elements. Follow the placement of these elements as illustrated in the samples.

  1. A *date* to indicate when the release was issued. Indicate when the information should be made public: "FOR IMMEDIATE RELEASE" or "FOR RELEASE ON [or AFTER] (date) and/or (time)."

  2. A press release should have a *title*. Type "NEWS RELEASE" in capitals at the center of the first page.

  3. A *contact* appears two lines below the title; type "CONTACT" flush left with the margin (or as illustrated in the samples). Include the name of the contact person for the release along with a telephone or fax number, or both. The name of the organization may also be included.

  4. A *headline* (subject line) appears two lines below the contact, centered, and usually in caps. If possible, include the company's business and the subject of the release: GRAND OPENING OF DOODLE'S HAIR SALON. Try to catch the reader's attention. This is your chance to advertise your story to the editor so he or she will decide to print it. If the story is complicated, use a subhead as well: Free Styling on January 10 by New York's Best.

  5. The *dateline* appears two lines below the subject line and is indented two spaces. It is composed of the city (and, if necessary, the state, in caps). The date may appear in upper and lower case, followed by a double dash.

  6. The *copy* begins on the same line, immediately after the dateline.

- The release should be typed on a single side of 8½ by 11-inch paper, double-spaced with a minimum of one inch margins all around. Exceptions to this rule do exist. In some industries, like publishing, an 8½ by 14-inch paper is sometimes used.

- If more than one page is required, center and type "(MORE)" or "(CONTINUED)" in capitals at the bottom of page one, and begin the next page flush left on the margin with a one-word title and page number: "Doodles 2."

- Short paragraphs are best.

- Use capitalization sparingly.

- Be consistent.

- At the end of the news release, center one of the following to indicate the end: # # # or (END).

- Use the active voice if possible.

- Write in an objective tone.

- Use simple, clear, and concise sentences.

- Edit. Eliminate all unnecessary words.

- Include the same, complete information when sending by email. Standards of spacing and arrangement are, of course, not as prescribed.

Hotel Summer Rates

[Emailed]

FOR IMMEDIATE RELEASE

Media Contact: Andria Zee
Best Choice Public Relations
212-555-0123
andria@bestchoice.com

Mexico Rare Hotels Announce Summer Savings

PUERTO VALLARTA, MEXICO July 15, 2006 — Mexico Rare Hotels, a collection of 23 small, boutique hotels in 24 destinations throughout the Mexican Republic, announces Sizzling Summer Savings at one of its eclectic lodgings within the collection by calling 1-800-555-0123 or online at www.mexicorarehotels.com.

EL CASSANTOS (Savings of 45%)

El CASSANTOS is a remarkable getaway that combines unique architecture inspired by Mexican masters with adventure, artistry, and the tranquility of nature. Spacious and luxurious accommodations include a freeform swimming pool and a variety of leisure activities, including horseback riding, water sports, and a luscious spa facility. Rates range from $250 per room, per night for a resort-view room to $1,500 per room, per night for a 3-bedroom casita.

This special is valid for travel from June 30 to September 30, 2006. For an additional person, add $25 USD to the rate (breakfast included), 17% tax and 5% services charge not included, subject to availability. The Bed & Breakfast Special is for a minimum stay of two nights and includes a full breakfast for two (adults only) and a massage (pay for one; get one free).

All rates and information can be found at www.mexicorarehotels.com where travelers and travel professionals can research and reserve the new hotels immediately and get extensive destination information, rates, and packages. Personal assistance is available in the US and Canada toll-free: 1-800-555-0123; Mexico toll-free 01-150-0123; or calling from other countries to +(00)-444-555-0123. Mexico Rare Hotels can also be reached by email at info@mexicorarehotels.com or via fax at +(00) 445-555-0123. The hotels are presented in the company's full-color directory, which is available on request.

#

PHOTOS AVAILABLE

For additional information, contact Andria Zee
Choice Public Relations, 212-555-0123
andria@choicespr.com

New Website Service

[Emailed]

CONTACT: Mark Little
mark@marklittlepr.com
202-555-0123

FOR IMMEDIATE RELEASE

YourTravel.com, Top Hotel Reservations Aggregator, Adds Amenities Filters to Website

BOSTON, MASSACHUSETTS (July 15, 2006) — Internet hotel room shoppers just got a boost with a new user-friendly tool with seven new amenities filters to search its popular website, including:
• Dataport
• Wireless Internet
• High Speed Internet
• Indoor Pool
• Outdoor Pool
• Fitness Facilities
• Pets Allowed

"These are now in place in Orlando, Phoenix, Dallas, San Francisco, and Chicago," said Manuel Casca, president of YourTravel of Minneapolis, Minnesota, the world's largest aggregators of hotel reservations and one of the world's fastest growing aggregators of hotel reservation information.

These new amenities filters join six basic search filters—distance, hotel, name (keywords), price, hotel rating, and preferred websites.

In addition to the new amenities filters, YourTravel has expanded the room and rate information when the user clicks the BookIt button. This expanded feature allows the customer to view all room and rates available from each website, not just the lowest, creating more booking flexibility.

"As more Americans are traveling in a market with increasing room rates, getting the right price at the right hotel is more and more important," adds Casca. "These new filters will make the customer's job much easier."

• YourTravel.com provides the only online, side-by-side hotel price comparison.
• The customer is able to search the best price from more than 20 different travel websites.
• The ease of use and the ability to locate the best price benefit both the business and leisure traveler, saving time and stretching their travel budget.
• The four-year-old company serves business and leisure travelers with hotel information for 3,250 cities in 104 countries, from Albania to Zimbabwe. Information from more than 20 different travel websites has been compiled into unbiased price comparisons with the lowest price highlighted. While YourTravel highlights the lowest price for each hotel, the user is able to select any travel website to book a room. Casca adds, "We don't just return the lowest rate, we return the most options in one search and then leave it in the hands of the consumer to make the choice."

# # #

Contact:
Mark Little
mark@marklittlepr.com
212-555-0123

QUESTIONS AND ANSWERS

*The more we proceed by plan the more
effectively we may hit by accident.*

—FRIEDRICH DÜRRENMATT

The question and answer, or Q&A, promotes understanding of a topic. It anticipates questions editors or general readers may have, states them, and provides the answers or explanations. It most commonly accompanies a complicated press release, and is also an effective tool for distribution within an organization to help personnel deal consistently with press questions.

In a number of forms—often just the questions—the Q&A is distributed to radio or television talk-show hosts or interviewers to interest them in interviewing a person and to help direct the interview into comprehensive areas of public interest.

The key to an effective Q&A is doing the proper research to learn what your public wants to know and what information the issuer wants to disseminate. A second form, FAQ (frequently asked questions), is often used in the same manner on websites, or in printed form.

When you are interested in proposing a topic of potential interest for a radio or television interview, e.g., to propose an author be interviewed about his new book or to reveal findings of a research project, use a modified form called "Talking Points." Instead

of using only questions and answers, the "Talking Points" format may also highlight salient issues and then list the supporting points below them.

DECIDE TO WRITE

Use this communication to:
- Suggest questions of general interest to an interviewer
- Promote an author of a book, play, research finding, etc.
- Stimulate reporters' interest
- Simplify and address common questions of a complicated news release

THINK ABOUT CONTENT

- Use a thought-provoking title to capture interest.
- Develop a list of the questions most likely to be asked about the topic. For an advanced personal computer, for example, the questions might include:
  — What advantages does it offer over other products now available?
  — When will it be available for home use?

—Where can it be purchased in our area?

—How easy will it be to operate?

—What kind of setup, instruction, etc. will it require?

—What will the price be?

—Who will buy it?

—Are other companies making a competitive product?

—What are the company's first-year sales projections?

—How long did it take to develop this product?

—How will this make consumers' lives better?

- Write short yet comprehensive answers to the questions for the people who will be interviewed.

- Be sure to have both questions and answers approved by the appropriate individual or organization officials before you distribute them to the media.

ELIMINATE WRONG MESSAGES

- Do not include technical terms without defining them.

- Remove all jargon.

CONSIDER SPECIAL SITUATIONS

Be sure the people who will be interviewed are prepared. Rehearse with them.

SELECT A FORMAT

- If the Q&A, FAQ, or Talking Points are sent with a press release, the design of the two documents should be complementary. They should be on matching or coordinating 8½ by 11-inch letterhead in the same format, with the same typeface.

- If the Q&A, FAQ, or Talking Points document is sent by email, it should be included within the email, and not as an attachment (unless requested). This increases the chances it will be read.

- Many other formats for explaining or distilling information may be used to create interest. Oversized postcards printed in glossy four-color ink might be used for a list of interview questions, for example.

Author Interview Talking Points

[Mailed on 8½ by 11-inch stationery]
CONTACT:
Sandra E. Lamb
(303) 555-0123
Email: sandylamb@email.com

Q&A

Suggested Topics

Television and Radio Producers' Reference

Sandra E. Lamb, author of *Personal Notes: How to Write from the Heart for Any Occasion*, enjoys outstanding reviews for bringing fresh wisdom and wit in answers radio and television audiences love. Perhaps your audience would be interested in hearing some of her "pithy," "excellent," and "knowledgeable" takes on one of these subjects:

Topic #1: How and what do you write to a friend or coworker going through bad times?

Talking Points
1. Write as soon as you hear and have confirmed the bad news, but if time has lapsed since the loss, write anyway.
2. Open with a simple, strong sentence expressing how sorry you are, naming the person, loss, or event you're writing about: "I was so sorry to hear that you lost your dear Harry, and my thoughts are with you at this time of sorrow," or "I was sorry to hear you are no longer director of operations."
3. Relate a fond memory in the case of a deceased person, if possible.
4. Offer specific help: "May I take over the Adams project until you get back to the office? I'll call on Thursday, to see what would be helpful, and if you have any special instructions."
5. Close on a warm note.

(more)

Author Interview Talking Points . . . *Continued*

Topic #2: Is your employer watching your email?

Talking Points

1. Your personal emails written at work can be read by your employer. The courts have usually found in favor of the employer owning emails sent from the workplace.
2. Personal emails written anywhere are not private. This is a very public forum, and as yet messages are not encrypted but float forever in cyberspace.
3. Know and follow your organization's rules for email use. Every organization should establish rules, and make those rules known to all employees.
4. Never violate someone's copyright by cutting-and-pasting from his or her email to send to someone else. You must have permission to use parts or all of someone else's email. The same rule applies to forwarding someone else's email.
5. Follow my 10 Golden Rules of Email to stay out of email interpersonal conflicts. Recognize when a message requires a human moment, and therefore a face-to-face meeting. Understand the communication bandwidth, and where email fits. Follow my rules of Netiquette.

Topic #3: Do you rate an A+ for E-manners?

Talking Points

1. First take the Email Genius Quiz. True or false?
   — Email is a great substitute for a face-to-face meeting, so if I don't want to have one, I can email.
   — If I wouldn't say it in person, I can email it.
   — Email's best feature is the ability to cut-and-paste and forward messages I get from other people or to forward jokes and files.
   — It's best to use instant email when I need an instant answer.
2. If you answered TRUE to any of these, you'll want to hear my instructions on how you can get into the Genius category. I'll explain why these practices are not only rude but also can get you a failing grade in E-manners.

(more)

Author Interview Talking Points . . . *Continued*

3. When should you email, when should you telephone, when should you voicemail, and when should you send a letter? Understand where email comes in the communication bandwidth. (Email is good for distanced business associates and to give information or ask a question when you don't need an immediate response.)
4. When shouldn't you use email? Personal issues shouldn't be the subjects of emails. Don't use emails when you need that human moment. Don't use email for messages with lots of emotional content.
5. How do you make your email more effective? Be brief without being abrupt. Keep messages to one subject and one screen. Make sure the subject line is precise and complete. Follow the sender's style. Check content, spelling, and punctuation before hitting the Send button.
6. Avoid mistakes, faux pas, and minefields. Sarcasm and humor aren't wise choices. Acronyms should be used with caution, and emoticons should be avoided.

Here are some other topics Sandra is prepared to talk about:

T: Why don't people RSVP? What should I do?
T: No one writes thank yous anymore. Why should I?
T: How can I teach my child to write thank yous?
T: How do I put real power in my resume?
T: How do I keep negativity out of my bad-news letter?
T: How do I write an attention-getting resume cover letter?
T: How do I say I'm sorry in writing?
T: How do I write a red-hot love letter?

To schedule an interview, CONTACT:

Sandra E. Lamb
303-555-0123, or
Email: sandylamb@email.com
(Please state "Interview Request" in the email subject line.)

###

64
BIOGRAPHY

*Let another man praise thee,
and not thine own mouth.*

—PROVERBS 27:2

 The biography or "bio" is an explanatory piece designed to give background information on a person. There are basically two forms to follow. The first is the newspaper or journalistic style. It is simple and comprehensive. The second form, a feature biography, gives information more as a personality profile.

Either piece may be accompanied by a fact sheet or timeline (see pages 362 and 364, respectively).

DECIDE TO WRITE
Use this piece:
- To get special media coverage
- As part of a media kit
- To give information to someone who will introduce the person for a speech
- With a book the person has authored

THINK ABOUT CONTENT
- Develop a logical outline.
- Write a commanding lead.
- Flesh out your ideas.
- Vary and simplify sentence structure and language.
- Craft for logical flow and comprehensive coverage.

- Back up all your claims, and pay off on your lead.
- Include some human interest facts.

For the newspaper-style bio:
- Open by identifying the person by name, title, and achievements relevant to the biography's point.
- State the person's educational and professional background.
- Include or exclude personal information, such as marital status, children, and academic standing, depending upon the audience.

For the feature-style bio:
- Use a more relaxed writing style, similar to that used for a magazine profile feature.
- Add human-interest details.
- Include quotes from the person.

SELECT A FORMAT
Use 8½ by 11-inch letterhead. If the biography is to be part of a media kit or mailing, use a typeface consistent with other pieces sent at the same time.

EDIT, EDIT, EDIT
Check for consistent verb and person tenses. Proofread, proofread, proofread.

Biography

[Emailed]

John Allen, CHE
President and CEO
Good Samaritan Hospital

John Allen is the president and CEO of Good Samaritan Hospital of Kearney, Neb., one of Nebraska's largest healthcare providers. The Catholic Health Initiative-affiliated Good Samaritan has been serving the central Nebraska-northern Kansas region for 80 years. Allen was appointed president and CEO in July 2004.

Allen most recently served as the president and CEO of Spencer Hospital in Spencer, Iowa. Previously, he served as senior vice president for administration at Indiana Hospital in Indiana, Penn.; vice president of general services at Central Vermont Hospital in Barre, Vt.; administrator of Olmsted Community Hospital in Rochester, Minn.; and administrator of Story County Hospital in Nevada, Iowa.

Allen holds master's degrees in hospital administration and industrial relations from the University of Minnesota and Iowa State University, respectively, and a bachelor's in sociology from the University of Kansas.

Allen and his wife, Carol, reside in Kearney. They have two grown children.

Also see ANNOUNCEMENT, page 21; BACKGROUNDER, page 360; MEDIA KIT, page 347; PITCH, page 338; PRESS RELEASE, page 350; and TIMELINE, page 364.

65

BACKGROUNDER

*Nothing is more simple than greatness;
indeed, to be simple is to be great.*

—EMERSON

The backgrounder gives pertinent and comprehensive information about products, places, and organizations. (For writing an information piece on a person, see "Biography," page 358.) This piece should be kept to one page.

DECIDE TO WRITE
Use this piece to enable readers to understand the subject.

THINK ABOUT CONTENT
- Vary language and sentence structure.
- Be consistent in tone and use the present tense.
- Make sure the information is accurate and complete. Check several sources, when possible, for every fact included.

- Construct information paragraphs as follows:
  — In paragraph one, the lead, make an important statement, then back it up with substantiating information: "ICQ, the city's largest employer, now has 88,999 employees."
  — In paragraph two, give the scope of the announcement, and back this up with facts.
  — In paragraph three, give the history or background, and summarize the developmental steps, functions, size, structure, and operation.
  — In paragraph four, cover the organization's philosophy, including objectives, goals, priorities, new areas, research, and development.
  — In paragraph five, the conclusion, include boilerplate data like the number and location of branch offices.
- Edit and proofread.

SELECT A FORMAT
Use 8$\frac{1}{2}$ by 11-inch letterhead if the document is to be mailed.

2

Background

Avon Worldwide Fund for Women's Health

As a company dedicated to the total well-being of women everywhere, Avon has created The Avon Worldwide Fund for Women's Health. The goal of this global initiative is to improve the health of women around the world. Under this plan, Avon's operations and facilities worldwide are encouraged to develop programs that address a leading health-related problem faced by women locally.

Avon's Breast Cancer Awareness Crusade in the United States, founded in October 1993, is a program that exemplifies the goals of The Avon Worldwide Fund for Women's Health. Its mission is to provide women across the country, particularly those who are medically underserved, with access to a full range of breast cancer education and early detection screening services.

Partnerships/Collaborations

Avon's Crusade is able to offer these vital services through the formation of innovative private/non-profit/public partnerships. The organizations with whom Avon collaborates are: the YWCA of the U.S.A. and the National Alliance of Breast Cancer Organizations (NABCO), the Federal Centers for Disease Control and Prevention (CDC) and the National Cancer Institute (NCI).

YWCA of the U.S.A.'s ENCOREplus Program

Avon's partnership with the YWCA of the U.S.A. was established with assistance from the Federal Centers for Disease Control and Prevention (CDC), to create and fund ENCOREplus. This program is available to qualified YWCA Associations that want to offer women in the community a structured program of education, early detection and post-diagnosis services for breast and cervical cancer. ENCOREplus provides each Association (76 are currently participating in 30 states) with comprehensive training in outreach, health education and referral mechanisms for women, particularly those who are underserved, to medical services at little or no cost. Avon offers volunteer support to ENCOREplus programs from its national sales force of Representatives.

- more -

Avon's Breast Cancer Awareness Crusade. Public Relations Society of America 1997 Silver Anvil Award–winning public service campaign.

FACT SHEET

Prove all things; hold fast that which is good.

—1 THESSALONIANS 5:21

The fact sheet breaks down complicated or very involved information into related sections so editors, reporters, interviewers, and others can quickly find the information they want. It often accompanies a complicated news release, or is part of a media kit distributed before a press conference.

DECIDE TO WRITE
Use the fact sheet:
- As part of a media or press kit
- To accompany a complex news release

THINK ABOUT CONTENT
- First develop a comprehensive outline. For a corporation, include name and description, address, number of employees, key officers, history, developmental changes, and locations. A fact sheet for international visitors to a city, for example, should include name and location, language, population, employment, government, climate, history, hotel accommodations, meeting and convention facilities, cultural attractions, sightseeing, and events. Also include notes about customs, dress, formalities, visas, and inoculation requirements.
- Make statements clear and concise.

EDIT, EDIT, EDIT
- Be sure all facts are triple-checked, and include sources as diverse as possible.
- Final proofreading is best done by using two experienced proofreaders: a reader who reads aloud while the other proofreader checks against the printed sheet. Do this a couple of times with different readers and copy checkers when the information is critical.

Fact Sheet

We want you to feel welcome at every Mobil Friendly Serve station. Every time!

Mobil

MOBIL FRIENDLY SERVE ACADEMY AND SCHOLARSHIP PROGRAM

FACT SHEET

Mobil Friendly Serve Academy

The Mobil Friendly Serve Academy is an innovative community service initiative by Mobil Oil to provide service industry education and employment for Orlando youth.

- Implemented by 13 Neighborhood Centers throughout Orlando, 50 student interns have enrolled in the program which will provide classroom education in career skills and on-the-job training at local Mobil Friendly Serve stations.

- Student interns will receive 22 hours of classroom training on topics including Good Citizenship, Assertiveness Training, Cultural Diversity, and Interviewing Techniques.

- Student interns will receive on-the-job training beginning in May at over 25 participating Mobil Friendly Serve stations throughout Orlando.

- The company's emphasis on superior customer service makes Mobil Friendly Serve stations an ideal training ground for young people interested in service industry careers.

- As Mobil Friendly Serve interns, students will greet customers and can offer services like cleaning the windshield, checking tire air pressure or picking up soda to go at the mart.

- The Mobil Friendly Serve internship will culminate with a graduation ceremony on August 11.

- Student interns will have the opportunity to continue employment with Mobil upon completion of the program.

- more -

Mobil Corporation Friendly Serve Academy Announcement, by Mobil Corporation with the Rowland Company. Public Relations Society of America 1996 Silver Anvil Award–winning community relations program.

67
TIMELINE

If the bugle gives an indistinct sound,
who will get ready for battle?

—1 CORINTHIANS 14:8

 When information lends itself to chronological organization, a timeline format allows for easy comprehension.

Timelines usually accompany complex news releases, and they are written so that editors and reporters can quickly grasp the sequence of events.

DECIDE TO WRITE

Use this communication:
- To clarify when events happened
- As part of a media kit

THINK ABOUT CONTENT
- Order important events or developments chronologically.
- Edit concisely.

Also see BACKGROUNDER, page 360; BIBLIOGRAPHY, page 366; BIOGRAPHY, page 358; FACT SHEET, page 362; and PRESS RELEASE, page 350.

Timeline

MOBIL FRIENDLY SERVE SCHOLARSHIP PROGRAM
OFFICIAL SELECTION PROCESS AND TIMELINE

7/31

- Deadline for applications; assume last of the applications with proper postmark will arrive at City of Orlando Youth Services no later than 8/4

- As applications arrive they will be screened by a Community and Youth Serviced staffer who will verify that the applications meet all of the required criteria

8/4

- Selection Committee made up of Community and Youth Service staffers will receive quantities of applications to review

8/7

- Selection Committee will determine top 30 applicants and send those applications to members of the Awards Panel for review

- Awards Panel will be made up of members of the Community and Youth Services Advisory Board and the Neighborhood Centers Advisory Board

8/9

- Each member of the Awards Panel will select his or her choice for the 19 scholarship awards and submit those recommendations to Herb Washington

8/10

- Herb Washington will present the tally of those recommendations to the Awards Panel in a special session; determination will be made for the 19 scholarship recipients

- Notification will be sent to 19 recipients by overnight mail

- Community and Youth Services may also notify employer or volunteer project supervisor for each of the recipients so that employer or supervisor can personally notify student of award prior to arrival of notification letter

8/11

- Notification letters arrive at homes of 19 scholarship recipients

- Mobil Friendly Serve interns who are scholarship recipients will be recognized at the 8/11 graduation ceremony

8/26

- Scholarship recipients will be honored by the Mayor at the August 26 Orlando City Council Meeting

- Mobil representative will present certificates to each of the recipients at that time

Mobil Corporation Friendly Serve Academy Announcement, by Mobil Corporation with the Rowland Company. Public Relations Society of America 1996 Silver Anvil Award–winning community relations program.

68

BIBLIOGRAPHY

Devise, wit; write, pen.

—WILLIAM SHAKESPEARE

A bibliography is a useful accompaniment to a biography (bio), a resume (to list what the person has authored or written), or even a backgrounder. A bibliography may list articles and books that have been published by or about the subject. When this piece is part of a media kit or is attached to a press release, the reporter, editor, or interviewer can quickly retrieve any additional information he or she needs. When the bibliography is part of a report, document, or book, it functions to list relevant sources for further study on the subject.

A bibliography lists sources; an annotated bibliography also includes a succinct description of the listing.

DECIDE TO WRITE
Use this piece:
- As part of a person's credentials or credits
- To accompany a resume

- As background information if a person is going to be introduced
- As part of a media kit
- To document relevant sources for a report, article, or book

THINK ABOUT CONTENT
- Use a standard format, such as one described in the current edition of the *Chicago Manual of Style,* for your listings.
- Be consistent throughout.

Also see BACKGROUNDER, page 360; BIOGRAPHY, page 358; MEDIA KIT, page 347; PRESS RELEASE, page 350; RESUME, page 118; and TIMELINE, page 364.

Bibliography

Annotated Bibliography

Azhar, M.Z., Varma, S.L., & Dharap, A.S. (1994). Religious psychotherapy in anxiety disorder patients. Acta Psychiatrica Scandinavica, 90, 1-3. Randomized 62 Muslim patients with generalized anxiety disorder to either traditional treatment (supportive psychotherapy and anxiolytic drugs) or traditional treatment plus religious psychotherapy. Religious psychotherapy involved use of prayer and reading verses of the Holy Koran specific to the person's situation. Patients receiving religious psychotherapy showed significantly more rapid improvement in anxiety symptoms than those receiving traditional therapy.

Bliss JR, McSherry E, Fassett J (1995). Chaplain intervention reduces costs in major DRGs: An experimental study. In Heffernan H, McSherry E, Fitzgerald R (eds), Proceedings NIH Clinical Center Conference on Spirituality and Health Care Outcomes, March 21, 1995. Randomized 331 open-heart surgery patients to either a chaplain intervention ("Modern Chaplain Care") or usual care. Patients in the intervention group had an average 2 day shorter post-op hospitalization, resulting in an overall cost savings of $4,200 per patient.

Byrd, R.C. (1988). Positive therapeutic effects of intercessory prayer in a coronary care unit population. Southern Medical Journal, 81, 826-829. Randomized 393 coronary care patients to either intercessory prayer or control groups. Patients didn't know they were being prayed for; doctors didn't know which patients were being prayed for; and the persons who were praying didn't know the patients they were praying for and had no contact with these patients. Compared with control patients, those who were prayed for had significantly less congestive heart failure, used fewer diuretics, and fewer cardiopulmonary arrests, had less pneumonia, used fewer antibiotics and were less frequently intubated.

Chu, C.C., & Klein, H.E. (1985). Psychosocial and environmental variables in outcome of black schizophrenics. Journal of the National Medical Association, 77, 793-796. Studying 128 Black schizophrenics and their families, investigators reported that Black urban patients were less likely to be re-hospitalized if their families encouraged them to continue religious worship while they were in the hospital (p.001).

Florell JL (1973). Crisis-intervention in orthopedic surgery: Empirical evidence of the effectiveness of a chaplain working with surgery patients. Bulletin of the American Protestant Hospital Association 37(2):29-36. Randomized patients either to a chaplain intervention which involved chaplain visits for 15 minutes/day per patient or to a control group ("business as usual"). The chaplain intervention reduced length of stay by 29% (p.001), patient-initiated call on RN time to one-third, and use of PRN pain medications to one-third.

John Templeton Foundation—The Mind/Body Medical Institute at Beth Israel Deaconess Medical Center—Harvard Medical School "Spirituality & Healing in Medicine II." Public Relations Society of America 1997 Silver Anvil Award–winning entry in the category of special events and observances.

69

SPEECH

*Oratory is the power to talk people out of their
sober and natural opinions.*

—CHATFIELD

 Public speaking is an effective way to gain
recognition and demonstrate leadership. It is
also a powerful tool for informing, inspiring,
persuading, helping to set policy, and initiating action.
A speech can be both provocative and memorable,
but a speech must be easily understood to be effective. For that reason, each speech should be custom
made to fit the audience, the speaker, and the occasion.
And remember, the best speeches go beyond spoken
words; they make a connection between the speaker
and the audience.

In speech writing, the rules for written English must
be replaced with the rules for spoken, conversational
English.

THINK ABOUT CONTENT

- Before starting the actual writing process, consider the audience, its composition, number,
needs, and educational background.
- Learn all you can about the time and setting for
the speech.

- Focus on a single theme.
- Research the subject thoroughly.
- Rehearse—on site, if possible—and make adjustments and corrections as needed.
- Look for ways to refit and reuse the speech with
other audiences or to use its contents in other ways
(for example, magazine or newspaper features).

WRITE THE SPEECH

Preparing to Write
- Consider the audience and the speaker's relation-
ship to it.
  - How much background will audience mem-
bers have?
  - Will uninvolved spouses and friends attend?
  - What will the age ranges be?
  - What will the audience's reference points,
interests, and attitudes be?

- If you are writing the speech for someone else, you will want to take some additional preparatory steps.
  — Interview the person who will deliver the speech, acting like a reporter.
  — Record the session and take notes.
  — Pay attention to how the person speaks, his or her style, manner, range, pronunciation, and delivery. Note if he or she is aggressive, soft-spoken, loud, or mild-mannered.
  — Listen for natural speech patterns, colloquialisms, expressions, and mannerisms.
  — Learn the speaker's attitude about giving the speech. Learn any apprehensions or fears he or she may have.
  — Select possible topic areas, considering any ideas the speaker may have. Include issues facing your industry, anecdotes, the speaker's areas of expertise, and special concerns.
  — Calculate the length of the speech. (A typewritten, double-spaced page takes between one minute and one and a half minutes to deliver.)
  — Interview the organizers of the event to learn every detail: the setting, time of day, other speeches and speakers, presentations, awards, and other activities. Ask what the audience will be doing during the speech: Will they be eating, drinking, standing, or sitting? If possible, visit the site and examine the setup.
  — Select the specific topic of the speech. Now the speechwriter must become an ideas person. Review other speeches from other such events, perhaps from previous years if this is an annual event. Sometimes the event will dictate the speech topic and content.
  — Present the ideas for approval, if necessary.
  — Research the subject. Gather all the material you can, making sure your references are the most comprehensive and current. Use the library as well as any organization files. Interview organization officials and other experts. Review other speeches the speaker has made on this or related topics.

The Speechwriting Process

- Outline the speech. Within the basic format of introduction, body, and summary, carefully detail the points. Here, for example, is an outline for a speech for a corporation's annual sales meeting:
  1. Opening remarks and welcome
     Recognition of sales managers
     Purpose of the meeting
  2. How are we growing?
     Last year's sales figures
     This year's sales figures
     Next year's sales projections
  3. How are you growing as a salesperson?
     Looking at the numbers
     Great accomplishments
     New goals
  4. Conclusion
     New challenges ahead
     This is how we will DO IT!
- Write out the speech. Make it conversational. Include interesting details and anecdotes, and points of review. To be most effective, keep the speech simple with logical points of progression.
  — The *lead* should get the audience's attention with a compelling statement, humorous anecdote (be careful using jokes), thought-provoking question, quotation, or human-interest story. The opening must lead into the theme and set up the message.
  — The *body* of the speech should be easy to follow, progress logically, and emphasize and review major points. It must also be personalized to the audience and contain emotional content that will get them involved and make them care.
  — The *conclusion* should reiterate the major points, summarize, and tie the end to the beginning—in short, pay off on your lead. It's best to leave the audience optimistically challenged.
- Repetition can help make a speech successful by emphasizing important points.
- Use solid transitions to keep the audience's attention.
- Repeat nouns instead of using pronouns.

- Use parallel phrases for clarity and emphasis: ". . . a government of the people, by the people, for the people."
- Stick to simple words and simple, declarative sentences.
- Construct sentences with the subject and verb together. Don't use construction like "He, with fear and trepidation, crept . . ." Instead use "He crept . . ." or "With fear and trepidation, he crept . . ."
- Limit subordinate phrases and clauses. These become tedious and will lose your audience.
- Build in as much flexibility as possible so the speaker can adjust to changes during the speech, if necessary.
- Incorporate visuals to add interest and keep the audience's attention. They should be keyed to the points of emphasis in the speech in order to reinforce and illustrate the message.
- Include cues in parentheses: (Slide #4. Pause.)
- Make sure your visuals will work well with the size, arrangement, and composition of the audience. Emphasize them with action words.

Before Speaking

- Practice the speech in front of a mirror and, if possible, in the setting with the visuals that will be used. Practice until the delivery is smooth and the speaker is comfortable.
- Rehearse the speech and change any problem areas.
- Test the speech on an audience sample and, if possible, at the speech site. Make sure all the details are in place. (Speeches have failed because of a bad electrical cord, failure of a PowerPoint visual, or a screeching microphone.)

ELIMINATE WRONG MESSAGES

- Do not try to include more than one central idea or theme in a speech. Be sure you can explain the speech in one sentence.
- Don't trust an outline if you are not a practiced speaker, or if you are writing a speech for someone else. Type it out, double-spaced, underlining points for emphasis. (Some speakers like all capital letters and large type size.)
- Do not exaggerate the facts or overdramatize.
- Do not wander into side issues.
- Do not include jokes that are not germane to the audience, occasion, and subject. The same applies to quotes. Throwing in a famous quote or two doesn't necessarily strengthen a speech, and may weaken it.
- Do not plagiarize. If you use a quote, give full credit to the author and source.
- Watch out for homophones that can be misunderstood by the audience: *scene* or *seen; sew, so,* or *sow,* etc.
- Eliminate things that don't work with the speaker's skill level or presentation manner, and limit any elements that are difficult for the speaker to deliver, such as words ending in *s.*

CONSIDER SPECIAL SITUATIONS

- If the media will attend, make copies of the speech available.
- Recycle the speech by using excerpts for press releases, magazine articles, newsletters, and trade publications.

70

PUBLIC SERVICE ANNOUNCEMENT

Writing good sentences means no dependent clauses, no dangling things, no flashbacks, and keeping the subject near the predicate. We throw in as many fresh words as we can get away with. Simple, short sentences don't always work. You have to do tricks with pacing, alternate long sentences with short, to keep it vital and alive.

—THEODORE GEISEL (DR. SEUSS)

The public service announcement, or PSA, is to broadcast public relations what the press release is to print public relations. It's the basic tool used to get broadcast coverage of an event or product.

The Federal Communications Commission (FCC) requires radio and television stations to serve the community and public interest. Part of their obligation is interpreted as broadcasting brief announcements of nonprofit events. While these were historically events sponsored by nonprofit organizations, they are increasingly becoming nonprofit events sponsored by for-profit organizations.

PSAs range from ten to sixty seconds in length, and may be written in either release or script form and produced in audiotape for radio or videotape for television. PSAs can lead to radio or television interviews of official representatives of the event, or in coverage of the event in a special feature segment.

Some PSAs feature health information or safety tips. All kinds of PSAs are opportunities for positive publicity.

DECIDE TO WRITE

Use this vehicle to offer information on:
- Public health discussions
- New health, safety, or product information
- Health, welfare, and/or enrichment services offered to the public

THINK ABOUT CONTENT

- Write as a news release, starting with an arresting lead, usually in the form of a teaser—a catchy phrase, question, or term—that gets the attention of the audience.
- Use action verbs and short, declarative sentences.
- State the facts.
- List any photo opportunities, audiotapes, videotapes, or interviewing sessions that are available.
- List any authorities or celebrities available for interviews.
- In writing the broadcast script, you must write for the eye as well as the ear, and your script must include all the instructions and clues for production of how to create the end product. Start with your idea, then visualize how it should appear.

- Topics must have general public interest, a consumer angle, or an element of current news.
- Events with a news angle, products with a release date (books, new telephone service, a charity race, a new drug), human-interest, or consumer topics all provide possibilities for PSAs.
- Hard news releases are based on factual current events, and soft news releases are based on entertainment topics and celebrities. Know which you are doing, so you can direct it to the proper producer, editor, or director.
- It is often best to telephone a radio or television producer and very briefly pitch your idea first. Be sure you have it boiled down to a very interesting 15–20 second statement or two to grab his attention. Present it in one of these media categories, and be sure to suggest the audiotape or videotape opportunities:
  1. Natural disaster or crisis
  2. Health, medical, safety, or well-being
  3. Economics that affect the public
  4. Good Samaritans—personal stories about people who have done something for the community
  5. Humor or special human-interest stories

CONSIDER SPECIAL SITUATIONS

- For television, suggest ways to make the information or event visually interesting.
- Suggest ideas for interviews, filming, or audio recording.
- Make videotapes and audiotapes available, if possible.
- Suggest writing the broadcast script, if necessary. If you write the script, use the standard abbreviations listed below.

Location Information

EXT	exterior (outdoors), followed by precise location
INT	interior (indoors), followed by precise location
ANGLE	person or thing camera focuses on

Shot directions

CU	close-up shot
ECU	extremely close-up shot
MS	medium shot
CS	close shot
LS	long shot
ELS	extremely long shot

Camera instructions

SIL	silent film
B-roll	camera pans, includes ambient sounds
OC	on camera
dolly in/out	camera moves in a straight line toward or away from the subject
truck right/left	camera moves right or left parallel to the object
pan right/left	camera head moves right or left
tilt up/down	camera head moves vertically, up or down

Transitions

wipe	new picture
dissolve	gradual replacement of one image with another
fade	gradually fading to or from black at the beginning or end of a scene

Other visual directions

Super	print that appears over visual on the screen
CHYRON	text on screen

Audio directions

SOF	sound on film
SOT	sound on tape, means the sound is the audio track from a video- or audiotape
SIL	silent film
SFX	special effects
VO	voice-over or voice only
music under	music volume is lowered beneath narration
music up and out	usually means the end of the production

SELECT A FORMAT

- Use $8\frac{1}{2}$ by 11-inch sheets, type title in caps at the top of the first page. Under the title center and list the script time.
- Divide the pages vertically with video directions on the left-hand side and audio script on the right-hand side.

71
MEDIA ALERT AND PHOTO OPPORTUNITY ALERT

Be sure you are right, then go ahead.

—DAVID CROCKETT

This communication—the media alert, tip sheet, or news advisory—often serves as a bare-bones, short-notice invitation, or as a follow-up to an invitation. The photo opportunity alert or photo tip sheet is basically the same communication geared to television or photo coverage. Make this as appealing as possible by adding pizzazz to the staging of the event.

THINK ABOUT CONTENT
- Include the information appropriate to an invitation.
- Answer the questions *who, what, where, when,* and *how.*
- Include a sentence or two of background information if it will fit on a single page.

DECIDE TO WRITE
Use this piece to:
- Get the television and print media interested in covering an event
- Follow up on an invitation for an event

Media Alert

Good Samaritan Hospital

Kearney, Nebraska   *www.gshs.org*

Media Advisory

Contact: Wendy Meyer, Corporate Communications
10 E 31 St., Kearney, NE 68847
Phone: (308) 555-0123 Fax: (308) 555-0124
wendymeyer@email.com

Good Samaritan Hand Washing Campaign Kicks Off In Local Schools Dec. 6

With flu season upon us, Good Samaritan Hospital is helping keep the community healthy through the "Give Health a Hand" campaign, which highlights the correct way to wash your hands and kill germs that can cause illness such as flu.

On Monday, Dec. 6, a nurse from Good Samaritan will be teaching kids the right way to wash up. In partnership with the Kearney Public School System, Holly Warth (Trauma Outreach Coordinator/RN) will demonstrate proper hand washing techniques and distribute hand washing kits and posters at local schools.

Demonstrations will be held at:
Meadowlark (3rd Grade) -- 10:45 a.m.
Windy Hills (3rd Grade) -- 2 p.m.
The demonstrations will last approximately 15 minutes.

Good Samaritan is kicking off the campaign in conjunction with National Hand Washing Awareness Week, which runs Dec. 5 - 11.

Warth and school nurse Susan Puckett will be available for interview after the demonstrations. Please contact Wendy Meyer or Jaime Naig (800-555-0123) for further information or to make interview arrangements.

###

Good Samaritan Hospital's "Give Health a Hand" campaign. Public Relations Society of America 2005 Bronze Anvil Award–winning media relations, consumer services, health care services program.

72

OPINION EDITORIAL

For they can conquer who believe they can.

—VIRGIL

The opinion editorial ("op-ed") or guest editorial column is a mainstay of many newspapers and magazines, appearing—as the name suggests—on newspaper editorial pages opposite pieces written by the publication's reporters and editors. In magazines these usually appear in a special section called mail, from our readers, etc.

Pieces selected to appear here affect the personal viewpoint of readers and include letters to the editor, contributing editorials, and articles with bylines.

While the op-ed by nature offers substantial latitude, it is important to study the particular publication you wish to write for, and then follow that specific publication's guidelines.

DECIDE TO WRITE

Use this venue to:

- Influence public opinion about a major political issue, societal ill, crisis, or current event
- Respond to or correct incorrect or inaccurate information presented in the publication
- Promote a particular point of view
- Point out that relevant information was omitted from an article
- Congratulate the editor or author on a position or piece

THINK ABOUT CONTENT

- Inquire before writing to learn the policy of a publication and its editorial policies about these pieces.
- Letters to the editor offer the opportunity for publicity and visibility. Keep that connection in mind when writing.
- Write to the specifications or guidelines of the particular publication.
- Be sure to get the approval of organization officials if your letter represents your organization.
- Take a positive approach and upbeat tone whenever possible.

- If you are refuting an editorial, reference the editorial title and date. State your position and support it with hard data and facts, giving the source and authorities, but use only one or two sources. Stick to the point and be as clear, objective, and brief as possible. Be passionate, but don't go overboard.

- In responding to mistakes or inaccuracies, refer to the publication date and page of the piece you are responding to. Quote the incorrect statement and then state the correct information. Make sure you document your statement with one or two sources. Finally, sign your letter with your name and, if applicable, title.

- Keep letters or articles brief and to the point. Most publications allow a maximum of 500 to 800 words per piece. Check with the publication.

ELIMINATE WRONG MESSAGES

- Don't fire off an immediate response to a negative article without reflection. Carefully weigh the decision and try to determine if a response is likely to fuel more negative press.

- Stay away from inflammatory or derogatory remarks.

- Do not threaten legal action.

- Unless you are doing a humorous piece or parody, refrain from hyperbole.

SELECT A FORMAT

Use $8^1/_2$ by 11-inch letterhead. Type your piece double-spaced with a minimum of one-inch margins.

CONSIDER SPECIAL SITUATIONS

Use the correct name and title of the editor, and address your op-ed piece directly to that person.

NEWSLETTER

*Your writing is both good and original;
but the part that is good is not original,
and the part that is original is not good.*

—SAMUEL JOHNSON

A newsletter is a publication for a defined and specific audience. Most are written for an "in" group, such as employees, neighbors, club and association members—people with a common interest. They are generally written in an informal journalistic style as news or features.

STUDY TYPES OF NEWSLETTERS

- Employee newsletters are usually produced by the organization to help create a sense of community. They usually include a mix of employee information and organization news.
- Community newsletters are usually directed at geographical neighbors to create unity by addressing common concerns and issues, and for the purpose of disseminating information.
- Association, club, or group newsletters exist to keep members of an identified group in touch. For example, the Rotarians, Toastmasters, Book-of-the-Month Club, Mystery Writers of America, and all sorts of small common-interest groups for runners, tennis players, health-club members, and genre writers use the newsletter to inspire, inform, and create camaraderie among their membership.

- Publicity newsletters exist to create their own publics. Hotels, vacation clubs, fan clubs, and politicians create newsletters to promote themselves.
- Self-interest newsletters make a profit by offering common-interest information, advice, and solutions to problems for a fee. Such newsletters exist for financial investors, public relations personnel, public speakers, bargain shoppers, writers, and many other kinds and groups of people.

THINK ABOUT CONTENT

- Know the audience thoroughly so the newsletter can be focused appropriately.
- Use a journalistic style of writing. However, there is no need to write in the inverted pyramid style of putting all the facts in the first sentence or paragraph.
- Informal writing is best for most readers.
- Article length depends upon the audience, although business-related newsletters tend to keep article length from 200 to 600 words.
- Create a mix of informational and entertaining pieces. Features should have a beginning, middle, and end. Make the lead a hook for the readers,

and follow it in logical order, explaining and elaborating on the lead.

- Give feature pieces more human interest than news pieces, and more color.

SELECT A FORMAT

- Almost any size may be used, but the major consideration here will be the cost of the paper you select. A standard finished size of 8½ by 11 inches, often folded to that size from a 11 by 17-inch sheet of paper is practical. An address label may be applied to make the piece a self-mailer.
- Computer-generated type or table-top publishing may be used. A banner on the front page and line art or photos will give the newsletter character, but keep it simple.

- Balance pages, taking care to not place all the photos or illustrations on one side of the page, or all in the center where they will seem to be falling into the fold.
- Place the most important items in the upper left-hand or lower right-hand positions on the page, since the eye falls to these spots first.
- Use white space to add interest and create an open, easy-and-quick-to-read feel.
- Online newsletters are becoming very popular because of their cost-saving character. Study many before creating one. This medium requires writing in a more concise manner.

Newsletter

BAYLOR COLLEGE OF MEDICINE

Inside Information

Volume 16, Number 15 • September 22, 1995

Baylor Launches United Way Campaign

The 1995 United Way campaign at Baylor will begin September 28 with a goal of raising $130,000 to benefit hundreds of programs that will touch thousands of lives. The campaign will run through October 27.

Co-chairs of the campaign are William R. Brinkley, Ph.D., Vice President for Graduate Sciences and Dean of The Graduate School of Biomedical Sciences, and Carlos Vallbona, M.D., Chairman of Community Medicine.

"Historically, Baylor has demonstrated extensive and compassionate support for the many fine programs United Way represents," Brinkley said. "Without these programs, many people would have nowhere to turn for help."

Vallbona pointed out that in addition to research and education, Baylor's mission includes a commitment to public service. "Everyone at Baylor can express concern for others through a donation to the United Way," he said.

Department coordinators will distribute pledge cards and envelopes. Contributions can be made by payroll deduction or single payment. Pledge cards, which allow you to designate your donation for a particular United Way agency, should be returned to department coordinators by October 27.

The United Way of the Texas Gulf Coast provides community services through 78 agencies in Fort Bend, Harris, Montgomery, and Waller counties. Baylor President William T. Butler, M.D., serves on the Board of Trustees of the United Way of the Texas Gulf Coast, and United Way of the Texas Gulf Coast President Judith L. Craven, M.D. (BCM '74), is a Baylor Assistant Professor of Community Medicine. ◆

"Our goal . . . is to promote awareness of healthy life styles."

Wellness Month Activities Offer Free Information, Prizes, and More

Join the more than 1,000 Baylor employees who will learn more about healthy life style habits during Wellness Month '95, held in October. The Health Promotion Section of the Office of Public Affairs is sponsoring a month's worth of events that promise healthy information, food, activities, and prizes.

"People can't change their habits overnight, but they can change a little at a time," said Harriet Spain, Assistant Director of Health Promotion. "Our goal during Wellness Month is to promote awareness of all aspects of healthy life styles and to let people know about the resources available at Baylor and in the community."

Donning a '60s theme of "Wellness Month '95: 31 Days of Peace, Love, and Health," the event will feature the health challenge competition, where employees collect tokens for participating in healthy life style activities, such as ordering the Wellness Month special at the Baylor cafeteria, donating blood, doing volunteer work, and going to aerobics classes. At the end of the month, tokens will be turned in for prize drawings. Prizes include dining and entertainment gift certificates, and a special grand prize. Employees can sign up to participate in the health challenge, October 2-6, from noon to 1 p.m. in the Baylor Cafeteria. Tie-dyed Wellness

WELLNESS MONTH '95

BAYLOR COLLEGE OF MEDICINE

Month T-shirts can be purchased at a reduced price at this time.

A highlight of Wellness Month will be the Health Fair on Thursday, October 26, from 10 a.m. to 2 p.m. Approximately 50 booths, staffed by Baylor and community professionals and volunteers, will offer free blood pressure and cholesterol screenings, as well as eye exams for glaucoma and a skin sun sensitivity test. Other activities during the Health Fair include a healthy food sampling, free information on various medical and health issues, and an aerobics demonstration by the Amateur Athletics Union, the national aerobics champions.

During all Wellness Month activities, drawings will be held for dining and entertainment gift certificates.

Each Baylor employee will receive a flyer explaining all of the Wellness Month activities. If you have questions after reading the flyer, contact Harriet Spain at 798-5770.

Wellness Month '95 Schedule of Activities

- **Tuesday, October 10**, noon until 1 p.m., "Herb Growing in Houston," DeBakey Building lobby.

- **Wednesday, October 11**, noon until 1 p.m., meditation workshop, Jaworski classroom.

- **Friday, October 13**, noon until 1 p.m., demonstration of healthy wok cooking by Dorothy Huang, a well-known local chef, DeBakey Building lobby.

- **October 16-19**, 11 a.m. until 2 p.m., free flu shots, DeBakey Building lobby.

- **Wednesday, October 18**, noon until 1 p.m., "Happy and Healthy Feet."

- **Thursday, October 19**, noon until 1 p.m., safe biking seminar sponsored by Planetary Cycles, DeBakey Building lobby.

- **Monday, October 23**, 10 a.m. until 2 p.m., mini massages offered on Massage Day, DeBakey Building lobby.

- **Thursday, October 26**, 10 a.m. until 2 p.m., Health Fair, DeBakey Building lobby. ◆

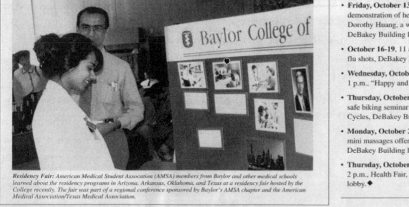

Residency Fair: American Medical Student Association (AMSA) members from Baylor and other medical schools learned about the residency programs in Arizona, Arkansas, Oklahoma, and Texas at a residency fair hosted by the College recently. The fair was part of a regional conference sponsored by Baylor's AMSA chapter and the American Medical Association/Texas Medical Association.

Inside Information, *the newsletter of the Baylor College of Medicine. Public Relations Society of America 1997 Bronze Anvil Award–winning newsletter.*

74

BROCHURE

The difficulty is not to write,
but to write what you mean,
not to affect your reader,
but to affect him precisely as you wish.

—ROBERT LOUIS STEVENSON

A brochure is a sales piece used in sales efforts, promotion, and media kits. It should present a description of the organization, its capabilities, product line, and goals.

The brochure should answer the questions:

- What is the organization?
- Where did it come from (background)?
- What does it have to offer (product or service)?

It should also tell the reader where the organization is located, its representatives, and why it is unique or special. Always give the reader information on how to contact the organization.

THINK ABOUT CONTENT

- Research, review, and collect scores of brochures, then note what you like or don't like about them.
- Decide what and how much you want to say.
- Identify the message in terms of features and benefits. Features are the nitty-gritty of the services or products; benefit statements describe what's in it for the reader.

- It's also important to be as economical with words as possible. The most effective brochures are often the shortest.
- Decide how you want your brochure to look. The visual appearance of your brochure must promote the message.
- Decide how many to produce, estimating what the shelf life of the brochure will be and how much you have to spend. You may want or need to get the professional help of a designer and printer to make these decisions.
- Write the copy, then review and rewrite it.
- Select a desktop publisher and/or printer and work with him or her to fit your copy into a finished brochure size allowing for photos, visuals, and displays.
- Edit the copy, collect any photos or artwork, and rough out a layout indicating the size and placement of the headings, graphics, and photos.
- Select a paper with the right look, feel, color, and durability. The cost of the stock may limit your choice, but select one that will work best with your type style, graphics, and color choices.

Brochure

How does "therapy" work?

Therapy works by helping you objectively look at behaviors, feelings and thoughts in situations which you find problematic. It helps you to learn more effective ways in dealing with those situations.

Therapy is a collaborative effort. You and your psychologist will identify your goals — what you want to have happen, and agree on how you'll know when you're making progress. Your psychologist will talk to you about the length of time it may take to help you see changes.

Progress, and change, can happen. Nine out of ten Americans surveyed by *Consumer Reports* said that psychotherapy had helped them. And in another recent major national study, half of the patients studied were making improvement after eight sessions of therapy, 75 percent after six months of therapy.

"My psychologist helped me to understand and deal with my feelings . . . Life is slowly getting back in balance."

"My son hasn't said a civil word to me in months . . ."

"You have breast cancer. In those four words, my life changed, from the inside out . . ."

"Ever since the big layoff, weird things started happening to me. I couldn't sleep or eat . . ."

Talk to someone who can help.
American Psychological Association

American Psychological Association's "Talk to Someone who Can Help." Public Relations Society of America 1997 Silver Anvil Award–winning institutional program.

XI. ELECTRONIC COMMUNICATIONS

75

EMAIL, ELECTRONIC, AND ONLINE COMMUNICATION

This is very true: for my words are my own, and my actions are my ministers'.

—CHARLES II

The revolution in electronic communications systems and tools requires that we have both better writing skills and additional, special skills for these new modes of communication because these new cultures have introduced the possibility, too, for serious errors. Therefore, be sure to scrupulously follow all principles of writing clear, brief, timely, and precise communications as set down in the individual chapters of this book.

Before you send a message, consider your message and response requirements, and select the best communication vehicle:

- If what you have to communicate requires a human moment (it's high in either emotional or personal content), requires dialogue, negotiation, or if the content is of a personnel, confidential, or financial nature, a face-to-face exchange is still best.
- The telephone is a good choice when you need an immediate answer, if the person you want to communicate with prefers voice contact, and/or if your message will benefit from the nuance of voice inflection (even leaving a voice message).

- Use email for informal interoffice, business to business, and informational messages and memos; or when speed, large distribution numbers, and creation of a permanent record are requirements of your message.
- To send a very personal message of praise, comfort, or support, a handwritten letter or note is best because writing it down adds the weight of care, contemplation, and a permanent record.

EMAIL MESSAGES

The three most important things to remember about email communications are: (1) you will be judged on the basis of your workplace email writing skills, (2) emails can be intercepted (and forwarded) to an unintended recipient, and (3) emails aren't truly ever deleted. So don't fill in the "To:" until your email has been completed to your satisfaction, and only hit "Send:" after you have thoroughly checked and edited it.

THINK ABOUT CONTENT

- See "Memo," page 159, and/or other communication chapters, and use the general rules presented in those chapters.
- Know your organization's rules for email use. If no policy is in place, create a well-thought-out one.
- Begin by answering these questions:
  — Does the organization limit employee email and online use?
  — In your organization, are messages confidential and owned by the sender, or are they organization-owned as part of the system? That is, is the sender the "custodian" or the "owner" of the email messages he or she sends?
  — Does the organization reserve the right to monitor, as owner of the system, all email?
- Use your organization's rules of etiquette, technical terms, approved abbreviations, and symbols where they exist.
- Remember, correct capitalization, spelling, and punctuation are part of a proper message, and all capitals equals a shout.
- Use email only for business messages in your business setting, if appropriate.
- Restrict your message to one subject whenever possible. Multiple subjects impede the receiver's response and create a filing problem.
- State the subject clearly and precisely in the subject line.
- Copy or highlight only the point of a received message you are responding to.
- Respond promptly, or use an acknowledgment message if your response will take you over 24 hours: "I got your message, and I'll get a response back tomorrow morning."
- Make sure your recipient can accept and open your attachments before you send them.
- Limit messages to one screen length whenever possible.

ELIMINATE WRONG EMAIL MESSAGES

- Do not write confidential or sensitive messages that you do not want people other than the intended recipient to read.
- Do not fire off messages without thoroughly thinking them through.
- Do not forward messages without the permission of the sender/author.
- Don't copy and paste copyrighted material into your messages without the author's permission.
- Don't use acronyms (BTW, FWIW, LOL, IMO) or emoticons (keyboard characters to create "faces" showing emotions) in business emails; and use them only very sparingly in personal emails.
- Don't forward jokes and other materials in business settings. Ask personal friends and associates if they wish to receive them before sending.
- Never send an angry (flame) message, or make a personal attack. Take time to cool down before emailing.
- Beware of posting personal information that could result in identity theft.

SELECT AN EMAIL FORMAT

- Use a business salutation to start your email, or follow your organization's established format.
- Learn and use your organization's special abbreviations and symbols, if any.

USING EMAIL GROUPS AND ELECTRONIC BULLETIN BOARDS

Electronic email groups and bulletin boards, where messages on a wide variety of subjects are posted, are common worldwide. Posting and discussion rules should be in place. You may be required to agree to comply with online group rules in order to participate. Carefully observe them at all times.

THINK ABOUT ONLINE MESSAGE CONTENT

- Tune in for a period of time before posting in an online group so you can learn the language, rules for participating, and symbols.
- Give your online message some reflection before sending.
- Evaluate your online message before you send it to be sure it adds new information or ideas. "Me too" messages usually waste a lot of people's time.
- Phrase your online posts in objective, positive terms whenever possible. Online messages can easily be misinterpreted, and offense can easily be taken.
- Online levity is an art form that's difficult to master. Become very familiar with the particular culture before you try it. Even then, consider that self-deprecating humor is usually safest.

VOICE MESSAGING

Create a clear, slow, short message with simple instructions on your voice message. Check your messages frequently and return customer or client calls promptly.

Many people resist leaving voice messages because they don't think through a message before calling.

CREATING YOUR ELECTRONIC VOICE MESSAGE

Your Recorded Message

- The best messages are brief, informative, clear, and business-like.
- Use a machine or message setting that doesn't make the caller wait.
- Test your voice mail regularly to be sure it's working properly.
- Keep it fresh and timely. Callers may think you're out of town for the month if they repeatedly get the same message.
- Get your messages frequently—once every hour is probably a good rule for most businesses.

Suggestions for Callers

- Before dialing, write down the message points you want to cover.
- Speak a little slower and louder than usual, and enunciate clearly. Be sure to address the *who, when, what, why, where,* and *how much* of your call.
- Listen to your message and edit it, if possible.
- Make your message short, and repeat your telephone number succinctly at the end. Here's the end of an effective message: ". . . I'll be in my office until 4:30 P.M. Eastern Standard Time if you want to discuss this further. My telephone number is two-one-two, five-five-five, zero-one-two-three. That's two-one-two, five-five-five, zero-one-two-three."

APPENDICES

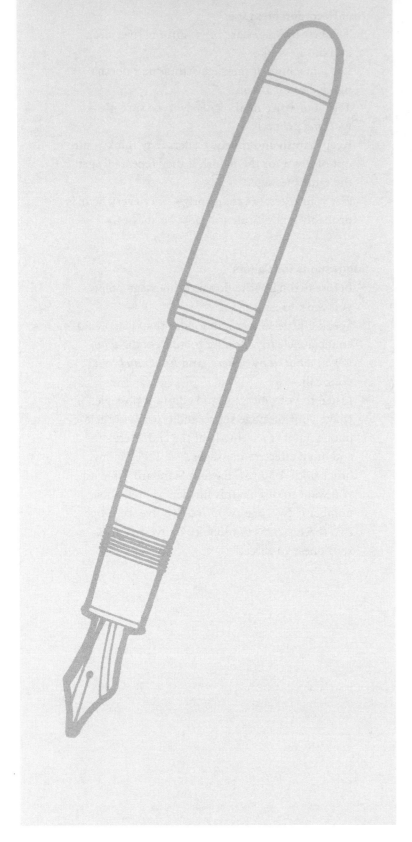

APPENDIX I
FORMS OF ADDRESS

Person	Title for Envelope/Inside Address	Salutation
Ambassador, American	The Honorable [Name] American Ambassador [in Canada and Latin America, the Ambassador of the United States of America] City, Country	Sir/Madam: Dear Mr./Madam Ambassador:
Ambassador, foreign	His/Her Excellency [Name] Ambassador of [Country] Washington, DC	Excellency: Dear Mr./Madame Ambassador: My dear Mr./Madame [Name]:
Archbishop, Roman Catholic	The Most Reverend [Name] Archbishop of [City] City, State	Dear Archbishop [Name]: Most Reverend and dear Sir: Your Excellency: Reverend Sir:
Bishop, Episcopal	The Right Reverend [Name] Bishop of [Diocese] City, State	Right Reverend Sir: Dear Bishop [Name]:
Bishop, Methodist	Bishop [Name] City, State	Your Excellency: Dear Bishop [Name]:
Bishop, Roman Catholic	The Most Reverend [Name] Bishop of [Diocese] City, State	Your Excellency: Most Reverend Sir: Dear Bishop [Name]:
Brother	Brother [Name] Address City, State	Dear Brother [Name]: Dear Brother:

Person	Title for Envelope/Inside Address	Salutation
Cabinet member, United States	The Honorable [Name] The Secretary of [Dept.] Washington, DC	Sir/Madam: Dear Mr./Madam Secretary: Dear Mr./Mrs. [Name]:
Cardinal, Roman Catholic	His Eminence [First Name] Cardinal [Last Name] Archbishop of [City] City, State	Your Eminence: My dear Cardinal: Dear Cardinal [Name]:
Clergyman, Protestant [except Episcopal]	The Reverend [or with a doctorate, Reverend Dr.] [Name] Address City, State	My dear Mr./Mrs./Ms. [or Dr.]: Dear Mr./Mrs./Ms.: Dear Pastor [Name]:
Consul	[Full Name], Esq. [Country] Consul City, State	Sir/Madam [*Madame* if foreign consul]: Dear Mr./Mrs./Ms. Consul:
Dean, college	Dean [or Dr.] [Name] College or University City, State	Sir/Madam: Dear Dean [Name]: Dear Dr. [Name]:
Doctor	Dr. [Name] [or Full Name], M.D. or Ph.D. or D.D. Address City, State	Dear Dr. [Name]:
Governor	The Honorable [Name] Governor of [State] City, State	Sir/Madam: My dear Governor [Name]: Dear Governor [Name]:
Judge	The Honorable [Name] Name of Court City, State	Sir/Madam: My dear Judge [Name]: Dear Judge [Name]:
Legislator	The Honorable [Name] Name of Legislative Body City, State	Sir/Madam: Dear Senator [Name]: My dear Mr./Ms./Mrs.: Dear Mr./Ms./Mrs.:
Mayor	The Honorable [Name] Mayor of [City] City, State	Sir/Madam: Dear Mayor [Name]:

Person	Title for Envelope/Inside Address	Salutation
Military officer	[Full or abbreviated rank] [Full Name], [Abbreviation for Service] Address City, State	Sir/Madam: Dear Major/Captain/ General/Admiral [Name]:
Monsignor	The Reverend Monsignor [Name], or The Rev. Msgr. [Name] City, State	Dear Monsignor [Name]: Monsignor [Name]: Reverend and dear Monsignor [Name]:
Nun	Sister [Name], [Initials of Order] Address City, State	Dear Sister [Name]: Dear Sister:
Patriarch, Eastern Orthodox	His Beatitude the Patriarch of [Diocese] Address City, State	Most Reverend Lord: Your Beatitude:
The Pope	His Holiness Pope [Name], or His Holiness the Pope Vatican City Rome, Italy	Your Holiness: Most Holy Father:
President, college or university	President [Full Name], or Dr. [Full Name] College or University City, State	Sir/Madam: Dear Dr. [Name]: Dear President [Name]:
President, Prime Minister [foreign country]	President [Name], or Prime Minister [Name] City, Country	Excellency: Dear Mr./Ms./Mrs. President: Madame Prime Minister:
President, United States	The President The White House Washington, DC 20500	Mr. President: Dear Mr./Ms./Mrs. President: Dear President [Name]:
Priest, Roman Catholic, Episcopal	The Reverend [Dr.] [Name] Address City, State	Reverend Father: Dear Father [Name]: Dear Father:

Person	Title for Envelope/Inside Address	Salutation
Professor	Prof. [Name] Department of [Subject] College or University City, State	Dear Sir/Madam: Dear Professor [Name]: Dear Dr. [Name]:
Rabbi	Rabbi [Name] Address City, State	Dear Rabbi [Name]: Dear Dr. [Name]:
Representative	The Honorable [Name] The House of Representatives Washington, DC 20515	Sir/Madam: Dear Mr./Ms./Mrs. [Name]: Dear Representative [Name]:
Secretary-General of the United Nations	His [or Her] Excellency [Name] Secretary-General of the United Nations United Nations Plaza New York, NY 10017	Excellency: Dear Mr./Ms./Mrs. Secretary-General:
Senator	The Honorable [Name] United States Senate Washington, DC 20510	Sir/Madam: Dear Senator [Name]:
Speaker of the House	The Honorable [Name] The House of Representatives Washington, DC 20515	Dear Mr./Madam Speaker:
Supreme Court Justice	The Honorable [Name], Associate [or Chief] Justice of the United States Supreme Court Washington, DC 20543	Sir/Madam: Dear Justice [Last Name]: Dear Mr./Ms./Mrs. Justice [Last Name]:
United Nations Representative	His/Her Excellency [Country] Representative to the United Nations United Nations New York, NY 10017	Excellency: Your Excellency: Ambassador: Sir/Madam [*Madame* if foreign]: Mr./Ms./Mrs. [Name]:

Person	Title for Envelope/Inside Address	Salutation
Vice President, United States	Vice President of the United States, or The Vice President of the United States Washington, DC	Dear Mr./Ms./Mrs.: Dear Mr./Madame Vice President [Name]:
Baron/Baroness	The Right Honorable Lord/Lady [Name]	My Lord/Lady: Dear Lord/Lady [Name]:
Baronet	Sir [Name], Bt.	Dear Sir: Dear Sir [Name]:
Wife of baronet	Lady [Name]	Dear Madame: Dear Lady [Name]:
Duke/Duchess	His/Her Grace, the Duke/ Duchess of [Duchy]	My Lord Duke/Madame: Dear Duke of [Duchy]: Dear Duchess:
Earl/Countess	The Right Honorable The Earl/Countess of [Place]	My Lord/Madame: Dear Lord [Name]: Dear Countess:
Knight	Sir [Name]	Dear Sir: Dear Sir [Name]:
Wife of knight	Lady [Name]	Dear Madame: Dear Lady [Name]:
Marquess/ Marchioness	The Most Honorable The Marquess/Marchioness of [Place]	My Lord/Madame: Dear Lord/Lady [Name]:
Viscount/ Viscountess	The Right Honorable The Viscount/Viscountess of [Place]	My Lord/Lady: Dear Lord/Lady [Name]:
Other royalty	His/Her Royal Highness The Prince/Princess of [Place]	Your Royal Highness:

ABBREVIATING TITLES

Educational degrees, memberships, military or civil honors, and titles that follow a name include these:

Abbreviation	Title
A.A.	associate of arts
A.B.	bachelor of arts (*artium baccalaureus*)
A.M.	master of arts (*artium magister*)
B.A.	bachelor of arts
B.D.	bachelor of divinity
B.F.A.	bachelor of fine arts
B.S.	bachelor of science
CEO	chief executive officer
CFO	chief financial officer
CPA	certified public accountant
D.B.	bachelor of divinity (*divinitatis baccalaureus*)
D.D.	doctor of divinity (*divinitatis doctor*)
D.D.S.	doctor of dental surgery
D.O.	doctor of osteopathy
D.S.O.	Distinguished Service Order
D.V.M.	doctor of veterinary medicine
Esq.	esquire
F.R.S.	fellow of the Royal Society
Hon.	the honorable
J.D.	doctor of law (*juris doctor*)
J.P.	justice of the peace
Kt.	knight
L.H.D.	doctor of humanities (*litterarum humaniorum doctor*)
Litt.D.	doctor of letters (*litterarum doctor*)
LL.B.	bachelor of laws (*legum baccalaureus*)
LL.D.	doctor of laws (*legum doctor*)
L.P.N.	licensed practical nurse
M.A.	master of arts
M.B.A.	master of business administration
M.H.A.	master of hospital administration
M.D.	doctor of medicine (*medicinae doctor*)
M.P.	member of parliament
MP	military police
M.P.H.	master of public health
M.S.	master of science
M.S.W.	master of social work
Ph.B.	bachelor of philosophy (*philosophiae baccalaureus*)
Ph.D.	doctor of philosophy (*philosophiae doctor*)
Ph.G.	graduate in pharmacy
PM	prime minister
Psy.D.	doctor of psychology
R.N.	registered nurse
Rev.	reverend
S.B.	bachelor of science (*scientiae baccalaureus*)
S.J.	Society of Jesus
S.M.	master of science (*scientiae magister*)
S.T.B.	bachelor of sacred theology (*sacrae theologiae baccalaureus*)
VP	vice president

ABBREVIATING U.S. MILITARY BRANCHES

USAF	United States Air Force
USCG	United States Coast Guard
USMC	United States Marine Corps.
USN	United States Navy

APPENDIX II

AVOIDING DISCRIMINATORY WORDS

Eliminate discriminatory words from your writing. Because word usage changes over time, words fall out of favor, change in meaning, become outmoded, or even become offensive instead of accepted, or accepted instead of offensive.

Keep current. Know the present meanings of words and how to use them. Know which words are too harsh, which are regional and aren't understood by all your readers, which are redundant or fog your intended meaning, and, yes, which are offensive and should not be used at all.

Develop a sense for the proper, precise word. Choose every word carefully, and eliminate every one that isn't working, is unnecessary, carries the wrong meaning, or is too vague.

Here are some word guidelines.

AVOID SEXIST LANGUAGE

Treat all readers equally. That means addressing men and women as equals in your communications. Think about why you should use these words. Then test your choices by reviewing the following sections.

Instead Of	Use	Why
Chairman	The chair is ... The representative is ... The leader is ... The person responsible is ... The moderator is ... The convener is ... The coordinator is ... The presiding officer is ... The head is ...	Avoid gender-specific terms.
Manpower	employees, workforce, personnel, workers, staff	Select the most inclusive and descriptive non-gendered word.
The employee may select *his* benefit category	Employees may select benefit categories ... Employees may select their benefit categories ...	Use plural forms to avoid gender reference. (Eliminate *his* and *her*.)

Instead Of	Use	Why

Dear Sir:
Gentlemen:
Madam:
	Dear Chairperson:
	Dear Editor:
	Dear Colleague:
	Dear Customer Service
	    Representative:
	Dear Service Manager:
	Dear Public Relations
	    Director:
		Use nongendered titles when gender is unknown.

Ms. C. Ross and Jim Burns ...	Ms. C. Ross and Mr. J. Burns ... Ross and Burns ... Cathy Ross and Jim Burns ...	Use parallel or equal construction for women and men.
The directress for the program ...	The director for the program ...	Eliminate gender connotation unless it is necessary to include it. (Don't use *poetess, priestess, deaconess,* or other words that imply the masculine form is standard and the feminine is exceptional.)
Mothering new employees ...	Nurturing new employees ...	Use inclusive, nonstereotypical terms.
Manhours worked ...	Hours worked ...	Rewrite to eliminate gender reference.

Hurricane Katrina did
    her worst damage ...
	Hurricane Katrina did
	    the worst damage ...
	The hurricane did
	    the worst damage ...
		Rewrite to avoid gender reference.

Since the beginning
    of mankind ...
	Since the beginning
	    of the human species ...
	Since the beginning
	    of humankind ...
	Since the first people ...
		Use an inclusive word.

Avoid the Generic *Man* Trap

When *man* denotes an adult male human, and that distinction is needed in your writing, use it, as in "The committee consisted of three women and one man." But don't use *man* when you mean both men and women. Here are four areas where you should be especially careful to use an inclusive term:

- Don't use *man* in general references to all people: "man of the hour" and "man for the job." Use an inclusive and correct word such as *person:* "*person of the hour," "person for the job.*"
- Don't use *man* to refer to all humans: "mankind prefers," "all mankind." Use inclusive terms like *all people* and *humankind.*
- Don't use *man* as a prefix or suffix when there's a more inclusive word: *manhours, manmade, foreman.* Use inclusive and correct words like *time* or *work hours, synthetic,* and *supervisor.*
- Some male-sounding words containing *man* or *his* have nonsexist origins. They derive from the Latin *manus,* which means hand. Don't change these in error:

Don't Substitute This	For This
herufacture	manufacture
heragement	management
heripulate	manipulate
herual	manual
heruscript	manuscript
herage	manage

If the resulting *her* word or *person* word is silly, find another substitute, or use the old word.

Instead of	Use This
freshperson	freshman, first-year student
herstory	history
personhole	manhole

Avoid the *He/She* Pronouns

The word used to substitute for a noun is a pronoun, and although we have no difficulty with the first-person pronoun (*I, we, me, us, our,* and *ours*) or the second-person pronoun (*you, your,* and *yours*), the third-person pronoun (*he, she, they, him, her, hers, it, its, their,* and *theirs*) can create problems for writers.

Although it has been common practice to address both sexes of readers as *he,* it is best to change your writing to avoid this problem.

Option 1: Use Plural Pronouns

Change

If the **reader** has questions, **he** should call this office.

To

If **readers** have questions, **they** should call this office.

Option 2: Reword to Omit Pronouns

Change the same sentence to

Readers should call this office with questions.

Option 3: Reword to Use Second- or First-Person Pronouns

If you elect to use first person or second person, be sure you are consistent throughout your communication and that first or second person works.

Use

If **you** have questions, call this office.

Or

Call this office if **you** have questions.

Or first person

I will call the office if **I** have questions.

Option 4: Replace Pronouns with The

Change

The **employee** may use **his** vacation request form.

To

The **employee** may use **the** vacation request form.

Option 5: Repeat the Noun

This becomes tedious for the reader, so it should be used very sparingly.

Example:

The **employee** may use the **employee's** vacation request form.

Option 6: Restructure the Sentence to Passive Voice

Passive voice should be used very sparingly and only if it emphasizes what you want to emphasize or provides needed variety in your sentence structure. It usually results in longer and indirect writing.

Example:

The vacation request form should be used by the **employee**.

Option 7: Substitute *One* for Pronouns

This may result in a loss of the conversational tone you want in your writing.

Example:

The **employee** has three choices; **one** should select first, second, and third.

Option 8: Use *His* or *Her*

Use *his or her* very rarely because it distances you—the writer—from your reader and can make your writing very tedious. *He/she* and *his/her* are cumbersome and should be avoided in most writing.

Example:

The **employee** should list **his or her** first, second, and third vacation choices.

Or

The **employee** has three choices; **he/she** should select first, second, and third.

Avoid Feminine Words

Some English words that come from Latin or other language roots have hang-on feminine equivalents, or feminine prefixes or suffixes. (This is especially true of the Romance languages: Spanish, French, Italian, Portuguese, and Romanian.) The current trend is to make one form of these words:

Instead of	Use
actress	actor
adultress	adulterer
authoress	author
blonde	blond
comedienne	comedian
conductress	conductor
fiancée	fiancé
goddess	god
heiress	heir
majorette	major
masseuse	masseur
songstress	singer
waitress	waiter

There are some more in the listing in the next section.

Avoid Gendered Terms

Our American culture produced a language loaded with masculine words that are often used to refer to either sex. When possible, take the sex out of your language by removing gender from occupations.

Choose words that are inclusive of both sexes, easy to pronounce, and make logical sense. For most of your writing, you will want to include nongendered substitutions like the ones on the following pages.

Instead Of	Use
actress	actor
adman	advertising writer, ad person, adsmith
administratrix	administrator
advanceman	advance agent, initiator
adventuress	adventurer
aircraftsman	aviator, aircraft engineer
airline stewardess	flight attendant
airman/woman	aviator, pilot, flier
airmanship	aviation skill, flying skill
alderman	public representative, council member/person
alumna/alumnus, alumnae/alumni	graduates, alums
ambassadress	ambassador
ancestress	ancestor
anchorman/woman	anchor
apeman	prehuman
assemblyman	assemblyperson, assembly worker, line person
authoress	author
aviatrix	aviator
bachelor's degree	undergraduate degree
bagboy	bagger, assistant
barman/maid	bartender, waiter
baseman	base player
bastard	(eliminate)
bedfellow	associate, partner
bellboy, bellman	bellhop
benefactress	benefactor
blindman	blind person
blonde	blond
bondsman	bondsperson, guarantor, insurer
bookman	author, scholar, librarian
bossman/lady	boss, supervisor
brakeman (bobsled)	brake operator
brakeman (railroad)	railroad worker, guard
brakeman (train)	conductor's assistant
brethren	laity
brewmaster	brew director, chief brewer, head brewer
bridesmaid	bride's attendant
brotherhood	human kinship, camaraderie

Instead Of	Use
brotherly	kind, helpful
brotherly love	charity, goodwill
brunette	brunet
bull session	talk-fest, get-together
busboy, busgirl	waiter's helper, waiter's assistant
businessman, businesswoman	business representative, business executive, businessperson
businessmen	businesspersons, businesspeople
busman	bus driver
cabin boy	crew member
cabman	cab driver, cabby
cameraman, camerawoman	camera operator, photographer
career woman	manager, supervisor (or name the job, profession, or title)
cattlemen	cattle breeders, cattle owners, cattle herders
cavemen	cave dwellers, cave people
chairman/woman	chairperson, chair, head, presider, presiding officer, convener, facilitator
chambermaid	housekeeper
choirgirl/boy	choir member
chorus girl/boy	member of the chorus, singer
churchman	lay officer
city fathers	city council, leaders, city officials
clansman	member of the clan
clergymen/women	ministers, clergy, clerics, pastors
coed	student
comedienne	comedian
committeemen	committee members
common man	commoner, average person
company man/woman	loyal employee, team player
concertmistress/master	concert leader, first violinist
conductress	conductor
confidante	confidant
confidence man	swindler
congressman	member of congress, representative

Instead Of	Use
contact man	contact person, liaison
copyboy, copygirl	copy clerk, runner, carrier, messenger
copyman	copy editor, copy writer
councilman	council member
counterman/girl	clerk, waiter
countryman	compatriot, citizen, patriot
cowboy/girl	cowhand, rider
craftsman	artisan, crafter, craftsperson
creatrix	creator, maker
crewman	crew member
dairyman	dairy farmer, dairy worker
dayman	day worker, day laborer
deaconess	deacon, elder
debutante	debutant
deliveryman	deliverer, delivery clerk
directress	director, administrator
distaff	(eliminate in reference to women)
divorcée	divorcé
doorman	doorkeeper, doorkeep
draftsman	drafter
drum majorette	drum major, baton twirler
Dutchman	Dutch person
elder statesman	senior political leader
elderman	elder
emperor, empress	ruler, monarch, sovereign, commander, leader
enchantress	enchanter, sorcerer, magician, fascinating woman
engineman	engineer, engine driver
Englishman	the English, Englander, Briton
enlisted man	enlistee, member, recruit
equestrienne	equestrian, rider, horseback rider
executrix	executor
expressman	delivery person
fair sex	(eliminate)
fall guy	scapegoat, stand-in
family of man	humankind, the human family
farmeress, farmerette	farmer
fraternal twins	nonidentical twins

Instead Of	Use
fatherland	homeland
favorite son	favorite candidate
feminine persuasion	female
feminine rhyme (poetry or music)	rhyme with an unstressed final syllable
fiancée	fiancé, betrothed
fighting man	fighter, soldier
filly	(eliminate in reference to girls or women)
fireman	firefighter, stoker (ships and trains)
fisherman	fisher, angler
five-man committee	five-person committee, five-member committee
flagman	flagger
floorman	floorwalker, person on duty
flyboy	aviator, pilot, flier
forefathers	ancestors, forebears, progenitors, foremothers and forefathers
foreman, forewoman (lady)	supervisor, boss, leader
forgotten man	(use specific noun: unemployed, poor, etc.)
founding father	founder, ancestor
Frenchmen	the French, French people
freshmen	first-year students, beginners
frogman	diver, sailor
front man	intermediary
frontiersman	pioneer, leader, settler
funnyman	comedian, humorist, comic
G-man	government employee
gagman	writer
gamesmanship	game playing, strategy
garbage man	garbage collector
gasman	gas deliverer, attendant
gateman	gate attendant
gentlemen's agreement	unwritten agreement, pact, agreement of honor
girl Friday, man Friday	aide, assistant, helper
goddess	god
governess	child caretaker, nurse
gownsman	gownsperson, academic person

Instead Of	Use
grandfather clause	preexisting condition clause
guardsman	guard, soldier
guildsman	guild member, guildsperson
gunman	shooter, killer, assassin
hackman	hackie, cabdriver
handyman	fixer, face-of-all-trades
hardwareman	retailer
hat-check girl	hat checker, attendant
headman	boss, president
headmaster	principal
heiress	heir, inheritor
helmsman	coxswain, guider, steerer
henchman	right arm, enforcer
heroine	hero
history of man	history
hooker	prostitute
horseman/woman	rider, equestrian
hostess	host
hotelman	hotel operator, manager, hotel worker, desk clerk
housewife	homemaker
huntress	hunter
husbandman	farmer, husbander
idea man	idea person, creator
infantryman	infantry soldier, foot soldier
inner man	inner self, inner person, psyche, soul
inside man	accomplice, undercover agent, spy
inspectress	inspector
instructress	instructor, teacher
insurance man	insurance agent
Irishmen	Irish people
jack-of-all-trades	handy person
jazz man	jazz player, musician
John Q. Public	the public
johnny-come-lately	newcomer, new arrival
johnny-on-the-spot	prompt person
journeyman	experienced person, journey-level tradesperson
juryman	juror, member of the jury
key man	key person
king's ransom	valuable

Instead Of	Use
king-size	huge, large
kinsmen	kin, kinfolk, relatives
laundress, laundryman	laundry worker
layman	layperson
laymen	laity, lay people
layout man	layout person
leadman	leader
learned man	learned person, scholar, sage
legman	runner, messenger
letterman	athlete of achievement, achiever
lighthouse man	lighthouse keeper
lineman	line repairer, technician, installer, football player
lioness (when referring to a person)	lion
longshoreman	stevedore, longshoreworker
lookout man	guard, sentry, lookout
lumberman, lumberjack	logger, woodcutter, forester
madam	(eliminate)
maid	house cleaner, house worker
maid of honor	honored attendant
maiden	first, untried, single
maiden name	family name, birth name
mailman	letter carrier, postal worker, mail carrier
maintenance man	janitor, repair person, caretaker
maitre d'	head waiter
majorette	major
makeup man	makeup person
male nurse	nurse
male/female hardware	couplings, plugs and sockets
man about town	(eliminate)
man among men	important person
man of action	human dynamo, go-getter
man of distinction	person of distinction
man of letters	literary person, writer, scholar, academic
man of the year	newsmaker of the year
man on horseback	dictator, tyrant

Instead Of	Use
man on the street	average citizen, pedestrian, average person
man (verb)	operate, staff
man's best friend	dog
man's law	the law
man's work	work
man-of-war	armed warship
man-sized	large
man-to-man	face-to-face, person-to-person, one-on-one
manageress	manager
maneater	flesh eater, cannibal
manhandle	mishandle, rough up, maltreat
manhole	utility hole, maintenance access
manhours	time, work hours, labor time
manhunt	search
mankind	humankind, people, humanity
manlike	humanlike
manmade	handmade, hand-built, synthetic, manufactured, machine-made, simulated
manpower	workers, personnel, workforce
marked man	target, marked person
marksman	sharpshooter
masculine persuasion	male
masculine rhyme (poetry, music)	rhyme with stressed or strong final syllable
masseuse	masseur, massage
master	expert
master key	skeleton key, passkey
master plan	plan, blueprint, plan of action, working plan, design
masterful	skillful
masterpiece	great work of art
master's degree	graduate degree, graduate-level degree
matron of honor	honored attendant
mayoress	mayor
meatman	butcher, meat cutter
mechanical man	robot, machine, mechanical device
mediatress, mediatrix	mediator

Instead Of	Use
medicine man	spirit healer, faith healer
men working	people working
meter maid	meter attendant, meter reader
middleman	go-between, contact person, negotiator, liaison, intermediary
midshipman	cadet
Miss	Ms.
modern man	people today, modern humans
mother country	homeland, native country
Mother Earth	earth, world
mother lode	main lode, pay lode
Mother Nature	nature
mother tongue	first language, native language
mother's son	parent's child
motherhood, fatherhood	parenthood
motorman	driver
Mrs.	Ms.
murderess	murderer
negress	black woman (only if necessary to distinguish)
newsboy	news deliverer, news carrier
newsman	reporter, newscaster
newspaperman	editor, reporter, journalist, writer
night watchman	guard, night guard, security guard, watcher
no-man's-land	desolate, uninhabited land
nobleman	nobleperson, member of nobility
Norseman	Norse person
number-one man	head, number one, chief
number-two man	second in command, chief
nurseryman	horticulturist, nursery
nymphomaniac	(eliminate)
oarsman	crew member, rower
odd man	extra person, eccentric
odd man out	person not included
office boy	messenger, clerk
oilman	oil executive, oil field worker
old wives' tale	superstition

Instead Of	Use
ombudsman	representative, researcher, mediator
one-upsmanship	the art of one-upping
organization man	loyal employee, team player
outdoorsman	outdoors person
paperboy	paper carrier
patrolman, policeman	police officer
patroness	patron, benefactor, sponsor
penmanship	handwriting
pitchman	promoter, hawker
plainclothesman	police officer, detective
playboy/girl	pleasure seeker, carouser
poetess	poet
postman	letter carrier, postal worker
postmistress	postal official
prehistoric man	prehistoric people
pressman	press operator
priestess	priest
prioress	prior
procuress	procurer
prodigal son	prodigal child (except for Biblical reference)
prophetess	prophet
proprietress	proprietor, owner, manager
publicity man	publicist
queen's English	proper English
queenly	regal, noble
radioman	radio operator
ranchman	rancher
rangeman	range rider, ranger
reman	restaff
Renaissance man	Renaissance person
repairman	repairer
rewrite man	editor, reviser, rewriter
rifleman	shooter, soldier
right-hand man	assistant, right arm, chief assistant
salesman/woman/lady	sales agent, sales associate, salesperson
Scotsman	Scot, Scotlander
sculptress	sculptor
seaman	sailor, mariner, seafarer
seamstress	tailor, sewer, mender, needleworker

Instead Of	Use
seductress	seducer
seeress	prophet, seer, clairvoyant
serviceman	sailor, soldier
shipmaster	commander, captain
showman	actor, director, producer
showmanship	showiness, stage presence
signalman	signal operator, signaler
sister ship	co-ship
snowman	snow creation
social man	social person
song-and-dance man	singer and dancer
songstress	singer
sorceress	sorcerer, enchanter
spaceman	astronaut, spacefarer, cosmonaut
spinster	(eliminate)
spokesman, spokeswoman	spokesperson, representative
sportsmanlike	sporting
sportsmanship	fair play, fairness
squaw	(eliminate)
starlet	young star, star in the theater
state policeman	state trooper, trooper
statesman	diplomat, mediator, leader (or a specific title)
statesmanlike	diplomatic
stewardess	flight attendant (aircraft), steward (ship, union shop)
straw man	straw, straw person
suffragette	suffragist
suffragettism	suffrage
suitor	pursuer
switchman	switch operator
taskmaster	supervisor, tyrant
temptress	tempter, enticer
testatrix	testator
tigress (when referring to a person)	tiger
timberman	timber worker, forester
to a man	to a person
toastmaster/mistress	speaker, toastmaker
Tom, Dick, and Harry	everyone, ordinary people

Instead Of	Use
tomcat	(eliminate)
tragedienne	tragedian, actor who plays tragic roles
traitoress, traitress	traitor, betrayer, turncoat
trashman	trash collector
tribesman	member of the tribe
triggerman	assassin, hoodlum
trollop	(eliminate)
Uncle Sam	U.S. or United States
usherette	usher
villainess	villain, scoundrel
virginal	(eliminate in reference to women)
vixen	(eliminate in reference to women)
waitress	waiter, server
wardress	warden, prison warden
warhorse	(eliminate in reference to women)
watchman	guard, watch
weak sister	weakling, coward
weaker sex	(eliminate)
weatherman	weathercaster, forecaster, meteorologist
Welshman	Welsh person
wench	(eliminate in reference to women)
woman lawyer	lawyer
woman stockbroker	stockbroker
workman	worker
workmanlike	efficient, skillful
workmen's compensation	workers' compensation
yeoman	guard, attendant, assistant
yes-man	endorser, follower, supporter
yokefellow	companion, coworker
young man	youth, teenager

There are many more, of course. Make your own logical nonsexist substitutions, using the most precise word that describes the function.

Try Out *Person* Words and Phrases Before Using

Person substitutions—chair*person*, spokes*person*—are generally acceptable, but they are sometimes contrived and awkward. Try out *person* words before using. Better alternatives almost always exist. But don't make substitutions if the cure is worse than the disease.

Don't Use Female or Male Words That Lower a Person's Status

This occurs more often in female words than male:

Don't Use	When You Mean
my girl	secretary
the girls	women employees
gals	women
females	women
female	woman, girl
males	men
the boys	men
boy	man
manly	strong, vigorous, etc.
sissy	——
tomboy	——
man and wife	husband and wife
men and ladies	men and women
lady	woman
biddy	older woman
divorcée	woman who is divorced

AVOID WORDS THAT STEREOTYPE BY RACE OR NATIONALITY

Nationality and heritage word usage changes with time. Those used 100 years ago, or even 15 years ago, may not be acceptable today.

First, use the racial or ethnic background of people only when it is necessary and relevant. Then the term preferred by the people you are describing should be used, and it should be used with sensitivity. Remember the principles:

* Treat all people equally.
* Use the race or ethnic background of people *only* when it is a vital part of your message.
* Refer to race or nationality objectively.
* Be as specific as possible.

Make sure your writing reflects that you are in touch. Here are some present generally accepted usages:

* *African American* and *black* are the terms preferred by most Americans of African and Caribbean descent, and these terms are usually interchangeable. If writing about cultural heritages, however, use *African American*. Do not use black as a singular noun: A *black* was hired in Department B. Do use it to differentiate: There are fifteen black and thirteen white committee members. No longer preferred are the terms *negro, colored,* or *Afro-American.*
* *American* implies citizenship. If the person being written about is of Chinese heritage but isn't an American citizen, don't use Chinese American.
* If necessary, terms like *Irish American, Italian American,* and others may be used.
* *Native American* is the inclusive, preferred term for general reference to aboriginal people of the United States. This includes Alaska native groups like Inuit and Aleut peoples, and peoples of Hawaii and American Samoa. In reference to heritage, many native Americans prefer to be identified by their tribal affiliation or nation, such as Navajo, Hopi, Sioux, Arapaho, or Zuni.
* *American Indian* is not accurate, since Indians are from India. It was a name given by Europeans, and isn't usually preferred.
* *Asian American* is the preferred term for U.S. citizens of Asian descent but be more specific if possible. Asia is a vast area, and many people prefer to be identified by their national heritage: *Korean American, Chinese American, Japanese American.*
* *Arab American* is acceptable, but select a more distinct national reference, if possible: Iraqis or Syrians, for example. It is important to remember that Iranians are not Arabs. Also, do not use Persian, except to refer to rugs, cats, or the Gulf.
* *Chinese* is preferred in referencing citizens of China. Do not use *Chinamen* or *Orientals.*
* *Russians* are citizens of Russia. There is no longer a Soviet Union, so there are no Soviets. Use the proper national term to describe people from this part of the world: Citizens of Ukraine are Ukrainians, citizens of Georgia are Georgians.
* *Jew* is used to describe a person descended from the ancient Hebrews with the ethnic heritage based on Judaism. Do not use the word as an adjective or a verb. The preferred term for a citizen of Israel is *Israeli,* and these citizens are descended from many heritages. Do not use *Jewess,* as it is both pejorative and patronizing.
* *Colored* or *Coloured* is used by South Africans to refer to other South Africans of mixed race. Do not use this term in referring to Americans of mixed race.
* *Illegal immigrants* is used to describe people who come into this country illegally, without a passport, visa, or other legal document that entitles them to visit, work, or live in the country. Be careful in using *illegal* or *alien,* because both are offensive and require certain knowledge of this fact. It is better to avoid these negative terms, but use *undocumented* or *without a passport,* when necessary.
* *Latino* and *Hispanic* are synonymous, inclusive ethnic names for groups in the United States who have a cultural Spanish heritage, including Mexicans, Cubans, Puerto Ricans, Central Americans, and South Americans. Latinos may be of any race, including white, black, Native American, Asian, etc. Some speak Spanish, others don't; some are immigrants, and others are U.S. born. It is important to remember that Spaniards are not Latinos.
* *Whites* is a racial designatation of people formerally referred to as the most inclusive definition of *Anglo.*

Don't Send Subtle Discriminatory Messages

Do not infer any of these untruths:

> *Jews are miserly.*
> *Italians are members of the Mafia.*
> *Hispanics are dishonest.*
> *Chicanos are unkempt.*
> *All blacks live in ghettos and are on welfare.*
> *Puerto Ricans are lazy.*
> *Germans are abrasive.*
> *The English are bullheaded.*
> *The French are arrogant.*
> *The Chinese are not able to manage.*
> *The Japanese are underhanded.*

Discriminatory statements are often subtle. Take this example:

> *"This study encompasses two ghetto areas.*
> *Our sample includes 300 black males ... "*

Or, statements may be discriminatory by implication:

> *"open-minded German"*
> *"neatly dressed Chicano"*
> *"generous Jew"*
> *"an industrious Puerto Rican"*
> *"Chinese manager"*

Never Use Discriminatory Words of Race, Nationality, or Sexual Preference

Other unacceptable words that refer to race, nationality, and sexual preference include:

Before You Use	Think About This
abortionist	Offensive term; use the most correct term, e.g., *abortion doctor, abortion provider, abortion practitioner, gynecologist who performs abortions.*
acknowledged/ admitted/avowed homosexual	Offensive. Use *openly gay* or *gay.*
adopted child	Do not use to define a child's relationship to the parents.

Before You Use	Think About This
alcoholic	Use the term *recovering alcoholic* if the person has stopped drinking; *reformed alcoholic* is incorrect and offensive.
alien	Do not use to describe someone who has entered the country illegally.
Amerasian	Originated to describe the child of an Asian mother and American father. Use *Asian American* instead.
American Indian	Use Native American instead.
Anglo	Use *white* instead. May be used to identify a person of English Anglo-Saxon heritage.
Asian	Use the country of citizenship, e.g., Chinese.
bi	Offensive. Use *bisexual.*
bitch	Offensive. Use *only* to refer to a female dog.
boy	Use only to describe a male person under 18 years of age.
braburner	Offensive term for feminist.
brave	Offensive term for Native American young men.
buck	Offensive term for black or Native American young men.
cabron	Offensively vulgar Spanish word for cuckold.
Canuck	Use Canadian or French Canadian.
chief	Use only in referring to the head of an official tribal government of Native Americans. Check first.
Chinese fire drill	Use another term to refer to mass confusion.
co-ed, coed	Do not use as a noun; use *student.*

Before You Use	Think About This
Colored	Do not use to refer to Americans of mixed racial ancestry. May be used to refer to people of some African countries. Use the country of origin when possible. Capitalize when used.
companion	Generally preferred to describe a person in a homosexual relationship.
culo	Offensive Spanish word for ass.
dark continent	Do not use to refer to Africa.
Dutch courage	Do not use to refer to cowardice.
Dutch treat	Do not use to refer to each person paying his or her own expenses.
dyke	Offensive word for *lesbian*.
Eastern Indians	Use *people of India* to distinguish from Native Americans.
Eskimos	Use specific names such as *Inuits* or *Aleuts* whenever possible.
ethnic	Do not use as a noun. Use only if relevant, and then use nationality or race.
fag	Offensive term for homosexual men.
gay	Use as a noun or adjective to describe homosexual men and sometimes women: *gay, gay men,* and *lesbians.* Use the choice of your reader.
ghetto	Offensive term for areas of a city where poor people live. Use the proper neighborhood name.
girl	Use only to describe a female person under 18 years of age.
gringo	Offensive Spanish word for white Americans.
guero	Offensive Spanish word for white Americans.
gyp/gypped/ gyp joint	Offensive words derived from *gypsy*.

Before You Use	Think About This
hick	Offensive term for rural person.
high yellow, high yeller	Offensive term for some black people.
hillbilly	Offensive term for rural person.
holy rollers	Offensive term for evangelical and charismatic Christians.
homo	Offensive term for homosexual person.
homosexual lifestyle, gay lifestyle	Offensive and erroneous terms. There is no single gay subculture, gay, nongay, or heterosexual lifestyle.
illegal	Use only to describe a violation of the law. Often misused to mean a rule or contract agreement has been broken.
illegals, illegal aliens	Offensive terms to refer to people who have entered the country without a passport, visa, or other document that permits them to enter.
illegitimate	Offensive term used to describe children of unmarried people.
Indians	Use this term for citizens of India. Use *Native Americans* when referring to aboriginal peoples of North America.
Injun	Offensive term for Native Americans.
inner city	Use carefully to refer only to the center of the city. Do not use to refer to or depict an area of the city inhabited by poor people. A better term is the neighborhood, district, or other appropriate name.
Jap	Offensive term that originated during World War II for Japanese people.

Before You Use	Think About This	Before You Use	Think About This
JAP	Offensive term short for "Jewish American Princess."	queer	Use only as an adjective when it is the preferred word of the subject and audience groups of your communication to describe sociopolitical activists who want to integrate pro-gay attitudes into all aspects of American life.
joto	Offensive Spanish term for gay person.		
kaffir	Offensive word used primarily in South Africa to refer to black people.		
lesbian	Use as a noun when appropriate for a woman with same-sex orientation.	racially diverse	Use to describe a group of people of different races.
mayate	Offensive Spanish word for black person.	racially mixed	Use to describe a person who has parents of different races.
mestizo	Not a term of choice by most people of European and Indian heritage.	real parents	Use *biological parents,* or *birth parents* only if those terms are accurate and necessary.
morocho	Offensive Spanish term for black person.	redskins	Offensive term for Native Americans.
mulatto	Offensive word for people of African and European heritage.	sangron	Offensive Spanish term for a disagreeable person.
natural parents	Use *biological parents,* or *birth parents* only if that term is accurate and necessary.	savages	Offensive term for Native Americans.
Negress	Offensive term for black woman.	sexual orientation	Generally preferred over the terms *sexual preference* and *sexual persuasion.*
Negro	Use only if chosen by the black people who are the subject and audience of your communication.	Spanish	Use only to refer to citizens of Spain. Do not use to describe Latinos.
New World	Some Native Americans object to the use of this term for North America, since it does not recognize their existence on the continent prior to the landing of Christopher Columbus.	Spanish speakers	Can be used to refer to any people who speak Spanish.
		step-	Do not use in stereotypical slang expressions like *wicked step-mother.*
Oriental	Do not use in referring to persons or groups unless it is part of a proper name.	tribe	Use only as a proper noun in referring to ethnic groups, or African or Eastern European nations, or language groups. Native American tribal names are used by themselves: Navajo, Hopi, Sioux. Native Americans generally prefer *nation.*
Persian	Do not use in reference to people. Refer instead to the correct country of citizenship.		
powwow	Use only to properly refer to Native American spiritual or social celebrations.	undocumented immigrant	Use as a synonym for illegal immigrant.

Before You Use	Think About This
WASP	This acronym for White Anglo-Saxon Protestant is derogatory.
Welsh, welsher	Offensive term of uncertain origin, which was used to refer to going back on one's word.
wetbacks	Offensive term used to describe Mexican people who enter the United States illegally.
white trash	Offensive term that should not be used to refer to poor or socially deprived white people.
Whitey (Whitie, Whity)	Contemptuous term used by blacks to describe Caucasians. Do not use it.
wimp	Offensive term used to describe a weak or boring person.
Wop	Offensive term for Italian or southern European people.
Yankee	May still be considered offensive by some when referring to people from the north and northeastern United States.
Yanqui	Offensive Spanish word for a white American.
Zambo	Offensive Spanish word for a person of African or Indian heritage.

AVOID AGE DISCRIMINATION

Know your reader, and avoid age terms that might offend:

Before Using This	Consider
adolescents	young people
elderly	people over seventy
golden ager	person over sixty-two
middle-aged	people between forty-five and sixty
oldster	people over sixty-five
senior citizens	people over sixty-two
teenagers	young people
youngster	young person

AVOID STEREOTYPING PEOPLE WITH DISABILITIES

Avoid derogatory, apologetic, or patronizing words:

Instead Of	Use
attack	epilepsy (or appropriate)
birth defect	congenital disability
bobo (Spanish)	mental disabilities
crazy	(Use specific medical term, e.g., paranoid, manic-depressive, psychotic, etc.)
crippled	disabled
deaf	individual who cannot hear
deaf and dumb	hearing and speech disabled
deaf-mute	individual who cannot hear or speak
deformed	(Describe specific condition.)
disfigured	(Describe specific condition.)
fits	seizures
handicapped	disabled
idiota (Spanish)	mental disability
imbecil (Spanish)	mental disability
invalid	(Describe specific disability.)
lame	disabled (Or, use word for specific condition.)
mentally deranged	(Use specific term, e.g., neurotic, paranoid, etc.)
mongoloid	Down's syndrome
normal	(A trait, not a person, is normal.)
retarded	mentally disabled
special	(Use the correct term when referring to people with disabilities.)
spells	epilepsy (or appropriate)

INDEX

MORE CAREER BOOKS AND WRITING GUIDES FROM TEN SPEED PRESS